# tiffin

●●●●●●

# tiffin

## 500 AUTHENTIC RECIPES
### CELEBRATING INDIA'S REGIONAL CUISINE

●●●●●●●

## SONAL VED

Foreword by
### CHEF FLOYD CARDOZ

●●●●●●

Illustrations by
### ABHILASHA DEWAN

BLACK DOG
& LEVENTHAL
PUBLISHERS

Black Dog & Leventhal Publishers
Hachette Book Group
1290 Avenue of the Americas
New York, NY 10104
www.hachettebookgroup.com
www.blackdogandleventhal.com

Originally published in 2018 by Roli Books in India
First U.S. Edition: October 2018

Black Dog & Leventhal Publishers is an imprint of Running Press, a division of
Hachette Book Group. The Black Dog & Leventhal Publishers name and logo
are trademarks of Hachette Book Group, Inc.

The publisher is not responsible for websites (or their content) that are not
owned by the publisher.

The Hachette Speakers Bureau provides a wide range of authors for speaking
events. To find out more, go to www.HachetteSpeakersBureau.com or call
(866) 376-6591.

Recipe photography copyright © 2018 by Anshika Varma

Print book interior design by Sneha Pamneja

ISBN: 978-0-316-41576-7

Printed in China

1010

10 9 8 7 6 5 4 3 2

# CONTENTS

●●●●●●

## FOREWORD

Growing up and staying in Bombay from the 1960s through 1980s, good Indian food, as I knew it then, was always regional. Cooked and eaten at home, it was delicious. As a young boy I would wait for my friends to invite me over for a meal...especially those who were from different parts/regions of India—from Maharashtra, Kashmir, Karnataka, Bengal, or Rajasthan. Some of these friends were Catholic, or Hindu, Muslim, Parsi, or Sikh. No matter who they were, or where they came from, there was always amazing food cooked and served at home.

My love for food grew from these meals.

There were other cuisines we enjoyed when we went out to eat at restaurants—especially Mughlai, Chinese, and South Indian, or sometimes street fare of Chole Bhature. To most of us this was what we called Indian food. The food at home was never considered "Indian cuisine" as it was more Goan or Kashmiri, or Maharashtrian. The nicer restaurants predominantly served "restaurant food," which was primarily Mughlai with a bit of tandoori or Punjabi food thrown in. These restaurants existed in every major city, with other options of lunch homes or smaller "hotels." Over the years the cuisine slowly evolved and Indian restaurants spread to other parts of the world, making the diners believe that this was

"Indian cuisine." It was in the early '80s that the luxury hotel chains first started experimenting with regional Indian food. These meals, though expensive, introduced people for the first time, to food and a style of cooking they had no idea even existed.

When I started to cook, I had no interest in cooking the "Indian food" that restaurants had made popular. Even after I moved to the United States, I did not have much interest in eating or cooking this "Indian Cuisine." When I married Barkha I was introduced to a regional variety, Sindhi cuisine. This was very different from anything I had ever eaten. It excited me as a cook and a food lover to rediscover and celebrate the diversity of our regional cuisine.

I love Indian cuisine, the variety it offers, the cooking techniques, and the use of flavor and texture. I want the world to enjoy and celebrate this multiplicity in food that India has to offer. However, the use of an all-encompassing term "Indian Cuisine" does this wide range a disservice. We don't group French, German, Italian, and Spanish cuisine into a broad group of "European cuisine." Calling our food "Indian Cuisine" does not cover the depth, or showcase the nuances of the wide variety. I want to champion this diversity and beauty of regional Indian food. There is so much to discover, so much to acknowledge.

When we opened The Bombay Canteen in Mumbai, I was certain we were going to cook Indian food. We started to look for lesser-known regional cuisines and cooking techniques. And in the process discovered gems that most of our guests liked, but also some that others thought were strange. However, we continued our push for this regional variety and celebrating the food of one of the states on the coastal belt of India, and decided to open O'Pedros. Today, many chefs and restaurateurs are embracing and experimenting with local regional ingredients and cuisines. The inspiration is endless and the possibilities even more.

Indian regional cuisine is here to stay! The more we can do to spread the word and share the cuisine, the better world cuisine will get. Tiffin is a book that is just scratching the surface; it is like opening Alibaba's cave, a treasure trove of recipes and memories that mean a lot to a billion people!

Every recipe contributed in this book has a context and a memory associated. Our chef at The Bombay Canteen, Thomas Zacharias, like myself, champions regional Indian food and his recipes remind him of the joy of eating with family and the glorious flavors of his home. Of festivals he celebrated with his grandmother and the aromas of her kitchen. My mom's shrimp curry takes me back to the lazy afternoon meals we had growing up in Bombay and Anjuna. It still reminds me of the home-grown coconuts, rice, and mangoes. It takes me back to the days when we climbed our neighbor's coconut tree to steal a few fresh coconuts (even though we had a yard full of coconut trees that we had access to). I still remember an Assamese harvest meal that we immensely enjoyed, but also wondered why not many people (me included) knew about their amazing pork curry!

Tiffin celebrates these regional offerings, showcasing food from Ladakh to Tamil Nadu, and from Maharashtra to Arunachal Pradesh. Introducing food and cooking techniques that most of us don't know exist or have experienced. I believe if we don't celebrate these cuisines and techniques they will die like so many dishes, never to be recognized again.

I have had the pleasure of working with Sonal Ved on various projects. She has put her heart and soul into this treasury of food that India has to offer to the world.

As a chef I am excited to see this compilation of recipes. I wish this was my daily Tiffin and I could enjoy these cuisines every day!

CHEF FLOYD CARDOZ

The journey of *Tiffin* begins in our own kitchen, between the pages of a family recipe book, and in the childhood memories of how our grandmothers cooked. As we hold a magnifying glass over the lunch tiffins of our friends at school and later of our colleagues at work, dishes that deck our dining tables, and sophisticated amuse-bouches at progressive Indian restaurants, we experience the diversity of Indian cuisine.

As a civilization, India is believed to be about 80,0000 years old. From prehistoric settlements to the emergence of the Indus Valley Civilization, the rise of religions, dynasties, empires, and, most recently, colonization—the country's past has had a deep impact on its cuisine. In *Tiffin*, we aim to highlight what these catalysts were and how they helped shape the cuisines of different parts of the country.

Influences on Indian cuisine can be found as early as the time of the Indus Valley Civilization. The legacy left behind by the Harappans manifests in ingredients, the shapes of the vessels used for cooking, and techniques such as charring or smoking. While selecting the 500 recipes in the book, we realized the wisdom of these early people: they cooked and ate out of pots that were dexterously crafted, and consumed superfoods such as turmeric, ginger, and gourd—ingredients that are not too different from what we cook with today.

As the subcontinent witnessed the arrival of traders and invaders, the cauldron of Indian cuisine was further stirred. From the Turks, who brought dates and nuts and used them to garnish and sweeten desserts, to the Arab traders, who brought coffee and asafoetida via the silk route, to the Portuguese, who brought fine bread—these people changed the culinary landscape of India. Their lessons and ingredients merged into the prevailing culinary story of the land, to make Indian cuisine diverse and rich.

While on the one hand, tribal people, inspired by forests, made simple yet nutritious recipes, on the other, Indian royals enriched their local cuisines with fine and nuanced recipes. The royal kitchens brought to the fore methods such as slow-cooking of meats and lentils, hand-pounding of spices, complex marination of meats, and mixing of aromatic spices to bring a refined touch to each dish. These methods continue to be a crucial part of our cooking. They include marinating meats overnight, pre-soaking lentils and pulses, and fermenting dough and batter to obtain the desired texture and flavour.

European traders and colonizers also left their mark. The arrival of the British and the subsequent culinary exchange between the *memsahibs* (married white women) and the *khansamas* (cooks) led to the emergence of a new cuisine, glimpses of which can be seen across Indian gymkhanas, or clubs, in Indian metros.

The cuisine further changed post-Independence, when India became one of the most powerful agrarian economies in the world. Today, there is an

obvious agricultural atmosphere in every part of the country. Ingredients such as rice, wheat, sugar, cashew nuts, corn, and soybeans are our top exports, and milk and dairy are available in plenty. Staples of Indian cuisine are celebrated the world over—from peppercorns from Malabar, to tea from Darjeeling, to berries from Mahabaleshwar, to chiles from Nagaland, and oranges from Arunachal Pradesh.

When we set out to choose the recipes to include in *Tiffin*, we kept the varied produce, techniques, and culinary styles in mind. While each section is well represented in terms of what the six regions have to offer, it is by no means exhaustive. How does one bottle up the goodness of such an old and diverse cuisine in just 500 recipes?

So we did the next best thing and put in a flavorful blend of favorite Indian recipes (of course there is butter chicken) and several lesser-known dishes by taking a leaf out of temple cuisine, street food, tribal recipes, and other dishes that you might not commonly find.

While most of these have been hand-picked by culinary experts from each region, we went beyond, and reached out to the best repositories of traditional recipes—wedding caterers, who are given the responsibility of serving contemporary and traditional spreads. Each of the contributor recipes, which includes those given by grandmothers, mothers, aunts, friends, cookbook authors, and chefs who champion regional Indian cooking, are

marked by a miniature cloche. A handy glossary and basic recipe section will help you wade through these recipes.

While the book has been divided regionally, the dishes are not to be savored insularly. In fact, most can be effortlessly paired with one another, without them clashing. When we have friends over for tea, we often daydream of matching a Benarasi *tamatar chaat* with a *khasta kachori* from Madhya Pradesh, next to a bowl of Indore-style fried *garadu* neighboring *bhutte ke kees* and Kutchi *kadak* toasts. And on Sundays, with brunch on our minds, we want our tables laden with *Bhojpuri dum aloo*, Bengali-style *lucchis*, Rajasthani *ghatte ki kadhi*, Assamese chicken-and-banana-flower stir-fry, and a South Indian payasam.

While compiling these recipes, we came to realize that what scientists say about Indian cuisine is perhaps true. The reason why it is so addictive is because it has few overlapping flavors. With such a diverse topography—with snowy terrains, arid deserts, beautiful coastlines, leafy tropical forests, and mountainous belts—the ingredients here are unlike those in any other part of the world. They are different from one another, even within the country, and this is reflected in the way the cuisine changes as you move from one location to another. But when all these blend together in a cauldron of diverse cultural history, they lead to a multifaceted cuisine that we call Indian.

# GLOSSARY

## DALS AND LEGUMES

### KALA CHANA / HORSE GRAM

Fibrous black *chana* is soaked and boiled before eating. The sprouted variety is tossed as a salad. A typical Indian way of eating it is to toss boiled black *chana* with lemon juice, butter, coriander, chiles, and spices.

### RAJMA / RED KIDNEY BEANS

Red kidney beans are soaked overnight, boiled and then added to curries. When cooked with a spicy tomato sauce and served with rice, it results in a classic North Indian comfort meal called *rajma-chawal*. The Bhainsku *rajma* variety from Uttarakhand is pink in color and speckled with black spots.

### MOONG DAL / GREEN GRAM

This lentil can be either split or whole. *Moong dal* is usually boiled or soaked before use. It can be turned into a curry or fermented into a crepe or a savory cake called *dhokla*. Also available without the skin, in yellow color, it is cooked in a similar fashion.

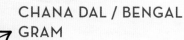

### CHANA DAL / BENGAL GRAM

One of the most basic pantry essentials, *chana dal* is split and polished in form. It is boiled to make curry, powdered to make chickpea flour or *besan*, and used in tempering.

### KABULI CHANA / CHICKPEAS

This beige-colored chickpea variety is soaked overnight and boiled before eating. It is tossed in Indian stir-fries and eaten with a refined flour-based bread called *puri*. Crushed Kabuli *chana* is used to give body to Indian cutlets called *tikkis*.

## MATKI / MOTH OR TURKISH BEAN

Moth or Turkish bean is soaked in water overnight to enable it to sprout. The bean is boiled, tempered, and turned into an Indian-style stir-fry or eaten as a salad.

## LOBIA / BLACK-EYED BEANS

Also known as cow peas, *lobia* is soaked and boiled, or sprouted, before eating. It is a rich source of calcium, folate, and proteins and is tempered before eating with *chapattis*.

## TOOR DAL / SPLIT PIGEON PEAS

This is the most common variety of lentil in the Indian pantry. It is usually boiled before use. Some recipes might call for soaking the *dal* in water overnight.

## SABUT MASOOR DAL / BROWN LENTIL

This whole brown seed-like lentil is boiled before use. It is cooked into a curry and creamed with dairy. When it is red in color and in split form, without the skin, it is known as split red lentil or *lal masoor*.

## URAD DAL / BLACK LENTIL

Whole *urad dal* resembles a black seed and is therefore known as black gram; it is also available in split and skinned form. The latter is off-white in color. This lentil can be turned into curries or be an excellent ingredient to ferment along with rice to make *idlis*, *dosas*, and other South Indian delicacies.

# SPICES

### KHUS KHUS / POPPY SEEDS

This ingredient is turned into a paste to add to gravies, soaked to texturize *tikkis*, and added to sweet dishes and savories alike. It is a versatile ingredient that is known for its cooling properties.

### LAL MIRCH / RED CHILE POWDER

Red chile powder is made of ground chiles from different parts of the country. The Kashmir and Guntur varieties are the most popular and potent. Traditionally, women who specialized in pounding chiles were hired to make this powder; now pre-packaged powder is available in Indian stores.

### HING / ASAFOETIDA

*Hing* is a type of resin that is added in minimal quantities to basic Indian tempering. It is used to gently flavor *dals*, curries, *rasams*, and other gravies. It is known to have digestive benefits.

### SAUNF / FENNEL SEEDS

Fennel seeds add a sprightly touch to any dish they are added to. They are one of the main components of a spice mix called Panch Phoran, which is popular in East India. Fennel seeds are also eaten raw as a mouth-freshener.

### LAUNG / CLOVES

It is aromatic and has tremendous medicinal benefits. Its oil is used to cure dental ailments, and is used in tempering.

### KALI MIRCH / BLACK PEPPERCORN

These black, round seeds are derived from the pepper plant. They can be ground in a mill and used to flavor bland dishes or added whole to the tempering for a rich spicy flavor.

## AJWAIN / CAROM SEEDS

*Ajwain* has several healing properties. From treating the common cold to digestion problems, the spice is used in powdered or whole form. In cooking, it adds a pungent flavor.

## DALCHINI / CINNAMON

*Dalchini* looks like the bark of a tree. Rightly so; it is procured from the inner bark of a tropical evergreen tree. It is used in whole form in tempering, or powdered and added for a rich, aromatic touch to gravies, *pilafs*, and curries.

## ELAICHI / CARDAMOM

Available in green and black forms, *elaichi* is a true Indian superfood. The black variety is known as *badi elaichi* and the green variety is known as *choti elaichi*. Crushed or whole, they are added to Indian tempering for *pilafs*, *biryanis*, Indian tea, and gravies. Powdered cardamom is added to desserts to add an earthy touch. *Elaichi* can instantly help cure nausea.

## TEJ PATTA / BAY LEAF

From detoxifying to slowing down aging, bay leaf is a variety of edible leaf with several health benefits. It is added at the tempering stage to hot oil, which absorbs its flavors. A lot of recipes pull out the bay leaf before serving the dish.

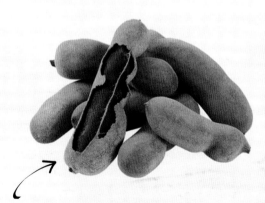

## IMLI / TAMARIND

This ingredient adds a sour, sweet taste to any dish it is added to. Available in pod form, it is usually pulped before use. Tamarind is highly tangy and added to sherbets, gravies, curries, and soups.

# SPICES

## CURRY LEAVES / KADHI PATTA

These leaves form the backbone of a typical Indian tempering. It is used in abundance to flavor dry stir-fries, especially in South Indian cuisine. Sometimes, dried curry leaves are also powdered to make *podi* (South Indian powder) to sprinkle on dosas, idlis, and *upmas*.

## METHI SEEDS / FENUGREEK SEEDS

These rough, coarse seeds from the *methi* or fenugreek plant are bitter but nutritious. They have high medicinal value, from helping with diabetes to acting as antioxidants. The seeds are soaked and blitzed into a paste or are used whole in tempering.

## KESAR / SAFFRON

This is one of the most expensive spices in India. It is used in sweet and savory preparations to give a unique floral fragrance and flavor. *Kesar* lets out an orange-yellow color to the dish it is added to.

## JAIPHAL / NUTMEG

Its outer coating is known as *javitri* or mace. Both the spices are used sparingly in Indian gravies, *pulaos*, and *biryanis*. They deliver a delicate earthy flavor to any dish they are added to.

## SHAHI JEERA / CARAWAY SEEDS

Caraway seeds are used in the tempering of Indian curries and gravies. They are bigger in size than regular cumin and deliver a more pronounced flavor.

## AMCHOOR / DRY MANGO POWDER

Tart, sour notes to a dish can be added with a gentle splattering of dry mango powder. It is made by grinding dry pieces of mango. *Amchoor* is known to aid acidity and boost digestion.

## CHIRONJI / CHAROLI

*Chironji* is a medicinal plant. Interestingly, it is used to add texture to several milk-based Indian desserts. It helps combat diarrhea and has several beauty benefits.

## CHAKRI PHOOL / STAR ANISE

Star anise delivers a fresh, sprightly flavor to any dish that it is added to. It is mostly used whole. The ingredient comes from a tree; it is plucked before ripening and dried before it is sold.

## DHANIYA SEEDS / CORIANDER SEEDS

Use them whole or powder them to make one of the most commonly used spices in the Indian kitchen. They are generously used in Indian gravies, curries, and *shorbas*.

## KOKUM

The product of a fruit tree, *kokum* is used fresh to make sherbet or dry as a souring agent. It is used in curries, gravies, and dals to enhance their flavor and give a lemon-like sour tang. *Kokum* is an essential ingredient to make *sol kadhi*.

## JEERA / CUMIN

*Jeera* belongs to the parsley and dill herb family. It is tiny and brown in color and is a must-have in an Indian spice box. *Jeera* is usually used in whole form in tempering, or powdered to flavor gravies and curries.

## PANCH PHORAN

A preferred tempering in East Indian cuisine, Panch Phoran is a mixture of five spices: fennel, cumin, *kalonji*, mustard, and fenugreek seeds.

## SAUNF / ANISEED

With a licorice-like taste, aniseed is aromatic and added in tempering of dishes, to flavor soups, pickles, and gravies.

## KALONJI / NIGELLA SEEDS

The nigella seed has a strong, pungent flavor. It has powerful healing benefits, from acting as a natural antioxidant to curing colds—there is little *kalonji* can't solve. It is also one of the integral ingredients for making Panch Phoran.

## RAI / MUSTARD SEEDS

These tiny seeds of mustard are black in color. They are blistered in hot oil in most Indian temperings and are one of the most commonly used spices. Mustard seeds are known to stimulate the appetite.

## VEGETABLES AND FRUITS

### KASHI PHAL / SAFED KADOO / ASH GOURD

An excellent source of vitamins, calcium, and minerals, ash gourd is an underdog Indian vegetable. It is used to make an Indian side dish called *subji*, to be eaten with *chapattis*.

### KARELA / BITTER GOURD

Bitter gourd is an acquired taste. The intensely bitter vegetable is juiced with the skin on and helps cure everything from indigestion to diabetes. When it is charred-fried, it loses its bitterness and turns into a wonderful Indian side dish.

### TARO ROOT

When eaten as a tuber, it is known as *arbi*, and when eaten as a leaf, it known as *patra*. The tuber is boiled before being used as a stir-fry, while the leaves are spiced and steamed to make a variety of Indian appetizers.

### BHINDI / OKRA

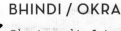

Okra is used in Asian and Indian cooking alike. It is one of the most frequently made vegetables in any Indian home. Most regions have their versions of cooking with this vegetable; South Indians stir-fry it with coconut, while North Indians add a dash of *amchoor* or dried mango powder.

### LAUKI / BOTTLE GOURD

It is a common Indian vegetable used as a side dish, or stir-fried at the base of a curry or dal. The bottle gourd has off-white flesh and seeds that are edible. Its juice is known to be a hydration hack during Indian summers.

### KASURI METHI / DRIED FENUGREEK LEAVES

Dried fenugreek leaves are used to finish several Indian gravies and curries. They have a distinct earthy aroma and flavor, which get added to the dish they are sprinkled on.

## PARWAL / POINTED GOURD

The pointed gourd has a neutral flavor and is used to make stir-fries. Interestingly, in Central India, people make a dessert out of this vegetable. *Parwal* is commonly available and inexpensive.

## METHI / FENUGREEK

Fenugreek leaves are available as mature leaves, and in micro-green form during winters in India. Both are used to make stir-fries and sometimes added to dal as well. They have a bitter aftertaste and are a good source of minerals and vitamins.

## TURIA / RIDGE GOURD

This variety of gourd is called so because of its corrugated texture. It is used to make side dishes and is a high source of vitamins.

## MAKHANA

## NADRU / LOTUS ROOT

The root of the lotus flower or lotus stem is finely sliced, boiled, and used to make various North Indian side dishes. It is a rich source of phytonutrients and minerals. The seeds of the plant are popped like popcorn to make a healthy snack called *makhana*.

## VEGETABLES AND FRUITS

### KAND / PURPLE YAM

This root vegetable grows underground. It is boiled or baked and used to make a variety of niche Indian dishes, like the famous Gujarati *undhiyu*. It is a rich source of vitamin A, vitamin C, and manganese.

### KATHAL / JACKFRUIT

This tropical fruit is eaten ripe, as it is, or eaten raw. It is often used by vegetarians to make dishes look meaty.

### BAEL / WOOD APPLE

Bael has a sticky, pulpy inside. It is seldom eaten raw and is commonly sweetened with sugar syrup and turned into a cooling summer drink.

### BAMBOO SHOOT

A Northeast Indian staple, bamboo shoots are not widely available. They are sold either in fermented or fresh form; in most cases they are turned into a stir-fry or added to soups.

## BAIGAN / EGGPLANT

Eggplants come in short, round, elongated, large, and plump shapes. Some are starkly purple, while some have white streaks on them. They are best mashed and turned into a famous dish called *bharta*, or chopped and stir-fried.

## KAIRI / RAW MANGO

Before the mango ripens, it is plucked out. This is a delicacy to be eaten on its own. In some regions such as Gujarat, it is baked or boiled and blitzed to make a cooling summer drink.

## SURAN / ELEPHANT-FOOT YAM

An unpleasant-looking vegetable, *suran* is a good source of carbohydrates. It goes through multiple rounds of cleansing, scrubbing, and boiling before it is used to make a stir-fry or mashed into a cutlet.

# MISCELLANEOUS

## GONGURA LEAVES

These refreshing leaves with bright red stems are commonly used to make *pachhadi* or stir-fry in South India. It is a variety of sorrel leaf and is sometimes also eaten in pickled form. It is a rich source of folate and vitamins.

## KURMURA / PUFFED RICE

Puffed rice is used to make one of the most common and popular varieties of Indian snacks, called *bhel*. It is light and sometimes tempered and mixed with *sev* for a quick snack.

## RAJGIRA / AMARANTH

A well-known Indian superfood, it is used to coat cutlets and *kebabs* for texture, powdered and used in flour form to make Indian breads, or cooked with jaggery syrup to make energy bars.

## SEV

## NYLON SEV

A fine vermicelli-like ingredient made out of fried gram flour, *sev* is used to garnish a variety of Indian chaats. When it is extremely fine-textured, it is known as nylon *sev*, due to its resemblance to nylon threads.

## TARBOOJ KE BEEJ / WATERMELON SEEDS

Watermelon seeds are extracted from the fruit, dried, and used to garnish desserts or main courses. They are also powdered and added to gravies for texture.

## SABUDANA / SAGO

A form of tapioca, *sabudana* is a pearl-shaped ingredient that is soaked in water before it is stir-fried with tempering. It is also added to desserts for texture. This ingredient is one of the few things that are allowed to be eaten during Indian fasts.

## DHANIYA / CORIANDER

A common variety of Indian herb, coriander has a cilantro-like texture, color, and flavor. Its roots are more flavorful than its leaves. It can be blended to make a green chutney too.

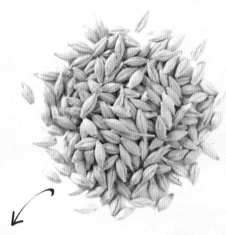

## JAU / BARLEY

Also known as *jau*, barley water has intense cooling properties. The grain is powdered to make flour for Indian bread. Sometimes, the grains are boiled and mashed to make *tikkis*.

## POHA / CHURA / FLATTENED RICE

Flattened rice is either soaked in water until it swells and used to make breakfast or toasted and tempered to make a dry snack.

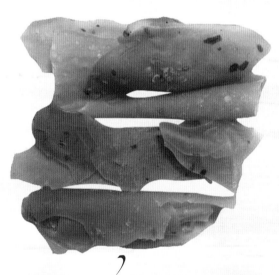

## RABODI

Dried sheets made out of corn are known as *rabodi*. It has a satisfyingly soft texture when added to curries and gravies. *Rabodi* is available in Indian stores and is used in Rajasthani dishes.

## TIL / SESAME SEEDS

Sesame seeds are also known as *til* and are available in white and black. They can be ground into a powder and added to an Indian mouth-freshener called *mukhwas*. Or they can be sprinkled on dishes as a garnish. When mixed with jaggery, sesame can turn into a sweet cracker as well.

## PAPAD / POPPADUM

A crispy snack that is made of a variety of Indian ingredients such as rice flour, *urad dal*, *moong dal*, corn, and *sago* is known as papad. It is either deep-fried or roasted on a live flame. It is eaten with an Indian meal to add texture to the experience.

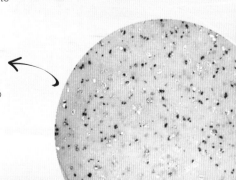

# SPICES

### KACHRI / WILD CUCUMBER

*Kachri* is a wild variety of cucumber found in arid deserts. Its powder is used to marinate meats and for chutney, while whole *kachri* is used in stir-fries or pickled to eat with Rajasthani meals.

### WHOLE SPICE MIX

A combination of spices such as cumin, cinnamon, cloves, peppercorn, star anise, bay leaves, and others used in Indian tempering makes this mix. It is available in pre-packaged form in Indian stores.

### KALA NAMAK / INDIAN BLACK SALT

Black salt is rich in minerals. It has a potent salty taste and is used to flavor chaats, chutneys, and sherbets.

### TIKKA MASALA / SPICE CAKE

*Tikka masala* is one of the most commonly used spice mixes in the Indian kitchen. It is a combination of various ground spices including chile powder, peppercorn, cinnamon, cloves, and more. The mix is usually mixed with yogurt or another liquid to form a marinade for meats.

### RASAM POWDER

A combination of various *dals* such as *toor* and *chana* and spices such as curry leaves and coriander seeds, *rasam* powder is the base spice to make a South Indian curry called *rasam*.

### HALDI / TURMERIC

One of the biggest superfoods in India, turmeric is known as powdered gold. It has high antioxidant, anti-bacterial, and anti-fungal properties and is used as a spice in tempering. Fresh turmeric is known as brain food, because it benefits memory and the nervous system.

# VEGETABLES & FRUITS

### TINDA / ROUND GOURD

This small, light green vegetable is chopped and used to make stir-fry. It is easily available, inexpensive, and commonly used in the Indian kitchen.

### SAIJAN KI PHALI / DRUMSTICK

The vegetable that grows on the moringa tree is one of the healthiest Indian superfoods. It is chopped and boiled or steamed and added to dals and gravies. Moringa leaves are blitzed into a powder and used to make drinks.

# GRAINS

### DALIA / CRACKED WHEAT

This is used to make Indian porridge or sweet dishes. It goes very well when paired with jaggery. Cracked wheat has a couscous-like texture and flavor. It is essentially a broken form of whole-wheat grain.

## FLOUR

### BESAN / GRAM FLOUR

Flour made out of powdered Bengal gram. Besan is used as a coating to batter-fry vegetables or fish. It is also made into a batter for crepes or pancakes.

### MAIDA / ALL-PURPOSE FLOUR

Also known as refined flour, *maida* is low in nutrition. It is used to make a variety of Indian breads such as *naan*, *parotta*, and *kulcha*. *Maida* is inexpensive and has a long shelf life.

### ATTA / WHOLE-WHEAT FLOUR

*Atta* is powdered grain. It is one of the most common types of flour in Indian pantries and is used across the country to make thin tortillas called *chapattis*.

### RICE FLOUR

Powdered rice in flour form. It is an excellent ingredient to coat seafood and plantains. Rice flour is also used to give body to desserts.

### SATTU

A rich Indian superfood, *sattu* is made of ground pulses, cereals, and lentils. It has an off-white color and is high in minerals and vitamins. It has high energy properties and is used to make sherbets, breads, and porridges.

### SUJI / SEMOLINA FLOUR

Also known as *rava*, semolina is used as a coating for various seafood- and meat-based dishes. It is also mixed with milk and sugar to make Indian sweet dishes. It is a common and inexpensive Indian pantry staple.

## BREADS

### PAV

Small loaves of bread usually served with spicy *bhaji* as a popular street food.

### CHAPATTI

*Chapatti* is a flat and slim Indian bread. It is made of whole-wheat flour and has a form like a Mexican tortilla, only it is much slimmer. It is eaten with almost everything—curries, gravies, *dal*, pickles, and *chutneys*.

### KULCHA

*Kulcha* is made of refined flour and is a leavened variety of bread. It is usually cooked in a *tandoor*, which is an Indian clay oven. *Kulchas* can be stuffed with onions, *paneer*, chiles, and garlic.

## TECHNIQUE

### DUMPUKTH

Slow-cooking by sealing the vessel to get the ingredients to give more flavor is known as *dumpukth*. Dough or a heavy lid is used to close a heavy-bottomed pan. Sometimes the dish is cooked overnight for the flavors to reach their highest potential.

### TADKA

*Tadka* is the Hindi word for tempering. Here, oil is heated, and a splattering of spices and herbs is added. This helps the hot oil to absorb the flavors, which are then released into the main dish.

# MISCELLANEOUS

## KASUNDI

*Kasundi* is made by fermenting mustard seeds. Strong, with a kick of umami, *kasundi* is India's answer to wasabi. Today, *kasundi* is eaten with fish cutlets, and used to marinate fish or meats, or as a dipping sauce.

## RAITA

A cooling Indian side made of yogurt. It is a dish that may or may not have finely chopped tomatoes, onions, cucumbers, and chiles. It is usually eaten with *parathas* or Indian rice dishes.

## NANNARI / SARSAPARILLA

Also known as sarsaparilla, *nannari* roots are medicinal and have immense cooling benefits. In South India, the root extract is turned into a sweet, summer drink.

## WARQ / SILVER LEAF

Silver leaf is any foil composed of a pure metal, usually silver or gold, and is used for garnishing. The leaves are edible but flavorless.

## SONTH / DRIED GINGER

Dried ginger powder has immense heating properties. It is a quick fix for the common cold and cough. It is added to gravies and curries for an earthy, gingery flavor. Sometimes it is also eaten with honey for medical benefits.

## GUR / JAGGERY

Jaggery is a variety of unrefined sugar. It is a healthier alternative to common sugar. Golden in color, jaggery is used to sweeten Indian desserts. It can also be cooked with water and turned into a syrup.

## KEWRA / VETIVIER WATER

An extract distilled from pandanus flowers, *kewra* is colorless. The liquid is added in minimal quantities to curries and gravies for aroma and a gently sweet flavor.

## SIRKA / VINEGAR

Vinegar extracted from rice, sugar cane, coconut, and other tropical Indian ingredients, *sirka* is a souring agent and is used in place of lemon juice to give dishes a tangy flavor.

## MANGODI

*Mangodi* is a ready-to-use ingredient made out of soaked, puréed, and dried lentils. It is added to Rajasthani dishes for texture. The granule-sized *mangodis* absorb the flavor of the curries and gravies they are added to.

## CHAACH / BUTTERMILK

A cooling drink made out of yogurt and water churned together. Buttermilk is sometimes tempered with curry leaves or seasoned with salt and cumin powder.

## PANEER

Also known as cottage cheese, is it a common variety of Indian cheese. *Paneer* is made by curdling milk with lemon juice and discarding the whey. It is used in cubed or crumbled form.

## DAHI / CURD

Solid-textured white mass obtained by adding culture to lukewarm milk. It has fewer bacterial strands than yogurt, but both are used interchangeably in Indian cuisine.

## KER & SANGRI

A local Marwari favorite is *ker sangri*—made with *ker*, a shrub berry, and *sangri*, the bean of a flowering tree called *khejar*. When *ker* and *sangri* are cooked together with a tempering of spices, the dish is eaten as a main course. The berry and bean are also pickled to eat later.

## KHOYA / WHOLE-MILK FUDGE

A coarse, fudgy dairy product obtained by cooking milk until the liquid from it begins to evaporate. *Khoya* is sweetened with sugar or jaggery to turn it into a sweet dish. Sometimes it is also added to gravies for texture.

## SHERBET

Not to be confused with the frozen dessert, Indian sherbet refers to a sweetened drink made from a variety of ingredients such as *kokum*, mango, lemongrass, fennel seeds, and so on.

## TODDY

Early morning coconut sap is collected and sold in bottles in coastal states in India, which have an abundance of coconut trees. Toddy is also turned into an alcoholic drink or used to ferment breads.

## SOYBEAN

An inexpensive form of protein, soybean is a product of the soybean plant. It is made into tofu, soy milk, fermented bean paste, tempeh, and other vegan-friendly edibles.

## PHITKARI / ALUM

Alum is available as loose powder or in block form. Commonly it is added to water to purify it, since alum makes the grits and impurities settle at the bottom. Alum is used to quick pickle or preserve ingredients. It is frequently used in the Indian kitchen to make a dish called *petha*.

## KOFTA

Roundels of meat balls added to gravies are known as *kofta*. In India, for vegetarians, *koftas* are also made using cottage cheese or potatoes, though traditionally they are made of minced meat.

## KORMA

The word comes from the Urdu word "to braise." It is a type of Indian gravy wherein meat or vegetables are braised in liquid, which could be yogurt, cream, stock, or water.

## IDLI STEAMER

A metal vessel that has built-in round molds, space at the bottom to hold water to allow steaming, and a lid. Raw idli batter is poured into the molds, and water is added at the bottom. The steam from the hot water cooks the dish.

# BASIC RECIPES

## MUSTARD SEED OIL

Cooking time: 10 minutes
Makes: 1¼ cups (300 ml)

INGREDIENTS

5 Tbsp (55 g) yellow mustard seeds
5 Tbsp (55 g) brown mustard seeds
1 Tbsp (9 g) mustard powder
1 cup (240 ml) olive oil

METHOD

1. In a blender, combine the yellow mustard seeds, brown mustard seeds, and mustard powder. Blitz together.
2. With the blender running, pour the olive oil through the blender cap and continue to churn the mixture until it emulsifies thoroughly.
3. Strain the oil through a fine-mesh sieve and discard the solids. Store for up to a week in the refrigerator.

## DUNGAAR

Cooking time: 20 minutes
For 1 recipe

INGREDIENTS

1 piece coal
1 Tbsp (15 g) ghee

METHOD

1. Heat the coal on a live flame until it turns red. This should take 8–9 minutes.
2. Carefully, with a pair of tongs, place the coal in the dish you want to smoke. You can place the hot coal in a metal bowl or a piece of aluminium foil.
3. Pour ghee over it and allow it to sizzle for a second. Cover the dish with a lid for 7–8 minutes, to allow it to smoke.

4. Open the lid and discard the piece of coal with the tongs, and stir the dish well. This will ensure the flavor is absorbed thoroughly.

## KHOYA / MAWA

Cooking time: 2 hours
Makes: 1 cup (200 g)

INGREDIENTS

5 cups (1.2 L) full-fat milk

METHOD

1. In a thick-bottomed pan over medium heat, heat milk and allow it to reach the boiling point.
2. Allow it to bubble on medium flame, stirring occasionally to prevent it from spilling over.
3. Scrape the milk solids from the side of the pan and keep adding them back to the pan.
4. Continue to do this for an hour and a half to two hours until all the milk has thoroughly reduced and all you have is milk mass.
5. Reduce the heat to low and monitor the pan, as it is likely to burn too quickly.
6. Once all the liquid has evaporated, remove the khoya from the pan and refrigerate until use.

## YOGURT

Cooking time: 10 minutes
Makes: 4 cups (960 ml)

INGREDIENTS

4 cups (960 ml) full-fat milk
1 Tbsp (15 g) yogurt culture

METHOD

1. Warm the milk slightly in a milk pot for 2 minutes on low heat.
2. Remove from the heat and let it rest for 3–4 minutes.
3. Stir in the yogurt culture and keep it covered in a warm place for 6–7 hours.

4. Refrigerate once it is set.
5. For sour yogurt: Allow fresh yogurt to stay at room temperature once it has set. Leaving it out for 3–4 hours will speed up its bacterial activity and turn the yogurt sour.

## CHAAT MASALA

Cooking time: 15 minutes
Makes: ½ cup (80 g)

INGREDIENTS

5 Tbsp (35 g) ground cumin (*jeera*)
1 Tbsp (15 g) peppercorns (*sabut kali mirch*)
2 Tbsp (60 g) dried mango powder (*amchoor*)
1 Tbsp (18 g) Indian black salt (*kala namak*)
½ tsp ground asafoetida (*hing*)
Salt, to taste

METHOD

1. On a hot standard pan on medium-high heat, tip in all the ingredients and toss for 1–2 minutes.
2. Remove from the pan and allow it to cool.
3. Blend it in a blender on high speed into a fine powder.
4. Run it through a fine sieve and discard the molasses.
5. Store in an airtight container for up to a month.

## RAW PAPAYA PASTE

Cooking time: 10 minutes
Makes: ¾ cup (180 g)

INGREDIENTS

1 cup (170 g) raw papaya (*papita*)
5 Tbsp (75 ml) water

METHOD

1. In a blender, beat both the ingredients into a fine purée. Add more water to smoothen, if needed.
2. Store in an ice tray by freezing into cubes.

## GINGER-GARLIC PASTE

Cooking time: 10 minutes
Makes: 4½ cups (400 g)

INGREDIENTS

1 cup (100 g) ginger (*adrak*), peeled
1 cup (136 g) garlic (*lasan*), peeled
2 Tbsp (30 ml) vegetable oil

METHOD

1. In a blender, blitz ginger and garlic together into a fine paste. Add a few tablespoons of water to loosen the paste.
2. Remove from the blender and pour oil on top to keep it fresh.
3. Refrigerate until use.

## RIPE OR RAW MANGO PURÉE

Cooking time: 5 minutes
Makes: ¾ cup (200 g)

INGREDIENTS

1 cup (165 g) raw or ripe mango (*kairi*)
A few ice cubes

METHOD

1. In a food processor, tip in raw or ripe mango. Add ice cubes instead of water and blend into a smooth purée.
2. Strain the purée using a sieve and discard the molasses.
3. Freeze until use.

## JIRALU MASALA

Cooking time: 10 minutes
Makes: ¼ cup (40 g)

INGREDIENTS

2 Tbsp (14 g) ground cumin (*jeera*)
½ Tbsp (9 g) Indian black salt (*kala namak*)
½ Tbsp (9 g) sea salt
1 tsp red chile powder
Pinch ground asafoetida (*hing*)
1 tsp dried mango powder (*amchoor*)

METHOD

1. In a blender, mix all the ingredients into a fine powder.
2. Store in an airtight container up to a week.

## LENTIL STOCK

Cooking time: 1½–2 hours
Makes: 4 cups (960 ml)

INGREDIENTS

6–7 cups (1.4 L–1.6 L) water
1 cup (200 g) mixed lentils, soaked in water for 2 hours
3 tsp salt

METHOD

1. Drain the lentils.
2. In a pot, mix all the ingredients and allow it to simmer on medium heat for an hour and a half to two hours.
3. Once the lentils are soft, drain and separate the stock.
4. Add the cooked lentils to make kebabs, pureé into dosa batter, or add to rice pulaos. Save the stock in a refrigerator.

## HUNG CURD

Cooking time: 5 minutes
Makes: ¾ cup (200 g)

INGREDIENTS

1 cup (240 g) yogurt (dahi)
1 sheet of cheesecloth

METHOD

1. Pour the yogurt into the cheesecloth and fasten it from the top.
2. Hang it loose and allow the water from the yogurt to trickle out slowly.
3. After 5–6 hours, transfer the yogurt still retained in the cheesecloth into a bowl and use it as hung curd.

## PANEER

Cooking time: 20 minutes
Makes: 1 cup (225 g)

INGREDIENTS

4 cups (960 ml) full-fat milk
Juice of 1 medium-size lemon (nimbu)

METHOD

1. In a deep-bottomed pan over a medium-high heat, heat milk and allow it to reach the boiling point.
2. Add lemon juice gradually, continuously stirring until the milk begins to curdle.
3. Once the water separates out thoroughly from the thick white mass called paneer, strain it with a cheesecloth.
4. Discard the whey and allow the paneer to rest inside the cheesecloth for 1–2 hours.
5. De-mold the mass from the cheesecloth and use.

## MINT–CILANTRO CHUTNEY

Cooking time: 10 minutes
Makes: ⅓ cup (100 g)

INGREDIENTS

1 cup (64 g) fresh mint leaves (pudina)
½ cup (8 g) fresh cilantro leaves (hara dhaniya)
3 green chiles
1 tsp cumin seeds (jeera)
2 Tbsp (30 ml) lemon juice (nimbu)
5 Tbsp (75 ml) water
½ tsp sugar
Salt, to taste

METHOD

1. In a blender, add all the ingredients and blitz into a thick paste.
2. Add more water if required.
3. Refrigerate until use.

## DATE-TAMARIND CHUTNEY

Cooking time: 30 minutes
Makes: ¾ cups (200 g)

### INGREDIENTS

1 cup (240 g) dates, seeded and finely chopped
½ cup tamarind (*imli*), seeded
½ cup (168 g) jaggery (*gur*), finely chopped
1½ cups (360 ml) water
2 tsp red chile powder
1 tsp ground cumin (*jeera*)
Salt, to taste

### METHOD

1. In a skillet, boil water and add dates, tamarind, and jaggery until the mixture reaches the boiling point. This should take 3–4 minutes.
2. Cool off the mixture and blitz it into a thick paste. Strain using a fine sieve and discard the molasses.
3. Add red chile powder, cumin powder, and salt, and stir well.
4. Refrigerate until use.

## GARAM MASALA

Cooking time: 15 minutes
Makes: ¾ cup (120 g)

### INGREDIENTS

5 Tbsp (30 g) cumin seeds (*jeera*)
4 Tbsp (30 g) green cardamom (*choti elaichi*)
2 Tbsp (30 g) peppercorns (*sabut kali mirch*)
2 Tbsp (10 g) coriander seeds (*dhaniya*)
1 Tbsp (6 g) fennel seeds (*saunf*)
1 Tbsp (8 g) cloves (*laung*)
2 (1-in. / 2.5-cm) cinnamon sticks (*dalchini*)
3 bay leaves (*tej patta*)
1 Tbsp (6 g) caraway seeds (*shahi jeera*)
2 tsp nutmeg powder
1 tsp dried ginger powder (*sonth*)

### METHOD

1. In a skillet over a low-medium heat, dry-roast all the spices for 3–4 minutes or until they are fragrant.
2. Ensure the pan is not too hot, or the spices will begin to burn.
3. Remove from the heat and allow the spices to cool down.
4. Blend them in a high-speed blender into a fine powder.
5. Run the mixture through a sieve and discard the molasses.
6. Stock the powder in an airtight jar for up to a month.

## GHEE

Cooking time: 1½–2 hours
Makes: 2–3 cups (480–720 ml)

### INGREDIENTS

16 cups (4 L) milk
3 Tbsp (45 g) yogurt (*dahi*)

### METHOD

1. In a heavy-bottomed pan over low-medium heat, heat 1 liter of milk until it reaches the boiling point. Allow it to cool at room temperature, so a thin sheet of milk cream or malai forms on top of it.
2. Save this in a bowl in a refrigerator. Repeat the process with other 3 liters of milk, boiling only a liter at a time. You can do this over 3 days and keep adding to your malai bowl.
3. Once you have about a cup of malai, add yogurt to it and allow it to rest for 4 hours at room temperature. This allows the malai to get cultured.
4. Using a wooden spoon, vigorously whisk the malai until the milk solids begin to separate from the whey. You can add 3–4 Tbsp of water in order to quicken this process.
5. Transfer the solid into a heavy-bottomed pan and continue to cook it on low heat.

6. Once this butter melts off, the milk solids will settle at the bottom and the ghee will rise on the top.
7. Run it through a sieve and collect the golden liquid in a bowl.
8. You can store the ghee at room temperature for up to a week.

## BUTTERMILK / CHAACH

Cooking time: 5 minutes
Makes: 1 glass (250 ml)

INGREDIENTS

½ cup (120 g) yogurt (*dahi*)
1 cup (240 ml) water

METHOD

1. In a bowl, mix both the ingredients.
2. Run a hand blender through the mixture until it blends thoroughly.
3. Refrigerate until use.

## TAMARIND PULP

Cooking time: 15 minutes
Makes: 1¼ cups (300 g)

INGREDIENTS

1 cup tamarind (*imli*)
2 cups (480 ml) water

METHOD

1. On a skillet over low-medium heat, heat water and soak tamarind in it for 30 minutes.
2. Drain and blend it into a liquid.
3. Strain and discard the molasses.
4. Refrigerate until use.

Note: Alternately, you can buy pre-made tamarind balls from an Indian grocery store. These are essentially balls of tamarind extract, rolled out and ready for use.

## COCONUT MILK

Cooking time: 15 minutes
Makes: 1 cup (240 ml)

INGREDIENTS

¾ cup (180 ml) water
2 cups (160 g) fresh coconut flesh (*nariyal*), grated

METHOD

1. In a blender, blitz all the ingredients together into a thick liquid.
2. Run this liquid through a cheesecloth and squeeze out the milk. The milk will drop right through the cloth.
3. Re-do this at least 2–3 times until all the milk has been extracted from the coconut flesh.
4. Refrigerate until use.

## BIRISTA

Cooking time: 1 hour
Makes: 3 cups (700 g)

INGREDIENTS

2 lb, 3 oz (1 kg) onion, thinly sliced
Vegetable oil, for frying

METHOD

1. In a skillet over low-medium heat, heat the vegetable oil. Add the onions and deep-fry until they are brown and crispy.
2. Spread them on a kitchen towel and allow it to soak the extra oil.
3. Freeze the onions for 10–15 minutes.
4. Remove from the refrigerator and stock in an airtight container for up to a week.

## SUGAR SYRUP

Cooking time: 1 hour
Makes: 2 cups (480 ml)

INGREDIENTS

3 cups (600 g) sugar
1½ cups (360 ml) water
2 tsp saffron threads (*kesar*)

METHOD

1. In a heavy-bottomed saucepan over medium-high heat, combine the sugar and water.
2. Cook, stirring continuously, and bring to a boil.
3. After 8–10 minutes, the sugar will dissolve into the water.
4. Allow it to boil for a few minutes more until the syrup thickens. This is your basic sugar syrup.
5. Check for its consistency by dipping a spoon into the syrup, touching it with your forefinger, pressing your thumb to your forefinger, and gently pulling them apart—when a single thread forms and does not break, it is ready.
6. To achieve a two-thread consistency, boil it further for 3–4 minutes. Check the consistency between your thumb and forefinger; pull them apart to see if two threads form; your sugar syrup with two-thread consistency is ready.
7. Finish by stirring in saffron threads.

## SAFFRON SYRUP

Cooking time: 5 minutes
Makes: 2 Tbsp (30 ml)

### INGREDIENTS

1 tsp saffron threads (*kesar*)
2 Tbsp (30 ml) milk or water

### METHOD

1. Take warm milk or water. Add saffron threads and stir well. Once the saffron releases its color and flavor into the milk or water, use it as needed.

## LAMB STOCK

Cooking time: 1½ hours
Makes: 4 cups (960 ml)

### INGREDIENTS

7 ounces (200 g) lamb bones
4 cups (960 ml) water
1 medium-size onion, sliced
1 large carrot (*gajar*), diced
1 medium-size stalk celery, diced
1 bay leaf (*tej patta*)
1 tsp peppercorns (*sabut kali mirch*)

METHOD

1. In a skillet over medium-high heat, heat enough water to submerge the bones. Bring it to a boil and add the bones to it. Allow it to boil for 5 minutes. Drain and discard this water.
2. Add the blanched bones to the other ingredients and pour more water on top. The water should cover the ingredients completely.
3. Bring the water to a rolling boil. Remove any scum that floats on top.
4. Pour more water if needed, and continue to boil the broth on low-medium heat for 1 hour. Keep adding more water if needed.
5. Strain and reserve the stock for use.

## COCONUT CHUTNEY

Cooking time: 20 minutes
Makes: 1 cup (240 g)

### INGREDIENTS

1 cup (80 g) fresh coconut (*nariyal*), grated
2 green chiles, finely chopped
1 tsp ginger (*adrak*)
Salt, to taste
1 Tbsp (15 ml) coconut oil (*nariyal*)
1 Tbsp (12.5 g) Bengal gram/split chickpeas (*chana dal*), roasted
1 tsp mustard seeds (*rai*)
1 dry red chile (*sookhi lal mirch*)
3 curry leaves (*kadhi patta*)

### METHOD

1. In a food processor, blend coconut, green chiles, ginger, and salt. Add a little water to adjust consistency. It should resemble a thick porridge and be coarse.
2. In a skillet over a medium-high heat, heat the coconut oil. Add the Bengal gram, mustard seeds, dry red chile, and curry leaves, and allow the ingredients to crackle.
3. Pour this hot tempering on the coconut mixture and stir well.

## RACHEDOMASALA PASTE

Cooking time: 10 minutes
Makes: ½ cup (120 g)

### INGREDIENTS

1 (1-in. / 2.5 cm) piece ginger (*adrak*)
5 garlic cloves (*lasan*)
10 dried red chiles (*sookhi lal mirch*)
1 tsp cumin seeds (*jeera*)
5 peppercorns (*sabut kali mirch*)
1 (1-in. / 2.5-cm) cinnamon stick (*dalchini*)
5 whole cloves (*laung*)
½ tsp fenugreek seeds (*methi dana*)
1 tsp sugar
3 Tbsp (45 ml) vinegar (*sirka*)
1 Tbsp (15 ml) coconut (*nariyal*) feni liquor
   (available at Indian markets)
Salt, to taste

### METHOD

1. In a blender, blitz all the ingredients into a
   fine paste.
2. Add 3–5 Tbsp of water to adjust consistency.
   Stock for 1–2 days in the refrigerator.

## PANCH PHORAN

Cooking time: 5 minutes
Makes: 5 Tbsp (50 g)

### INGREDIENTS

1 Tbsp (6 g) cumin seeds (*jeera*)
1 Tbsp (11 g) mustard seeds (*rai*)
1 Tbsp (6 g) fennel seeds (*saunf*)
1 Tbsp (10 g) nigella seeds (*kalonji*)
1 tsp fenugreek seeds (*methi dana*)

### METHOD

In a bowl, mix all the ingredients together.
Store in an airtight container.

## TOMATO PURÉE

Cooking time: 20 minutes
Makes: ½ cup (120 g)

### INGREDIENTS

4 medium-size tomatoes
Water, for boiling

### METHOD

1. Dice the tomatoes and discard the seeds.
2. In a skillet over medium heat, boil enough
   water to completely cover the tomatoes and
   boil it for 30 minutes.
3. Remove from the pan; drain and reserve the
   water.
4. Allow the tomatoes to cool and blitz in a
   blender. Add the reserved water if needed to
   adjust consistency—it should be like ketchup.
5. Run it through a sieve and discard the
   molasses and leftover water. Save the tomato
   purée for use.

## DHANSAK MASALA

Cooking time: 20 minutes
Makes: 4 cups (500 g)

### INGREDIENTS

1 cup (250 g) coriander seeds (*dhaniya*)
½ cup (125 g) cumin seeds (*jeera*)
½ cup (125 g) dried red chiles (*sookhi lal mirch*)
6 tsp caraway seeds (*shahi jeera*)
1 Tbsp (10 g) fenugreek seeds (*methi dana*)
2 tsp black stone flower (*pathar ke phool*)
1 Tbsp (15 g) peppercorns (*sabut kali mirch*)
4 tsp poppy seeds (*khus khus*)
2 Tbsp (30 g) ground cinnamon (*dalchini*)
4 Tbsp (30 g) cloves (*laung*)
1 cup (30 g) bay leaves (*tej patta*)
¼ cup (30 g) star anise (*chakri ke phool*)
1 tsp mace powder (*javitri*)
1 tsp nutmeg powder (*jaiphal*)

### METHOD

1. In a skillet over low-medium heat, dry-roast all
   the spices for 5–10 minutes until fragrant.
1. Blend into a fine powder in a blender and stock
   in an airtight jar for a week.

## WHOLE-WHEAT FLOUR DOUGH

Cooking time: 20 minutes
Makes: 2 cups (200 g)

INGREDIENTS

2 cups (250 g) whole-wheat flour (*atta*)
¾ cup (180 ml) water
1 Tbsp (15 ml) vegetable oil

METHOD

1.  In a bowl, mix all the ingredients and knead into a tight dough.
2.  To make chapattis: Break the dough into 10–15 table-tennis ball–size dough balls.
3.  Place them on a rolling board and flatten them with your palms. Using a rolling pin, enlarge the circles into disks the size of your hands.
4.  Use extra dry flour to ensure they don't stick to the rolling board.
5.  Lift the chapattis and cook them on a hot griddle over medium heat on both sides until light brown spots appear on the surface. You can make parathas in the same way; simply fold the large, raw chapatti dough into a triangle, overlapping the layers, and roll it in this shape.
6.  Apply 1 tsp ghee on top before serving.
7.  To make puris: Cut coin-size roundels of the dough, 20–25 and roll them into smooth balls.
8.  Place them on a rolling board and flatten them with your palms. Using a rolling pin, enlarge the circles into disks the size of your palm.
9.  Use extra dry flour to ensure they don't stick to the rolling board.
10. Lift the disks, and in a deep pan, deep-fry them in hot oil before serving.

## SAMOSA PASTRY / PUFF

Cooking time: 10 minutes
Makes: 12 samosas

INGREDIENTS

2 cups (250 g) all-purpose flour (*maida*)
½ cup (120 g) ghee
1 tsp carom seeds (*ajwain*)
2 tsp salt
Water, for kneading

METHOD

1.  In a medium-size bowl, combine the flour, ghee, carom seeds, and salt. Rub with your fingertips until the mixture resembles bread crumbs. Gradually add some water and knead into a medium-soft dough.
2.  Divide the dough into small rounds. Roll each round into a small disk and cut into half-moons. Make a cone out of each half-moon and stuff each with filling. Seal the edges to resemble a triangle, to conceal the filling inside.

# north india

●●●●

UTTAR PRADESH . JAMMU & KASHMIR . PUNJAB . DELHI .
HIMACHAL PRADESH . UTTARAKHAND . HARYANA

A famed ambassador of Indian cuisine abroad, North India is known for its rich gravies, heavily-spiced preparations, meat-based fare and flavor-steeped food. Dishes such as butter chicken, *dal makhani*, naan, and *murg mussalam*, among others, are a mainstay at Indian restuarants all over the world.

At the northernmost tip of the county, Kashmir is known for its delicate recipes and hospitable culture, which are innately warmth-inducing. *Wazwan*, the multi-course Kashmiri meal, is a standout feature. Literally translating to "cooking shop" (with "waz" meaning "cooking" and "wan" meaning "shop"), a typical *wazwan* meal has thirty-six courses. It includes a mix of vegetable and meat dishes, some cooked overnight under the supervision of speciality chefs called "vaste waze." The food served contains a rich blend of spices such as cloves, cinnamon, dried ginger, fennel, and saffron (one of the finest and most expensive varieties in the world is grown in Kashmir).

Although food scarcity is a reality in this region, owning to its harsh winters and frequent curfews due to political turmoil, the local produce compensates with a variety of greens, sweet river fish, dried pulses, and underdog vegetables such as lotus root, turnip, knol khol, and boombh that are used in dishes ranging from appetizers to mains. Kashmiri cuisine also beautifully incorporates sundried fruits such as apricots, apples, and plums, which are used throughout the year.

While the western side of the state, adjoining Pakistan, retains the essence of typical "Indian" cuisine with a tempering of tadkas, garnishes of finely-chopped coriander and mint leaves, and usage of lemon juice for finishing; the east of the state, in Ladakh, has cuisine that is heavily influenced by Tibet, owing to its proximity to the border. Here you will find momos, *baozi*-like *tingmo* bread, herbal teas, and brothy noodles like *thukpa* and *thenthuk*.

One of the best-kept secrets of Ladakhi cuisine is the variety of indigenous pastas that are found here. In Ladakh you will discover *bhatsa marku* and *skyu*. While the former is a Tibetan-style buttered mac-and-cheese dish made of yak dairy, *skyu* is a whole-wheat pasta shaped like orecchiette, only denser. The locals like to sauté *skyu* with copious amounts of mountain cheese and vegetables. In the Spiti Valley

(in the neighboring state of Himachal Pradesh), you will find *kev* that resembles *strozzapreti* and is tossed with typical Indian spices.

Himachal Pradesh's cuisine is a combination of the finesse of Kashmiri food with the robustness of the adjoining region of Punjab. Here, where the weather is extreme, you will also find influences of Tibetan food. People in fecund regions cook using a variety of peas, beans, cauliflower, cabbage, and other winter vegetables. Bone-in meats are at the core of soupy broths, which are flavored either with typical Indian spices such as clove, cinnamon, and ginger, or Chinese sauces, depending on which part of the state you are in.

Dharamsala, fondly called Dhasa, in rhyme with Tibet's capital, Lhasa, is home to the fourteenth Dalai Lama, the Tibetan spiritual guru who has made India his home. In the past six decades since he escaped his country to seek refuge in India, thousands of Tibetans have followed suit, and Dharamsala today offers authentic Tibetan cuisine with dishes such as *momos*, *thukpa*, and butter tea. The town also has a thriving coffee culture, which can be seen in the number of indigenous coffee outlets.

The jewel in the crown of North Indian cuisine is undoubtedly that of Awadh (present-day Lucknow and its adjoining areas). One of the most refined cuisines in the world, Awadhi fare is characterized by delicate flavors, elaborate meat marinades, and slow cooking of food, sometimes overnight.

The delicate cuisine of Awadh was initially devised to suit the fine palates of the nawabs who ruled this region in the 18th and 19th centuries. Awadh's valuable contributions to Indian cuisine include the *kakori* kebab, *sheermal*, korma, *shammi* kebab, *gulathi*, and biryani, among others.

Another interesting cuisine that hails from this region is that of the Kayasth community. When the British arrived in India, the Kayasths were one of the first to adopt their language, manners, and food habits. This led to the development of a unique cuisine that had Hindu, Muslim, and colonial influences. The Kayasths are known for their lavish hospitality and meat-eating culture; they were ahead of their time when it came to cooking. Not only did they champion faux meat by disguising vegetarian fare to look and feel like meat so they could blend in with the Mughals, they also strictly ate seasonal produce.

Chaat is another standout feature of North Indian fare. Savory hors d'oeuvres that are mostly a combination of potatoes, peas, yogurt, chutneys, and spices are a hallmark of Indian cuisine. While the origin of chaat is debatable, a popular story goes that chaat originated in Shah Jahan's kitchen in Delhi, when he wished to eat something loaded with spices but light on the stomach. It is no coincidence then that North Indian chaat, especially from cities such as Agra, Lucknow, Meerut, Varanasi, and Mathura, is famous.

The Mughals were gourmets and took their food very seriously. It is believed that Akbar preferred to drink water only from the Ganges. The food of the royals was tasted by a food taster before it was presented to them. The first Mughal emperor, Babur, was dismayed at the lack of variety of fruit in India. As the *Baburnama* states, he wrote, "There is no ice, cold water, good food or bread in the markets." But he also wrote, "When the mango is good it is really good... In fact, the mango is the best fruit of Hindustan." While he created a courier system to Samarkand that ensured a steady supply of melons, mulberries, and grapes among other fruits, he fell in love with the Indian mango. Subsequent Mughals introduced the idea of orchards in Delhi and Agra, to fulfil a sense of nostalgia for their homeland in Central Asia. In fact, Akbar was one of the first kings to staff horticulturists from Persia and Central Asia to take care of his fruit farms.

Delhi, being the capital of the Mughal Empire for over 150 years, became the main inheritor of the empire's culinary legacy. The streets of Old Delhi are lined with eateries whose owners claim they are descended from the chefs who worked in the Mughal kitchens. Some of the finest biryanis, *haleem*, and kebabs are still found in Delhi.

But contrary to popular belief, butter chicken has not trickled down from Mughal cookbooks. Butter chicken originated in Peshawar in present-day Pakistan in a shop called Mukhey da Dhaba, later called Moti Mahal. When owner Kundan Lal Gujral moved to Delhi after 1947, he brought his butter chicken recipe with him. The dish was originally made to preserve tandoori chicken from drying out by saving it in a tomato and cream gravy, but worked out so well on its own that it became iconic.

Other regions in North India, such as Haryana, Uttarakhand, and Punjab, have a rich farming and dairy culture. The Green Revolution in Punjab in the mid-1960s was a catalyst in making India self-sufficient, by pushing production of wheat and rice. Today, India is one of the most powerful agrarian economies in the world, with farming (and its allied activities) a primary source of livelihood for 80 percent of rural India's population, and its contribution to GDP about 15 percent. Cuisine in these regions includes meat, indigenous cheeses, and homemade cream and butter, as dairy is a rich part of the agricultural economy. The popular highway eateries (dhabas) originated in Punjab and were the first of their kind, as the linking of the cities in India began. Characterized by cots to sit on while eating rustic, simple, and comforting food, dhabas continue to be a unique part of the North Indian culinary experience.

From Awadhi, Lucknowi, Punjabi, Mughlai, and Kayasth cuisines to street-style chaats, if there is one region that can be called the heart of Indian cuisine, it is truly North India. No wonder then that it finds so much representation, from tony restaurants in London to cheap eats in Hanoi—you can't go too far without digging into butter chicken and naan.

APPETIZERS

## THANDA TAMATAR SOUP 🍲
Cold tomato soup.

Cooking time: 45 minutes | Serves: 4-6    Origin: Uttar Pradesh

INGREDIENTS

1 tsp butter
½ tsp ginger paste (*adrak*)
½ tsp garlic paste (*lasan*)
1 cup (240 g) chopped tomato
1 cup (240 ml) water
Salt, to taste
Freshly ground black pepper (*kali mirch*), to taste
Few drops freshly squeezed lemon juice (*nimbu*)
2 Tbsp (30 ml) heavy cream
Dash ground cinnamon (*dalchini*)
1 small sprig fresh cilantro (*hara dhaniya*)

METHOD

1. In a saucepan over medium-high heat, melt the butter.
2. Add the ginger paste and garlic paste. Sauté for 2–3 minutes until fragrant.
3. Add the tomato and water. Cook until the tomato becomes soft and mushy.
4. Add the sugar and season to taste with salt and pepper. Stir well to combine. Remove from the heat and set aside to cool.
5. When the tomato is cool enough to handle, transfer to a blender and add a few ice cubes. Blend the soup and strain it through a fine-mesh sieve.
6. Stir in the lemon juice and refrigerate to cool.
7. Before serving, add the cream and a dash of cinnamon. Garnish with the cilantro.

## GAHAT KA SHORBA
Healthy soup, rich in protein.

Cooking time: 1 hour | Serves: 4      Origin: Himachal Pradesh

INGREDIENTS

1 tsp vegetable oil
1 tsp cumin seeds (*jeera*)
2 tsp ginger-garlic paste (*adrak-lasan*)
¼ cup (42.5 g) tomato, finely chopped
¼ cup (42.5 g) onion, finely chopped
Pinch ground asafoetida (*hing*)
1 tsp mustard paste (*rai*)
½ cup coriander roots, finely chopped
1 tsp ground cumin (*jeera*)
1 tsp ground coriander (*dhaniya*)
4 cups (960 ml) water
Salt, to taste
1 cup (200 g) horse gram (*chana dal*), soaked in water for 30 minutes
Freshly ground black pepper, to taste

METHOD

1. In a saucepan, over low-medium heat, heat the oil. Add the cumin seeds. Sauté until the seeds begin to crackle.
2. Add the ginger-garlic paste, tomato, and onion. Sauté for 2 minutes.
3. Add asafoetida, mustard paste, coriander roots, cumin, and coriander and sauté for 1 minute.
4. Add 4 cups of water, salt, and horse gram.
5. Reduce the heat to low and allow the soup to bubble until the horse gram is thoroughly cooked. This should take an hour.
6. Season with pepper and serve hot.

# RIKAUCHHE 🍲
Steamed and pan-fried black lentil chips in yogurt sauce.

Cooking time: 40 minutes | Serves: 8-10  Origin: Uttar Pradesh

## INGREDIENTS

1 cup (200 g) black lentils (*urad dal*), soaked in water for at least 3 hours, preferably overnight, drained

¾ cup (180 ml) vegetable oil, plus more for preparing the colander and wok

1½ tsp fenugreek seeds (*methi dana*)

1½ tsp ginger paste (*adrak*)

1½ tsp garlic paste (*lasan*)

1 Tbsp (7 g) ground turmeric (*haldi*)

1 Tbsp (18 g) salt

1½ tsp red chile powder

½ cup (120 g) yogurt (*dahi*)

½ cup (120 ml) water

1 Tbsp (7 g) ground cumin (*jeera*)

2-3 green chiles, chopped

1 Tbsp (1 g) fresh cilantro leaves (*hara dhaniya*), finely chopped

## METHOD

1. In a blender or food processor, grind the black lentils into a fine paste.
2. Grease a heatproof colander with a little vegetable oil and put it over a pot of boiling water.
3. Divide the gram paste into 2 or 3 portions and shape each into a long cylinder. Put the cylinders in the colander and cover with a plate. Steam until stiff and a little hard. Remove and cut the cylinders into slices (they should look like thick chips).
4. In a skillet over low-medium heat, heat the vegetable oil for panfrying.
5. Working in batches if needed, add the chips and panfry until golden brown. Transfer to paper towels to drain.
6. Heat 2 Tbsp (30 ml) of vegetable oil in a wok until it starts to smoke.
7. Add the fenugreek seeds. When the seeds turn brown, add the ginger paste, garlic paste, turmeric, salt, red chile powder, and yogurt. Sauté until the spices are cooked and the oil floats on the top.
8. Add the fried chips and water. Cook, stirring, for 5 minutes until well blended. Serve hot, garnished with cumin, green chiles, and cilantro.

## PANEER DAHIVADA

Deep-fried paneer cakes served with dollops of yogurt, relishes, and spices.

Cooking time: 40 minutes | Serves: 2 Origin: Uttar Pradesh

INGREDIENTS

1 cup (240 g) paneer; available at Indian markets, page 28)
1 medium-size potato, boiled
1 Tbsp (7.5 g) cornflour
1 green chile, finely chopped
1 tsp ginger paste (*adrak*)
Salt, to taste
Vegetable oil, for frying
2 cups (480 g) yogurt (*dahi*)
5 Tbsp (75 g) date-tamarind chutney (page 29)
5 Tbsp (75 g) mint-cilantro chutney (page 28)
5 tsp red chile powder
5 tsp ground cumin (*jeera*)
5 tsp Indian black salt (*kala namak*)

METHOD

1. In a medium-size bowl, combine the paneer, potato, cornflour, green chile, and ginger paste. Season to taste with salt. Mash well.
2. Divide the mixture into equal small portions. Shape each portion into a flat cake.
3. In a deep skillet over medium-high heat, heat the vegetable oil for frying.
4. Carefully add the cakes to the hot oil and deep-fry until golden brown. Transfer to paper towels to drain.
5. To assemble the dish, place a fried cake on a plate. Top it with a spoonful each of yogurt, date-tamarind chutney, mint-cilantro chutney, a pinch each of red chile powder, cumin, and black salt. Serve. Repeat with the remaining cakes.

## BENARASI TAMATAR CHAAT

Mashed tomato street food drizzled with sugar syrup and tamarind relish.

Cooking time: 30 minutes | Serves: 2 Origin: Uttar Pradesh

INGREDIENTS

4 dried red chiles (*sookhi lal mirch*), soaked in water for 30 minutes, drained
1 (1-in. / 2.5-cm) piece peeled fresh ginger (*adrak*)
1 Tbsp (15 ml) vegetable oil
2 Tbsp (30 g) whole-milk fudge (*khoya*; available at Indian markets; page 25)
1 Tbsp (9 g) cashews (*kaju*)
1½ tsp poppy seeds (*khus khus*)
2 tsp garam masala
1 cup (240 g) finely chopped tomato
¾ cup (82.5 g) finely chopped potato
Salt, to taste
1 tsp red chile powder
¼ cup (4 g) fresh cilantro leaves (*hara dhaniya*), finely chopped
3 Tbsp (45 ml) sugar syrup (page 30)
3 Tbsp (45 g) date-tamarind chutney (page 29)
1 tsp ground cumin (*jeera*)
½ cup (120 g) *nimki* (available at Indian markets)

METHOD

1. In a food processor, grind the dried red chiles and ginger into a smooth paste. Set aside.
2. In a skillet over low heat, heat the vegetable oil.
3. Add the prepared chile-ginger paste, whole-milk fudge, cashews, and poppy seeds. Cook for 4–5 minutes, stirring.
4. Add the garam masala and tomato. Season to taste with salt. Cook, stirring, for 2 minutes. With a potato masher, gently smash the tomato.
5. Add the potato and cook for 4–5 minutes. Use the potato masher once more, this time for 30 seconds, keeping the potato coarse.
6. Stir in the red chile powder and cilantro. Remove from the heat and set aside.
7. Drizzle the mashed tomato mixture with the sugar syrup, garnish with the date-tamarind chutney, cumin, and nimki. Serve hot.

# BENARASI DAL KACHORI

Deep-fried black lentil and whole-wheat flour puffed bread.

Cooking time: 30 minutes | Serves: 4    Origin: Uttar Pradesh

## INGREDIENTS

1 cup (125 g) whole-wheat flour (*atta*)
3 Tbsp (45 g) ghee
½ cup (100 g) black lentils (*urad dal*), soaked in
   water overnight, drained
½ cup (85 g) semolina (*suji*)
1 tsp carom seeds (*ajwain*)
1 tsp red chile powder
Salt, to taste
Ghee, for frying

## METHOD

1. In a small bowl, combine the flour and ghee. Rub with your fingertips until the ghee is well incorporated and the mixture resembles bread crumbs.

2. In a blender or food processor, grind the drained black lentils into a fine paste. Add the paste to the flour mixture along with the semolina, carom seeds, and red chile powder. Season to taste with salt. Knead the mixture with enough water to form a medium-soft dough. Divide the dough into small rounds and roll into small disks (*puris*).

3. In a deep skillet over medium-high heat, heat the ghee for frying.

4. Working in batches, gently place the disks into the hot ghee. Deep-fry until they puff up, about 30 seconds for each disk. With a slotted spoon, transfer to paper towels to drain. Serve hot.

# CHURA MATTAR

Flattened rice soaked in milk and cream, tempered, and tossed with green peas.

Cooking time: 30 minutes | Serves: 2    Origin: Uttar Pradesh

## INGREDIENTS

½ cup (120 ml) milk
½ cup (120 ml) heavy cream
1 cup (200 g) flattened rice (*poha/chura*), rinsed
1 Tbsp (15 g) ghee
1 tsp cumin seeds (*jeera*)
1 tsp ginger paste (*adrak*)
1 green chile, finely chopped
½ cup (80 g) green peas (*hara mattar*), boiled
1 tsp garam masala
1 tsp chaat masala
1 tsp freshly ground pepper (*kali mirch*)
Salt, to taste
Juice of 1 lemon (*nimbu*)
¼ cup (4 g) fresh cilantro leaves (*hara dhaniya*),
   finely chopped

## METHOD

1. In a medium-size bowl, combine the milk and cream. Add the rice and soak for 8 minutes. Drain. Save the milk and cream mixture to add to rich curries later.

2. In a skillet over medium-high heat, heat the ghee.

3. Add the cumin seeds. Cook until the seeds begin to crackle.

4. Add the ginger paste and green chile. Stir-fry for 1 minute.

5. Add the boiled green peas. Cook for 5–7 minutes.

6. Stir in the garam masala, chaat masala, and pepper. Season to taste with salt. Add the soaked rice. Cook for 3–4 minutes until the rice is soft.

7. Stir in the lemon juice and cilantro. Serve hot.

## BHARWA GUCCHI 🍲

Gourmet stuffed mushrooms laced in yogurt sauce.

Cooking time: 40 minutes | Serves: 4-6   Origin: Uttar Pradesh

### INGREDIENTS

8–10 large dried morel mushrooms (*gucchi*)

**For the filling**

Vegetable oil, for frying

¼ cup (15 g) spring onion (*hara pyaz*),
   finely chopped

¼ cup (4 g) fresh cilantro leaves (*hara dhaniya*),
   finely chopped

3 Tbsp (18 g) finely chopped fresh mint leaves
   (*pudina*)

2 Tbsp (30 ml) freshly squeezed lemon juice
   (*nimbu*)

1 Tbsp (30 g) whole-milk fudge (*khoya*; available
   at Indian markets; page 25)

Salt, to taste

**For the gravy**

½ cup (120 g) ghee

2 whole cloves (*laung*)

2 green cardamom pods (*choti elaichi*)

½ cup (30 g) finely minced or grated spring onion
   (*hara pyaz*)

2 tsp ginger paste (*adrak*)

2 tsp garlic paste (*lasan*)

2 tsp green chile paste

¼ cup (60 g) cashew butter (*kaju*)

¾ cup (180 g) hung curd (page 28) or thick Greek-
   style yogurt (*dahi*), whisked

Salt, to taste

1½ tsp garam masala

Few saffron threads (*kesar*), soaked in 3 Tbsp
   (45 ml) warm milk

### METHOD

1. Wash and hydrate the morel mushrooms in warm water and then boil them in fresh water for 10 minutes. Drain and set aside.

2. **To make the filling:** In a skillet over low-medium heat, heat 1 tsp vegetable oil.

3. Add the spring onion. Stir-fry until golden. Transfer to a small bowl.

4. To the spring onion, add the cilantro, mint, lemon juice, and whole-milk fudge. Season to taste with salt. Stir to combine. Stuff each mushroom with an equal amount of filling. Set aside.

5. **To make the gravy:** Wipe out the skillet and return it to medium-high heat.

6. Add 1 Tbsp (15 g) of ghee to melt. When it starts to smoke, remove the skillet from the heat and let cool slightly. Return the skillet to low-medium heat and add the cloves and green cardamom pods. Fry until they change color. Remove the whole spices from the ghee and discard.

7. Return the skillet to the heat and add the remaining 7 Tbsp (105 g) of ghee to the skillet and the spring onion. Sauté until translucent.

8. Add the ginger paste, garlic paste, and green chile paste. Stir-fry until the water evaporates.

9. Stir in the cashew butter. Fry until well blended and the color changes.

10. Reduce the heat to low. Add the yogurt and season to taste with salt. Stir and simmer until it reaches a sauce-like consistency.

11. Add the garam masala and the saffron milk. Stir to mix well.

12. Add the stuffed morel mushrooms to the gravy and ¼ cup (60 ml) of hot water. Simmer for 10 minutes, coating the morels with the gravy. Serve hot.

●●

# PUNJABI SAMOSA
Deep-fried spiced potato triangles wrapped in puff pastry.

Cooking time: 40 minutes | Makes: 15        Origin: Punjab

## INGREDIENTS

For the filling
1 Tbsp (15 ml) vegetable oil, plus more for
   deep-frying
1 tsp cumin seeds (*jeera*)
2 green chiles, finely chopped
1 tsp ginger paste (*adrak*)
1 tsp ground turmeric (*haldi*)
1 tsp red chile powder
2 cups (450 g) mashed potatoes
2 tsp garam masala
1 tsp chaat masala
Juice of 1 lemon (*nimbu*)
¼ cup (4 g) fresh cilantro leaves (*hara dhaniya*)
Salt, to taste
1 package samosa pastry sheets (samosa patti;
   available at Indian markets and online, page 33)
Vegetable oil, for frying

## METHOD

1. **To make the filling:** In a skillet over medium-high heat, heat 1 Tbsp (15 ml) of vegetable oil.
2. Add the cumin seeds. Cook until the seeds begin to crackle.
3. Add the green chiles, ginger paste, turmeric, and red chile powder. Stir well to combine.
4. Add the mashed potatoes, garam masala, chaat masala, lemon juice, and cilantro. Season to taste with the salt. Mix well. Set aside.
5. Place a spoonful of the mixture on a samosa pastry sheet and wrap to enclose it in a triangular shape like spanakopita. Repeat until all filling and pastry are used up.
6. In a wok over medium-high heat, heat the vegetable oil for deep-frying.
7. Working in batches if needed, carefully add the stuffed somosas to the hot oil and deep-fry until golden. Transfer to paper towels to drain.
8. Serve hot with mint-cilantro chutney (page 28).

## HARA BHARA KEBAB

A quick party starter is also the best way to indulge your kids in healthy eating.

Cooking time: 40 minutes | Serves: 3    Origin: Uttar Pradesh

### INGREDIENTS

2 cups (60 g) fresh spinach, boiled
1 cup (160 g) green peas (*hara matter*), boiled
1 cup (225 g) boiled potato cubes
1 cup (64 g) fresh mint leaves (*pudina*)
1 cup (16 g) fresh cilantro leaves (*hara dhaniya*), finely chopped
½ cup (120 g) chickpea flour (*besan*)
1 Tbsp (15 g) ginger-garlic paste (*adrak-lasan*)
1 Tbsp (8 g) red chile powder
1 Tbsp (10 g) chaat masala
1 tsp red chile paste
1 tsp ground cumin (*jeera*)
1 tsp dried mango powder (*amchoor*)
1 tsp garam masala
Salt, to taste
Vegetable oil, for frying

### METHOD

1. In a large bowl, combine everything except the vegetable oil and mash it well with a potato masher.
2. Roll the mixture into 12 round medium-size patties.
3. In a skillet over low-medium heat, heat the vegetable oil for frying.
4. Carefully add the patties to the hot oil and shallow-fry until golden.
5. Serve hot with mint-cilantro chutney (page 28), if desired.

## AMRITSARI BUN CHAAT 📷

Potato burger served with chutney, peanuts, and pomegranate.

Cooking time: 20 minutes | Serves: 2-4    Origin: Punjab

### INGREDIENTS

½ cup (1 stick; 120 g) butter, divided
4 burger buns
2 potatoes, boiled, mashed
2 tsp red chile powder
2 tsp ground coriander (*dhaniya*)
2 tsp chaat masala
2 tsp ground cumin (*jeera*)
1 tsp Indian black salt (*kala namak*)
Salt, to taste
1 medium-size onion, sliced
2 tsp garlic chutney (page 270)
2 Tbsp (30 g) date-tamarind chutney (page 29)
2 Tbsp (30 g) mint-cilantro chutney (page 28)
½ cup (120 g) spicy peanuts
2 Tbsp (30 g) fresh pomegranate seeds (*anar*)
½ cup (120 g) *nylon sev* (available at Indian markets)
½ cup (8 g) fresh cilantro leaves (*hara dhaniya*), finely chopped

### METHOD

1. Butter the burger buns and toast them gently in a hot skillet over medium heat. Set aside.
2. In a medium-size bowl, stir together the potatoes, red chile powder, coriander, chaat masala, cumin, black salt, and salt.
3. Divide the mixture into small portions and shape each into a flat cake.
4. Return the skillet to medium-high heat. Add the remaining butter. Working in batches, add the cakes to the hot skillet with any remaining butter from step 1 and panfry on both sides until golden brown. Place a cake on a bun bottom. Top with sliced onion and the chutneys.
5. Place the spicy peanuts, pomegranate seeds, sev, and cilantro over this and serve immediately with the bun top.

## MONJI KALIA

Kohlrabi in a spiced curd-based stew.

Cooking time: 30 minutes | Serves: 4-6 Origin: Jammu & Kashmir

### INGREDIENTS

1¼ cups (300 ml) vegetable oil, divided
2 lb, 3 oz (1 kg) kohlrabi (*ganth gobhi*), peeled, and
  cut into 1-in. (2.5-cm) cubes
4 whole cloves (*laung*)
2 black cardamom pods (*badi elaichi*), crushed
Pinch ground asafoetida (*hing*)
1 cup (240 ml) water
1 Tbsp (7 g) aniseed powder (*saunf*)
1 tsp ground turmeric (*haldi*)
1 tsp ground ginger (*sonth*)
½ tsp garam masala
Salt, to taste
2 Tbsp (30 g) yogurt (*dahi*)
2 Tbsp (30 ml) milk
3 green cardamom pods (*choti elaichi*)

### METHOD

1. In a skillet over low-medium heat, heat 1 cup
   (240 ml) of vegetable oil.
2. Add the kohlrabi and fry until golden. Transfer
   to paper towels to drain. Set aside.
3. In a deep pot over low-medium heat, heat 3
   Tbsp (45 ml) of vegetable oil.
4. Add the cloves, black cardamom pods, and
   asafoetida. Sauté until fragrant.
5. Add the water and cover the pot to prevent the
   oil from spattering.
6. Carefully remove the lid and add the fried
   kohlrabi, aniseed powder, turmeric, ginger, and
   garam masala. Season to taste with salt. Increase
   the heat to medium and cook for 10 minutes.
7. In a small bowl, whisk the yogurt and milk.
   Pour this into the pot. Stir continuously and
   bring to a boil. Cook for 5 minutes more and
   remove from heat.
8. In a small skillet over medium-high heat, heat
   the remaining 1 Tbsp (15 ml) of vegetable oil.
9. Add the green cardamom pods and sauté until
   they change color. Remove and add to the stew
   pot. Serve hot.

## RESHMI KEBAB ZAFRANI

Minced chicken kebabs on skewers.

Cooking time: 40 minutes | Serves: 4      Origin: Uttar Pradesh

### INGREDIENTS

2 lb, 3 oz (1 kg) minced chicken
2 eggs, whisked
2 tsp ground cumin (*jeera*)
1 tsp yellow chile powder
½ tsp ground white pepper (*safed mirch*)
Salt, to taste
3 Tbsp (45 g) cashew paste (*kaju*)
4 tsp ginger paste (*adrak*)
4 tsp onion paste
1 tsp garam masala
Pinch saffron threads (*kesar*), soaked in 2 Tbsp
  warm milk
5 Tbsp (20 g) fresh cilantro (*hara dhaniya*),
  finely chopped
½ cup (120 g) processed cheese, grated

### METHOD

1. In a large bowl, combine the chicken mince,
   eggs, cumin, yellow chile powder, white pepper,
   salt, cashew paste, ginger paste, onion paste,
   garam masala, saffron, cilantro, and cheese. Mix
   well. Set aside for 30 minutes.
2. Shape the chicken mince mixture along the
   length of the skewers to shape into kebabs.
3. Preheat the oven to 350°F (180°C).
4. Skewer the kebabs and place them on a baking
   sheet. Roast for 20–25 minutes.
5. Remove from skewers and serve hot.

## AMRITSARI MALAI CHAAP

Skewered soya nuggets.

| Cooking time: 30 minutes | Serves: 2 | Origin: Punjab |
| --- | --- | --- |

### INGREDIENTS

1 cup (240 ml) heavy cream
½ cup (120 g) yogurt (*dahi*)
1 Tbsp (15 g) ginger-garlic paste (*adrak-lasan*)
1 tsp dried fenugreek leaves (*kasuri methi*)
1 tsp red chile powder
1 tsp ground cumin (*jeera*)
Salt, to taste
15 soya nuggets, boiled, drained

### METHOD

1. In a medium-size bowl, stir together the cream, yogurt, ginger-garlic paste, dried fenugreek leaves, red chile powder, and cumin. Season to taste with salt.
2. Add the soya nuggets, stir to coat, and refrigerate to marinate for 4 hours.
3. Preheat the oven to 350°F (180°C).
4. Skewer the soya nuggets and place them on a baking sheet. Roast for 15–17 minutes.
5. Serve hot.

## AMRITSARI MACHI

Spicy fried fish fillet.

| Cooking time: 30 minutes | Serves: 2 | Origin: Punjab |
| --- | --- | --- |

### INGREDIENTS

2 sole fillets
Juice of 1 lemon (*nimbu*)
1 Tbsp (15 g) ginger-garlic paste (*adrak-lasan*)
1 tsp carom seeds (*ajwain*)
1 tsp red chile powder
1 tsp ground turmeric (*haldi*)
Pinch ground asafoetida (*hing*)
1 Tbsp (7.5 g) chickpea flour (*besan*)
1 tsp rice flour
Salt, to taste
Vegetable oil, for frying
1 Tbsp (10 g) chaat masala

### METHOD

1. In a medium-size bowl, combine the fish, lemon juice, ginger-garlic paste, carom seeds, red chile powder, turmeric, asafoetida, chickpea flour, and rice flour. Season to taste with salt and marinate the fish for 10 minutes.
2. In a deep skillet over medium heat, heat the vegetable oil for frying.
3. Carefully add the fish to the hot oil and deep-fry until golden on both sides.
4. Sprinkle with the chaat masala before serving.

# CHICKEN THUKPA 📷

Light yet filling soup loaded with vegetables, meats, and condiments.

Cooking time: 35 minutes | Serves: 2  Origin: Jammu & Kashmir

INGREDIENTS

3 Tbsp (45 ml) vegetable oil
2 whole chicken legs (thighs and drumsticks)
1 medium-size onion, finely chopped
½ cup (30 g) chopped spring onion (*hara pyaz*)
4 garlic cloves (*lasan*), minced
2 green chiles, finely chopped
1 tsp minced peeled fresh ginger (*adrak*)
1 cup (240 ml) vegetable broth
Juice of 1 lemon (*nimbu*)
Salt, to taste
1 tsp soy sauce
1 tsp honey
½ cup (120 g) noodles, cooked according to the
   package directions
¼ cup (60 g) assorted chopped vegetables
¾ tsp finely chopped fresh cilantro leaves
   (*hara dhaniya*)

METHOD

1. In a soup pot over medium-high heat, heat the vegetable oil.
2. Add the chicken and panfry for 10 minutes, turning.
3. Add the onion, spring onion, garlic, green chiles, and ginger. Cook, stirring, for 3–4 minutes.
4. Pour in the vegetable broth and add the lemon juice, salt to taste, soy sauce, and honey. Stir well to combine. Reduce the heat to low and cover the pot. Cook the broth for about 15 minutes.
5. Remove the chicken from the broth and shred it. Add the shredded chicken back to the broth along with the vegetables and noodles. Let bubble for 10 minutes more.
6. Serve hot, garnished with cilantro.

# THENTHUK

Al dente strips of dough floating in hot soy-hinted vegetable soup.

Cooking time: 30 minutes | Serves: 2  Origin: Jammu & Kashmir

INGREDIENTS

**For the dough**
½ cup (62.5 g) all-purpose flour (*maida*)
1 tsp freshly ground black pepper (*kali mirch*)
Salt, to taste
1 tsp vegetable oil
5 Tbsp (75 ml) water
**For the soup**
3 Tbsp (45 ml) vegetable oil
1 green chile, finely chopped
1 tsp ginger-garlic paste (*adrak-lasan*)
1 medium-size onion, finely chopped
1 medium-size tomato, finely chopped
1 medium-size carrot (*gajar*), julienned
1 green bell pepper, julienned
¼ cup (17.5 g) shredded cabbage (*bandh gobhi*)
2 cups (480 ml) vegetable broth
1 Tbsp (15 ml) soy sauce
1 tsp chile sauce
Salt, to taste

METHOD

1. **To make the dough:** In a medium-size bowl, combine the flour, pepper, salt to taste, vegetable oil, and water. Knead to make a medium-soft dough. Let rest for 5–7 minutes.
2. Roll the dough into a thin disk and cut into long noodle-like strips with a sharp knife. Set aside.
3. **To make the soup:** In a soup pot over medium-high heat, heat the vegetable oil.
4. Add the green chile, ginger-garlic paste, onion, and tomato. Sauté the mixture for 2–3 minutes.
5. Add the carrot, green bell pepper, cabbage, and vegetable broth. Let the soup bubble for 2–3 minutes.
6. Stir in the soy sauce, chile sauce, and dough strips. Season to taste with salt. Cook for 7–8 minutes. Taste and adjust the seasoning and serve hot.

## GOLE KE SEEKH KEBAB ♨
Smoked minced meatballs

Cooking time: 30 minutes | Makes: 15     Origin: Uttar Pradesh

### INGREDIENTS

½ cup (120 g) raw papaya with skin
Salt, to taste
2 cups (480 g) minced lamb or beef (*keema*)
1½ tsp ginger paste (*adrak*)
1½ tsp garlic paste (*lasan*)
3–4 medium-size onions, sliced, fried, ground to
   a paste
½ cup (60 g) chickpea flour (*besan*), toasted
1½ Tbsp (12 g) red chile powder
½ cup (120 ml) heavy cream
6 green cardamom pods (*choti elaichi*), divided
4 whole cloves (*laung*), divided
2 whole mace (*javitri*)
1 black cardamom pod (*badi elaichi*)
1 (1-in. / 2.5-cm) cinnamon stick (*dalchini*)
Pinch ground nutmeg (*jaiphal*)
1 Tbsp (5 g) dried unsweetened shredded coconut
   (*nariyal*)
1 Tbsp (9 g) poppy seeds (*khus khus*)
7–8 cashews (*kaju*)
2 bay leaves (*tej patta*)
1 recipe Dungaar (page 26)
7 Tbsp (105 g) ghee
1 Tbsp (15 ml) vetivier water (*kewra*; available at
   Indian markets)
1 Tbsp (15 g) yogurt (*dahi*), whipped

### METHOD

1.  In a mortar and pestle or food processor, grind the papaya with salt to taste into a fine paste. Transfer to a large heatproof pan with a tight-fitting lid, add the minced meat, and stir to combine.
2.  Add the ginger paste, garlic paste, onion paste, chickpea flour, red chile powder, and cream. Mix thoroughly. Set aside for 15 minutes.
3.  Meanwhile, place a griddle over low-medium heat. Add 3 green cardamom pods, 2 cloves, the mace, black cardamom pod, cinnamon stick, nutmeg, coconut, poppy seeds, cashews, and bay leaves. Roast until fragrant. Transfer to a blender or mortar and pestle, add a little water, and grind the ingredients into a fine paste. Blend this paste into the minced meat mixture into a smooth paste.
4.  Meanwhile, prepare the dungaar. Working on a heatproof surface, make a hollow in the center of the meat paste mixture. Place the prepared dungaar. Cover the pan so the smoke is properly infused into the paste with all the aromas. Add the vetivier water and mix well.
5.  In a small bowl, stir together the yogurt and ghee. Set aside.
6.  Preheat a grill to medium heat.
7.  Divide the minced paste into about 15 equal portions. Shape each portion into a ball. Skewer 7–8 balls on a metal skewer. Repeat with the remaining balls. Place the skewers on the grill. Cook, turning every few minutes, so the kebabs are evenly cooked. Baste them with the ghee-yogurt mixture, allowing a few drops to drip onto the fire. Serve hot.

# HIMACHALI LAMB SOUP

A hearty meat soup with vegetables and noodles.

Cooking time: 30 minutes | Serves: 2 Origin: Jammu & Kashmir

INGREDIENTS

1 tsp vegetable oil
1 medium-size onion, finely sliced
1 Tbsp (15 g) garlic paste (*lasan*)
1 tsp green chile paste
1½ cups (360 ml) lamb or chicken broth
1 tsp soy sauce
1 tsp vinegar (*sirka*)
1 cup (150 g) shredded cooked lamb or chicken
½ cup (88 g) rice noodles
¼ cup (22.5 g) finely chopped cabbage
   (*bandh gobhi*)
¼ cup (32.5 g) finely chopped carrot (*gajar*)
¼ cup (4 g) fresh cilantro leaves (*hara dhaniya*),
   finely chopped
Salt, to taste
Freshly ground black pepper (*kali mirch*), to taste

METHOD

1. In a soup pot over medium-high heat, heat the vegetable oil.
2. Add the onion, garlic paste, and green chile paste.
3. Sauté for 2–3 minutes.
4. Stir in the broth, soy sauce, and vinegar. Bring the mixture to a boil.
5. Add the shredded meat and let the mixture bubble for about 20 minutes, or until the meat is thoroughly heated. Add the rice noodles, cabbage, and carrots. Mix well. Reduce the heat to low and simmer for 4–5 minutes, or until the noodles are cooked.
6. Serve hot, garnished with cilantro, and seasoned to taste with salt and pepper.

# KABARGAH

Lamb chops dipped in yogurt and deep-fried.

Cooking time: 45 minutes | Serves: 4-6 Origin: Jammu & Kashmir

INGREDIENTS

2 lb, 3 oz (1 kg) 3-in.-by-5-in. (7.5-cm-by-12.5-cm)
   lamb chops
2 cups (480 ml) milk
4 whole cloves (*laung*)
3 black cardamom pods (*badi elaichi*), crushed
2 (1-in. / 2.5-cm) cinnamon sticks (*dalchini*)
2 bay leaves (*tej patta*)
2 tsp salt, plus more for seasoning
1 tsp garam masala
Pinch ground asafoetida (*hing*)
½ cup (120 g) yogurt (*dahi*)
½ tsp red chile powder
1½ cups (360 g) ghee
Silver leaves, for garnishing (*warq*; optional;
   page 24; available at Indian markets)

METHOD

1. In a large pot over medium heat, combine the lamb, milk, cloves, black cardamom pods, cinnamon sticks, bay leaves, salt, garam masala, and asafoetida. Cook until the milk is absorbed. Remove the pot from the heat and transfer the chops to a large plate. Remove the whole spices that remain and set aside.
2. In a small bowl, whisk the yogurt, red chile powder, and a pinch of salt until smooth.
3. In a large skillet over low-medium heat, heat the ghee.
4. Dip each chop into the yogurt batter and fry until cooked through and rich brown in color. Transfer to paper towels to drain. Serve hot, garnished with silver leaves (if using).

## BOTI KEBAB

Succulent melt-in-the-mouth lamb kebabs.

Cooking time: 1 hour | Makes: 4     Origin: Uttar Pradesh

INGREDIENTS

2 lb, 3 oz (1 kg) boneless lamb cubes, rinsed
½ cup (120 g) ginger-garlic paste (*adrak-lasan*)
5 Tbsp (75 ml) freshly squeezed lemon juice
  (*nimbu*)
¼ cup (60 g) raw papaya paste
Salt, to taste
¼ cup (60 g) hung curd (page 28)
½ cup (120 ml) vegetable oil
2 tsp red chile powder
1 tsp ground white pepper (*safed mirch*)
1 tsp ground cumin (*jeera*)
1 tsp ground cardamom
Melted butter, for basting

METHOD

1.  In a large bowl, combine the lamb, ginger-garlic
    paste, lemon juice, and raw papaya paste.
    Season to taste with salt. Mix to combine and
    set aside for 30 minutes.
2.  Prepare a second marinade: In another large
    bowl, whisk the yogurt, vegetable oil, red chile
    powder, white pepper, cumin, and cardamom.
3.  Add the lamb and mix to coat. Refrigerate for
    2 hours.
4.  Preheat the oven to 400°F (200°C).
5.  Skewer the lamb cubes and roast (or grill) for
    15–20 minutes. Baste with butter and roast for
    3–5 minutes more, or until tender. Remove from
    the skewers and serve hot.

## KAKORI KEBAB

Skewered grilled lamb kebabs.

Cooking time: 40 minutes | Makes: 6     Origin: Uttar Pradesh

INGREDIENTS

1 cup (240 g) minced lamb
1 green chile, finely chopped
2 Tbsp (15 g) chickpea flour (*besan*)
1 Tbsp (15 g) ginger-garlic paste (*adrak-lasan*)
1 Tbsp (15 g) raw papaya paste
1 Tbsp (6 g) garam masala
1 tsp freshly ground black pepper (*kali mirch*)
1 tsp ground cumin (*jeera*)
Pinch ground mace (*javitri*)
Pinch ground nutmeg (*jaiphal*)
Salt, to taste
½ egg
5 Tbsp (75 g) ghee, melted

METHOD

1.  In a medium-size bowl, mix together the lamb,
    green chile, chickpea flour, ginger-garlic paste,
    papaya paste, garam masala, pepper, cumin,
    mace, and nutmeg. Season to taste with salt.
2.  Add the egg (divide the egg after whisking in a
    small bowl). Knead the mixture into a soft
    dough and marinate for 1 hour in the refrigerator.
3.  Preheat the oven to 400°F (200°C).
4.  Skewer lumps of the kebab mixture on metal
    skewers and place them on a rimmed baking
    sheet. Brush with ghee and bake for 35–40
    minutes, basting with more ghee midway
    through the baking time to avoid excessive
    dryness.

## KACHCHE KEEME KE KEBAB 🍽

Panfried minced meat cakes.

Cooking time: 40 minutes | Makes: 20–25 Origin: Uttar Pradesh

### INGREDIENTS

5 whole cloves (*laung*)
5 green cardamom pods (*choti elaichi*)
4 dried red chiles (*sookhi lal mirch*)
3 black cardamom pods (*badi elaichi*)
2 whole mace (*javitri*)
1 (1-in. / 2.5-cm) cinnamon stick (*dalchini*)
¼ tsp ground nutmeg (*jaiphal*)
2 Tbsp (12 g) cumin seeds (*jeera*)
1 Tbsp (15 g) peppercorns (*sabut kali mirch*)
1 Tbsp (9 g) poppy seeds (*khus khus*)
1 cup coconut flesh (*nariyal*), dry-roasted
1 (2-in. / 5-cm) piece grated peeled fresh
   ginger (*adrak*)
8 garlic cloves (*lasan*), minced
5 Tbsp (75 g) grated raw papaya
1 medium-size onion, sliced and fried (*birista*;
   page 30)
¾ cup (90 g) chickpea flour (*besan*), toasted
½ cup (120 g) yogurt (*dahi*)
2 lb, 3 oz (1 kg) minced lamb or beef (*keema*)
1 Tbsp (15 g) salt
Green chiles to taste, chopped
Chopped fresh mint leaves (*pudina*), to taste
Ghee, for panfrying

### METHOD

1. Preheat a griddle over low-medium heat.
2. On the hot griddle, combine the cloves, green cardamom pods, dried red chiles, black cardamom pods, mace, cinnamon stick, nutmeg, cumin seeds, peppercorns, poppy seeds, and coconut. Dry-roast until fragrant, stirring frequently. Transfer to a food processor or spice grinder and process until ground. Transfer to a medium-size bowl to cool.
3. To the bowl, add the ginger, garlic, papaya, fried onion, chickpea flour, yogurt, and minced meat. Season to taste with salt, green chiles, and mint. Mix well to combine all the ingredients. Divide the mixture into 20–25 small portions. With greased palms, shape each into a flat cake (*tikki*).
4. Wipe out the griddle, if needed, and place it over medium-high heat and add just a little ghee to melt.
5. Working in batches, panfry the cakes until golden brown on both sides. Remove and repeat until all are fried, adding more ghee as needed. Serve hot.

# POULTRY AND EGGS

## MURGH MUSALLAM 🍲

Slow-cooked chicken stuffed with spices and dried fruits.

Cooking time: 1 hour | Serves: 4-6    Origin: Uttar Pradesh

### INGREDIENTS

**For the stuffing**
½ cup (120 g) ghee
4 whole cloves (*laung*)
2 (1-in. / 2.5-cm) cinnamon sticks (*dalchini*)
2 black cardamom pods (*badi elaichi*)
2 bay leaves (*tej patta*)
½ tsp ground mace (*javitri*)
½ cup (120 g) sliced onion
2 tsp ginger paste (*adrak*)
10 cashews (*kaju*), ground to a paste with little water
1 Tbsp (9 g) poppy seeds (*khus khus*), ground to a paste with little water
½ cup (47.5 g) dried unsweetened shredded coconut (*nariyal*), ground to a paste
1 tsp ground coriander (*dhaniya*)
Salt, to taste
10 almonds (*badam*), blanched, peeled, and sliced
40 raisins (*kishmish*), chopped

**For the chicken**
1 whole chicken, skin removed
½ cup (120 g) ghee
11 oz (300 g) onions, sliced
2 tsp garlic paste (*lasan*)
2 tsp ginger paste (*adrak*)
2 tsp red chile powder
1 tsp ground coriander (*dhaniya*)
Salt, to taste
1 cup (240 ml) milk
1½ cups (360 ml) coconut cream (*nariyal*)
1½ cups (360 g) yogurt (*dahi*), whisked

### METHOD

1. **To make the stuffing:** In a skillet over medium-high heat, heat the ghee.

2. Add the cloves, cinnamon sticks, black cardamom pods, bay leaves, and mace. Cook until the spices begin to crackle. With a slotted spoon, remove from the pan and set aside to cool. When cool, transfer to a spice grinder or mortar and pestle, add a little water, and grind together into a smooth paste. Set aside.

3. Return the skillet and ghee to medium-high heat. Add the onion and sauté until golden brown. With a slotted spoon, transfer the onion to a food processor. Let cool slightly and process to a smooth paste. Set aside.

4. Return the skillet and ghee to medium-high heat again. Add the ginger paste, cashew paste, poppy seed paste, coconut paste, and coriander. Season to taste with salt. Sauté until the mix turns light brown in color.

5. Add the almonds and raisins. Stir well to combine.

6. Add the spice paste and onion paste. Stir to combine. Remove the pan from the heat.

7. **To make the chicken:** Stuff the chicken with the stuffing mixture. Close the cavity with cocktail picks. Tie the chicken with kitchen string so it does not lose shape and holds in the stuffing.

8. In a Dutch oven over medium-high heat, heat the ghee.

9. Add the onions and fry until translucent.

10. Add the ginger paste and garlic paste. Fry until the water evaporates.

11. Stir in the red chile powder and coriander.

12. Add the stuffed chicken. Fry carefully, browning it all over. Season to taste with salt.

13. Add the milk and bring to a boil.

14. Add the coconut cream. Reduce the heat to low. Cover the pot and simmer the chicken until it becomes very tender but the flesh does not come off the bone and a little gravy is left.

15. Stir in the whisked yogurt to the gravy. Reduce the heat to very low and cook until the gravy is thick and the ghee comes to the surface. Serve hot.

# ADRAKI MURGH 🍲

Chicken in ginger-flavored tomato gravy.

Cooking time: 1 hour | Serves: 4          Origin: Uttar Pradesh

## INGREDIENTS

**For the marinade**
1½ cups (360 g) yogurt (*dahi*), whisked
½ cup (120 ml) malt vinegar (*sirka*)
3 green cardamom pods (*choti elaichi*), seeds
  removed and ground into a powder
2 tsp ginger paste (*adrak*)
1 tsp garlic paste (*lasan*)
1 tsp ground coriander (*dhaniya*)
1 tsp ground cumin (*jeera*)
1 tsp red chile powder

**For the chicken**
1 whole cut-up broiler chicken, skin removed
½ cup (120 g) ghee
2 tsp cumin seeds (*jeera*)
1½ cups (360 g) peeled, chopped, blanched tomato
Salt, to taste
1½ tsp red food color

## METHOD

1. **To make the marinade:** In a large bowl, whisk
   the yogurt, vinegar, green cardamom powder,
   ginger paste, garlic paste, coriander, cumin, and
   red chile powder.
2. **To make the chicken:** Add the chicken to the
   marinade. Stir to coat. Refrigerate for 2 hours.
3. In a large skillet over medium-high heat, heat
   the ghee.
4. Add the cumin seeds. Cook until the seeds
   begin to crackle.
5. Add the chicken along with the marinade. Stir
   until well mixed.
6. Stir in the tomato and season to taste with salt.
   Reduce the heat to medium and cook until the
   chicken is cooked through and the gravy
   thickens.
7. Stir in the food color and mix well. Serve hot.

# KALI MIRCH KA MURGH 📷 🍲

Black pepper-flavored chicken with vegetables.

Cooking time: 1 hour | Serves: 4-6          Origin: Uttar Pradesh

## INGREDIENTS

4 medium-size boneless, skinless chicken breasts,
  rinsed
Zest of 1 lemon (*nimbu*), divided
Juice of 1 lemon (*nimbu*), divided
1 head garlic (*lasan*), peeled and minced, divided
2 tsp peppercorns (*sabut kali mirch*), freshly
  ground, divided
2 Tbsp (30 ml) olive oil, divided
Salt, to taste
4 small potatoes, halved
6 French green beans (haricots verts), cut into
  (1-in. / 2.5-cm) pieces
1 carrot (*gajar*), cut into small dice
1 small red onion, cut into ½-in. (1.25-cm) wedges
½ cup (120 ml) chicken broth

## METHOD

1. With a sharp knife, make small random slits
   in the chicken breasts to allow the flavors to
   seep in.
2. In a small bowl, stir together half the lemon zest
   and juice, half the garlic, half the ground
   peppercorns, and 1 Tbsp (15 ml) of olive oil.
   Season to taste with salt. Rub this mixture over
   the chicken breasts and set aside.
3. In the skillet over low-medium heat, heat the
   remaining 1 Tbsp (15 ml) of olive oil.
4. Add the remaining garlic. Sauté for a few
   seconds until fragrant.
5. Toss in the potatoes. Season to taste with salt.
   Cook until the potatoes begin to soften.
6. Add the green beans, carrot, red onion, and the
   remaining ground peppercorns, lemon juice,
   and zest.
7. Arrange the chicken pieces over the vegetables.
   Pour in the chicken broth. Adjust the heat to
   low and cover the skillet. Cook until the chicken
   starts to fall apart.
8. Serve hot.

## MURGH ZAFRANI

Chicken in saffron sauce.

| Cooking time: 1 hour | Serves: 4-6 | Origin: Uttar Pradesh |
| --- | --- | --- |

INGREDIENTS

½ cup (120 g) ghee
12 whole cloves (*laung*)
6 green cardamom pods (*choti elaichi*)
2 (1-in. / 2.5-cm) cinnamon sticks (*dalchini*)
2 Tbsp (20 g) chopped garlic (*lasan*)
¾ cup (180 g) sliced onion
½ tsp ground nutmeg (*jaiphal*)
5 tsp ginger paste (*adrak*)
4 tsp garlic paste (*lasan*)
½ tsp red chile powder
Salt, to taste
1 whole cut-up broiler chicken
2 cups (480 ml) chicken broth
Few strands saffron (*kesar*), crushed and soaked
  in ¼ cup (60 ml) hot water

METHOD

1. In a Dutch oven over medium-high heat, heat the ghee.
2. Add the cloves, green cardamom pods, and cinnamon sticks. Cook until the spices begin to crackle.
3. Add the garlic and fry until it browns.
4. Add the onion and nutmeg. Sauté until the onion is golden brown.
5. Stir in the ginger paste, garlic paste, and red chile powder. Season to taste with salt.
6. Add the chicken to the pot, stir, and cook until the moisture evaporates.
7. Add the chicken broth and bring to a boil. Reduce the heat to low. Cover the pot and cook until the chicken is tender.
8. Remove the pot from the heat and set aside to cool. Remove the chicken and strain the gravy through a fine-mesh strainer. Discard whatever is left in the strainer.
9. Return the chicken pieces and strained gravy to the pot. Simmer until the gravy is reduced by half and has a sauce-like consistency.
10. Stir in the saffron water and serve.

## LAHORI CHARGHA

Whole chicken marinated and deep-fried.

| Cooking time: 1 hour | Serves: 4 | Origin: Punjab |
| --- | --- | --- |

INGREDIENTS

1 whole chicken
5 Tbsp (75 g) yogurt (*dahi*)
1 Tbsp (15 ml) vinegar (*sirka*)
2 Tbsp (30 g) ginger-garlic paste (*adrak-lasan*)
1 Tbsp (6 g) ground coriander (*dhaniya*)
1 Tbsp (6 g) garam masala
2 tsp red chile powder
1 tsp ground turmeric (*haldi*)
1 tsp ground cumin (*jeera*)
1 tsp chaat masala
1 tsp dried fenugreek leaves (*kasuri methi*)
2 Tbsp (30 ml) heavy cream
Salt, to taste
Vegetable oil, for frying

METHOD

1. With a sharp knife, make incisions over the whole bird for the marinade to penetrate.
2. In a small bowl, stir together the yogurt, vinegar, ginger-garlic paste, coriander, garam masala, red chile powder, turmeric, cumin, chaat masala, dried fenugreek leaves, and cream. Season to taste with salt. Rub the paste over the chicken and marinate overnight in the refrigerator.
3. In a steamer, steam the whole bird for 20 minutes.
4. In a large deep pan over medium-high heat, heat the vegetable oil for frying.
5. Add the steamed bird, adjust the heat to low, and deep-fry for 20–25 minutes, or until cooked through and golden brown.
6. Serve hot, carved into pieces.

## CHAWLA'S LUDHIANA CHICKEN
Baked chicken in yogurt and cashew gravy.

| Cooking time: 1 hour | Serves: 2 | Origin: Punjab |
| --- | --- | --- |

### INGREDIENTS

1 lb, 2 oz (500 g) bone-in chicken pieces
Juice of 1 lemon (*nimbu*)
Salt, to taste
1 Tbsp (15 g) ghee
1 tsp caraway seeds (*shahi jeera*)
3 Tbsp (45 g) onion paste
2 bay leaves (*tej patta*)
1 Tbsp (15 g) ginger-garlic paste (*adrak-lasan*)
1 Tbsp (15 g) dried fenugreek leaves (*kasuri methi*)
½ cup (120 g) cashews (*kaju*)
½ cup (120 g) yogurt (*dahi*)
Freshly ground black pepper (*kali mirch*), to taste

### METHOD

1. In a large bowl, mix the chicken with the lemon juice and season to taste with salt. Refrigerate to marinate for 4 hours.
2. Preheat the oven to 400°F (200°C).
3. Transfer the chicken to a baking sheet and bake for 20 minutes.
4. In a skillet over medium-high heat, heat the ghee.
5. Add the caraway seeds. Cook until the seeds begin to crackle.
6. Add the onion paste, bay leaves, and ginger-garlic paste. Sauté until the onion turns golden.
7. In a blender, blitz the dried fenugreek leaves and cashews into a smooth paste with some water.
8. Add this paste to the skillet and sauté the mixture well.
9. Add the chicken and yogurt and allow the chicken to absorb the flavors. Cook until the water from the yogurt evaporates.
10. Season to taste with salt and pepper. Serve hot.

## TANDOORI CHICKEN 🍲
Street-style barbequed chicken.

| Cooking time: 40 minutes | Serves: 4 | Origin: Delhi |
| --- | --- | --- |

### INGREDIENTS

6 Tbsp (90 g) yogurt (*dahi*)
2 tsp ginger-garlic paste (*adrak-lasan*)
1 tsp green chile paste
1 tsp red chile powder
2 tsp ground coriander (*dhaniya*)
1 tsp garam masala
1 Tbsp (8 g) tandoori masala
1 tsp ground cumin (*jeera*)
Salt, to taste
1 whole chicken (cut into 8 pieces)
1 tsp lemon juice (*nimbu*)
Oil, for basting
1 Tbsp (8 g) chaat masala

### METHOD

1. In a medium-size bowl, combine the yogurt, ginger-garlic paste, green chile paste, red chile powder, coriander, garam masala, tandoori masala, and cumin. Season to taste with salt. Whisk together to form a thick marinade.
2. Rub the marinate over the chicken and refrigerate for 3–4 hours.
3. Preheat the oven to 350°F (180°C).
4. Grill the pieces for 25–30 minutes.
5. Halfway, remove the chicken from the oven and baste it with oil.
6. Once done, sprinkle chaat masala on top and serve hot.

# MURGH MAKHANI 🍲

The very popular Butter Chicken or chicken in a creamy tomato-based sauce.

Cooking time: 30 minutes | Serves: 3      Origin: Delhi

### INGREDIENTS

2 lb, 3 oz (1 kg) tomatoes, finely chopped
2 Tbsp (30 g) butter
2 tsp red chile powder
¾ cup (180 ml) heavy cream
2 cups (280 g) Tandoori Chicken (page 64)
Salt, to taste
¼ cup (4 g) fresh cilantro leaves (*hara dhaniya*), finely chopped

### METHOD

1. In a saucepan over low-medium heat, cover the tomatoes in water and boil until soft. Set aside to cool. Blitz into a fine purée.
2. In a wok over medium heat, heat the butter.
3. Add the tomato purée and red chile powder. Cook for 7–8 minutes.
4. Add the cream and tandoori chicken. Season to taste with salt. Cook for 10–15 minutes and garnish with cilantro.
5. Serve hot.

# ACHARI MURGH

Indian pickle-flavored chicken.

Cooking time: 30 minutes | Serves: 2-4    Origin: Uttar Pradesh

### INGREDIENTS

2 dried red chiles (*sookhi lal mirch*)
1 tsp fenugreek seeds (*methi dana*)
1 tsp mustard seeds (*rai*)
1 tsp fennel seeds (*saunf*)
1 tsp onion seeds (*kalonji*)
1 Tbsp (15 g) Indian pickle (*achar*)
1 tsp ground turmeric (*haldi*)
1 cup (240 g) yogurt (*dahi*)
Salt, to taste
3 green chiles, slit
8 ounces (250 g) chicken, cubed
1 Tbsp (15 ml) vegetable oil
¼ cup (60 g) finely chopped onions
1 Tbsp (15 g) ginger-garlic paste (*adrak-lasan*)
1 tsp red chile powder
1 tsp ground coriander (*dhaniya*)
1 cup (240 ml) water
¼ cup (4 g) fresh cilantro leaves (*hara dhaniya*), finely chopped

### METHOD

1. In a food processor or blender, blend the dried red chiles, fenugreek seeds, mustard seeds, fennel seeds, and onion seeds into a powder.
2. In a medium-size bowl, combine 1 Tbsp of the prepared spice powder, Indian pickle, turmeric, yogurt, salt, and green chiles. Add the chicken. Toss well and marinate for 3 hours.
3. In a skillet over low-medium heat, heat the vegetable oil.
4. Add the onions and sauté for 2 minutes. Add the ginger-garlic paste, red chile powder, and coriander. Stir well. Cook for 3 minutes.
5. Add the marinated chicken and water. Reduce the heat to low and simmer until the chicken is cooked through and the water from the marinade evaporates.
6. Garnish with cilantro. Serve hot.

## PATIALA CHICKEN

Chicken in tomato gravy with fluffy omelet bits, garnished with cheese.

Cooking time: 1 hour | Serves: 2      Origin: Punjab

### INGREDIENTS

2 eggs
¼ cup (4 g) fresh cilantro leaves (*hara dhaniya*), chopped
Salt, to taste
Freshly ground black pepper (*kali mirch*), to taste
2 Tbsp (30 ml) vegetable oil, divided
1 tsp cumin seeds (*jeera*)
¼ cup (42.5 g) finely chopped onion
1 Tbsp (15 g) ginger-garlic paste (*adrak-lasan*)
1 Tbsp (6 g) garam masala
1 tsp ground turmeric (*haldi*)
1 tsp red chile powder
1 cup (140 g) cubed chicken
1 cup (240 g) tomato purée
2 tsp dried fenugreek leaves (*kasuri methi*)
2 Tbsp (30 ml) heavy cream
¼ cup (60 g) grated cheese

### METHOD

1. In a small bowl, whisk the eggs and cilantro. Season to taste with salt and pepper. Whisk well to combine.
2. In a skillet over medium heat, heat 1 Tbsp (15 ml) of vegetable oil.
3. Pour in the whisked egg and make an omelet. Remove when golden brown on both sides. Set aside to cool. Tear into pieces.
4. Return the skillet to medium-high heat and add the remaining 1 Tbsp (15 ml) of vegetable oil.
5. Add cumin seeds. When the seeds begin to crackle, add the onions and ginger-garlic paste. Cook until golden-brown.
6. Stir in the garam masala, turmeric, red chile powder, and chicken. Season to taste with salt. Mix well. Cover the skillet and reduce the heat to low. Cook for 15–17 minutes, stirring occasionally.
7. Stir in the tomato purée and dried fenugreek leaves. Cover and cook for 10 minutes more.
8. Once the chicken is done, add the cream and omelet pieces.
9. Serve hot, garnished with cheese.

## KOKUR NADUR 📷

Chicken cooked with lotus stems in a spicy gravy.

Cooking time: 40 minutes | Serves: 4-6 Origin: Jammu & Kashmir

### INGREDIENTS

2 lb, 3 oz (1 kg) medium-size lotus stems (*bhein*), cut into 2-in. (5-cm) pieces (available in some specialty Indian markets and online)
1¼ cups (300 ml) vegetable oil, divided
1 whole cut-up broiler chicken
1½ tsp red chile powder mixed with a little water
1½ cups (360 ml) water, plus more for mixing with the red chile powder
4 whole cloves (*laung*)
2 black cardamom pods (*badi elaichi*), crushed
2 bay leaves (*tej patta*)
1 Tbsp (7 g) aniseed powder (*saunf*)
1 tsp ground ginger (*sonth*)
Pinch ground asafoetida (*hing*)
Salt, to taste
½ tsp spice cake (tikki masala), crushed (page 22)

### METHOD

1. Wash the lotus stems well to remove all traces of mud. Set aside to drain.
2. In a deep skillet over medium-high heat, heat 1 cup (240 ml) of vegetable oil for frying.
3. Add the chicken to the hot oil and fry until golden brown. Remove and set aside.
4. In the same oil, fry the lotus stems until golden brown. Remove and set aside.
5. In a heavy-bottomed pot or skillet over high heat, heat the remaining ¼ cup of vegetable oil.
6. Add the red chile powder. Stir for a few seconds, add the water, and bring to a boil.
7. Add the fried chicken and lotus stems along with the cloves, black cardamom pods, bay leaves, aniseed powder, ginger, and asafoetida. Season to taste with salt. Cook for 10–15 minutes. When the gravy thickens, stir in the spice cake and cook for 1–2 minutes more, stirring gently. Serve hot.

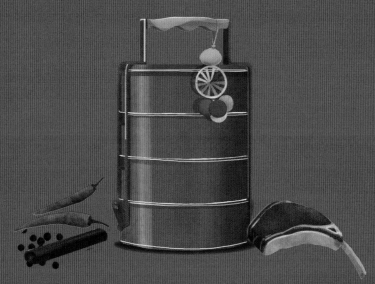

MEAT AND PORK

## KEEMA AKBARI ♨

Almond and cashew-flavored minced meat.

Cooking time: 1 hour 30 minutes | Serves: 6 Origin: Uttar Pradesh

### INGREDIENTS

½ cup (120 g) ghee
½ cup (85 g) minced onion
1 Tbsp (10 g) chopped garlic (*lasan*)
1 lb, 10½ oz (750 g) minced lamb
1 cup (240 g) yogurt (*dahi*), whisked
1 tsp ground black cardamom
1 tsp freshly ground black pepper (*kali mirch*)
4 green chiles, sliced
Salt, to taste
15 almonds (*badam*), blanched and peeled
12 cashews (*kaju*)
1 Tbsp (9 g) poppy seeds (*khus khus*), roasted

### METHOD

1. In a skillet over low heat, heat the ghee.
2. Add the onion and garlic. Sauté until the onion is translucent.
3. Add the lamb. Cook until completely dry.
4. Add the yogurt, cardamom, pepper, and green chiles. Season to taste with salt. Simmer until the yogurt is completely absorbed and the lamb is tender.
5. While the mince cooks, in a blender, combine the almonds, cashews, and poppy seeds with a little water. Blend into a smooth paste, adding more water as needed. Transfer the paste to the lamb mixture. Stir to combine. Reduce the heat to very low and simmer for 3 minutes more, stirring constantly, being very careful the paste does not burn. Serve hot.

## RAAN ♨

Tender leg of lamb flavored with spices.

Cooking time: 1 hour 30 minutes | Serves: 6-8 Origin: Uttar Pradesh

### INGREDIENTS

2 lb, 3 oz (1 kg) leg of lamb (*raan*), pricked well all over with a fork
1 (3-in. / 7.5-cm) piece raw papaya, ground to a paste
Salt, to taste
4 large onions, 1 finely grated to a paste; 3 sliced and fried until golden (*birista*; page 30)
3 Tbsp (22.5 g) chickpea flour (*besan*), toasted
1 Tbsp (15 g) grated, peeled fresh ginger (*adrak*)
1 Tbsp (15 g) garlic paste (*lasan*)
2 cups (480 g) yogurt (*dahi*), plus more as needed
6 Tbsp (90 g) ghee
1 tsp caraway seeds (*shahi jeera*)
1 Tbsp (15 g) coriander seeds (*dhaniya*), toasted

### METHOD

1. Rub the leg of lamb with the papaya paste and salt. Place in a large resealable plastic bag.
2. In a medium-size bowl, combine the grated onion, fried onions, chickpea flour, ginger, garlic paste, and yogurt. Mix well to combine. Cover the meat with this mixture. Seal the bag, turn the meat to coat, and refrigerate to marinate overnight, or for at least 4 hours.
3. When ready to cook, on your pressure cooker, select Sauté and preheat the cooking pot.
4. Add the ghee to melt.
5. Add the caraway seeds and coriander seeds. Cook until the seeds begin to splutter.
6. Add the meat along with the marinade and cook until brown.
7. Lock the lid in place and close the pressure release valve. Select Manual/Pressure Cook and cook for 3 minutes. Reduce the pressure to Low and cook for 20 minutes more, or until the meat falls off the bones and the mixture is dry. Let the pressure release, open the lid; if the lamb is not tender, add more yogurt and cook for 10 minutes more.
8. Serve hot.

# CHANDRAJI'S MEAT CURRY 📷 🍲

Succulent, tender lamb enriched with whole
spices in yogurt sauce.

Cooking time: 1 hour 30 minutes | Serves: 3 Origin: Uttar Pradesh

## INGREDIENTS

2 Tbsp (30 ml) mustard seed oil (page 26)

2 lb, 3 oz (1 kg) bone-in lamb pieces

1 Tbsp (15 g) ghee

2 cups (480 g) sliced onion

6–7 whole cloves (*laung*)

4 dried red chiles (*sookhi lal mirch*)

3 (1-in. / 2.5-cm) cinnamon sticks (*dalchini*)

3 bay leaves (*tej patta*)

2–3 star anise (*chakri ke phool*)

2 black cardamom pods (*badi elaichi*)

1 Tbsp (15 g) peppercorns (*sabut kali mirch*)

2 tsp coriander seeds (*dhaniya*)

1 tsp cumin seeds (*jeera*)

Pinch ground mace (*javitri*)

2 Tbsp (30 g) ginger-garlic paste (*adrak-lasan*)

1 cup (240 g) yogurt (*dahi*)

¾ oz (20 g) lotus seeds (*makhana*; available at
  Indian markets or online)

1 tsp Kashmiri red chile powder

Salt, to taste

¼ cup (4 g) fresh cilantro leaves (*hara dhaniya*),
  finely chopped

## METHOD

1. In a skillet over medium-high heat, heat the
   mustard seed oil until it starts to smoke.

2. Add the lamb. Sear until golden brown on all
   sides. Remove from the pan and set aside.

3. Return the skillet to low heat. Add the ghee and
   onion. Sauté until golden brown.

4. Add the cloves, dried red chiles, cinnamon
   sticks, bay leaves, star anise, black cardamom
   pods, peppercorns, coriander seeds, cumin
   seeds, and mace. Continue to sauté until the
   onion turns dark brown.

5. Add the ginger-garlic paste and cook, stirring,
   for 1 minute.

6. Add the sautéed lamb back to the skillet and
   continue to cook.

7. In a medium-size bowl, whisk the yogurt with 7
   fl oz (210 ml) of water to make a loose slurry.
   Gradually add this liquid to the pan and
   simmer—do not add the liquid all at once.

8. While the lamb cooks, toast the lotus seeds in a
   covered pan on medium heat for 5 minutes or
   until they pop. Ensure you don't burn them (as
   they cook very quickly). Transfer to a food
   processor. Let cool and grind into a powder.

9. Gradually add the lotus seed powder to the
   mixture, stirring. If the curry turns too dry, add
   more water.

10. Add the Kashmiri red chile powder and season
    to taste with salt. Cook, on low heat, until the
    lamb is succulent and tender.

11. Serve hot, garnished with cilantro.

# CHUQANDAR GOSHT 🍲

Lamb cooked with beets.

Cooking time: 1 hour 30 minutes | Serves: 3 Origin: Uttar Pradesh

## INGREDIENTS

4 Tbsp (45 ml) vegetable oil

8–10 peppercorns (*sabut kali mirch*)

2 bay leaves (*tej patta*)

4 whole cloves (*laung*)

3 medium-size onions, finely sliced

2 Tbsp (30 g) ginger-garlic paste (*adrak-lasan*)

2 green chiles, slit lengtwise

1 lb, 2 oz (500 g) lamb, cut into bite-size pieces

Salt, to taste

1½ tsp red chile powder

1 tsp ground turmeric (*haldi*)

1 tsp ground coriander (*dhaniya*)

4 small beets (*chuqandar*), peeled and sliced

1 cup (240 g) tomatoes, chopped

1 cup (240 ml) water, or as needed

1 bunch fresh cilantro leaves (*hara dhaniya*), finely chopped

## METHOD

1. On your pressure cooker, select Sauté and preheat the cooking pot.

2. Add the vegetable oil to heat.

3. Add the peppercorns, bay leaves, and cloves.

4. Add the onions. Sauté until golden brown.

5. Add the ginger-garlic paste and green chiles. Sauté until the paste turns brown.

6. Add the lamb and season to taste with salt. Cook, stirring, until the moisture dries up and the meat is light brown.

7. Add the red chile powder, turmeric, and coriander. Stir well. Add the beets and tomatoes. Stir well to combine.

8. Pour in ½–1 cup (120–240 ml) of water. Lock the lid in place and close the pressure release valve. Select Manual/Pressure Cook and cook for 18 minutes, or until the meat is tender.

9. Release the pressure and remove the lid. Simmer until the oil separates and floats on the top. Add a little water so a thick gravy forms. Serve hot, garnished with cilantro.

# MUGHLAI-STYLE WHITE LAMB

Aromatic lamb in a yogurt-laced saffron sauce.

Cooking time: 1 hour 30 minutes | Serves: 4 Origin: Uttar Pradesh

## INGREDIENTS

2 lb, 3 oz, (1 kg) lamb, cubed

2 cups (480 g) yogurt (*dahi*)

½ cup (120 g) ghee

2½ Tbsp (15 g) garam masala

2 Tbsp (30 g) ginger-garlic paste (*adrak-lasan*)

1 Tbsp (8 g) red chile powder

1 cup (170 g) finely chopped onion

2 Tbsp (30 g) dried red chiles (*sookhi lal mirch*), ground to a powder

10 white peppercorns (*safed mirch*)

Salt, to taste

2 Tbsp (18 g) poppy seeds (*khus khus*)

½ cup (120 g) whole-milk fudge (*khoya*; available at Indian markets; page 25)

¼ cup (34 g) cashews (*kaju*)

Pinch saffron threads (*kesar*), diluted in 2 Tbsp (30 ml) milk

Silver leaves, for garnishing (*warq*; page 24)

## METHOD

1. Fill a medium-size pot about halfway with water and bring to a rolling boil over high heat. Add the lamb and boil for 15 minutes. Transfer the meat to a medium-size bowl and cover with the yogurt. Refrigerate for 1 hour.

2. In a skillet over medium-high heat, heat the ghee.

3. Add the garam masala, ginger-garlic paste, red chile powder, and onion. Sauté for 1 minute.

4. Add the lamb with the yogurt, the ground dried red chiles, and white peppercorns. Season to taste with salt. Reduce the heat to low and cook for 40 minutes.

5. Add the poppy seeds and cook for 20 minutes more.

6. Add the whole-milk fudge. Continue to cook, stirring, until the meat is thoroughly cooked.

7. Stir in the cashews and saffron milk. Serve hot, garnished with silver leaves (*warq*).

# TERAI PASANDA
Escalopes of the leg of lamb.

Cooking time: 1 hour 20 minutes | Serves: 8  Origin: Uttar Pradesh

## INGREDIENTS

½ cup (100 g) raw papaya, minced

½ tsp salt

2 lb, 3 oz (1 kg) leg of lamb (*raan*), thinly sliced

4–5 whole dried red chiles (*sabut lal mirch*), medium-size

1½ tsp coriander seeds (*dhaniya*)

2 whole cloves (*laung*)

1 cup (240 g) ghee

2 lb, 3 oz (1 kg) onions, finely chopped

1½ cups (360 g) yogurt (*dahi*)

1 cup (120 g) roasted chickpea (*chana*), powdered

2 tsp garam masala

2 Tbsp (30 g) ginger-garlic paste (*adrak-lasan*)

1 tsp red chile powder

2 tsp coriander paste (*dhaniya*)

Salt, to taste

10–12 drops vetivier (*kewra*) water for garnishing

1 recipe dungaar (page 26), using 1 tsp ghee

1 medium-size onion, cut into rings

¼ cup (16 g) fresh mint leaves (*pudina*), finely chopped

## METHOD

1. In a medium-size bowl, combine the minced raw papaya and salt. Add the meat. Smear the meat with the paste and marinate in the refrigerator for at least 1 hour in summer and 3 hours in winter.

2. In a pan over low-medium heat, dry-roast the whole red chiles, coriander seeds, and cloves. Set aside to cool. Using a grinder or food processor, grind to a fine powder.

3. In a skillet over medium-high heat, heat the ghee.

4. Add the onion. Cook until golden brown. Add the marinated meat. Stirring occasionaly, cook for 20 minutes.

5. Add the yogurt, roasted chickpea powder, garam masala, ginger-garlic paste, red chile powder, and coriander paste. Reduce the heat to low. Continue to cook for 60 minutes, or until the meat is tender. Season to taste with salt. Add the vetivier water.

6. Meanwhile, prepare the dungaar and place it inside the dish. This should be done just before serving.

7. Serve hot, garnished with onion rings and mint leaves.

## MEAT BHATINDA 📷
Mildly spiced dry lamb dish.

Cooking time: 1 hour | Serves: 3          Origin: Punjab

INGREDIENTS

2 Tbsp (30 ml) vegetable oil
1 medium-size onion, sliced
1 bay leaf (*tej patta*)
10 oz (300 g) bone-in lamb pieces
1 cup (240 ml) water
1 Tbsp (15 g) ginger-garlic paste (*adrak-lasan*)
Salt, to taste
1 tsp ground turmeric (*haldi*)
2 green chiles, finely chopped
¾ cup (180 g) thick yogurt (*dahi*)
1 Tbsp (6 g) garam masala
¼ cup (4 g) fresh cilantro leaves (*hara dhaniya*),
   finely chopped

METHOD

1.  In a skillet over medium-high heat, heat the
    vegetable oil.
2.  Add the onion and bay leaf. Sauté until golden
    brown.
3.  Add the lamb and stir well.
4.  Add the water. Cook for 3–4 minutes.
5.  Stir in the ginger-garlic paste and season to
    taste with salt. Reduce the heat to low and cook
    for 30 minutes, or until the lamb begins to
    soften.
6.  Add the turmeric, green chiles, and yogurt.
    Mix well. Simmer until all the ingredients are
    thoroughly cooked and the water from the
    yogurt evaporates.
7.  Stir in the garam masala and cook until the
    lamb is fully done.
8.  Serve hot, garnished with cilantro.

## SYUN METHI
Lamb cooked with fenugreek.

Cooking time: 1 hour | Serves: 6          Origin: Jammu & Kashmir

INGREDIENTS

2 lb, 3 oz (1 kg) lamb with bones, cut into 2-in.
   (5-cm) cubes, rinsed
2 cups (480 ml) water, plus more for the fenugreek
   leaves
Salt, to taste
3 bay leaves (*tej patta*)
3 black cardamom pods (*badi elaichi*)
3 whole cloves (*laung*)
1 (2-in. / 5-cm) cinnamon stick (*dalchini*)
2 tsp aniseed powder (*saunf*)
2 tsp ground ginger (*sonth*)
1 tsp ground turmeric (*haldi*)
1 tsp garam masala
Pinch ground asafoetida (*hing*)
1 lb, 2 oz (500 g) fenugreek leaves (*methi*), rinsed
½ cup (120 g) ghee
3 green chiles, sliced

METHOD

1.  In a large deep pot over high heat, combine the
    lamb, water, salt, bay leaves, black cardamom
    pods, cloves, cinnamon stick, aniseed powder,
    ginger, turmeric, garam masala, and asafoetida.
    Cook for 15 minutes, or until the lamb is almost
    done. With a slotted spoon, transfer the lamb
    pieces to a bowl and set aside. Strain the stock
    and set aside.
2.  In a small saucepan over high heat combine the
    fenugreek leaves with enough water to cover.
    Bring to a boil, strain, and process into a paste.
3.  In a deep skillet over low-medium heat, heat
    the ghee.
4.  Add the fenugreek paste. Sauté for 5 minutes,
    stirring frequently.
5.  Add the lamb. Sauté for 5 minutes more.
6.  Add the stock. Cook until the lamb is tender.
    Remove from the heat.
7.  Serve hot, garnished with green chiles.

## NALLI DUMPUKTH 🍲
Slow-braised lamb shanks with mild spices.

Cooking time: 1 hour 30 minutes | Serves: 6 Origin: Uttar Pradesh

### INGREDIENTS

1 cup (125 g) whole-wheat flour (*atta*), plus more
   for dusting
Water, as needed to make dough
¾ cup (180 g) ghee
6 green cardamom pods (*choti elaichi*), cracked
4 whole cloves (*laung*)
3 Tbsp (45 g) ginger paste (*adrak*)
3 Tbsp (45 g) garlic paste (*lasan*)
10 lamb shanks
Salt, to taste
1 cup (240 g) yogurt (*dahi*)
¼ cup (60 g) fried onion paste
1½ tsp red chile powder
3 cups (720 ml) beef broth
¾ cup (180 ml) tomato purée
1 Tbsp (15 g) cashew butter (*kaju*)
1 tsp garam masala
1½ tsp julienned peeled fresh ginger (*adrak*)
½ tsp saffron threads (*kesar*), soaked in
   3 Tbsp (45 ml) warm milk

### METHOD

1. In a small bowl, combine the flour with just enough water to form a dough. Knead into a tight dough and set aside.
2. In a saucepan over low-medium heat, heat the ghee.
3. When hot, add the green cardamom pods and cloves. Cook until they begin to crackle.
4. Add the ginger paste and garlic paste. Sauté until the water evaporates.
5. Add the lamb and season to taste with salt.
6. Stir in the yogurt, fried onion paste, and red chile powder. Cook for 5 minutes.
7. Add the beef broth and bring the mixture to a boil. Reduce the heat to low and simmer until the meat is tender. Remove the cooked meat from the gravy and arrange in an ovenproof casserole dish.
8. Strain the gravy into another pan. Stir in the tomato purée and place the pan over medium heat. Cook, stirring, until the gravy thickens.
9. Stir in the cashew butter and garam masala. Cook for 2–3 minutes. Pour the gravy over the lamb.
10. Mix the ginger into the saffron milk and add to the lamb.
11. Preheat the oven to 350°F (180°C).
12. Dust a work surface with flour. Roll out the dough to a size large enough to cover your casserole dish. Place the dough on top of the dish and seal tightly around the edges.
13. Bake for 15–20 minutes until the dough is golden brown.

# TAR GOSHT
Rich lamb curry.

Cooking time: 1 hour | Serves: 6-8      Origin: Uttar Pradesh

INGREDIENTS

For the stock (*yakhni*)
2 lb, 3 oz (1 kg) trotters (*payas*)
6 cups (1.5 L) water
For the lamb curry
2 cups (480 ml) vegetable oil
2 bay leaves (*tej patta*)
5 whole cloves (*laung*)
4 green cardamom pods (*choti elaichi*)
2 cups (480 g) sliced onions
1½ Tbsp (22 g) garlic paste (*lasan*)
1½ Tbsp (22 g) ginger paste (*adrak*)
4 lb, 6 oz (2 kg) lamb, cut into pieces
1 cup (240 g) onion paste
1 cup (240 g) yogurt (*dahi*)
3½ Tbsp (21 g) garam masala
3 tsp yellow chile powder
3 tsp red chile powder
1 tsp ground turmeric (*haldi*)
3 Tbsp (18 g) ground coriander (*dhaniya*)
Salt, to taste

METHOD

1.  **To make the stock (*yakhni*):** In a pressure cooker cooking pot, combine the trotters with the water. Lock the lid in place and close the pressure release valve. Select Manual / Pressure Cook and cook for 12 minutes. Let the pressure release. Remove the lid and strain to get a stock.
2.  **To make the lamb curry:** In a skillet over medium-high heat, heat the vegetable oil. Add the bay leaves, cloves, and green cardamom. Add the onions. Stir-fry until golden brown. Remove from the heat. Set aside to cool.
3.  Using a food processor grind the mixture to a paste.
4.  Add the ginger paste and garlic paste. Stir well. Add the meat, raw onion paste, fried onion paste, and stock along with the yogurt and all the spice powders. Season to taste with salt. Stir-fry until the oil rises to the surface.
5.  Transfer to pressure cooker cooking pot. Lock the lid and close the pressure release valve. Select Manual / Pressure Cook and cook for 6 minutes or until the meat is tender. Let the pressure release. Remove the lid and serve hot.

# GUSHTABA
Lamb balls in a yogurt gravy.

Cooking time: 1 hour | Serves: 6-8      Origin: Jammu & Kashmir

INGREDIENTS

2 lb, 3 oz (1 kg) lamb, boneless from leg
1 cup (240 g) meat fat or white butter
5 green cardamom pods (*choti elaichi*), divided
1 tsp ginger powder (*sonth*)
Salt, to taste
10 lamb bones
12 cups (3 L) water
½ cup (120 g) ghee
2 tsp garlic paste (*lasan*)
2 tsp fried onion paste (*birista*; page 30)
3 cloves (*laung*)
1 (1-in. / 2.5-cm) cinnamon stick (*dalchini*)
2 bay leaves (*tej patta*)
3 tsp fennel powder (*saunf*)
2 cups (480 ml) milk
1 cup (240 g) yogurt (*dahi*), whisked
2 tsp dried mint (*pudina*)

METHOD

1.  Pound the boneless meat on a smooth stone with a wooden mallet (or use a grinder or food processor). Add the meat fat, 2 green cardamom pods, ginger, and salt. Keep pounding till you get a smooth pulp.
2.  Divide the mixture into equal portions and shape into round balls. Set aside.
3.  **To make the stock,** boil the bones in the water for 30 minutes and strain. Set aside.
4.  In a large skillet over medium-high heat, heat the ghee. Add the salt, garlic paste, fried onion paste, cloves, cinnamon stick, the remaining 3 green cardamom pods, and bay leaves.
5.  Add the stock and keep stirring. Add the fennel powder, milk, and whisked yogurt. Stir well to combine. Carefully add the lamb balls (*gushtabas*), one by one, and boil for 30 minutes, or until the balls are tender and the gravy is thick. Simmer for 15 minutes.
6.  Garnish with dried mint and serve hot with steamed rice.

# FISH AND SEAFOOD

## GAAD NADUR

Kashmiri-style fried fish tossed with lotus stems.

Cooking time: 30 minutes | Serves: 2  Origin: Jammu & Kashmir

INGREDIENTS

10 oz (300 g) mackerel fillets (*surmai*)
Salt, to taste
Vegetable oil, for frying
½ cup (120 g) fried onions (*birista*; page 30)
1½ tsp whole spice mix (page 22)
2 tsp garlic paste (*lasan*)
1 cup (240 g) lotus stems (*bhein*), sliced, boiled
   (available in some specialty Indian markets
   and online)
1 Tbsp (15 g) Kashmiri veri masala (available at
   Indian markets)
2 tsp ground turmeric (*haldi*)
2 tsp red chile powder
2–3 pieces kokum, soaked in ½ cup (120 ml) water
   for 1 hour

METHOD

1. Season the fish on both sides with salt. Set aside
   for 10 minutes.
2. In a large skillet over low-medium heat, heat the
   vegetable oil for frying.
3. Add the fillets. Cook on both sides until golden.
   Transfer to paper towels to drain.
4. In a food processor, blend the fried onions into
   a paste.
5. In a clean skillet over low-medium heat, heat 1
   Tbsp (15 ml) of vegetable oil.
6. Add the whole spice mix. Cook until the seeds
   begin to crackle.
7. Add the garlic paste. Sauté for 2 minutes.
8. Add the lotus stems, Kashmiri veri masala,
   turmeric, and red chile powder. Mix well. Reduce
   the heat to medium and cook for 10 minutes.
9. Discard the kokum and add the soaking water
   to the skillet. Cook for 3–4 minutes.
10. Add the onion paste. Cook the mixture for 5
    minutes more.
11. Add the fried fish, taste and adjust the
    seasonings as needed, and cook until the fish is
    heated through.
12. Serve hot.

## KULLU TROUT

Dill-flavored trout cooked in mustard seed oil.

Cooking time: 30 minutes | Serves: 2  Origin: Jammu & Kashmir

INGREDIENTS

2 Tbsp (30 ml) mustard seed oil (page 26), divided
1 tsp dried dill
1 tsp ground coriander (*dhaniya*)
1 tsp red pepper flakes
½ tsp lemon zest (*nimbu*)
Salt, to taste
1 whole trout, cleaned thoroughly
1 tsp mustard seeds (*rai*)
2 Tbsp (20 g) diced onion
1 Tbsp (1 g) fresh cilantro leaves (*hara dhaniya*)
   finely chopped
Juice of 1 lemon (*nimbu*)

METHOD

1. In a shallow bowl (big enough to hold the fish),
   combine 1 Tbsp (15 ml) of mustard seed oil, the
   dill, coriander, red pepper flakes, and lemon
   zest. Season to taste with salt and stir to
   combine. Add the fish, turn to coat, and marinate
   for 10 minutes.
2. In a large skillet over low-medium heat, cook
   the fish in its own juices for 10 minutes on each
   side, or until golden and crisp. Remove the fish
   and set aside.
3. Return the skillet to the heat and add the
   remaining 1 Tbsp (15 ml) of mustard seed oil.
   Add the mustard seeds and onion. Sauté until
   the onion turns golden.
4. Add the cilantro, lemon juice, and the fried fish.
   Taste and adjust the seasoning. Gently stir to
   combine.
5. Serve hot.

## AMRITSARI FISH CURRY 📷 🍲

A rich gravy-based fish dish.

Cooking time: 50 minutes | Serves: 4          Origin: Punjab

INGREDIENTS

8 pieces catfish (*singhara*)

3 Tbsp (45 ml) mustard seed oil (page 26), plus
   more for frying

1 Tbsp (15 g) ginger-garlic paste (*adrak-lasan*),
   divided

1 tsp red chile powder, divided

1 Tbsp (8 g) cornstarch

1 Tbsp (7.5 g) chickpea flour (*besan*)

2 tsp red pepper flakes

1 tsp dried fenugreek leaves (*kasuri methi*)

1 tsp rice flour

½ tsp ground coriander (*dhaniya*)

1 egg

Salt, to taste

½ tsp carom seeds (*ajwain*)

1 cup (170 g) chopped onion

½ tsp ground cumin (*jeera*)

½ cup (120 g) chopped tomato

1 cup (240 ml) water

Juice of 1 lemon (*nimbu*)

½ tsp chaat masala

¼ cup (4 g) fresh cilantro leaves (*hara dhaniya*),
   finely chopped

METHOD

1. In a large bowl, combine the catfish, 3 Tbsp of
   mustard seed oil, 1½ tsp of ginger-garlic paste,
   ½ tsp of red chile powder, the cornstarch,
   chickpea flour, red pepper flakes, dried fenugreek
   leaves, rice flour, coriander, and egg. Season to
   taste with salt. Gently stir to combine.

2. In a skillet over medium heat, heat more
   mustard seed oil for frying.

3. Add the fish and fry until crisp on both sides.
   Transfer to paper towels to drain.

4. Take a spoonful of the same oil in a skillet. Heat
   it over medium heat and add the carom seeds.
   Cook until they begin to crackle.

5. Add the onion. Sauté until golden.

6. Add the remaining 1½ tsp of ginger-garlic
   paste, ½ tsp of red chile powder, and the cumin.
   Sauté until the masalas are well-cooked.

7. Stir in the tomato. Cook for 15 minutes more.

8. Add the water. Reduce the heat to low and
   simmer the gravy for 20 minutes.

9. Add the fried fish and cook until heated through.

10. Finish with lemon juice, chaat masala, and
    cilantro.

## PUNJABI FISH CURRY

A light yogurt-based fish dish.

Cooking time: 30 minutes | Serves: 4          Origin: Punjab

INGREDIENTS

1 medium-size onion, diced

1 green chile

2 tsp minced garlic (*lasan*)

1 tsp ground turmeric (*haldi*)

Salt, to taste

8 catfish steaks (*singhara*)

Vegetable oil, for frying

2 tsp ground coriander (*dhaniya*)

2 tsp ground cumin (*jeera*)

2 tsp red chile powder

3 Tbsp (45 ml) water

½ cup (120 g) yogurt (*dahi*)

1 Tbsp (6 g) garam masala

½ cup (8 g) fresh cilantro leaves (*hara dhaniya*),
   finely chopped

METHOD

1. In a blender, combine the onion, green chile,
   and garlic. Blitz together until a smooth paste
   forms. Set aside.

2. In a small bowl, stir together the turmeric and
   salt to taste. Rub this mixture over the catfish
   fillets.

3. In a deep skillet over medium heat, heat the
   vegetable oil for frying.

4. Carefully add the fish to the hot oil and deep-fry
   until golden brown on both sides. Transfer to
   a plate.

5. In another skillet over medium heat, heat
   2-3 Tbsp of vegetable oil.

6. Add the onion-chile paste, coriander, cumin,
   and red chile powder. Season to taste with salt
   and stir well to combine.

7. Add the water and allow it to absorb the
   masalas. Stir in the yogurt and cook until the
   water from it has absorbed.

8. Add the fish steaks and give it a gentle stir.

9. Finish with garam masala and cilantro.
   Serve hot.

# FISH MUSALLAM 📷 🍲

Baked fish stuffed with spices.

Cooking time: 1 hour | Serves: 6          Origin: Uttar Pradesh

## INGREDIENTS

6 lb, 9 oz (3 kg) whole Singhada, or Sole, washed,
   insides cleaned, and scaled
1½ cups (180 g) roasted chickpea flour (*besan*)
Few drops yellow food coloring
1 recipe Dungaar (page 26)
1 cup + 1 Tbsp (255 g) ghee
2 cups (480 g) sliced onion
10 green cardamom pods (*choti elaichi*)
10 peppercorns (*sabut kali mirch*)
10 dried red chiles (*sookhi lal mirch*)
5 whole cloves (*laung*)
5 black cardamom pods (*badi elaichi*)
5 tsp (15 g) poppy seeds (*khus khus*)
5 tsp (25 g) charoli seeds (*chironji*)
1 Tbsp (15 g) coriander seeds (*dhaniya*)
1 tsp ground mace (*javitri*)
1 (1-in. / 2.5-cm) piece fresh peeled ginger (*adrak*)
1½ cups (360 g) yogurt (*dahi*)
¾ cup (180 ml) heavy cream
Salt, to taste

## METHOD

1. Rub the fish inside and out, with ¾ cup (90 g) of chickpea flour and then wash it off under running water. Do this twice or three times. Cover the fish with the yellow food color and put it on a large baking tray.
2. Prepare the dungaar (page 26). Meanwhile, place the fish on a thoroughly heatproof surface and using heavy-duty grill gloves and tongs, carefully place the prepared dungaar. Pour 1 cup (240 g) or less of ghee on it, in order to sizzle the coal and emit smoke. Cover the fish tight.
3. Preheat the oven to 300°F (150°C).
4. In a skillet over medium-high heat, heat the remaining 1 Tbsp (15 g) of ghee.
5. Add the onion and fry until golden brown. Transfer to a food processor. Add the green cardamom pods, peppercorns, dried red chiles, cloves, black cardamom pods, poppy seeds, charoli seeds, coriander seeds, mace, and ginger. Process into a smooth paste. Transfer to a medium-size bowl.
6. Add the remaining ¾ cup (90 g) of chickpea flour, the yogurt, and cream. Season to taste with salt. Whisk to combine. Uncover the fish and fill the inside of the fish with this mixture. Use any extra filling to rub all over the fish.
7. Bake until one side browns. Turn the fish over and bake until the other side browns. Serve hot.

## AWADHI FISH CURRY
Crispy fried fish fillets in a regal yogurt curry.

Cooking time: 50 minutes | Serves: 3     Origin: Uttar Pradesh

### INGREDIENTS

1 tsp freshly squeezed lemon juice (*nimbu*)
1 tsp garlic paste (*lasan*)
1 tsp ginger paste (*adrak*)
1 tsp red chile powder
1 Tbsp (7.5 g) chickpea flour (*besan*)
Salt, to taste
5 medium-size sole fillets
Vegetable oil, for frying
2 tsp ginger-garlic paste (*adrak-lasan*)
1 tsp fenugreek seeds (*methi dana*)
1 medium-size onion, finely chopped
1 tsp red chile powder
1 tsp ground coriander (*dhaniya*)
½ tsp ground turmeric (*haldi*)
2 medium-size tomatoes, finely chopped
¼ cup (60 g) hung curd (page 28)
1 tsp garam masala

### METHOD

1. In a shallow bowl (big enough to hold the fish), mix the lemon juice, garlic paste, ginger paste, red chile powder, and chickpea flour. Season to taste with salt. Add the fish, rub this mix onto it, and marinate for 15 minutes.
2. In a heavy-bottomed skillet over medium-high heat, heat the vegetable oil for frying.
3. Add the fish. Deep-fry until golden on both sides. Transfer to paper towels to drain. Set aside.
4. In a clean skillet over medium-high heat, heat 1 Tbsp (15 ml) of vegetable oil.
5. Add the ginger-garlic paste and fenugreek seeds. Sauté for 2 minutes.
6. Add the onion, red chile powder, coriander, and turmeric. Sauté for 3–4 minutes.
7. Add the tomatoes. Cook for 4–5 minutes more.
8. Remove from the heat and set aside to cool. Transfer to a blender or food processor and blend the mix into a smooth paste.
9. Return the skillet to the heat and add 1 Tbsp (15 ml) of vegetable oil.
10. Add the spice-vegetable paste. Sauté for 1 minute.
11. Add the yogurt and fish. Sprinkle on the garam masala. Mix well. Reduce the heat to low and simmer for 5–6 minutes.
12. Serve hot.

# FISH KOFTA
Fish-ball curry.

Cooking time: 20 minutes | Serves: 4-6    Origin: Uttar Pradesh

## INGREDIENTS

1¾ lb (800 g) firm white fish fillets, cleaned
6 medium-size potatoes, boiled and mashed
2 tsp ground coriander (*dhaniya*)
½ tsp red chile powder
Salt, to taste
3 Tbsp (45 g) ghee or vegetable oil, divided
2 medium-size onions, chopped
2 eggs, whisked, divided
1 tsp freshly squeezed lemon juice (*nimbu*)
¼ cup (4 g) fresh cilantro leaves (*hara dhaniya*),
    finely chopped
2 Tbsp (15 g) bread crumbs
Vegetable oil, for frying

## METHOD

1. In a medium-size bowl, cut the fish into pieces.
   Using a potato masher or wooden spoon, mash
   well.
2. Add the mashed potatoes to the fish. Combine
   with the coriander and chile powder. Season to
   taste with salt. Mix well.
3. In a skillet over low-medium heat, heat 1 Tbsp
   of ghee or oil.
4. Add the fish and potato mixture. Stir-fry for a
   few minutes until the moisture is absorbed,
   taking care not to burn. Remove from the heat
   and set aside.
5. In a separate saucepan over medium heat, heat
   the remaining 2 Tbsp (30 g) of the ghee or oil.
6. Add the onions. Sauté until golden brown.
   Using a slotted spoon transfer the onions to the
   fish mixture. Add half of the whisked egg to the
   mixture. Stir well to combine.
7. Add the lemon juice and mix lightly until
   combined. Sprinkle over the cilantro.
8. With damp hands, shape into sausage-like
   koftas, about 3-in. (7.5-cm) long and ¾-in. (2-cm)
   thick.
9. Place the remaining whisked egg in a shallow
   bowl. Spread the bread crumbs on a plate. Dip
   the koftas first in the beaten egg mixture, then
   roll in the bread crumbs until coated.
10. In a wok over medium-high heat, heat the
    vegetable oil for deep-frying.
11. Working in batches, carefully lower the koftas
    into the hot oil and deep-fry for 2–3 minutes, or
    until light brown all over. Remove with a slotted
    spoon and drain on paper towels.

VEGETARIAN

## DAL MAKHANI
Butter rich black dal.

Cooking time: 1 hour 15 minutes | Serves: 3     Origin: Punjab

### INGREDIENTS

2 cups (400 g) whole black lentils (*sabut urad*)

7 cups (1.7 L) water, plus more as needed

1 Tbsp (15 g) julienned peeled fresh ginger (*adrak*)

2 Tbsp (30 g) butter

1 Tbsp (15 g) ghee

2 tsp cumin seeds (*jeera*)

2 cups (500 g) tomato purée

3 tsp red chile powder

Salt, to taste

1 tsp dried fenugreek leaves (*kasuri methi*)

½ cup (120 g) homemade cream or heavy cream

### METHOD

1. In your pressure cooker cooking pot, combine the black lentils, water, and ginger. Lock the lid in place and close the pressure release valve. Select Manual/Pressure Cook and cook for 9 minutes. Release the pressure and remove the lid.
2. In a skillet over medium-high heat, melt the butter and ghee together.
3. Add the cumin seeds. Cook until the seeds begin to crackle.
4. Stir in the tomato purée and red chile powder. Cook for 5–6 minutes, stirring well.
5. Add the black lentils and more water as needed to adjust the consistency (which should be like a porridge). Reduce the heat to low and simmer the dish for 50 minutes.
6. Finish with salt to taste, the fenugreek leaves, and cream. Serve hot.

## ARHAR DAL
The classic yellow lentils, simple and flavorful.

Cooking time: 30 minutes | Serves: 4     Origin: Uttar Pradesh

### INGREDIENTS

2 Tbsp (30 g) ghee

Pinch ground asafoetida (*hing*)

1 tsp cumin seeds (*jeera*)

1 dried red chile (*sookhi lal mirch*), optional

½ tsp sugar

1 tsp ground turmeric (*haldi*)

1 cup (200 g) split pigeon pea (*toor* dal),
    soaked in water for 30 minutes

Salt, to taste

3¼ cups (800 ml) water

**For the tempering**

1 Tbsp (15 g) ghee

1 tsp red chile powder

¼ cup (4 g) fresh cilantro leaves (*hara dhaniya*),
    finely chopped for garnishing

### METHOD

1. In your pressure cooker, select sauté and preheat the cooking pot.
2. Add the ghee to melt.
3. Add the asafoetida, cumin seeds, dried red chile (if using), sugar, and turmeric. Sauté for 1 minute. Season to taste with salt.
4. Add the dal. Roast the ingredients until the dal starts to stick to the cooking pot.
5. Add the water.
6. Lock the lid in place and close the pressure release valve. Select Manul / Pressure cook and cook for 20 minutes. Let the pressure release. Remove the lid.
7. **For the tempering:** In a small ladle, heat 1 Tbsp (15 ml) of ghee and add the red chile powder. Remove immediately.
8. Pour over the cooked dal.
9. Garnish with cilantro and serve hot with steamed rice.

# DHABA DAL
Street-style lentils, a staple of dhabas.

| Cooking time: 40 minutes | Serves: 3 | Origin: Punjab |
| --- | --- | --- |

## INGREDIENTS

1 cup (200 g) split black lentils (*urad dal*), cooked
1 tsp ground turmeric (*haldi*)
Salt, to taste
2 Tbsp (30 g) white butter
2 tsp cumin seeds (*jeera*)
1 Tbsp (15 g) ginger-garlic paste (*adrak-lasan*)
1 medium-size onion, finely chopped
1 green chile, finely chopped
1 medium-size tomato, finely chopped
½ cup (125 g) tomato purée
4 cups (960 ml) water, plus more as needed
1 Tbsp (6 g) garam masala
½ cup (8 g) fresh cilantro leaves (*hara dhaniya*),
  finely chopped

## METHOD

1.  In a small bowl, mix together the cooked lentils and turmeric. Season to taste with salt and set aside.
2.  In a skillet over medium heat, melt the butter.
3.  Add the cumin seeds. Cook until they begin to crackle.
4.  Add the ginger-garlic paste and onion. Sauté until the onion turns golden brown.
5.  Add the green chile and tomato. Cook for 10 minutes more.
6.  Add the cooked lentils and stir them into the tomato and spices.
7.  Stir in the tomato purée and water. Reduce the heat to low and cook for 30 minutes. Add more water if it turns too dry.
8.  Finish with salt to taste, the garam masala, and cilantro. Serve hot.

# LAHORI CHANA
Chickpeas flavored with fennel seeds.

| Cooking time: 40 minutes | Serves: 2 | Origin: Punjab |
| --- | --- | --- |

## INGREDIENTS

1 cup (200 g) dried chickpeas (*safed chana*)
3 cups (720 ml) water
1 Tbsp (15 g) whole spice mix (page 22)
1 Tbsp (6 g) ground coriander (*dhaniya*)
2 dried red chiles (*sookhi lal mirch*)
1 Tbsp (15 g) ginger-garlic paste (*adrak-lasan*)
Salt, to taste
Juice of 1 lemon (*nimbu*)
1 tsp fennel seeds (*saunf*)
1 Tbsp (15 ml) vegetable oil
1 tsp cumin seeds (*jeera*)
¼ cup (42.5 g) finely chopped onion
1 green chile, finely chopped

## METHOD

1.  In your pressure cooker cooking pot, combine the chickpeas, water, whole spice mix, coriander, dried red chiles, and ginger-garlic paste. Season to taste with salt. Lock the lid in place and close the pressure release valve. Select Manual/Pressure Cook and cook for 12 minutes. Release the pressure and remove the lid. Transfer the chickpeas to a medium-size bowl and let cool.
2.  Once cool, smash gently with a potato masher. Add the lemon juice and fennel seeds. Mix well and set aside
3.  In a skillet over medium-high heat, heat the vegetable oil.
4.  Add the cumin seeds. Cook until the seeds begin to crackle.
5.  Add the onion and green chile. Sauté for 1–2 minutes.
6.  Add the mashed chickpea mixture. Mix well. Reduce the heat to low and simmer for 7–10 minutes. Serve hot.

# RAJMA 🍲
A wholesome kidney bean gravy.

Cooking time: 30 minutes | Serves: 4      Origin: Punjab

## INGREDIENTS

1 Tbsp (15 g) ghee

1 medium-size onion, grated

1½ tsp ginger-garlic (*adrak-lasan*) paste

2 tsp ground coriander (*dhaniya*)

1 tsp red chile powder

2 medium-size tomatoes, finely chopped

1 cup (200 g) kidney beans, (*rajma*), soaked
   overnight and boiled

2 cups (480 ml) water

Salt, to taste

¼ cup (4 g) fresh cilantro leaves (*hara dhaniya*),
   finely chopped

## METHOD

1. In a skillet over medium-high heat, heat the ghee.
2. Add the onions. Sauté until golden brown. Add the ginger-garlic paste, coriander, and red chile powder. Sauté for 3–4 minutes.
3. Add the tomatoes and cook for 15–17 minutes until the tomatoes have softened.
4. Add the kidney beans and water. Season to taste with salt. Allow the gravy to bubble until the ghee begins to leave the sides of the pan.
5. Garnish with cilantro and serve hot with rice.

# LANGARWALI DAL
Traditional lentils served at gurudwaras.

Cooking time: 40 minutes | Serves: 2      Origin: Punjab

## INGREDIENTS

1 cup (200 g) Bengal gram (split chickpeas;
   *chana dal*), soaked in water for 1 hour, drained

1 cup (200 g) black lentils (*urad dal*), soaked in
   water for 1 hour, drained

3 cups (720 ml) water

1 tsp ground turmeric (*haldi*)

1 Tbsp (15 g) ghee

1 tsp cumin seeds (*jeera*)

1 Tbsp (6 g) minced peeled fresh ginger (*adrak*)

1 medium-size tomato, finely chopped

1 Tbsp (6 g) ground coriander (*dhaniya*)

1 tsp red chile powder

1 tsp garam masala

¾ tsp finely chopped fresh cilantro leaves
   (*hara dhaniya*)

Salt, to taste

## METHOD

1. In your pressure cooker cooking pot, combine the drained chickpeas and lentils, water, and turmeric. Season to taste with salt. Lock the lid in place and close the pressure release valve. Select Manual/Pressure Cook and cook for 9 minutes. Release the pressure and set aside to cool.
2. In a skillet over medium-high heat, heat the ghee.
3. Add the cumin seeds. Cook until the seeds begin to crackle.
4. Add the ginger. Sauté until it changes color.
5. Stir in the tomato, coriander, red chile powder, and garam masala. Sauté the mixture for 5–6 minutes until the tomato is thoroughly cooked.
6. Add the cooked chickpeas and lentils along with the cooking water and stir well to combine. Reduce the heat to low and simmer for 20 minutes. Stir in the cilantro. Taste and season with salt if needed. Serve hot.

## TAKEY PAISE

Chickpea flour coins coated with spices.

Cooking time: 40 minutes | Makes: 10-15 Origin: Uttar Pradesh

INGREDIENTS

For the chickpea coins
2 cups (240 g) chickpea flour (*besan*)
1 tsp red chile powder
1 tsp ground asafoetida (*hing*)
1 tsp ground cumin (*jeera*)
⅓ cup (55 g) grated onion
Salt, to taste
1 cup (240 ml) warm water
For the masala
1 Tbsp (15 ml) mustard seed oil (page 26)
½ medium-size onion, grated
1 tsp ground coriander (*dhaniya*)
½ tsp ground turmeric (*haldi*)
½ tsp red chile powder
Salt, to taste
Chopped fresh cilantro leaves (*hara dhaniya*),
    for garnishing

METHOD

1.  **To make the chickpea coins:** In a medium-size
    bowl, combine the chickpea flour, red chile
    powder, asafoetida, cumin, and onion. Season to
    taste with salt. Gradually pour in the warm
    water and knead the mixture into a smooth
    dough. It should be sticky, but not loose.
2.  Wrap the dough in plastic wrap and let rest for
    2 hours.
3.  Divide the dough equally into 10–15 small
    portions and roll into long sausage-like shapes.
4.  Fill a large saucepan with water. Place it over
    high heat and bring to a boil. Reduce the heat
    so the water simmers. Working in batches,
    add fistfuls of the rolls and simmer for 30
    minutes. Drain the rolls and cut them into
    ½-in. (1.25-cm) coins.
5.  **To make the masala:** In a skillet over low-
    medium heat, heat the mustard seed oil.
6.  Add the grated onion, coriander, turmeric,
    and red chile powder. Cook, stirring well, for
    30 seconds.
7.  Add the coins and gently mix. Season to taste
    with salt. Cook until heated through. Serve hot,
    garnished with cilantro.

## CHUQANDAR KA BHARTA

Tangy beet mash flavored with cumin.

Cooking time: 30 minutes | Serves: 6    Origin: Uttar Pradesh

INGREDIENTS

3–4 medium-size beets (*chuqandar*), boiled,
    peeled, and grated
2 medium-size onions, chopped
3–4 green chiles, chopped
1 Tbsp (1 g) fresh cilantro leaves (*hara dhaniya*),
    finely chopped
2 tsp cumin seeds (*jeera*), roasted, ground
¾ tsp red chile powder
Salt, to taste
1 Tbsp (15 ml) vegetable oil
Pinch cumin seeds (*jeera*)
1 Tbsp (15 ml) freshly squeezed lemon juice
    (*nimbu*)

METHOD

1.  In a large bowl, combine the beets, onions,
    green chiles, cilantro, ground cumin seeds, and
    red chile powder. Season to taste with salt.
2.  In a skillet over low-medium heat, heat the
    vegetable oil.
3.  Add the cumin seeds. Cook until the seeds
    begin to crackle.
4.  Adjust the heat to medium and add the beet
    mixture. Sauté until light brown.
5.  Add the lemon juice and mix well. Remove from
    the heat.
6.  Serve hot, with roti (Indian flatbread) or steamed
    rice, as desired.

## BENARASI ALOO 📷

Deep-fried baby potatoes tossed in spices.

Cooking time: 30 minutes | Serves: 2    Origin: Uttar Pradesh

INGREDIENTS

1 tsp vegetable oil

1 tsp cumin seeds (*jeera*)

1 tsp fennel seeds (*saunf*)

1 Tbsp (15 g) tamarind paste (*imli*)

1 Tbsp (6 g) garam masala

1 tsp ground turmeric (*haldi*)

Pinch ground cardamom

2 cups deep-fried baby potatoes

2 Tbsp (30 ml) heavy cream

2 tsp dried fenugreek leaves (*kasuri methi*)

Salt, to taste

1 Tbsp (15 g) cashew nut powder (*kaju*)

¼ cup (4 g) fresh cilantro leaves (*hara dhaniya*),
   finely chopped

METHOD

1.  In a skillet over medium-high heat, heat the
    vegetable oil.

2.  Add the cumin seeds and fennel seeds. Cook
    until the seeds begin to crackle. Reduce the
    heat to low.

3.  Stir in the tamarind paste, garam masala,
    turmeric, and cardamom. Stir well to combine
    and cook for 3–4 minutes.

4.  Add the deep-fried potatoes, cream, and dried
    fenugreek leaves. Season to taste with salt and
    garnish with the cashew powder and cilantro
    leaves. Serve hot.

## BHUNNE ALOO 🍲

Dry-roasted potatoes with hint of garlic.

Cooking time: 30 minutes | Serves: 4    Origin: Uttar Pradesh

INGREDIENTS

3 Tbsp (45 ml) mustard seed oil (page 26)

1 Tbsp (15 g) cumin seeds (*jeera*)

2 lb, 3 oz (1 kg) potatoes, unpeeled, cubed

2 tsp ground coriander (*dhaniya*)

2 tsp red chile powder

Salt, to taste

1 tsp dried mango powder (*amchoor*)

4 garlic cloves (*lasan*), minced

3 Tbsp (45 ml) warm water

METHOD

1.  In a skillet over low-medium heat, heat the
    mustard seed oil.

2.  Add the cumin seeds. Cook until the seeds
    stop crackling.

3.  Add the potatoes and stir well to combine.

4.  Stir in the coriander and red chile powder.
    Season to taste with salt. Cover the skillet,
    reduce the heat to low, and cook for 12–15
    minutes. Open the lid and carefully stir with a
    flat spoon, ensuring the potatoes remain intact.

5.  Sprinkle in the dried mango powder and gently
    stir once again. Dry-roast in the pan until brown
    and crisp.

6.  In a small bowl stir together the garlic and
    warm water. Sprinkle over the potatoes.

7.  Serve hot.

## AMRITSARI ALOO WADI

Dried lentil dumplings and potatoes in a curry.

Cooking time: 30 minutes | Serves: 2          Origin: Punjab

INGREDIENTS

2 Tbsp (30 g) ghee
1 tsp cumin seeds (*jeera*)
1 medium-size onion, sliced
2 tsp ginger paste (*adrak*)
2 tsp ground coriander (*dhaniya*)
1 tsp ground turmeric (*haldi*)
1 tsp ground cumin (*jeera*)
1 tsp red chile powder
2 medium-size potatoes, cubed
¾ cup (180 ml) water
1 cup (240 g) tomato purée
Salt, to taste
½ cup (120 g) dried lentil dumplings (*wadi*),
    boiled, drained (available online and at
    Indian markets)
1 tsp garam masala
¼ cup (4 g) fresh cilantro leaves (*hara dhaniya*),
    finely chopped

METHOD

1.  In a skillet over medium-high heat, heat the
    ghee.
2.  Add the cumin seeds. Cook until the seeds
    begin to crackle.
3.  Add the onion and ginger paste. Sauté until the
    onion turns golden.
4.  Stir in the coriander, turmeric, cumin, and red
    chile powder. Add the potatoes. Stir to combine
    and sauté for 4 minutes.
5.  Add the water and tomato purée. Season to
    taste with salt. Cook for 8–10 minutes, or until
    the potatoes are tender.
6.  Toss in the boiled lentil dumplings, garam
    masala, and cilantro. Cook until heated through.
7.  Serve hot.

## BAIGAN PATIALA

Eggplant cooked whole in tangy sauce.

Cooking time: 40 minutes | Serves: 2          Origin: Punjab

INGREDIENTS

4 dried red chiles (*sookhi lal mirch*)
2 Tbsp (20 g) desiccated coconut powder (*nariyal*)
1 tsp cumin seeds (*jeera*)
1 tsp fennel seeds (*saunf*)
1 tsp onion seeds (*kalonji*; available online and at
    some Indian markets)
2 Tbsp (30 ml) vegetable oil
½ tsp mustard seeds (*rai*)
2 curry leaves (*kadhi patta*)
2 tsp garlic paste (*lasan*)
1 cup (240 ml) water
5–6 small eggplants (*baigan*), stem ends trimmed,
    with 4 criss-cross incisions made in each
2 Tbsp (30 g) tamarind paste (*imli*)
Salt, to taste
2 Tbsp (30 g) fried onions (*birista*; page 30)

METHOD

1.  In a skillet over medium-high heat, dry-roast
    the dried red chiles, desiccated coconut powder,
    cumin seeds, fennel seeds, and onion seeds.
2.  Transfer to a spice grinder or mortar and pestle,
    let cool, and grind into a fine powder.
3.  Return the skillet to the heat and add the
    vegetable oil.
4.  Add the mustard seeds and curry leaves. Cook
    until the seeds begin to crackle.
5.  Add the garlic paste, the ground spices, and
    water. Stir to combine.
6.  Add the eggplants. Cover the skillet and reduce
    the heat to medium. Cook for 15–20 minutes,
    stirring occasionally.
7.  Stir in the tamarind paste. Cover the skillet and
    continue to cook until the eggplants are soft.
    Season to taste with salt and garnish with the
    fried onions.
8.  Serve hot.

## PATIALA PAPAD KI SUBZI

Panfried poppadums stuffed with vegetables in smooth tomato gravy.

Cooking time: 40 minutes | Serves: 2          Origin: Punjab

### INGREDIENTS

For the stuffing

2 Tbsp (30 ml) vegetable oil, divided
1 tsp cumin seeds (*jeera*)
1 Tbsp (9 g) raisins (*kishmish*)
½ cup (55 g) grated carrot (*gajar*)
½ cup (55 g) grated cauliflower (*phool gobhi*)
½ cup (35 g) grated cabbage (*bandh gobhi*)
¼ cup (25 g) chopped French green beans
  (haricots verts)
½ cup (120 g) grated paneer (available at
  Indian markets; page 28)
2 tsp garam masala
1 tsp red chile powder
1 tsp ground turmeric (*haldi*)
Salt, to taste
3 Tbsp (3 g) fresh cilantro leaves (*hara dhaniya*),
  finely chopped
4–5 sheets poppadums (*papad*; available at
  Indian markets)

For the gravy

1 Tbsp (15 g) ghee
1 tsp cumin seeds (*jeera*)
½ tsp fennel seeds (*saunf*)
½ cup (120 g) onion paste
2 tsp ginger-garlic paste (*adrak-lasan*)
1 Tbsp (6 g) gram masala
1 tsp red chile powder
1 tsp ground turmeric (*haldi*)
1 cup (240 g) tomato purée
Salt, to taste
½ cup (120 ml) heavy cream
1 Tbsp (15 g) butter
¼ cup (4 g) fresh cilantro leaves (*hara dhaniya*),
  finely chopped
¼ cup (60 g) grated paneer (available at Indian
  markets; page 28)

### METHOD

1. **To make the stuffing:** In a medium-size saucepan over medium-high heat, heat 1 Tbsp (15 ml) of vegetable oil.
2. Add the cumin seeds and raisins. Cook until the seeds begin to crackle.
3. Add the carrot, cauliflower, cabbage, green beans, and paneer. Sauté for 2–3 minutes.
4. Stir in the garam masala, red chile powder, and turmeric. Season to taste with salt. Stir well to combine. Reduce the heat to medium and cook for 5 minutes.
5. Add the cilantro.
6. Take a spoonful of the stuffing and place it in the middle of the poppadum. Roll it into a cigar shape and seal the sides by moistening the edges of the sheet with water. Repeat with the remaining sheets and stuffing.
7. In a skillet over medium-high heat, heat the remaining 1 Tbsp of vegetable oil.
8. Add the stuffed poppadums. Panfry until cooked. Remove from the heat and set aside.
9. **To make the gravy:** In a medium-size saucepan over medium-high heat, heat the ghee.
10. Add the cumin seeds and fennel seeds. Cook until the seeds begin to crackle.
11. Add the onion paste, ginger-garlic paste, garam masala, red chile powder, and turmeric. Mix well to combine.
12. Stir in the tomato purée and mix well. Reduce the heat to medium and cook for 12–15 minutes.
13. Add enough water to create texture. Increase the heat to high and cook for 2–3 minutes more. Season to taste with salt.
14. Add the stuffed poppadum rolls and gently stir to combine.
15. Add the cream and butter. Stir and remove the pan from the heat.
16. Serve hot, garnished with cilantro and grated paneer.

# SARSON KA SAAG
Classic seasonal mustard leaf dish.

Cooking time: 40 minutes | Serves: 2     Origin: Punjab

## INGREDIENTS

2 cups (112 g) fresh mustard greens
½ cup (15 g) fresh spinach
½ cup (49 g) lamb's quarters (*bathua*)
1 green chile, minced, divided
1 cup (240 ml) water
Salt, to taste
1 Tbsp (15 g) ghee
1 medium-size onion, finely chopped
1½ tsp peeled fresh ginger (*adrak*), minced
1½ tsp minced garlic (*lasan*)
1 Tbsp (9 g) maize flour (*makkai*)

## METHOD

1. In your pressure cooker cooking pot, combine the mustard greens, spinach, lamb's quarters, half the green chile, and water. Season to taste with salt. Lock the lid in place and close the pressure release valve. Select Manual/Pressure Cook and cook for 6 minutes. Let the pressure release, remove the lid, and let cool. Mash gently and set aside.
2. In a skillet over medium heat, heat the ghee.
3. Add the onion, ginger, garlic, and remaining half of the chile. Stir well to combine.
4. Add the mashed greens. Cook for 5–7 minutes.
5. Sprinkle in the maize flour to thicken the mixture. Taste to adjust the seasoning and serve hot with makkai ki roti (see page 111).

# PUNJABI BHINDI MASALA
Spicy fried okra.

Cooking time: 40 minutes | Serves: 2     Origin: Punjab

## INGREDIENTS

1 Tbsp (15 ml) vegetable oil
1 cup (330 g) chopped okra (*bhindi*)
1 tsp cumin seeds (*jeera*)
1 medium-size onion, finely chopped
1 green chile, finely chopped
1 Tbsp (15 g) ginger-garlic paste (*adrak-lasan*)
1 Tbsp (6 g) ground coriander (*dhaniya*)
1 Tbsp (13.5 g) dried fenugreek leaves (*kasuri methi*)
2 tsp red chile powder
½ tsp ground turmeric (*haldi*)
2 medium-size tomatoes, finely chopped
Salt, to taste
1 Tbsp (15 g) Punjabi chole masala (available at Indian markets)
1 tsp dried mango powder (*amchoor*)
¼ cup (4 g) fresh cilantro leaves (*hara dhaniya*), finely chopped

## METHOD

1. In a skillet over medium-high heat, heat the vegetable oil.
2. Add the okra. Stir-fry until golden brown. Transfer to a bowl and set aside.
3. Return the skillet to the heat. To the remaining oil, add the cumin seeds. Cook until the seeds begin to crackle.
4. Add the onion, green chile, and ginger-garlic paste. Sauté until the onion turns golden brown.
5. Add the coriander, dried fenugreek leaves, red chile powder, and turmeric. Sauté until fragrant.
6. Stir in the tomatoes and season to taste with salt. Cook for about 10 minutes until the tomatoes cook well.
7. Add the okra, chole masala, and dried mango powder. Cook for 2–3 minutes more.
8. Garnish with cilantro and serve hot.

# BAIGAN BHARTA 🍲
Roasted spiced eggplant.

| Cooking time: 40 minutes | Serves: 2 | Origin: Punjab |
| --- | --- | --- |

INGREDIENTS

1 (½ lb / 500 g) eggplant (*brinjal*), large, round;
   make four 1-in. (2.5 cm) deep slits
2 Tbsp (30 ml) vegetable oil plus
   1 tsp for applying on eggplant, divided
1 large onion, cut into medium-size cubes
1½ tsp ginger (*adrak*), chopped
1 tsp green chiles, chopped
½ cup (80 g) green peas (*hara mattar*), boiled
Salt, to taste
3 tomatoes, 2 chopped into 8 pieces plus
   1 medium-size, grated
¼ tsp ground turmeric (*haldi*)
½ tsp red chile powder
1 Tbsp (4 g) fresh cilantro (*hara dhaniya*),
   finely chopped

METHOD

1. On the outer surface of the eggplant apply 1 tsp vegetable oil. Roast over medium-high heat until soft. Cool, peel, and mash. Set aside.
2. In a skillet over medium-high heat, heat 1 Tbsp (15 ml) vegetable oil.
3. Add the onion, ginger, and green chiles. Cook until light brown. Add the green peas and season to taste with salt. Cook for 1 minute. Add the chopped tomatoes. Cook for 30 seconds. Remove from the skillet and set aside
4. In the same skillet heat the remaining 1 Tbsp (15 ml) vegetable oil.
5. Add the turmeric, red chile powder, and grated tomato. Cook for 1 minute. Add the mashed eggplant. Cook until semi thick.
6. Add the onion mixture and cilantro. Mix lightly for a minute. Serve hot.

# MATTAR PANEER 🍲
Paneer with peas in gravy.

| Cooking time: 40 minutes | Serves: 2 | Origin: Delhi |
| --- | --- | --- |

INGREDIENTS

4 Tbsp (60 ml) vegetable oil, divided
4 cups (240 g) paneer, cut into slices
2 bay leaves (*tej patta*)
2 medium-size onions, grated
1 tsp ginger (*adrak*) paste
¾ tsp red chile powder
¾ tsp ground turmeric (*haldi*)
3 medium-size tomatoes, puréed
2 Tbsp (30 g) yogurt (*dahi*), beaten
2 Tbsp (30 g) heavy cream
2 cups (320 g) green peas (*hara mattar*), boiled
Pinch sugar
1½ cups (360 ml) water
Salt, to taste
¼ tsp garam masala
1 Tbsp (4 g) fresh cilantro (*hara dhaniya*),
   finely chopped

METHOD

1. In a non-stick pan over medium heat, heat 1 Tbsp vegetable oil for 30 seconds.
2. Add the paneer and fry, on both sides until light brown. Transfer to paper towels to drain. Set aside.
3. In a skillet over low-medium heat, heat the remaining 3 Tbsp (45 ml) of vegetable oil. Add the bay leaves, onion, and ginger paste. Stirring occasionally, cook until light golden brown. Add the red chile powder and turmeric. Mix well to combine.
4. Add the tomato purée and cook until the oil separates. Add the beaten yogurt and stir well.
5. Stir in the cream, green peas, and paneer. Let simmer for 1 minute.
6. Add the water and sugar. Season to taste with salt. Simmer until all the ingredients are thoroughly cooked. Add the garam masala and stir well. Garnish with cilantro and serve hot.

## GAJAR METHI KI SUBZI
Blushing pink carrots stir-fried with fenugreek.

Cooking time: 30 minutes | Serves: 3      Origin: Haryana

INGREDIENTS

1 Tbsp (15 ml) vegetable oil
1 tsp cumin seeds (*jeera*)
1 medium-size onion, sliced
1 green chile, finely chopped
2 tsp ginger-garlic paste (*adrak-lasan*)
2 cups (240 g) fresh fenugreek leaves (*methi*),
   finely chopped
2 tsp ground coriander (*dhaniya*)
1 tsp ground turmeric (*haldi*)
1 tsp red chile powder
1 cup (130 g) carrots batons (*gajar*)
Salt, to taste

METHOD

1. In a skillet over medium-high heat, heat the vegetable oil.
2. Add the cumin seeds. Cook until the seeds begin to crackle.
3. Add the onion, green chile, and ginger-garlic paste. Sauté for 4–5 minutes.
4. Add the fenugreek leaves. Sauté for 5–7 minutes more, or until the leaves begin to wilt.
5. Add the coriander, turmeric, and red chile powder. Cook, stirring, for 30 seconds.
6. Add the carrots. Reduce the heat to low and cook for 10 minutes, or until cooked through.
7. Season to taste with salt. Serve hot.

## HAAK
Kashmiri collard greens with garlic.

Cooking time: 30 minutes | Serves: 4   Origin: Jammu & Kashmir

INGREDIENTS

1 Tbsp (15 ml) mustard seed oil (page 26)
2 Tbsp (20 g) minced garlic (*lasan*), plus whole
   cloves for garnishing (optional)
10 dried red chiles (*sookhi lal mirch*)
   plus 1 for garnishing
5 cups (150 g) fresh Kashmiri collard greens
   (*haak*), shredded
Salt, to taste
1 cup (240 ml) water
½ tsp dried ginger powder (*sonth*)

METHOD

1. On your pressure cooker, select Sauté and preheat the cooking pot.
2. Add the mustard seed oil and garlic. Sauté, stirring, until golden brown.
3. Add the dried red chiles. Cook for 30 seconds.
4. Add the Kashmiri collard greens and season to taste with salt. Stir until the greens wilt and begins to release its water.
5. Add the water. Lock the lid in place and close the pressure valve. Select Manual/Pressure Cook and cook for 6 minutes.
6. Release the pressure. Stir in the dried ginger powder and taste to adjust the seasoning.
7. Garnish with whole fried garlic cloves and dried red chile, if desired. Serve hot.

## TURAI MASALA
Spicy, delicious ridge gourd.

Cooking time: 20 minutes | Serves: 2     Origin: Uttar Pradesh

### INGREDIENTS

1 tsp vegetable oil

1 tsp cumin seeds (*jeera*)

1 green chile, sliced

1 tsp ground turmeric

2 tsp ginger-garlic paste (*adrak-lasan*)

1 Tbsp (6 g) ground coriander (*dhaniya*)

1 tsp red chile powder

1 cup (240 g) ridge gourd, sliced

½ cup (120 ml) tomato purée

1 tsp garam masala

Salt, to taste

¼ cup (4 g) fresh cilantro leaves (*hara dhaniya*),
   finely chopped

### METHOD

1. In a skillet over low-medium heat, heat the vegetable oil.
2. Add the cumin seeds and green chile. Cook until the seeds begin to crackle.
3. Add the turmeric, ginger-garlic paste, coriander, and red chile powder. Sauté for 1 minute.
4. Add the ridge gourd pieces. Stir in ¼ cup water and allow the vegetable to cook. This should take about 10 minutes.
5. Add the tomato purée and continue to simmer.
6. Add the garam masala and season to taste with salt. Garnish with cilantro and serve hot.

## SKYU
Ladakhi-style pasta loaded with vegetables.

Cooking time: 40 minutes | Serves: 2   Origin: Jammu & Kashmir

### INGREDIENTS

3 cups (375 g) whole-wheat flour (*atta*)

1 Tbsp (15 ml) vegetable oil

1 Tbsp (15 g) ginger-garlic paste (*adrak-lasan*)

1 medium-size onion, chopped

1 medium-size tomato, chopped

1 medium-size potato, chopped

1 tsp red chile powder

1 tsp ground turmeric (*haldi*)

1 tsp garam masala

Salt, to taste

½ cup (120 ml) water

1 cup (160 g) green peas (*hara mattar*)

½ cup (120 ml) milk

### METHOD

1. In a medium-size bowl, mix the flour with enough water to knead into a soft dough.
2. Divide the dough equally into 25–30 small pieces. Roll the pieces into small balls and press with your finger to make orecchiette-shaped (like little ears) pasta.
3. In a skillet over low-medium heat, heat the vegetable oil.
4. Add the ginger-garlic paste, onion, tomato, and potato. Sauté for 5 minutes.
5. Stir in the red chile powder, turmeric, and garam masala. Season to taste with salt. Sauté for about 6 minutes, or until all the vegetables are cooked.
6. Add the water and green peas. Cover the skillet, reduce the heat to low, and cook for 10 minutes.
7. Add the milk and pasta pieces. Let bubble for about 8 minutes, or until the pasta is cooked.
8. Serve hot.

RICE AND BREADS

# KOFTA BIRYANI 🍲
Meatballs cooked with fragrant rice.

| Cooking time: 2 hours \| Serves: 6 | Origin: Uttar Pradesh |
|---|---|

## INGREDIENTS

For the koftas
2 cups (480 g) minced lamb or beef (*keema*)
½ cup (60 g) chickpea flour (*besan*), toasted
2 tsp salt, divided
2 Tbsp (30 g) ginger paste (*adrak*), divided
2 Tbsp (30 g) garlic paste (*lasan*), divided
2 tsp red chile powder, divided
1 Tbsp (6 g) garam masala, divided
2 Tbsp (30 g) yogurt (*dahi*), divided
4 medium-size onions, sliced, fried until lightly
  golden (*birista*; page 30)
¾ cup (180 ml) vegetable oil

For the rice
2 qt (1.9 L) water
8–10 whole cloves (laung)
2–3 bay leaves (*tej patta*)
2 black cardamom pods (*badi elaichi*)
1 (1-in. / 2.5-cm) cinnamon stick (*dalchini*)
1 tsp peppercorns (*sabut kali mirch*)
Salt, to taste
2 cups (400 g) basmati rice, rinsed, soaked in
  water for 2 hours, drained
1 small whole mace (*javitri*)
10 green cardamom pods (*choti elaichi*)
1 tsp ghee
Few saffron threads (*kesar*) or orange food color,
  soaked in 2 Tbsp (30 ml) vetivier water (*kewra
  jal*; available at Indian markets)

## METHOD

1. **To make the koftas:** In a food processor, grind the mince into a fine paste.
2. Add the chickpea flour, 1 tsp of salt, 1 Tbsp (15 g) of ginger paste, 1 Tbsp (15 g) of garlic paste, 1 tsp of red chile powder, 2 tsp of garam masala, 1 Tbsp (15 g) of yogurt, and 1 Tbsp (15 g) of fried onion paste. Mix all the ingredients thoroughly until well blended.
3. Divide the mixture equally into small portions and shape each portion into a ball, a little smaller than a golf ball.
4. In a deep skillet over medium heat, heat the vegetable oil.
5. Reduce the heat to low, add the meatballs, and deep-fry until golden brown and cooked through. With a slotted spoon, transfer to paper towels to drain. Set aside.
6. In the same oil, add the remaining 1 Tbsp (15 g) of ginger paste and 1 Tbsp (15 g) of garlic paste. Sauté until the oil floats on top.
7. Add the remaining 1 tsp of salt, fried onion paste, 1 Tbsp (15 g) of yogurt, 1 tsp of red chile powder, 1 tsp of garam masala, and about ¼ cup (60 ml) of water. Mix well. Gently place the koftas (meatballs) into the skillet again and cook gently until the mixture is dry and the oil floats on top.
8. **To make the rice:** In a deep saucepan over high heat, combine the water, cloves, bay leaves, black cardamom pods, cinnamon stick, and peppercorns. Season to taste with salt. Bring the water to a boil.
9. Add the rice and cook until the rice is firm to the bite. Drain the rice and spread it on a baking sheet.
10. In a spice grinder or mortar and pestle, grind the mace and green cardamom pods into a fine powder. Set aside.
11. In the rice pot, sprinkle the ghee on the bottom and spread out a portion of the rice. Place a few koftas with a little garam masala over the rice. Sprinkle with a little mace-cardamom powder. Add another layer of rice and more koftas and masala. Sprinkle with a little mace-cardamom powder. Repeat the layers ending with a rice layer.
12. With the back of a spoon make 3 holes in the rice layers and pour in the saffron mixture. Cover the pot tightly and cook on high heat for 2 minutes. Reduce the heat to very low and cook until steam starts emerging from the pot. Check the rice for doneness. Remove from the heat. Keep the pot closed for a few minutes. Uncover and mix the rice with the spices taking care not to break koftas.
13. Serve hot.

# AKHA JEERA CHAAMP PULAO 🍲
Pilaf with masala lamb chops.

Cooking time: 1 hour | Serves: 6-8        Origin: Uttar Pradesh

## INGREDIENTS

**For the green paste**
12 green chiles
2 Tbsp (2 g) fresh cilantro leaves (*hara dhaniya*)
1 Tbsp (4 g) fresh mint leaves (*pudina*)
4 tsp ginger-garlic paste (*adrak-lasan*)
**For the lamb chops and pilaf**
3 cups (720 ml) water
2 lb, 3 oz (1 kg) double lamb chops
5 green cardamom pods (*choti elaichi*)
5 whole cloves (*laung*)
4 (2-in. / 5-cm) cinnamon sticks (*dalchini*)
1 tsp peppercorns (*sabut kali mirch*)
Salt, to taste
1 cup (240 ml) vegetable oil
2 tsp cumin seeds (*jeera*)
3 medium-size onions, sliced
1 tsp garam masala
3 cups (600 g) basmati rice, rinsed, soaked in
　　water for 30 minutes, drained

## METHOD

1. **To make the green paste:** In a food processor, combine the green chiles, cilantro, mint, ginger-garlic paste, and just a touch of water. Process into a fine paste. Set aside.

2. **To make the lamb chops:** In a large pot over medium heat, combine the water, lamb chops, green cardamom pods, cloves, cinnamon sticks, and peppercorns. Season to taste with salt. Cook until the meat is tender. Remove the chops and set aside. Strain the stock into another pan.

3. In a large skillet over low heat, heat the vegetable oil.

4. Add the cumin seeds. Cook until they begin to crackle.

5. Add the onions. Sauté until golden.

6. Stir in the garam masala and the green paste. Cook until the water evaporates.

7. Increase the heat to medium-high. Add the cooked chops and stir-fry, adding a few tablespoons (45 ml) of water when the mixture starts sticking to the bottom of the pan. Repeat this process twice.

8. Measure the strained stock. Add enough warm water to make a total of 5½ cups (1.3 L). Pour the liquid into the skillet. Bring to a rapid boil and add the rice. Stir to mix well. Reduce the heat to low. Cover and cook until the rice is tender and the liquid is completely absorbed. Serve hot.

# YAKHNI PULAO 🍛
Kashmiri-style lamb rice.

Cooking time: 1 hour | Serves: 8-10    Origin: Jammu & Kashmir

## INGREDIENTS

5 medium-size onions, divided
2 lb, 3 oz (1 kg) lamb, cubed
12 peppercorns (*sabut kali mirch*)
6 green cardamom pods (*choti elaichi*)
5 garlic cloves (*lasan*)
4 black cardamom pods (*badi elaichi*)
2 (2-in. / 5-cm) cinnamon sticks (*dalchini*)
2 bay leaves (*tej patta*)
1 (1-in. / 2.5-cm) piece peeled fresh ginger (*adrak*), chopped
2 Tbsp (12 g) fennel seeds (*saunf*)
1 Tbsp (6 g) cumin seeds (*jeera*)
1 Tbsp (15 g) yogurt (*dahi*)
¾ tsp ground mace (*javitri*)
Salt, to taste
1 cup (240 ml) vegetable oil
1½ tsp garlic paste (*lasan*)
1½ tsp ginger paste (*adrak*)
1 tsp red chile powder
2 lb, 3 oz (1 kg) basmati rice, rinsed, soaked in water for 30 minutes, drained

## METHOD

1. Coarsely chop 1 onion and place it in your pressure cooker cooking pot. Finely slice the remaining 4 onions and set aside.

2. To the cooking pot, add the lamb, peppercorns, green cardamom pods, garlic, black cardamom pods, cinnamon sticks, bay leaves, ginger, fennel seeds, cumin seeds, yogurt, and mace. Season to taste with salt. Fill the cooking pot halfway with water. Lock the lid in place and close the pressure release valve. Select Manual/Pressure Cook and cook for 25 minutes, or until the meat is tender.

3. Release the pressure and remove the lid. Remove the meat pieces from the stock and discard any whole spices sticking to them. Strain the stock and save it for later use.

4. In a pot or a deep skillet over medium-high heat, heat the vegetable oil.

5. Add the sliced onions and fry until golden. With a slotted spoon, transfer to paper towels to drain.

6. Return the skillet, with the oil remaining in it, to medium-high heat. Add the garlic paste, ginger paste, red chile powder, half the fried onions, and the cooked lamb. Fry, stirring, until the lamb is lightly browned and the moisture evaporates.

7. Add the drained rice. Cook, stirring, for 2–3 minutes.

8. Pour in the strained stock. Add water, as needed, so the liquid is at least 3–4 in. (7.5–10 cm) above the rice. Cover and cook for 2–3 minutes. Reduce the heat to low and simmer until the rice is soft and the water evaporates. Serve hot, garnished with the remaining fried onions.

# SHAHJEHANI BIRYANI 🍲

Baked basmati rice flavored with spices and layered with rich lamb sauce.

Cooking time: 2 hours | Serves: 12-14    Origin: Uttar Pradesh

## INGREDIENTS

**For the meat**

½ cup (120 g) ghee, plus more for greasing a casserole dish

12 dried red chiles (*sookhi lal mirch*), ground to a paste with water

¾ cup (180 g) onion paste

¼ cup (36.25 g) blanched almonds (*badam*), peeled and ground to a paste

2 Tbsp (30 g) ginger paste (*adrak*)

2 Tbsp (30 g) garlic paste (*lasan*)

2 Tbsp (30 g) poppy seed paste (*khus khus*)

1 Tbsp (7 g) ground cumin (*jeera*)

1½ tsp ground cardamom

1½ tsp ground cinnamon (*dalchini*)

½ tsp ground nutmeg (*jaiphal*)

1½ tsp ground cloves (*laung*)

2 tsp freshly ground black pepper (*kali mirch*)

½ cup (120 ml) water, plus more as needed

4 lb, 6 oz (2 kg) lamb, deboned and cubed

Salt, to taste

½ cup (120 g) yogurt (*dahi*)

**For the rice**

4 cups (800 g) basmati rice, washed, soaked in water for 30 minutes, drained

2 qt (1.9 L) water

8 green cardamom pods (*choti elaichi*), cracked

2 (1-in. / 2.5-cm) cinnamon sticks (*dalchini*)

1 tsp vetivier water (*kewra*; available at Indian markets)

½ tsp saffron threads (*kesar*), soaked in ½ cup (120 ml) hot milk

¾ cup (180 ml) heavy cream

1 tsp cumin seeds (*jeera*)

**For garnishing**

2 large onions, sliced and fried until golden brown (*birista*; page 30)

½ cup (120 g) raisins (*kishmish*), fried

## METHOD

1. **To make the meat:** In a large skillet or sauté pan over low-medium heat, heat the ghee.

2. Add all the pastes and spices (through pepper). Cook, stirring constantly, until fragrant and the ghee separates and rises to the top.

3. Stir in the water and mix well. Reduce the heat to low and simmer until all the water evaporates and the spices and pastes are well toasted.

4. Add the lamb and season to taste with salt. Stir to coat the lamb evenly with the paste. Cook until the meat browns. Add a little water if the meat sticks to the bottom of the pan.

5. Stir in the yogurt. Cook until the meat is tender and a very thick gravy remains.

6. **To make the rice:** In a medium-size saucepan over low-medium heat, combine the rice, water, green cardamom pods, cinnamon sticks, and vetivier essence. Bring to a boil. Reduce the heat to medium and cook until the rice is almost tender and the water is absorbed.

7. Preheat the oven to 325°F (170°C). Grease a large ovenproof casserole dish with ghee.

8. Spread half the rice in the prepared dish. Pour ¼ cup (60 ml) of the saffron liquid, 6 Tbsp (90 ml) of cream, and ½ tsp cumin seeds over the top. Spread the cooked lamb evenly over the rice. Make a final layer with the remaining rice, saffron liquid, cream, and cumin seeds.

9. Cover the dish tightly with aluminum foil, pressing it down.

10. Bake for 35 minutes. Serve hot, garnished with fried onions and raisins.

# KHICHIDA
Slow-cooked medley of lentils, mutton, and barley.

Cooking time: 1 hour | Serves: 8          Origin: Uttar Pradesh

## INGREDIENTS

1 cup barley (*jau*), soaked overnight

6 cups (1.5 L) water

1 cup (200 g) Bengal gram (split chickpeas; *chana dal*), soaked in water overnight, drained

1 cup (200 g) dried split pea lentils (*matar dal*), soaked in water overnight, drained

1 cup (200 g) split red lentils (*masoor dal*), soaked in water overnight, drained

1 cup (200 g) black gram lentils (*sabut urad dal*), soaked in water overnight, drained

1 cup (200 g) Indian brown lentils (*sabut masoor dal*), soaked in water overnight, drained

1 cup (160 g) cracked wheat (*dalia*), washed

2 tsp ground turmeric (*haldi*), divided

2 tsp red chile powder, divided

2 tsp garam masala, divided

2 Tbsp (30 g) ginger-garlic paste (*adrak-lasan*), divided

1 small onion, ground to a paste

Salt, to taste

1 cup (240 ml) mustard seed oil (page 26)

2 cups (480 g) onions, sliced for mutton

2 lb, 3 oz (1 kg) mutton (*raan*), boneless, chopped into tiny pieces

⅔ cup (150 g) yogurt (*dahi*), for the garnishing

1 large onion, finely sliced, fried (*birista*; page 30)

Silver leaves, for garnishing (*warq*; optional; page 24; available at Indian markets)

4 green chiles, deseeded, finely chopped

¼ cup (4 g) fresh cilantro leaves (*hara dhaniya*), finely chopped

1 piece ginger, finely sliced

2 lemons (*nimbu*), optional

## METHOD

1. Drain the barley and grind it manually, either in a stone mill or an electric blender, to a coarse texture. Place in a bowl. Set aside.

2. In a large pot over low heat, heat the water. Add the barley, all the 5 lentils, cracked wheat, half the turmeric, half the red chile powder, half the garam masala, half the ginger-garlic paste, and onion paste. Season to taste with salt. Stirring occasionaly, let the mixture simmer for 2 hours.

3. In a wok over low-medium heat, heat the mustard seed oil.

4. Add the onion. Cook until deep pink. Add the remaining ginger-garlic paste and salt. Add the mutton pieces and cook for at least 20 minutes.

5. Add the yogurt, the remaining garam masala, red chile powder, and turmeric. Stir well.

6. Cook until the oil begins to leave the sides of the mutton spice mixture. Set aside to cool.

7. Shred the mutton into very tiny pieces using your hands.

8. Add this cooked shredded mutton to the lentil, wheat, barley mixture and return to low heat for 15–20 minutes, stirring constantly.

9. Decorate with *warq* (if using) just before serving.

10. Garnish with fried onions, green chiles, cilantro and ginger. A dash of lemon juice could be added (if using). Serve hot.

## ALLAHABAD KI TEHRI

Basmati rice loaded with vegetables.

Cooking time: 40 minutes | Serves: 4    Origin: Uttar Pradesh

### INGREDIENTS

1 Tbsp (15 ml) mustard seed oil (page 26)
1 Tbsp (15 g) whole spice mix (page 22)
1 bay leaf (*tej patta*)
1½ tsp ginger-garlic paste (*adrak-lasan*)
2 green chiles, finely chopped
1 Tbsp (6 g) ground coriander (*dhaniya*)
2 tsp red chile powder
2 tsp ground asafoetida (*hing*)
1 tsp ground cumin (*jeera*)
½ cup (55 g) cubed potato
½ cup (65 g) diced carrot (*gajar*)
½ cup (50 g) chopped green beans
½ cup (50 g) diced cauliflower (*phool gobhi*)
Salt, to taste
½ cup (120 g) yogurt (*dahi*)
2 cups (400 g) basmati rice, rinsed
4 cups (960 ml) vegetable broth
3 Tbsp (45 g) ghee
¼ cup (4 g) fresh cilantro leaves (*hara dhaniya*),
   finely chopped
Juice of 1 lemon (*nimbu*)

### METHOD

1. In a skillet over medium-high heat, heat the mustard seed oil.
2. Add the whole spice mix and bay leaf. Cook until the seeds begin to crackle.
3. Add the ginger-garlic paste, green chiles, coriander, red chile powder, asafoetida, and cumin. Cook, stirring, for 2 minutes.
4. Add the potato, carrot, green beans, and cauliflower. Cook for 1 minute, stirring well to coat the vegetables with the spices.
5. Season to taste with salt and stir in the yogurt. Cook for 4–5 minutes more.
6. Add the rice and vegetable broth. Cook for 25–27 minutes, or until the water evaporates and the rice is tender.
7. Mix in the ghee, cilantro, and lemon juice.
8. Serve hot.

## KANGUCHI PULAO

Mushrooms cooked with fragrant rice.

Cooking time: 30 minutes | Serves: 4-6 Origin: Jammu & Kashmir

### INGREDIENTS

5 Tbsp (75 g) ghee
5 Tbsp (45 g) blanched almonds (*badam*)
6 whole cloves (*laung*)
6 green cardamom pods (*choti elaichi*)
4 black cardamom pods (*badi elaichi*), crushed
3 (1-in. / 2.5-cm) cinnamon sticks (*dalchini*)
3 bay leaves (*tej patta*)
3½ oz (100 g) morel mushrooms (*gucchi*), slit
   lengthwise and rinsed
Pinch ground asafoetida (*hing*)
Salt, to taste
1½ cups (300 g) rice, rinsed, soaked in water,
   drained
3 cups (720 ml) water
1 tsp ground ginger (*sonth*)
2 pinches saffron threads (*kesar*)
1 tsp garam masala

### METHOD

1. In a heavy-bottomed pot over medium-high heat, heat the ghee.
2. Add the almonds, cloves, green and black cardamom pods, cinnamon sticks, and bay leaves. Cook until the spices begin to crackle.
3. Add the mushrooms and asafoetida. Season to taste with salt. Sauté for 1 minute.
4. Add the rice and stir gently.
5. Pour in the water and bring to a boil.
6. Stir in the ginger.
7. In a cup or small bowl, mix the saffron threads with 2 tsp of hot water and crush with a spoon. Add to the rice mixture. Cover the pot and cook for 15 minutes.
8. When most of the water is absorbed, reduce the heat to low and cook until the rice is tender. Sprinkle with the garam masala just before serving.

## PANEER PARATHA

A classic cottage-cheese stuffed bread.

Cooking time: 20 minutes | Makes: 3-4          Origin: Delhi

INGREDIENTS

1 medium-size onion, finely chopped
1 green chile, finely chopped
1 cup (225 g) paneer, crumbled
1 tsp ground coriander (*dhaniya*)
1 tsp dried mango powder (*amchoor*)
Salt, to taste
1 cup (125 g) whole-wheat flour (*atta*)
2 Tbsp (30 g) ghee

METHOD

1. In a medium-size bowl, combine the onion, green chile, paneer, coriander, and dried mango powder. Season to taste with salt.
2. In another medium-size bowl knead the flour with just enough water to form a soft dough.
3. Divide the dough into equal portions and roll out each small roundel of dough into a small chapatti. Place the paneer filling in the center.
4. Bring the edges together and pat it flat with your plam. Roll once again into a larger flatbread (*paratha*).
5. Heat a griddle over high heat until really hot.
6. Heat the ghee and panfry the paratha on both sides until golden.
7. Serve with pickle, curd and butter, if desired.

## BESAN KI ROTI 🍲

Chickpea and whole-wheat panfried flatbread.

Cooking time: 30 minutes | Makes: 3-4          Origin: Punjab

INGREDIENTS

For the roti
1 cup (120 g) chickpea flour (*besan*), plus more for dusting the work surface
1 cup (125 g) whole-wheat flour (*atta*)
Salt, to taste
2 Tbsp (30 ml) vegetable oil
1 medium-size onion, finely chopped
1 green chile, finely chopped
4 sprigs fresh cilantro (*hara dhaniya*), finely chopped
Ghee, for panfrying
For the garlic chutney
1 head garlic (*lasan*), peeled
2 dried red chiles (*sookhi lal mirch*)
2 tsp mustard seed oil (page 26)
½ tsp salt

METHOD

1. **To make the roti:** In a medium-size bowl, mix the chickpea flour and whole-wheat flour. Season to taste with salt.
2. Stir in the vegetable oil, onion, green chile, and cilantro. Dust the work surface with a little chickpea flour and turn the dough out. Knead into a hard dough, adding a little water as needed. Divide the dough into 6 small portions and roll each into a 4-in. (10-cm) disk.
3. Heat a griddle over high heat until really hot.
4. Working with one disk at a time, cook on each side until brown specs start to appear. Smear some ghee on the top and bottom and panfry until each side is golden brown and crisp. Repeat with the remaining bread and ghee.
5. **To make the garlic chutney:** In a blender or food processor combine all the chutney ingredients and process into a smooth paste.
6. Serve the flatbreads hot, with the garlic chutney.

# MAKKAI KI ROTI 🍲
Maize-flour flatbread.

Cooking time: 20 minutes | Makes: 4          Origin: Punjab

INGREDIENTS

1½ cups (200 g) maize flour (*makkai*)
¼ cup (30 g) chickpea flour (*besan*)
1 cup (16 g) fresh cilantro leaves (*hara dhaniya*),
   finely chopped
1 tsp carom seeds (*ajwain*)
Salt, to taste
Warm water, as needed to bind the dough
2 tsp ghee

METHOD

1. In a large bowl sift the maize flour. Combine with the chickpea flour.
2. Add cilantro leaves and carom seeds. Season to taste with salt.
3. Add warm water little by little and knead into a stiff and smooth dough.
4. Divide the dough into 4 portions. Press the dough balls with your palms and flatten them. Roll each into a small but thick flatbread.
5. Heat a griddle over high heat until really hot.
6. Working with one flatbread at a time, cook with ghee until light brown on both sides. Serve with Sarson ka Saag (see page 96), white butter, and jaggery, if desired.

# LEHSUNI NAAN
Garlic-flavored leavened flatbread.

Cooking time: 45 minutes | Makes: 3-4    Origin: Uttar Pradesh

INGREDIENTS

1 cup (120 g) all-purpose flour (*maida*)
2 tsp sugar
Pinch salt
3 Tbsp (45 g) ghee, divided
¼ cup (62.5 ml) milk
1 tsp baking powder
2 Tbsp (30 g) yogurt (*dahi*)
Warm water, to knead
2 Tbsp butter

METHOD

1. In a large bowl mix the flour with sugar, salt, 1 Tbsp (15 g) ghee, milk, and baking powder. Mix it thoroughly. Add water little by little and knead it into a tight and smooth dough.
2. Add 1 Tbsp (15 g) ghee and knead once again. Cover the dough with a wet cheesecloth for 2 hours.
3. Divide the dough into roundels and roll each into an elongated-shaped bread. Sprinkle sesame and garlic.
4. Heat a griddle over high heat until really hot. Melt the remainig 1 Tbsp (15 g) of ghee and roast the naan on both sides.
5. Brush butter on hot naans and serve with butter chicken (see page 65), if desired.

# AMRITSARI KULCHA 📷
Flatbread stuffed with potato and paneer.

Cooking time: 40 minutes | Makes: 3-4      Origin: Punjab

## INGREDIENTS

For the dough
1 cup (125 g) all-purpose flour (*maida*)
1 tsp sugar
1 tsp baking powder
½ tsp baking soda
3 Tbsp (45 g) ghee
¼ cup (60 g) yogurt (*dahi*)
¼ cup (60 ml) milk
Salt, to taste

For the filling
1 cup (225 g) mashed potatoes
1 green chile, finely chopped
1 tsp ground cumin (*jeera*)
1 tsp red chile powder
1 tsp chaat masala
½ medium-size onion, finely chopped
¼ cup (4 g) fresh cilantro leaves (*hara dhaniya*),
    finely chopped
¼ cup (60 g) finely chopped paneer
Salt, to taste
Butter, for serving

## METHOD

1. **To make the dough:** In a medium-size bowl, combine the flour, sugar, baking powder, baking soda, ghee, yogurt, and milk. Season to taste with salt. Mix together and knead into a medium-soft dough. Set aside for 1 hour.

2. **To make the filling:** In another medium-size bowl, stir together the mashed potatoes, green chile, cumin, red chile powder, chaat masala, onion, cilantro, and paneer. Season to taste with salt.

3. Divide the dough into small roundels. Roll each into a 4-in. (10-cm) disk. Place a spoonful of filling in the center of each and join all the edges to seal the filling inside.

4. Roll it back into a round, the size of your palm, and pat it with your fingertips.

5. Heat a griddle over medium-high heat.

6. Working in batches, cook the stuffed disks on both sides until golden brown. Serve hot, with lots of butter.

DESSERTS

## GONDH KA HALWA

Sweet fudge balls made of cracked wheat and edible gum.

Cooking time: 40 minutes | Serves: 2     Origin: Punjab

INGREDIENTS

½ cup (80 g) cracked wheat (*daliya*)
½ cup (120 g) ghee
½ cup (100 g) edible gum (*gondh*)
4 cups (960 ml) milk
1 cup (225 g) packed brown sugar
Pinch ground nutmeg (*jaiphal*)
Pinch ground cardamom
3 Tbsp (30 g) almonds (*badam*), slivered

METHOD

1. In a blender, blitz the cracked wheat for 4–5 seconds.
2. In a medium-size saucepan over medium heat, heat the ghee.
3. Add the edible gum and fry for 1 minute. With a slotted spoon, transfer the edible gum to a small bowl.
4. Return the skillet and ghee to the heat and add the cracked wheat powder. Sauté for 3 minutes until dark brown.
5. Pour in the milk and cook, stirring continuously.
6. Add the fried edible gum. Cook for 3–4 minutes, stirring, until it begins to thicken slightly.
7. Add the brown sugar. Continue to cook, stirring, until the mixture begins to leave the ghee.
8. Add the nutmeg, cardamom, and almonds. Stir well to combine.
9. Remove from the heat and divide the mixture into small equal portions. Shape the portions into balls while the mixture is still warm.
10. Serve warm.

## CHANE KA HALWA

Melt-in-your-mouth Bengal gram (split chickpea) sweet garnished with dried fruits.

Cooking time: 40 minutes | Serves: 6     Origin: Uttar Pradesh

INGREDIENTS

1 cup (200 g) Bengal gram (split chickpeas; *chana dal*), soaked in water for 3 hours, drained
4 cups (960 ml) milk
1 cup (240 g) ghee
2–3 green cardamom pods (*choti elaichi*), peels and seeds separated, seeds ground
1 (1-in. / 2.5-cm) cinnamon stick (*dalchini*)
1 cup (200 g) sugar
Silver leaves, for garnishing (*warq*; optional; page 24; available at Indian markets)
Mixed dried fruits, chopped, for garnishing

METHOD

1. In your pressure cooker cooking pot, combine the drained chickpeas and milk. Lock the lid in place and close the pressure release valve. Select Manual/Pressure Cook and cook for 30 minutes, or until soft. Release the pressure and remove the lid. Select Sauté and continue to cook until the milk is completely absorbed and the mix is dry. Transfer the chickpeas to a food processor and let cool. Once cool, grind into a smooth paste.
2. In a wok over low-medium heat, heat the ghee.
3. Add the green cardamom pod peels, the cinnamon stick, and the chickpea paste. Stir-fry until the mixture turns brownish and the ghee separates from the sides.
4. Add the sugar and ground green cardamom seeds. Stir-fry for 5 minutes.
5. Serve hot, garnished with silver leaves (if using) and chopped dried fruits.

## AGRE KA PETHA

India's answer to a Turkish delight.

Cooking time: 1 hour | Makes: 12-14    Origin: Uttar Pradesh

INGREDIENTS

2 cups (480 g) ash gourd (*kashi phal / safed kadoo*)
   deseeded and cubed into 12 pieces
1 tsp alum powder (*phitakiree*)
2 cup (400 g) sugar
1 Tbsp (15 ml) milk
2 cups (480 ml) water
1 Tbsp (15 ml) freshly squeezed lemon juice
   (*nimbu*)

METHOD

1. Prick the ash gourd pieces with a fork. Place the
   vegetable in a pan and submerge in water.
2. Place the pan over low-medium heat, add the
   alum powder, and boil the vegetable for 10
   minutes.
3. Drain. Wash thoroughly with fresh water.
4. In another pan over low heat, add the sugar and
   water. Allow it to bubble.
5. Add the lemon juice and allow the scum to float
   on top of the water surface. Scoop it out with
   a spoon.
6. Add the vegetable pieces and allow the sugar
   syrup to reach a two-thread consistency, about
   30 minutes (page 31).
7. Remove the *petha* from the sugar syrup and
   allow it to cool down. Keep the pieces separately
   to avoid sticking.
8. Serve when dry.

## ATTE KA HALWA 📷

A smooth and sweet whole-wheat flour pudding.

Cooking time: 20 minutes | Serves: 3    Origin: Punjab

INGREDIENTS

1 cup (240 ml) water
1 cup (240 ml) milk
1 cup (200 g) caster (superfine) sugar
1 cup (240 g) ghee
1 cup (125 g) whole-wheat flour (*atta*)
1 tsp ground cardamom (*choti elaichi*)
1 tsp rose water
2 Tbsp (10 g) powdered nuts

METHOD

1. In a large bowl, stir together the water, milk,
   and sugar. Set aside.
2. In a skillet over medium heat, heat the ghee.
3. Add the flour. Sauté until it turns deep brown.
4. Stir in the cardamom. Cook for 2–3 minutes
   more, stirring.
5. Add the milk mixture. Cook, stirring
   continuously, until all the water is absorbed and
   the ghee begins to leave the sides of the pan.
6. Stir in the rose water and powdered nuts.
   Serve hot.

## KAMAL GATTE KA HALWA

Lotus seed fudge topped with dried fruits.

Cooking time: 35 minutes | Serves: 2    Origin: Uttar Pradesh

INGREDIENTS

3 Tbsp plus ¾ tsp (50 g) ghee, plus more for the
  baking sheet
½ cup (16 g) lotus seeds (*makhana*), soaked in
  water overnight
½ cup (100 g) sugar
Assorted dried nuts, slivered, for garnishing

METHOD

1. Grease a baking sheet with ghee and set aside.
2. Drain and peel the lotus seeds. Place them in a
   food processor and process into a paste.
   Set aside.
3. In a skillet over medium heat, heat the ghee.
4. Stir in the lotus seed paste. Cook, stirring, for
   7–10 minutes. The paste will begin to get sticky
   as you keep stirring.
5. Once the mixture begins to thicken, add the
   sugar. Cook, stirring continuously, until the
   sugar melts. Continue to cook for 4–5 minutes
   more, stirring.
6. If the mixture looks dark, do not worry.
7. Remove from the heat and transfer to the
   prepared baking sheet.
8. Sprinkle with the dried fruits and cut into
   squares.
9. Serve at room temperature.

## ARSA

Deep-fried doughnuts sweetened with jaggery.

Cooking time: 30 minutes | Makes: 10    Origin: Uttarakhand

INGREDIENTS

1½ cups (300 g) rice, soaked in water for 4 hours,
  drained, and dried thoroughly
1 cup (240 ml) water
½ cup (118 g) jaggery (*gur*; unrefined cane sugar)
Vegetable oil, for deep-frying

METHOD

1. In a blender or food processor, grind the dried
   rice into a fine powder.
2. In a saucepan over medium heat, combine the
   water and jaggery. Cook until the jaggery melts
   and the syrup begins to thicken. Remove from
   the heat and set aside.
3. In a medium-size bowl, combine the rice powder
   and jaggery syrup. Knead the mixture into a
   tight dough.
4. Cut the dough and roll it into 10 table tennis-
   ball-size balls.
5. In a deep skillet over low-medium heat, heat the
   vegetable oil for deep-frying.
6. Carefully add the dough balls to the hot oil and
   fry until golden. Transfer to paper towels to
   drain. Cool to room temperature before serving.

## PIYAU BARE 🍲

Deep-fried black lentil nuggets soaked in sugar syrup and served with cream.

Cooking time: 40 minutes | Serves: 8-10   Origin: Uttar Pradesh

### INGREDIENTS

1 cup (200 g) black lentils (*urad dal*), soaked in water for 2 hours, drained
3 cups (600 g) sugar
2 cups (480 ml) water
Pinch orange food color
Few saffron threads (*kesar*), soaked in 1 Tbsp (15 ml) milk (page 31)
1 Tbsp (15 ml) vetivier water (*kewra*; available at Indian markets)
1 cup (240 ml) vegetable oil
2 cups (480 ml) heavy cream, whipped

### METHOD

1. In a blender or food processor, process the black lentils into a fine paste. Whip it a little to make it fluffy and light.
2. In a deep saucepan over high heat, combine the sugar and water. Bring the mixture to a boil and continue to boil until the syrup reaches a one-thread consistency (page 31). Remove from the heat and add the orange color, saffron mix, and vetivier essence. Mix well and set aside.
3. In a wok over medium-high heat, heat the vegetable oil.
4. Working in batches, gently drop 1½-tsp portions of batter (small nuggets) into the hot oil. Deep-fry until lightly golden. (The nuggets should be light and fluffy. Add a little water to the batter, if the consistency is too thick.) Remove the nuggets with a slotted spoon and transfer to paper towels to drain.
5. When the nuggets are done, soak them in the sugar syrup for a few minutes.
6. Remove and serve with whipped cream.

## CHAWAL KI KHEER

Rice pudding.

Cooking time: 1 hour | Serves: 2                   Origin: Delhi

### INGREDIENTS

2 cups (480 ml) milk
¾ cup (150 g) rice, soaked in water for 2 hours, drained
5 Tbsp (93.75 g) sweetened condensed milk
Pinch ground cardamom
1 tsp saffron threads (*kesar*)
2 Tbsp (20 g) assorted dried fruit powder

### METHOD

1. In a saucepan over medium-low heat, bring the milk to a boil.
2. Add the rice. Cook, stirring occasionally so the ingredients do not burn. Once the milk begins to thicken, stir in the sweetened condensed milk and cardamom. Reduce the heat to low and continue to cook for 40 minutes until the kheer has thickened to your desired consistency.
3. Stir in the saffron threads and dried fruit powder. Gently simmer the kheer for 2–3 minutes more. Serve hot or cold.

## MEWA KA ZARDA 📷 🍽

Baked rice pudding enriched with dried fruits.

Cooking time: 40 minutes | Serves: 4-6    Origin: Uttar Pradesh

INGREDIENTS

1 cup (240 ml) vegetable oil
2 cups (400 g) basmati rice, rinsed, soaked in water
    for 1 hour, drained
4 cups (960 ml) milk
½ tsp ground cardamom
¼ tsp ground nutmeg (*jaiphal*)
¼ tsp ground mace (*javitri*)
½ tsp saffron threads (*kesar*), soaked in 2 Tbsp
    (30 ml) hot milk
½ cup (120 g) charoli seeds (*chironji*), coarsely
    ground (optional)
20 almonds (*badam*), blanched, peeled, sliced
20 cashews (*kaju*), sliced
20 raisins (*kishmish*), soaked in water for
    15 minutes, drained
2 cups (400 g) sugar

METHOD

1.  In a deep saucepan over medium heat, heat the
    vegetable oil.
2.  Add the drained rice. Sauté for 3 minutes.
3.  Pour in the milk. Cover the pan and cook until
    the rice is tender and the milk is fully absorbed.
4.  Preheat the oven to 200°F (100°C).
5.  When the rice is cooked, stir in the cardamom,
    nutmeg, mace, saffron milk, charoli seeds (if
    using), almonds, cashews, raisins, and sugar.
    Mix well. Transfer the contents to a baking dish
    and cover tightly with aluminum foil.
6.  Bake for 10–12 minutes.
7.  Serve hot.

## BADNAAM KULFI

Cool wispy milky foam flavored with saffron.

Cooking time: 40 minutes | Serves: 2      Origin: Uttar Pradesh

INGREDIENTS

1 cup (240 ml) full-fat milk
1 cup (240 ml) heavy cream
1 Tbsp (7.5 g) cornflour
½ cup (60 g) powdered sugar
1 tsp saffron threads (*kesar*)
3 Tbsp (45 g) whole-milk fudge (*khoya*; available at
    Indian markets; page 25)
2 Tbsp (30 g) assorted sliced dried fruits

METHOD

1.  In a medium-size saucepan over medium-high
    heat, bring the milk to a rolling boil.
2.  Add the cream and cornflour. Stir well to
    combine.
3.  Add the powdered sugar, saffron threads, and
    whole-milk fudge. Mix well. Bring the milk to
    another boil. Remove from the heat and set
    aside to cool.
4.  Transfer to plastic container and cover with
    plastic wrap. Freeze until set.
5.  Once set, bring it out of the freezer and break it
    up using an electric handheld mixer.
6.  Repeat this freezing and breaking technique
    4 times.
7.  To finish the badnaam kulfi, beat it one final
    time and sprinkle it with dried fruits. Serve
    immediately in its beaten form.

## PANJIRI

Edible gum with roasted seeds and nuts.

Cooking time: 35 minutes | Serves: 2        Origin: Punjab

INGREDIENTS

½ cup (120 g) ghee
¼ cup (60 g) edible gum (*gondh*)
1 cup (32 g) lotus seeds (*makhana*)
5 Tbsp (45 g) almonds (*badam*)
5 Tbsp (45 g) watermelon seeds (*magaz*)
1 cup (125 g) whole-wheat flour (*atta*)
1 tsp carom seeds (*ajwain*)
5 Tbsp (37.5g) powdered sugar

METHOD

1. In a skillet over medium heat, heat the ghee.
2. Add the edible gum and roast until puffed. With a slotted spoon, transfer to a food processor and pulse to grind.
3. Return the skillet and ghee to medium heat. Add the lotus seeds. Fry for 4–5 minutes. With a slotted spoon, remove from the pan and set aside.
4. Add the almonds. Fry for 4–5 minutes. With a slotted spoon, remove from the pan and set aside.
5. Add the watermelon seeds. Fry for 4–5 minutes. With a slotted spoon, remove from the pan and set aside. Return the skillet and any leftover ghee to the heat. Add the wheat flour and carom seeds. Toast for 3–4 minutes, or until the flour turns light brown.
6. Transfer to a plate and mix all the roasted ingredients together. Let cool.
7. Add the powdered sugar and mix well.
8. Store in airtight jars.

## PUNJABI PINNI

Whole-wheat and whole-milk fudge balls.

Cooking time: 30 minutes | Makes: 8        Origin: Punjab

INGREDIENTS

½ cup (120 g) ghee
1 cup (125 g) whole-wheat flour (*atta*)
1 cup (240 g) whole-milk fudge (*khoya*; available at Indian markets; page 25)
½ cup (60 g) powdered sugar
¼ cup (60 g) assorted dried fruits
1 tsp ground cardamom

METHOD

1. In a skillet over medium-high heat, heat the ghee.
2. Add the flour. Toast for 10–12 minutes, or until deep brown. Transfer to a bowl.
3. Return the skillet to the heat. Add the whole-milk fudge and dry-roast until light brown. Add to the toasted flour and stir to combine.
4. Add the powdered sugar, dried fruits, and cardamom to the bowl. Let come to room temperature.
5. Mix all the ingredients well and roll into small balls. Store in an airtight container for 4–5 days.

# GAJAR KA HALWA
Shredded carrot pudding.

Cooking time: 20 minutes | Serves: 2      Origin: Punjab

## INGREDIENTS

2 lb, 3 oz (1 kg) carrots, washed, peeled, shredded
2½ cups (600 ml) milk
1 tsp ground cardamom (*choti elaichi*), divided
½ cup (100 g) sugar
½ cup (112.5 g) brown sugar
4 Tbsp (60 g) ghee
⅓ cup (30 g) almonds (*badam*), slivered
⅛ cup (25 g) raisins (*kishmish*)
⅓ cup (40 g) walnuts (*akhrot*), chopped
½ tsp ground cloves (*laung*)
½ tsp ground nutmeg (*jaiphal*)
½ tsp ground cinnamon (*dalchini*)

## METHOD

1. In a pan over medium-high heat, boil the shredded carrots with the milk. Simmer and cook for 20–25 minutes, stirring continuously until the liquid evaporates.
2. Add half the ground cardamom, brown sugar, and regular sugar. Stir continuously for 10–12 minutes. Remove and set the mixture aside.
3. In a wok over medium heat, heat the ghee.
4. Fry the slivered almonds until golden.
5. Add the prepared carrot mixture, raisins, walnuts, cloves, nutmeg, and cinnamon. Cook until the mixture begins to separate from the sides and caramalizes into a deep red color.
6. Serve hot, garnished with the remaining cardamom.

# ATTA BISCUITS
Healthy whole-wheat cookies.

Cooking time: 40 minutes | Makes: 10      Origin: Punjab

## INGREDIENTS

1 cup (125 g) whole-wheat flour (*atta*), plus more for the work surface
4 Tbsp (32 g) all-purpose flour (*maida*)
7 Tbsp (52.5 g) sugar, powdered
2 Tbsp (14 g) bran
7 Tbsp (105 g) unsalted butter
½ tsp salt
½ tsp baking soda
½ cup (120 ml) cold milk, plus more as needed

## METHOD

1. In a medium-size bowl, combine the wheat flour, all-purpose flour, powdered sugar, bran, butter, salt, baking soda, and milk. Knead into a tight dough. Add more milk, if needed. Let the dough rest for 10 minutes.
2. Preheat the oven to 400°F (200°C).
3. Dust a work surface with flour, and roll out the dough. Cut out 10 small pieces using a square cookie cutter and place on a baking sheet.
4. Bake the cookies for 20 minutes, or until done. Transfer to a wire rack to cool completely before storing in an airtight container.

# ACCOMPANIMENTS

## MOOLI KA RAITA

A cooling side dish made with yogurt.

Cooking time: 15 minutes | Serves: 2      Origin: Punjab

INGREDIENTS

2 cups (480 g) yogurt (*dahi*)
½ cup (125 g) grated radish (*mooli*)
1 green chile, finely chopped
½ medium-size onion, finely chopped
1 Tbsp (1 g) fresh cilantro leaves (*hara dhaniya*),
 finely chopped
1 Tbsp (6 g) fresh mint leaves (*pudina*), finely
 chopped
1 tsp Indian black salt (*kala namak*)
Salt, to taste

METHOD

1. In a small bowl, combine all the ingredients and stir well.
2. Refrigerate the raita for 2 hours before serving. Season to taste with salt and serve.

## SEA BUCKTHORN AND APPLE JAM

Himachali apple and sea buckthorn preserve.

Cooking time: 40 minutes | Serves: 4   Origin: Himachal Pradesh

INGREDIENTS

1½ cups (360 ml) water
1 cup (240 g) sea buckthorn
2 medium-size apples, peeled and chopped
1 cup (200 g) sugar
2 Tbsp (30 g) honey

METHOD

1. In a medium-size pot over high heat, bring the water to a boil.
2. Add the sea buckthorn and apples. Let bubble for 10 minutes.
3. Remove from the heat and cool to room temperature. Strain the fruits (reserve the cooking water), transfer to a blender, and blend into a coarse pulp. Add water from the pot, if needed. Transfer the mixture back to the pot.
4. Stir in the sugar and honey. Heat the fruit mixture over medium-low heat for 25–30 minutes, stirring occasionally to avoid burning. Remove and set aside to cool.
5. Refrigerate the preserves in a sterilized jar. Serve at room temperature.

# BUKNU
A versatile and popular spice mix.

Cooking time: 10 minutes | Serves: 4     Origin: Uttar Pradesh

## INGREDIENTS

1 tsp mustard seed oil (page 26)
2 Tbsp (14 g) ground turmeric (*haldi*)
2 Tbsp (14 g) ground cumin (*jeera*)
2 Tbsp (30 g) carom seeds (*ajwain*)
2 Tbsp (12 g) fennel seeds (*saunf*)
2 Tbsp (12 g) ground cardamom
1 Tbsp (9 g) dried amla powder, (available at Indian markets and online)
1 Tbsp (30) dried mango powder (*amchoor*)
1 Tbsp (5.5 g) ground ginger (*sonth*)
Pinch ground asafoetida (*hing*)
½ cup (120 g) salt
Indian black salt (*kala namak*), to taste

## METHOD

1. In a skillet over low heat, heat the mustard seed oil.
2. Add the turmeric, cumin, carom seeds, fennel seeds, cardamom, dried amla powder, dried mango powder, ginger, and asafoetida. Toast for 3–4 minutes.
3. Transfer to a spice grinder or mortar and pestle and let cool. Blend the mix into a fine powder. Combine the powder with the salts and store in an airtight container until use.

# KANJI
Fermented probiotic carrot drink.

Cooking time: 10 minutes | Serves: 3     Origin: Uttar Pradesh

## INGREDIENTS

1 Tbsp (11 g) brown mustard seeds (*rai*), crushed
1 Tbsp (15 g) black carrot batons (*gajar*)
1 medium-size beet (*chuqandar*), cut into batons
7 cups (1.7 L) water
Sea salt, to taste

## METHOD

1. In a clean coffee grinder or spice grinder, grind the mustard seeds.
2. In a sterilized 2-qt (1.9-L) glass jar, combine the ground mustard seeds, carrot, beet, and water. Season to taste with sea salt.
3. Cover the jar with a piece of cheesecloth and secure it with a rubber band. Place it in a sunny spot to bathe in sunlight every morning for a week. Stir the kanji every day.
4. Once it develops a tangy flavor, strain the drink and keep the pickles refrigerated separately to eat later.
5. Transfer the liquid to a storage container, chill, and drink immediately.

# MALIHABADI AAM KA PANNA

Raw mango-based cool summer drink.

Cooking time: 40 minutes | Serves: 2     Origin: Uttar Pradesh

## INGREDIENTS

2 medium-size mangoes (*kairi*)
4 cups (960 ml) water
3 Tbsp (37.5 g) sugar
1 tsp Indian black salt (*kala namak*)
1 tsp ground cumin (*jeera*)

## METHOD

1. Preheat the oven to 350°F (180°C).
2. Make four slits in the mango lengthwise and place them on a baking sheet. Bake for 40 minutes.
3. Press the charred mango skin to extract the pulp into a large bowl.
4. Stir in the water, mixing well.
5. Add the sugar, black salt, and cumin. Whisk to combine. Serve chilled.

# SHIKANJI

Lemonade with medicinal qualities.

Cooking time: 10 minutes | Serves: 3     Origin: Uttar Pradesh

## INGREDIENTS

¾ cup (180 ml) fresh lime juice
⅓ cup (21 g) fresh mint leaves, plus sprigs
   for garnish
⅓ cup (67 g) sugar
½ tsp grated black salt (*kala namak*),
   optional
½ tsp kosher salt
¼ tsp dried mango (*amchoor*) powder
¼ tsp freshly ground black pepper
¼ tsp ground cumin (*jeera*)
4 cups (960 ml) seltzer or water, chilled
Lemon slices, for serving

## METHOD

1. In a blender, combine the lime juice, mint leaves, sugar, black salt (if using), kosher salt, dried mango powder, pepper, and cumin. Purée until smooth. Pour into a pitcher and top with seltzer.
2. Garnish with lime slices and mint sprigs.

## KASHMIRI KAWAH

Hot almond and saffron-infused tea.

Cooking time: 10 minutes | Serves: 4  Origin: Jammu & Kashmir

INGREDIENTS

1 tsp saffron threads (*kesar*)
4 cups (960 ml) water
3 green cardamom pods (*choti elaichi*)
2 whole cloves (*laung*)
2 Tbsp (25 g) sugar
1 (1-in. / 2.5-cm) cinnamon stick (*dalchini*)
4 tsp (20 g) Kashmiri tea leaves
¼ cup (60 g) almonds (*badam*), sliced

METHOD

1. In a small bowl, mix the saffron threads with 2 Tbsp (30 ml) of warm water. Stir well.
2. In a saucepan over high heat, combine the 4 cups (960 ml) of water, green cardamom pods, cloves, sugar, and cinnamon stick. Bring to a boil.
3. Add the tea leaves. Boil for 2 minutes more.
4. Strain the liquid and add the saffron water. Mix well.
5. Serve hot, garnished with almonds.

## SWEET ROSE LASSI 📷

Cool yogurt drink.

Cooking time: 10 minutes | Serves: 2          Origin: Punjab

INGREDIENTS

2 cups (480 g) chilled yogurt (*dahi*)
5 Tbsp (75 g) rose syrup
1 Tbsp (7.5 g) powdered sugar
Pinch salt
Fresh food-grade rose petals, for garnishing

METHOD

1. In a small bowl, whisk the yogurt, rose syrup, powdered sugar, and salt. Whisk well and serve in tall glasses garnished with rose petals.

# central india
● ● ● ●

MADHYA PRADESH . CHHATTISGARH

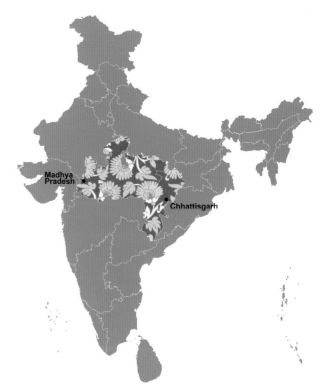

Chhattisgarh and Madhya Pradesh lie at the heart of India. Madhya Pradesh, like a large part of country, relies on wheat as one of the most important components of its meals, while Chhattisgarh is known as the "rice bowl of India." Being one of the largest producers of rice in the country, the state incorporates the grain in various forms. From the breakfast staple *faara*, to flatbreads like *chusela* (used to soak up curries and gravies), to *dehati bada* and chai-time crisps, rice is soaked, blitzed, pulverized, steamed, fried, and roasted.

The culinary traditions of Chhattisgarh are further enhanced by the varied rustic tribal recipes. The Gondi and Bastar tribes that are native to this region rely on forest yields, seasonal vegetables and fruits, and minimally-cooked and -spiced dishes. On special occasions, they make mithais such as *khaza*—a popular tribal delicacy—which is crisp like a sweet cookie. Another standout recipe is the Bastar *boda* curry. Inspired by the tribes of Bastar, the curry is cooked using indigenous mushrooms (*boda*), also known as desi mushrooms, which grow on mucky forest land in the monsoon. During the rainy season, or what is locally known as *haduk*, the tribes hunt various kinds of fungi, bamboo shoots, and greens. Since monsoons are lean months, when seeds are sowed and harvest is yet to come, forest produce is their best bet.

Apart from usage of foraged ingredients, usage of millets is another striking feature of Chhattisgarhi cuisine. Finger millet or "ragi" forms an integral part of the local diet. In summer, when the forests get hot, cooling off with a ragi soup known as *mandya paej* is mandatory. Ragi, an Indian superfood, is not only known for its energy-giving benefits, but is also a natural coolant.

Chhattisgarh was carved out of Madhya Pradesh in 2000, and the latter has a distinct style of cooking. While Chhattisgarhi cuisine is rustic, food from Madhya Pradesh is a flavor and texture riot. Each city here celebrates a robust food culture—this is largely because Madhya Pradesh is the second-largest state (by land mass) in India and each region has a unique historical background.

Gwalior has been ruled by a number of rulers, from the Tomars, to the Mughals, to the Marathas and finally the Scindia family, who were the last rulers of Gwalior State. This eventful past resulted in the development of a cuisine that took inspiration from all its previous rulers and is a medley of North Indian, Maharashtrian, and even Nepalese food (due to the intermarriage between many members of the Scindia family and the Nepalase Rana family).

*Gajak* (sesame-jaggery bar) is a popular winter snack that originated from the Bhind region of Madhya Pradesh and today is widely available in shops in every big city in the state. In Bundelkhand, Mughal, and Rajput tribal influences can be seen in the cuisine, with recipes such as *murar ke kebab*, sesame rice, and Bundeli *gosht*. Cuisine from Malwa (a plateau, encompassing central Madhya Pradesh and southeastern Rajasthan) has strong Rajasthani influences, especially dishes such as *mawa baati*, *bhutte ke kees* (known as *makai ki khichdi* in Rajasthan), and *amli ki kadhi*, although this one is not blended with yogurt, which is the case with many Marwari gravies—instead the sourness comes from tamarind pulp.

For non-vegetarians, the city of Bhopal is a gastronomical paradise. Muslim influence is obvious in Bhopali cuisine; it was the second-largest Muslim-ruled princely state after Hyderabad. The street food in Bhopal is rich with meaty samosas, kebabs, and spicy meat skewers. Kamar Bhai's *paya* soup shop is a famous eatery that doles out distinctly flavorsome mutton trotters soup, loaded with bits of meat.

Traditional techniques such as slow cooking, prolonged marination of meats, smoking, and hand-pounding of spices are still in common use in Bhopal. Typical dishes from the city include *rizala*, which is a combination of chicken and coriander; *filfora*, a coarse mutton curry; well-spiced keema; and *kewra*-scented korma. In the days when shikaar was the norm, Bhopal was also known for its game meat, including quail- and partridge-based recipes.

Another culinary hotspot in Madhya Pradesh is a little-known gem, Indore. With delightful chaats, dry namkeens, street-side desserts, and cooked snacks, the city leaves you impressed with the kind of food it churns out.

To catch the essence of this city, travelers often walk through Sarafa Bazaar, a jewelry market by day and a food market by night. The noisy, colorful bazaar is a buzzing spot for hungry souls, and serves dishes that range from amplified versions of Punjabi lassi, known here as *ghamandi* lassi or *shahi shikanji*, to humble Maharashtrian poha—sprinkled with grated coconut and pomegranate gems.

One of our favorites is the egg benjo, essentially a masala omelet stuffed inside a burger bun with veggies. There is also fried *garadu* (crispy cubes of root vegetable sprinkled with chaat masala), namkeen chaat, *moong bhajiya,* and more. What ties these together is a magical dust from Indore called *jeeravan* masala, a specialty blend that is a combination of dry mango powder, black salt, and cinnamon, and gives various street chaats immense character.

Overall, Madhya Pradesh is so steeped in the culinary arts that each city here has something unique to offer—be it spicy sev from Ratlam, chicken samosas from Jabalpur, bafauri from Bhojpur, or mawa batti from Gwalior—there is a culinary gem waiting to be discovered in every corner of the state. This also applies to the larger Central Indian region which serves together an array of flavors from Madhya Pradesh, along with charming and rustic Chhattisgarhi fare.

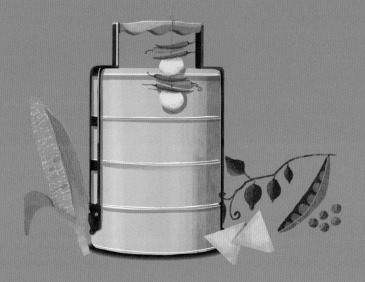

APPETIZERS

## MANDYA PAEJ

Hearty millet flour soup.

Cooking time: 10 minutes | Serves: 2     Origin: Chhattisgarh

INGREDIENTS

2 Tbsp (15 g) millet flour (*ragi*)
2 cups (480 ml) water
2 tsp flattened rice (*poha/chura*)
Salt, to taste

METHOD

1. In a saucepan over medium heat, dry-roast the flour until it turns light brown.
2. Slowly, incorporating a few spoonfuls at a time, stir in the water.
3. Add the rice. Cook for 3–4 minutes. Turn off the heat once the porridge begins to thicken. Season well with salt. Serve hot, like a soup, with lasan chutney (page 270), if desired.

## FARA

Light rice-flour breakfast dumpling.

Cooking time: 30 minutes | Serves: 2     Origin: Chhattisgarh

INGREDIENTS

1½ cups (360 ml) water
½ cup (80 g) rice flour
Salt, to taste
1 tsp vegetable oil
2 curry leaves (*kadhi patta*)
1 green chile, finely chopped
1 tsp mustard seeds (*rai*)

METHOD

1. In a saucepan over high heat, bring the water to a rolling boil. Remove from the heat and add the rice flour and salt to taste. Stir vigorously until the rice absorbs all the water. Transfer to a plate and knead it into a tight dough. Make 4–5 elongated sticks with the dough. Place the dough sticks in a steamer and steam for 12 minutes. Transfer to a serving plate when done.
2. In a skillet over low-medium heat, heat the vegetable oil.
3. Add the curry leaves, green chile, and mustard seeds. Sauté until the spices begin to crackle. Pour this tempering over the steamed fara. Serve hot with mint-cilantro chutney (page 28), if desired.

# MAHERI

Perfect monsoon porridge.

Cooking time: 15 minutes | Serves: 3   Origin: Madhya Pradesh

INGREDIENTS

1 Tbsp (15 g) ghee
1 tsp cumin seeds (*jeera*)
Pinch ground asafoetida (*hing*)
1 tsp ground turmeric (*haldi*)
¾ cup (150 g) millet (*ragi*), soaked in water for
  30 minutes, drained
3 cups (720 ml) buttermilk (*chaach*, page 30)
Salt, to taste

METHOD

1. On your pressure cooker, select Sauté to preheat
   the cooking pot.
2. Add the ghee to melt.
3. Add the cumin seeds and asafoetida. Cook until
   the seeds begin to crackle.
4. Add the turmeric and millet. Sauté for 2 minutes.
5. Add the buttermilk and season to taste with
   salt. Lock the lid in place and close the pressure
   release valve. Select Manual/Pressure cook and
   cook for 6 minutes.
6. Release the pressure and remove the lid.
   Serve hot.

# INDORI POHA

Street-style spiced flattened rice with fennel.

Cooking time: 20 minutes | Serves: 2   Origin: Madhya Pradesh

INGREDIENTS

1 Tbsp (15 ml) vegetable oil
1 tsp mustard seeds (*rai*)
1 tsp cumin seeds (*jeera*)
1 tsp fennel seeds (*saunf*)
2 curry leaves (*kadhi patta*)
1 green chile, finely chopped
1 tsp ground turmeric (*haldi*)
1 tsp red chile powder
1 tsp grated peeled fresh ginger (*adrak*)
1 tsp grated garlic (*lasan*)
½ cup (85 g) finely chopped onion
2 cups (400 g) flattened rice (*poha/chura*)
Salt, to taste
¼ cup (4 g) fresh cilantro leaves (*hara dhaniya*),
  finely chopped
¼ cup (45 g) pomegranate seeds (*anar*)

METHOD

1. In a skillet over low-medium heat, heat the
   vegetable oil.
2. Add the mustard seeds, cumin seeds, fennel
   seeds, curry leaves, and green chile. Cook until
   the seeds begin to crackle.
3. Stir in the turmeric, red chile powder, ginger,
   garlic, and onion. Sauté until fragrant.
4. Add the rice. Stir until everything turns a
   beautiful sunny yellow. Cook for 2–3 minutes.
5. Season to taste with salt and garnish with
   pomegranate seeds and cilantro before serving.

## BHOJPURI-STYLE BHARBHARA

Savory chickpea pancakes with peas and onions.

Cooking time: 30 minutes | Makes: 5  Origin: Madhya Pradesh

INGREDIENTS

½ cup (60 g) chickpea flour (*besan*)
½ cup (80 g) green peas (*hara mattar*), boiled
1 medium-size onion, finely chopped
1 green chile, finely chopped
1 tsp red chile powder
1 tsp chaat masala
1 tsp ground cumin (*jeera*)
Salt, to taste
Water, as needed
1 Tbsp (15 ml) vegetable oil

METHOD

1. In a medium-size bowl, combine the chickpea flour, green peas, onion, green chile, and spices. Season to taste with salt. Stir in enough water to achieve a pancake batter-like consistency.
2. In a skillet over medium heat, heat the vegetable oil.
3. Pour in the batter in mini pancake portions. Cook on both sides until golden brown and crisp. Serve hot with mint-cilantro chutney (page 28), if desired.

## KHASTA KACHORI

Lentil-stuffed fritters.

Cooking time: 35 minutes | Makes: 10 Origin: Madhya Pradesh

INGREDIENTS

1 cup (200 g) green gram (*moong dal*), boiled
1 cup (200 g) black lentils (*urad dal*), boiled
3 green chiles, finely chopped
2 Tbsp (30 g) ginger-garlic paste (*adrak-lasan*)
2 tsp dried mango powder (*amchoor*)
1 Tbsp (6 g) ground coriander (*dhaniya*)
1 tsp fennel seeds (*saunf*)
1 tsp ground turmeric (*haldi*)
1 tsp garam masala
1 tsp ground cumin (*jeera*)
Salt, to taste
1½ cups (360 g) whole-wheat flour (*atta*)
Water, for kneading
Oil, for frying

METHOD

1. In a medium-size bowl, combine the green gram, black lentils, green chiles, ginger-garlic paste, dried mango powder, coriander, fennel seeds, turmeric, garam masala, and cumin. Mash together slightly and season to taste with salt. Set aside.
2. In a medium-size bowl combine the whole-wheat flour with just enough water to knead the dough. Divide the dough into 10 small roundels and roll them out into small rotis, about the size of your palm. Place a spoonful of filling at the center of each dough circle and bring all the edges together. Roll out into small kachoris.
3. In a deep skillet over medium-high heat, heat the vegetable oil for frying.
4. Carefully add the kachoris to the hot oil and deep-fry until golden. Serve with date-tamarind and mint-cilantro chutneys (pages 28, 29), if desired.

## MOONG BHAJIYA
Spiced lentil fritters.

Cooking time: 30 minutes | Makes: 10  Origin: Madhya Pradesh

INGREDIENTS

1 cup (200 g) green gram (*moong dal*), soaked in
  water overnight, drained
1 cup (225 g) mashed potatoes
2 green chiles, finely chopped
1 Tbsp (15 g) ginger-garlic paste (*adrak-lasan*)
¼ cup (4 g) fresh cilantro leaves (*hara dhaniya*),
  finely chopped
¼ cup (42.5 g) finely chopped onion
Salt, to taste
Freshly ground black pepper (*kali mirch*), to taste
Vegetable oil, for frying

METHOD

1. In a food processor, combine the green gram,
   potatoes, green chiles, and ginger-garlic paste.
   Pulse for a few seconds until you get a slightly
   chunky consistency. Transfer the mixture to a
   medium-size bowl.
2. Stir in the cilantro and onion. Season to taste
   with salt and pepper.
3. In a deep skillet over medium heat, heat the
   vegetable oil for frying
4. Carefully drop spoonfuls of the prepared
   mixture into the hot oil (should make ten small
   fritters). Gently fry until beautifully golden.
   Transfer to paper towels to drain. Serve hot with
   mint-cilantro chutney (page 28), if desired.

## FRIED GARADU
Indore-style spiced potato wedges.

Cooking time: 15 minutes | Serves: 2  Origin: Madhya Pradesh

INGREDIENTS

Vegetable oil, for frying
2 cups (220 g) cubed yams
1 Tbsp (10 g) *jiralu* masala (available at Indian
  markets, page 27)
Juice of 1 lemon (*nimbu*)
Salt, to taste
¼ cup (4 g) fresh cilantro leaves (*hara dhaniya*),
  finely chopped

METHOD

1. In a skillet over low-medium heat, heat the
   vegetable oil for frying.
2. Carefully add the yam to the hot oil and deep-
   fry until golden brown. Transfer to paper towels
   to drain and sprinkle with the jiralu masala,
   lemon juice, and salt.
3. Garnish with cilantro and serve hot.

## BHUTTE KE KEES

Grated corn with pomegranate and coconut.

Cooking time: 30 minutes | Serves: 2  Origin: Madhya Pradesh

INGREDIENTS

2 large fresh ears corn
2 Tbsp (30 g) ghee
1 green chile, finely chopped
2 tsp ginger-garlic paste (*adrak-lasan*)
1 tsp cumin seeds (*jeera*)
Pinch ground asafoetida (*hing*)
1 cup (240 ml) milk
Salt, to taste
5 Tbsp (25 g) grated fresh coconut (*nariyal*)
¼ cup (4 g) fresh cilantro leaves (*hara dhaniya*),
   finely chopped
½ cup (90 g) pomegranate seeds (*anar*)
5 Tbsp (75 g) nylon sev (available at Indian
   markets)

METHOD

1. Using a grater, carefully grate the corn into a
   bowl and set aside.
2. In a skillet over low heat, heat the ghee.
3. Add the green chile, ginger-garlic paste, cumin
   seeds, and asafoetida. Sauté until the seeds
   begin to crackle.
4. Stir in the grated corn.
5. Slowly add the milk and allow it to boil until all
   the milk is absorbed.
6. Season to taste with salt and garnish with
   coconut, cilantro, pomegranate seeds, and
   nylon sev. Serve hot.

## INDORE NAMKEEN CHAAT

Local favorite dried snack salad.

Cooking time: 10 minutes | Serves: 2  Origin: Madhya Pradesh

INGREDIENTS

1 cup (240 g) Indore namkeen (available at Indian
   markets)
½ cup (85 g) finely chopped onion
½ cup (120 g) finely chopped tomato
½ cup (67.5 g) finely chopped cucumber
½ cup (112.5 g) cubed boiled potato
1 tsp red chile powder
1 tsp chaat masala
Juice of 1 lemon (*nimbu*)
Salt, to taste
¼ cup (4 g) fresh cilantro leaves (*hara dhaniya*),
   finely chopped
¼ cup (45 g) pomegranate seeds (*anar*)
2 Tbsp (30 g) nylon sev (available at Indian
   markets)

METHOD

1. In a medium-size bowl, toss together the Indore
   namkeen, onion, tomato, cucumber, and potato.
2. Add the red chile powder, chaat masala, and
   lemon juice. Season to taste with salt. Toss well
   to combine.
3. Garnish with cilantro, pomegranate seeds, and
   nylon sev.

## RATLAMI SEV

Deep-fried chickpea snack with spices.

Cooking time: 40 minutes | Serves: 4   Origin: Madhya Pradesh

INGREDIENTS

1 Tbsp (15 g) whole spice mix (page 22)
1 tsp peppercorns (*sabut kali mirch*)
½ tsp cumin seeds (*jeera*)
½ tsp fennel seeds (*saunf*)
½ tsp carom seeds (*ajwain*)
1 dried red chile (*sookhi lal mirch*)
2 cups (240 g) chickpea flour (*besan*)
1 tsp ginger-garlic paste (*adrak-lasan*)
Pinch ground asafoetida (*hing*)
1 tsp baking soda
Juice of 1 lemon (*nimbu*)
Salt, to taste
Water, as needed
Vegetable oil, for frying

METHOD

1. In a heavy-bottomed skillet over low-medium heat, combine the whole spice mix, peppercorns, cumin seeds, fennel seeds, carom seeds, and dried red chile. Dry-roast until the seeds begin to crackle and the mixture is fragrant. Transfer to a blender or mortar and pestle, cool, and grind into a fine powder.
2. In a medium-size bowl, stir together the chickpea flour, ginger-garlic paste, asafoetida, baking soda, lemon juice, and the prepared spice powder. Season to taste with salt. Add very little water to make a soft dough. Fill a murukku press or churros syringe with this dough.
3. In a deep skillet over low-medium heat, heat the vegetable oil for frying.
4. Press thin strings of the spiced dough into the hot oil and deep-fry until golden and crispy. Transfer to paper towels to drain and serve hot.

## DEHATI BADA

Rustic dough fritter with spinach.

Cooking time: 30 minutes | Makes: 6      Origin: Chhattisgarh

INGREDIENTS

1 cup (200 g) rice, soaked in water overnight, drained
3 cups (600 g) split black lentils (*urad dal*), soaked in water overnight, drained
Salt, to taste
2 green chiles, finely chopped
1 cup (30 g) fresh spinach, finely chopped
1 tsp red chile powder
Pinch baking soda
Vegetable oil, for frying

METHOD

1. In a food processor, combine the rice and black lentils. Grind into a smooth paste. Transfer to a large bowl and season to taste with salt.
2. Add the green chiles, spinach, red chile powder, and baking soda. Stir to combine.
3. In a deep skillet over low-medium heat, heat the vegetable oil for frying.
4. Carefully drop spoonfuls of the batter into the hot oil (should make 6 small vadas). Deep-fry until golden brown. Serve hot with date-tamarind and mint-cilantro chutneys (pages 28, 29), if desired.

## BHOPALI PAYA SOUP
Mildly spiced goat trotter soup.

| Cooking time: 1 hour | Serves: 3 | Origin: Madhya Pradesh |
|---|---|---|

### INGREDIENTS

1 Tbsp (15 ml) vegetable oil
8 peppercorns (*sabut kali mirch*)
3 whole cloves (*laung*)
2 cinnamon sticks (*dalchini*)
½ cup (120 g) sliced onion
1½ Tbsp (23 g) garlic-chile paste (*lasan mirch*)
1 Tbsp (6 g) ground coriander (*dhaniya*)
2 tsp ground turmeric (*haldi*)
2 tsp ground cumin (*jeera*)
1 medium-size tomato, finely chopped
6 pieces goat trotters, thoroughly washed with hot
    water until absolutely clean
Salt, to taste
6 cups (1.4 L) water
¼ cup (4 g) fresh cilantro leaves (*hara dhaniya*),
    finely chopped

### METHOD

1. On your pressure cooker, select Sauté to preheat
   the cooking pot.
2. Add the vegetable oil to heat.
3. Add the peppercorns, cloves, and cinnamon
   sticks. Cook until the spices begin to crackle.
4. Add the onion and garlic-chile paste. Sauté for
   1–2 minutes.
5. Add the coriander, turmeric, and cumin. Sauté
   for 1 minute more.
6. Add the tomato and trotters. Season to taste
   with salt and sauté until the spices have coated
   the trotters well.
7. Add the water. Lock the lid in place and close
   the pressure release valve. Select Manual/
   Pressure Cook and cook the soup for 18 minutes.
8. Release the pressure and remove the lid. Adjust
   the seasoning. Garnish with cilantro and serve
   hot with naan (page 111), if desired.

## JABALPURI CHICKEN SAMOSA 📷
Pastry-encased chicken patties.

| Cooking time: 30 minutes | Makes: 10 | Origin: Madhya Pradesh |
|---|---|---|

### INGREDIENTS

2 tsp vegetable oil
1 medium-size onion, finely chopped
1 green chile, finely chopped
1 Tbsp (15 g) ginger-garlic paste (*adrak-lasan*)
1 tsp ground turmeric (*haldi*)
1 tsp red chile powder
1 cup (140 g) shredded cooked chicken
¼ cup (4 g) fresh cilantro leaves (*dhaniya*),
    finely chopped
Juice of 1 lemon (*nimbu*)
1 tsp chaat masala
Salt, to taste
10 samosa pastry sheets (samosa *patti*; available at
    Indian markets and online, page 33)
Vegetable oil, for frying

### METHOD

1. In a skillet over medium-high heat, heat the
   vegetable oil.
2. Add the onion, green chile, and ginger-garlic
   paste. Sauté until the onion turns golden.
3. Stir in the turmeric and red chile powder. Sauté
   for 2 minutes more.
4. Add the chicken, cilantro, lemon juice, and
   chaat masala. Season to taste with salt. Cook for
   3 minutes more. Remove from the heat and set
   aside.
5. Stuff this mixture into the samosa patties.
   Carefully wrap to enclose it in a triangular
   shape like spanakopita. Repeat until all the
   filling and pastry are used up.
6. In a deep skillet over low-medium heat, heat the
   vegetable oil for frying.
7. Carefully add the folded samosa patties to the
   hot oil and deep-fry until golden. Serve hot with
   date-tamarind and mint-cilantro chutneys
   (pages 28, 29), if desired.

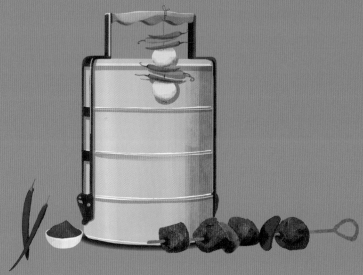

# POULTRY AND EGGS

## CHICKEN CURRY—BHOPALI STYLE

Chicken in an aromatic yogurt curry.

Cooking time: 30 minutes | Serves: 2-4  Origin: Madhya Pradesh

### INGREDIENTS

2 Tbsp (30 ml) vegetable oil, divided
1 (½-in. / 1.25-cm) piece peeled fresh ginger,
  chopped, plus 1 Tbsp (15 g) julienned peeled
  fresh ginger (*adrak*)
3 garlic cloves (*lasan*), chopped
½ medium-size onion, diced
1 tsp cumin seeds (*jeera*)
1 tsp coriander seeds (*dhaniya*)
1 tsp peppercorns (*sabut kali mirch*)
1 tsp ground cinnamon (*dalchini*)
1 tsp ground cloves (*laung*)
1 tsp ground turmeric (*haldi*)
1 tsp red chile powder
½ tsp ground mace (*javitri*)
Pinch ground nutmeg (*jaiphal*)
1 bay leaf (*tej patta*)
1 lb, 2 oz (500 g) cubed chicken
1 cup (240 g) yogurt (*dahi*)
Salt, to taste
¼ cup (4 g) fresh cilantro leaves (*hara dhaniya*),
  finely chopped
Juice of 1 lemon (*nimbu*)
3 Tbsp (45 g) fried onions (*birista*; page 30), for
  garnishing

### METHOD

1. In a skillet over medium-high heat, heat 1 Tbsp (15 ml) of vegetable oil.
2. Add the chopped ginger, garlic, onion, cumin seeds, coriander seeds, peppercorns, cinnamon, cloves, turmeric, red chile powder, mace, nutmeg, and bay leaf. Stir-fry for 4–5 minutes. Transfer to a blender and blend into a fine paste.
3. Return the skillet to medium heat and add the remaining 1 Tbsp (15 ml) of vegetable oil.
4. Add the spice paste and cook for 2 minutes.
5. Add the chicken. Cook, stirring, until the meat is well coated with the spices.
6. Stir in the yogurt and season to taste with salt.

Cover the skillet and cook until the meat is tender, the gravy thickens, and the water from the yogurt has evaporated. Remove from the heat.

7. Serve hot, garnished with julienned ginger, cilantro, lemon juice, and *birista*.

· · · · · · · · · · · ·

## CHHATTISGARHI CHICKEN CURRY

Semi-fried chicken in a robust chile curry.

Cooking time: 15 minutes | Serves: 2   Origin: Chhattisgarh

### INGREDIENTS

1 Tbsp (15 ml) vegetable oil
2 green chiles, finely chopped
1 medium-size onion, finely chopped
½ lb (250 g) bone-in chicken pieces
1 Tbsp (15 g) red chile paste
1 Tbsp (6 g) ground coriander (*dhaniya*)
1 tsp ground turmeric (*haldi*)
1 ground cumin (*jeera*)
Salt, to taste
1 cup (240 ml) water
1 Tbsp (6 g) garam masala
1 Tbsp (13.5 g) dried fenugreek leaves
  (*kasuri methi*)

### METHOD

1. In a skillet over medium heat, heat the vegetable oil.
2. Add the green chiles and onion. Sauté for 2 minutes.
3. Add the chicken. Cook, stirring, until the oil coats all the pieces. Let cook for 10 minutes until partially done.
4. Add the red chile paste, coriander, turmeric, and cumin. Season to taste with salt. Continue to cook the chicken for 4–5 minutes.
5. Add the water. Reduce the heat as needed and simmer the curry for 10 minutes.
6. Finish with salt, garam masala, and the dried fenugreek leaves and serve.

## BHOPALI RIZALA

A rich and creamy chicken dish from the Bhopal royal kitchen.

Cooking time: 45 minutes | Serves: 5   Origin: Madhya Pradesh

INGREDIENTS

⅓ cup (100 ml) vegetable oil
3 tsp ginger (*adrak*) paste
3 tsp garlic (*lasan*) paste
1 tsp ground turmeric (*haldi*)
2 tsp ground coriander (*dhaniya*)
Salt, to taste
2 lb, 3 oz (1 kg) chicken, cut into bite-size pieces
3½ oz (100 g) green chiles
7 cups (112 g) fresh cilantro leaves (*hara dhaniya*), chopped
1 cup (240 g) *birista* (blended in a paste; page 30)
2 tsp poppy seeds (*khus khus*), soaked, finely ground
1 tsp garam masala
1 cup (240 g) yogurt (*dahi*), whipped
1 egg, hardboiled, peeled, halved
Juice of 2 lemons (*nimbu*)

METHOD

1. In a skillet over low-medium heat, heat the vegetable oil.
2. Add the ginger and garlic pastes, turmeric, coriander, and salt to taste.
3. Continue to fry, sprinkling water if necessary, until the mixture turns golden brown.
4. Add the chicken pieces and continue to fry till the liquid dries out and the chicken turns golden brown.
5. Add the green chiles, cilantro, *birista* paste, ground poppy seeds, garam masala, and yogurt. Cook on medium heat until the oil floats on top.
6. Garnish with a hardboiled egg and lemon juice.

## EGG BANJO 📷

Masala omelet burger with ketchup and mint chutney.

Cooking time: 15 minutes | Makes: 2   Origin: Madhya Pradesh

INGREDIENTS

2 eggs
¼ cup (4 g) fresh cilantro leaves (*hara dhaniya*), finely chopped
1 tsp cumin seeds (*jeera*)
1 tsp julienned peeled fresh ginger (*adrak*)
1 tsp red chile powder
1 green chile, finely chopped
Salt, to taste
2 tsp olive oil
1 Tbsp (15 g) butter
2 burger buns, split
½ cup (120 g) sliced onion
1 medium-size tomato, sliced
1 Tbsp (20 g) ketchup

METHOD

1. In a small bowl, whisk the eggs, cilantro, cumin seeds, ginger, red chile powder, and green chile. Season to taste with salt.
2. In a small skillet over medium heat, heat the olive oil.
3. Pour half the egg batter into the skillet and spread it evenly. Cook on both sides until golden brown. Remove and set aside. Repeat with the remaining egg batter.
4. Butter one half of each bun and place an omelet on top. Layer with onion and tomato slices.
5. Apply ketchup to the other halves of the buns and close the sandwiches. Cut the burgers in half and serve with mint-cilantro chutney (page 28), if desired.

MEAT AND PORK

## BHOPALI KEEMA

Minced mutton stew with fried green chiles.

Cooking time: 35 minutes | Serves: 3   Origin: Madhya Pradesh

### INGREDIENTS

1 Tbsp (6 g) garam masala
1 Tbsp (30 g) dried mango powder (*amchoor*)
2 tsp red chile powder
Juice of 1 lemon (*nimbu*)
5 green chiles, slit
Vegetable oil, for frying
1 Tbsp (15 g) ghee
1 Tbsp (15 g) ginger-garlic paste (*adrak-lasan*)
1½ cups (360 g) minced mutton (*keema*)
1 large onion, finely chopped
1 large tomato, finely chopped
Salt, to taste
1 Tbsp (6 g) julienned peeled fresh ginger
¼ cup (4 g) fresh cilantro leaves (*hara dhaniya*),
   finely chopped

### METHOD

1.  In a small bowl, stir together the garam masala, dried mango powder, red chile powder, and lemon juice. Stuff the green chiles with this mixture.
2.  In a deep skillet over low-medium heat, heat the vegetable oil for frying.
3.  Carefully add the stuffed chiles to the hot oil and shallow-fry until charred.
4.  In another skillet over low-medium heat, heat the ghee.
5.  Add the ginger-garlic paste. Sauté until fragrant.
6.  Add the mutton. Cook for 12–15 minutes until the meat is thoroughly cooked.
7.  Add the onion and tomato. Sauté until they soften. Season to taste with salt.
8.  Add the fried green chiles and simmer for 2–3 minutes more.
9.  Garnish with ginger and cilantro to serve.

## FILFORA

Coarsely ground lamb curry.

Cooking time: 2 hours | Serves: 6-7   Origin: Madhya Pradesh

### INGREDIENTS

5 cups (80 g) fresh cilantro leaves (*hara dhaniya*),
   finely chopped
4 cups (256 g) fresh mint leaves (*pudina*), chopped
9 oz (250 g) green chiles, chopped
2 tsp ginger paste (*adrak*)
2 tsp garlic paste (*lasan*)
1 lb, 2 oz (500 g) tomatoes, finely chopped
1 cup (240 g) yogurt (*dahi*)
2 lb, 3 oz (1 kg) leg of lamb, pounded
¼ cup (50 g) raw papaya (*kachcha papita*),
   ground to paste (optional)
½ cup (100 ml) vegetable oil
2 medium-size onions, finely chopped
1 tsp garam masala
Salt, to taste

### METHOD

1.  In a large bowl, mix the cilantro, mint leaves, green chiles, ginger paste, garlic paste, and tomatoes.
2.  Add the yogurt and the pounded lamb. Using your hands mix well. Refrigerate overnight. If you don't have enough time, add the raw papaya paste as this will tenderize the mutton within 3 hours.
3.  In a skillet over low-medium heat, heat the vegetable oil.
4.  Add the onions and garam masala. Sauté until brown. Season to taste with salt.
5.  Reduce the heat to low. Add the lamb mixture and, stirring occasionally, simmer for 1½ hours. Serve hot.

## BHOPALI KORMA
Vetivier-hinted mutton korma.

Cooking time: 1 hour | Serves: 2     Origin: Madhya Pradesh

INGREDIENTS

For the mutton
2 cups (480 g) mutton, cubed
2 Tbsp (30 g) ginger-garlic paste (*adrak-lasan*)
2 cups (480 ml) water
Salt, to taste
For the paste
1 cup (240 g) fried onion (*birista*; page 30)
1 cup (240 g) yogurt (*dahi*)
8 peppercorns (*sabut kalimirch*)
2 tsp coriander seeds (*dhaniya*)
2 tsp cumin seeds (*jeera*)
1 cinnamon stick (*dalchini*)
2 tsp cardamom seeds (*elaichi*)
1 tsp ground mace (*javitri*)
2 bay leaves
Salt, to taste
For the gravy
2 Tbsp (30 g) ghee
1½ tsp red chile powder
1½ tsp fennel seeds (*saunf*)
Pinch ground nutmeg (*jaiphal*)
Pinch ground mace (*javitri*)
1 cup (240 g) yogurt (*dahi*)
2 tsp vetivier water (*kewra*)

METHOD

1. **To make the mutton:** In a pressure cooker, combine the mutton and ginger-garlic paste, water, and salt to taste. Lock the lid in place and close the pressure release valve. Select Manual/Pressure Cook and cook for 5 minutes.
2. Release the pressure and remove the lid. Remove the mutton pieces and reserve the stock.
3. **To make the paste:** In a blender, add the fried onions, yogurt, peppercorns, coriander seeds, cumin seeds, cinammon stick, cardamom seeds, mace, bay leaves, and salt to taste. Blitz until a paste forms.
4. **To make the gravy:** In a skillet over medium heat, heat the ghee. Add the red chile powder, fennel seeds, nutmeg, and mace. Sauté for 4–5 minutes.
5. Stir in the yogurt and cook for 7–8 minutes more.

6. Add the onion-spice paste and stir to combine. Continue to cook the gravy for 10 minutes.
7. Add the mutton pieces. Reduce the heat to low and simmer for 15 minutes. Adjust seasoning and finish with vetivier water. Serve hot.

· · · · · · · · · · · · ·

## BUNDELI GOSHT 📷
Goat curry, traditionally cooked in a clay pot.

Cooking time: 1 hour 30 minutes | Serves: 3
Origin: Madhya Pradesh

INGREDIENTS

2 Tbsp (30 g) ghee
1 Tbsp (15 g) whole spice mix (page 22)
1 tsp cumin seeds (*jeera*)
2 Tbsp (30 g) ginger-garlic paste (*adrak-lasan*)
5 Tbsp (75 g) onions, sliced and deep-fried (*birista*; page 30)
1 medium-size tomato, finely chopped
1 green chile, finely chopped
1 Tbsp (6 g) garam masala
1 tsp red chile powder
1 tsp ground turmeric (*haldi*)
2 cups (480 g) cubed mutton
6 cups (1.4 L) water
2 cups (400 g) chickpeas (*chana*), boiled
Salt, to taste
Freshly ground black pepper (*kali mirch*), to taste

METHOD

1. In a heavy-bottomed skillet over low-medium heat, heat the ghee.
2. Add the whole spice mix and cumin seeds. Cook until the spices begin to crackle.
3. Add the ginger-garlic paste and fried onions. Stir well.
4. Stir in the tomato, green chile, garam masala, red chile powder, and turmeric. Sauté for 8–9 minutes.
5. Add the mutton. Sauté until the masalas have coated the meat well.
6. Add the water. Reduce the heat to medium and cook the mutton for 40–45 minutes until fully done.
7. Add the boiled chickpeas and cook for 5 minutes more. Finish to taste with salt and pepper before serving.

# FISH AND SEAFOOD

## BHOJPURI FISH CURRY
Fish curry with aromatic spices.

Cooking time: 30 minutes | Serves: 4  Origin: Madhya Pradesh

### INGREDIENTS

6 dried red chiles (*sookhi lal mirch*)
2 Tbsp (22 g) mustard seeds (*rai*)
2 tsp coriander seeds (*dhaniya*)
1½ tsp cumin seeds (*jeera*)
1 tsp ground turmeric (*haldi*)
1 tsp freshly ground black pepper (*kali mirch*)
1 Tbsp (15 g) garlic paste (*lasan*)
1 tsp ginger paste (*adrak*)
8 rohu fish fillets, or carp or other white-fleshed
    fish (available at some Indian markets)
2 Tbsp (30 ml) mustard seed oil (page 26)
1 bay leaf (*tej patta*)
2 medium-size tomatoes, finely chopped
Salt, to taste
Juice of ½ lemon (*nimbu*)
¼ cup (4 g) fresh cilantro leaves (*hara dhaniya*),
    finely chopped

### METHOD

1. In a blender or mortar and pestle, combine the dried red chiles, mustard seeds, coriander seeds, cumin seeds, turmeric, pepper, garlic paste, and ginger paste. Blend into a fine paste. Rub this paste all over the fish and let marinate for 10 minutes.
2. In a skillet over medium heat, heat the mustard seed oil.
3. Working in batches, add the marinated fish and fry until golden and crispy. Remove and set aside.
4. Return the skillet to medium heat and add the bay leaf and any leftover paste to the oil left in the skillet. Sauté for 10 minutes.
5. Stir in the tomatoes and cook until soft. Finish with salt to taste, lemon juice, cilantro, and the fried fish. Cook until heated through and serve.

## MAHI BE-NAZEER 📷 🍽

A rich fish gravy.

Cooking time: 30 minutes | Serves: 4  Origin: Madhya Pradesh

### INGREDIENTS

½ cup (72 g) almonds (*badam*)

½ cup (120 g) yogurt (*dahi*)

3 Tbsp (45 ml) heavy cream

Salt, to taste

8 pieces fish (rohu preferably), cubed

1 cup (240 g) ghee

1 cup (240 g) sliced onion

1 Tbsp (15 g) garlic paste (*lasan*)

1 Tbsp (15 g) ginger paste (*adrak*)

1 Tbsp (6 g) ground coriander (*dhaniya*)

2 tsp red chile powder

1 tsp ground cardamom (*elaichi*)

½ tsp ground cumin (*jeera*)

¼ tsp ground cloves (*laung*)

¼ tsp ground cinnamon (*dalchini*)

1 Tbsp (15 ml) vetivier water (*kewra*; available at Indian markets)

### METHOD

1. In a food processor, blend the almonds, yogurt, cream, and salt into a fine paste. Rub this on the fish and let marinate for 10 minutes.

2. In a skillet over medium heat, heat the ghee.

3. Add the onion. Sauté until golden brown. Use a slotted spoon to transfer the onion to a food processor or mortar and pestle and grind into a fine paste.

4. Return the skillet and remaining ghee to medium heat and add the garlic paste, ginger paste, coriander, red chile powder, cardamom, cumin, cloves, and cinnamon. Sauté until the fat begins to float on the top.

5. Add the marinated fish and brown onion paste. Stir well to combine. Reduce the heat to low and cook uncovered for 10–15 minutes, stirring occasionally.

6. Finish with vetivier water and serve.

VEGETARIAN

# DAL BAFLA

Ghee-laden dough balls served with spiced pigeon peas.

Cooking time: 1 hour | Serves: 2     Origin: Madhya Pradesh

## INGREDIENTS

**For the bafla**

1 cup (125 g) whole-wheat flour (*atta*)
¼ cup (62.5 g) maize flour (*makkai*)
1 Tbsp (15 g) ghee
1 tsp cumin seeds (*jeera*)
Pinch carom seeds (*ajwain*)
Salt, to taste
Water, as needed

**For the dal (pigeon peas)**

1 Tbsp (15 ml) vegetable oil
Pinch ground asafoetida (*hing*)
1 tsp mustard seeds (*rai*)
1 tsp ground turmeric (*haldi*)
1 tsp red chile powder
1 cup (200 g) split pigeon peas (*toor dal*), soaked for 2 hours in water, drained
Water, as needed
Salt, to taste
¼ cup (4 g) fresh cilantro leaves (*hara dhaniya*), finely chopped

## METHOD

1. Preheat the oven to 400°F (200°C).
2. **To make the bafla:** In a medium-size bowl, mix together the bafla ingredients to form a smooth dough. Divide the dough into 6–8 small balls.
3. Fill a saucepan with water and place it over high heat. Bring to a rolling boil.
4. Add the dough balls. Once they begin to float on top of the water's surface, remove them from water and drain. Once dry, transfer to a baking sheet and bake for 20 minutes until crisp and golden.
5. **To make the dal (pigeon peas):** In a skillet over medium heat, heat the vegetable oil.
6. Add the asafoetida, mustard seeds, turmeric, and red chile powder. Stir to combine.
7. Add the pigeon peas and enough water to just cover. Bring to a boil and season to taste with salt. Reduce the heat to low and let simmer for 30 minutes, or until the pigeon peas soften.
8. Finish with cilantro. Serve the dal with the hot bafla.

# BURHANPURI DAL

Lentils spiked with whole spices.

Cooking time: 40 minutes | Serves: 2   Origin: Madhya Pradesh

## INGREDIENTS

3 Tbsp (45 g) ghee, divided
1 Tbsp (10 g) ground cinnamon (*dalchini*) and clove (*laung*) mix
1 Tbsp (15 g) ginger-garlic paste (*adrak-lasan*)
1 Tbsp (6 g) garam masala
1 tsp ground turmeric (*haldi*)
1 medium-size tomato, finely chopped
1 cup (200 g) black lentils (*urad dal*)
2 cups (480 ml) water
1 tsp cumin seeds (*jeera*)
1 tsp coriander seeds (*dhaniya*)
Salt, to taste

## METHOD

1. On your pressure cooker, select Sauté and add 1 Tbsp (15 g) of ghee to melt.
2. Add the cinnamon-clove mix, ginger-garlic paste, garam masala, and turmeric. Sauté for 5–6 minutes.
3. Add the tomato. Sauté until soft.
4. Add the black lentils and stir-fry once.
5. Add the water. Lock the lid in place and close the pressure release valve. Select Manual/Pressure Cook for 9 minutes. Let the pressure release and remove the lid.
6. In a small skillet over low-medium heat, heat the remaining 2 Tbsp (30 g) of ghee.
7. Add the cumin seeds and coriander seeds. Cook until the seeds begin to crackle. Add the seeds to the lentils and stir in the spices well. Season to taste with salt and serve.

## ARBI KI KADHI
Taro root curry.

Cooking time: 30 minutes | Serves: 2     Origin: Chhattisgarh

### INGREDIENTS

1 cup (240 g) yogurt (*dahi*)
2 Tbsp (16 g) water chestnut flour (*singhada*)
2 tsp red chile powder
1 tsp ground turmeric (*haldi*)
Salt, to taste
1 Tbsp (15 ml) vegetable oil
1 tsp cumin seeds (*jeera*)
1–2 dried red chiles (*sookhi lal mirch*)
1 cup (240 g) taro root (*arbi*), peeled, sliced and
    fried
¼ cup (4 g) fresh cilantro leaves (*hara dhaniya*),
    finely chopped

### METHOD

1. In a small bowl, whisk the yogurt, water chestnut flour, red chile powder, and turmeric. Season to taste with salt. Set aside.
2. In a small skillet over low-medium heat, heat the vegetable oil.
3. Add the cumin seeds and dried red chiles. Cook until the seeds begin to crackle.
4. Stir in the yogurt mixture. Season to taste with salt and cook for 8–9 minutes.
5. Add the fried taro root. Simmer for 3–4 minutes and garnish with cilantro before serving.

## BATKAR KADHI
Yogurt-lentil curry tempered with spices.

Cooking time: 50 minutes | Serves: 2     Origin: Chhattisgarh

### INGREDIENTS

1 cup (200 g) split red gram (*masoor dal*)
3 cups (720 ml) water, divided
Salt, to taste
1 Tbsp (7.5 g) chickpea flour (*besan*)
1 cup (240 g) yogurt (*dahi*)
1 Tbsp (15 ml) vegetable oil
2 dried red chiles (*sookhi lal mirch*)
2 green chiles, minced
1 tsp mustard seeds (*rai*)
Pinch fenugreek seeds (*methi*)
1 tsp ground turmeric (*haldi*)
1 tsp red chile powder
4 garlic cloves (*lasan*), minced

### METHOD

1. In your pressure cooker cooking pot, combine the red gram, 2 cups (480 ml) of water, and a pinch of salt. Lock the lid in place and close the pressure release valve. Select Manual/Pressure Cook and cook for 6 minutes.
2. Let the pressure release and remove the lid. Set aside to cool. When cool, drain.
3. In a small bowl, whisk the chickpea flour with the remaining 1 cup (240 ml) of water and the yogurt until smooth. Set aside.
4. In a skillet over low-medium heat, heat the vegetable oil.
5. Add the dried red chiles, green chiles, mustard seeds, and fenugreek seeds. Cook until the seeds begin to crackle.
6. Add the turmeric, red chile powder, and garlic. Cook, stirring, for 1 minute.
7. Add the cooked red gram and the yogurt mixture. Stir to combine and season to taste with salt. Reduce the heat to low and let the mixture bubble for 20 minutes. Serve hot with aromatic steamed rice, if desired.

## BHOJPURI DUM ALOO
Festive-season potato gravy.

Cooking time: 1 hour | Serves: 2          Origin: Madhya Pradesh

### INGREDIENTS

**For the filling**

1 Tbsp (15 g) ghee

½ medium-size onion, finely chopped

2 Tbsp (30 g) ginger-garlic paste (*adrak-lasan*)

½ cup (112.5 g) grated boiled peeled potato

2 tsp garam masala

1 tsp red chile powder

1 tsp ground turmeric (*haldi*)

1 lb, 1 oz (480 g) boiled baby potatoes, halved,
  centers scooped out slightly, shells deep-fried

1 Tbsp (15 ml) freshly squeezed lemon juice
  (*nimbu*)

Salt, to taste

**For the gravy**

1 Tbsp (15 ml) vegetable oil

1 Tbsp (15 g) whole spice mix (page 22)

1 bay leaf (*tej patta*)

1 tsp cumin seeds (*jeera*)

½ medium-size onion, finely chopped

2 Tbsp (30 g) ginger-garlic paste (*adrak-lasan*)

2 tsp garam masala

1 tsp ground turmeric (*haldi*)

1 tsp red chile powder

¾ cup (180 g) yogurt (*dahi*)

Salt, to taste

### METHOD

1. **To make the filling:** In a skillet over medium heat, heat the ghee.
2. Add the onion and ginger-garlic paste. Sauté for 4–5 minutes.
3. Add the grated potato, garam masala, red chile powder, turmeric, and scooped-out centers of baby potatoes. Sauté for 5 minutes more. Season with the lemon juice and salt to taste.
4. Stuff the filling into the fried potato shells and cover with another shell.
5. **To make the gravy:** In a skillet over low-medium heat, heat the vegetable oil.
6. Add the whole spice mix, bay leaf, and cumin seeds. Cook until the seeds begin to crackle.
7. Add the onion and ginger-garlic paste. Sauté for 2–3 minutes.
8. Stir in the garam masala, turmeric, red chile powder, and yogurt. Season to taste with salt. Reduce the heat to low and let the gravy bubble for 7–9 minutes.
9. Once the water from the yogurt evaporates, add the stuffed potatoes and simmer the dum aloo for 4–7 minutes until warmed through. Serve hot.

# BASTAR BODA CURRY
Earthy mushroom curry.

Cooking time: 30 minutes | Serves: 2      Origin: Chhattisgarh

## INGREDIENTS

1 Tbsp (15 ml) mustard seed oil (page 26)
1 Tbsp (15 g) julienned peeled fresh ginger (*adrak*)
1 Tbsp (15 g) sliced garlic (*lasan*)
1 cup (100 g) mushrooms
½ cup (85 g) finely chopped onion
1 green chile, finely chopped
3 Tbsp (45 g) cilantro paste
1 Tbsp (6 g) ground coriander (*dhaniya*)
2 tsp red chile powder
1 tsp ground turmeric (*haldi*)
1 tsp ground cumin (*jeera*)
1 tsp garam masala
1 medium-size tomato, finely chopped
Salt, to taste

## METHOD

1. In a skillet over medium-high heat, heat the mustard seed oil.
2. Add the ginger and garlic. Cook until fragrant.
3. Add the mushrooms. Reduce the heat to low and cook for 10 minutes. Transfer the mushrooms to a plate.
4. Return the skillet to medium heat. Add the onion, green chile, and cilantro paste. Sauté for 2–3 minutes.
5. Stir in the coriander, red chile powder, turmeric, cumin, and garam masala. Cook, stirring, for 2–3 minutes.
6. Add the tomato and cook until softened.
7. Stir in the mushrooms and season to taste with salt. Serve hot.

# MALWA-STYLE AMLI KADHI
Sour curry with chickpea flour and spices.

Cooking time: 20 minutes | Serves: 2   Origin: Madhya Pradesh

## INGREDIENTS

1 Tbsp (15 ml) vegetable oil
1 tsp cumin seeds (*jeera*)
1 tsp fenugreek seeds (*methi*)
1 tsp coriander seeds (*dhaniya*)
2–3 curry leaves (*kadhi patta*)
2 green chiles, finely chopped
¼ cup (60 g) tamarind pulp (*imli*; page 30)
1 Tbsp (7.5 g) chickpea flour (*besan*), mixed with water to form a paste
3 Tbsp (45 g) powdered jaggery (*gur*; unrefined cane sugar)
Salt, to taste

## METHOD

1. In a skillet over low-medium heat, heat the vegetable oil.
2. Add the cumin seeds, fenugreek seeds, coriander seeds, curry leaves, and green chiles. Cook until the seeds begin to crackle.
3. Stir in the tamarind pulp. Sauté for 1–2 minutes.
4. Add the chickpea flour paste and jaggery. Stir vigorously to ensure there are no lumps. Add water as needed to adjust the soup-like consistency of the kadhi. Season to taste with salt. Reduce the heat to low and simmer the curry for 15–17 minutes. Serve hot.

# RICE AND BREADS

# BAFAURI
Light and healthy steamed buns.

Cooking time: 20 minutes | Makes: 8     Origin: Chhattisgarh

## INGREDIENTS

½ cup (100 g) Bengal gram (split chickpeas;
  *chana dal*), soaked in water for 5 hours, drained
½ cup (30 g) finely chopped spring onion
  (*hara pyaz*)
¼ cup (4 g) fresh cilantro leaves (*hara dhaniya*),
  finely chopped
2 green chiles, finely chopped
1 Tbsp (15 g) ginger-garlic paste (*adrak-lasan*)
1 tsp carom seeds (*ajwain*)
1 tsp baking soda
1 tsp ground turmeric (*haldi*)
Salt, to taste
Freshly ground black pepper (*kali mirch*), to taste
Water, as needed

## METHOD

1. In a blender or food processor, grind the chickpeas into a smooth paste.
2. Add the remaining ingredients and process until well combined.
3. Add enough water to adjust the consistency—it should be as thick as pancake batter.
4. Using a ladle, pour a thin layer of batter into idli steamer molds and steam for 20 minutes. Unmold and serve hot.

. . . . . . . . . .

# CHUSELA
Rice flour puris.

Cooking time: 30 minutes | Makes: 8     Origin: Chhattisgarh

## INGREDIENTS

1 cup (160 g) rice flour
Water, for kneading
Salt, to taste
Vegetable oil, for deep-frying

## METHOD

1. In a small bowl, mix the rice flour, water, and salt to taste. Knead into a tight dough. Cut into 8 small roundels and roll them into puris (flatbreads).
2. In a deep skillet over medium-high heat, heat the vegetable oil for frying.
3. Carefully add the puris to the hot oil and deep-fry until golden on both sides. Serve.

. . . . . . . . . . . .

# CHANA DAL KI PURI
Chickpea-stuffed fritters.

Cooking time: 30 minutes | Makes: 8   Origin: Madhya Pradesh

## INGREDIENTS

1 cup (125 g) whole-wheat flour (*atta*)
1 Tbsp (15 g) ghee, plus more for frying
Salt, to taste
Water, for kneading
1 cup (200 g) Bengal gram (split chickpeas;
  *chana dal*), boiled
2 tsp cumin seeds (*jeera*)
2 tsp carom seeds (*ajwain*)
1 tsp nigella seeds (*kalonji*)

## METHOD

1. In a medium-size bowl, combine the flour, ghee, salt, and enough water to knead the mixture into a soft dough.
2. In a small bowl, combine the chickpeas, cumin seeds, carom seeds, and nigella seeds. Season to taste with salt.
3. Cut the dough into 6–8 small roundels and flatten each with your fingers.
4. Place a spoonful of the chickpea mixture in the center and seal it by rolling the dough into a ball again. Roll out the dough into 8 small puris.
5. In a skillet over low-medium heat, heat the ghee for frying.
6. Add the puris and fry until golden brown on both sides.

# ANGAAKAR ROTI

Gluten-free rotis spiked with fresh cilantro.

Cooking time: 20 minutes | Makes: 8  Origin: Madhya Pradesh

INGREDIENTS

1 cup (160 g) rice flour
3–4 Tbsp (32–42 g) chopped onion
2 green chiles, finely chopped
2–3 Tbsp (2–3 g) fresh cilantro leaves (*hara dhaniya*), finely chopped
Salt, to taste
Water, for kneading
1 Tbsp (15 ml) vegetable oil, plus more for frying

METHOD

1. In a small bowl, combine the rice flour, onion, green chiles, cilantro, and salt to taste. Add enough water to knead it into a tight dough and finish with the vegetable oil.
2. Cut the dough into 8 small roundels and roll them into flat rotis, patting with your fingers (like pancakes).
3. Place a large skillet over medium heat, add enough vegetable oil to coat the bottom of the skillet.
4. Cook the rotis on both sides until golden brown. Serve hot.

# BEDMI PURI

Fried and spiced breakfast bread.

Cooking time: 20 minutes | Makes: 8  Origin: Madhya Pradesh

INGREDIENTS

1½ cups plus 2 Tbsp (200 g) whole-wheat flour (*atta*)
½ cup (100 g) black lentils (*urad dal*), soaked in water, drained, and ground to a paste
1 Tbsp (15 ml) vegetable oil, plus more for frying
2 Tbsp (21 g) semolina (*suji*)
1 Tbsp (10 g) rice flour
1 tsp ground fennel seed (*saunf*)
1 tsp red chile powder
1 tsp ground coriander (*dhaniya*)
¼ cup (4 g) fresh cilantro leaves (*hara dhaniya*), finely chopped
Water, as needed

METHOD

1. In a medium-size bowl, combine the wheat flour, black lentil paste, vegetable oil, semolina, rice flour, ground fennel seed, red chile powder, coriander, and cilantro. Mix well.
2. Add enough water to knead the mixture into a tight dough. Cut the dough into 8 small roundels and roll them into small puris.
3. In a deep skillet over medium-high heat, heat the vegetable oil for frying.
4. Carefully add the puris to the hot oil and fry until golden on both sides.

## PALAK PURI
Spinach-infused fried bread.

Cooking time: 30 minutes | Makes: 15 Origin: Madhya Pradesh

### INGREDIENTS

1 cup (240 ml) spinach purée
2 cups (250 g) all-purpose flour (*maida*)
1 tsp ginger paste (*adrak*)
1 green chile, finely chopped
2 Tbsp (30 g) yogurt (*dahi*)
Salt, to taste
Water, for kneading
Vegetable oil, for frying

### METHOD

1.  In a medium-size bowl, combine the spinach purée, flour, ginger paste, green chile, and yogurt. Season to taste with salt. Add water as needed and knead into a tight dough. Set aside for 15 minutes.
2.  Cut the dough into 15 small roundels and roll out into puris.
3.  In a deep skillet over medium-high heat, heat the vegetable oil for frying.
4.  Carefully add the puris to the hot oil and deep-fry until golden brown on both sides. Serve hot.

## DUBRAJ RICE CHICKEN PULAO 📷
Aromatic rice laced with flavorful chicken.

Cooking time: 30 minutes | Serves: 2  Origin: Madhya Pradesh

### INGREDIENTS

1 cup (240 g) cubed chicken
1 cup (240 g) yogurt (*dahi*)
1 green chile, finely chopped
¼ cup (16 g) fresh mint leaves (*pudina*), finely chopped
¼ cup (4 g) fresh cilantro leaves (*hara dhaniya*), finely chopped, plus more for garnishing
8 peppercorns (*sabut kali mirch*)
1 Tbsp (15 g) butter
1 Tbsp (15 g) ginger-garlic paste (*adrak-lasan*)
1 Tbsp (6 g) garam masala
1½ tsp red chile powder
½ tsp green cardamom seeds (*choti elaichi*)
1 Tbsp (15 g) ghee
1 cup (200 g) Dubraj rice (a short-grained aromatic rice, found mainly in Madhya Pradesh, soaked in water for 30 minutes, drained
3 cups (720 ml) water
Salt, to taste

### METHOD

1.  In a medium-size bowl, combine the chicken, yogurt, green chile, mint, cilantro, peppercorns, butter, ginger-garlic paste, garam masala, red chile powder, and green cardamom seeds. Refrigerate to marinate for 2 hours.
2.  In a skillet over medium heat, heat the ghee.
3.  Add the chicken along with the marinade. Stir-fry for 2–3 minutes.
4.  Add the rice and water. Season to taste with salt. Cook until the rice in soft, the water has evaporated, and the meat is tender. Serve hot, garnished with cilantro.

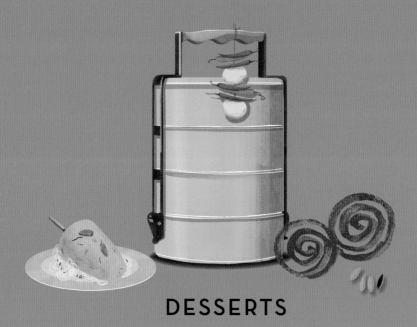

DESSERTS

## DOODH FARA

Indian-style tres leches.

Cooking time: 1 hour | Serves: 3        Origin: Chhattisgarh

### INGREDIENTS

½ cup (120 g) mawa (available at Indian markets, page 26)
4 Tbsp (50 g) caster (superfine) sugar, divided
1 Tbsp (9 g) finely chopped cashews (*kaju*)
½ cup (120 ml) water
¾ cup (120 g) rice flour
2 cups (480 ml) milk
1 tsp ground cardamom

### METHOD

1.  In a skillet over medium heat, roast the mawa until it turns light brown.
2.  Add 1 Tbsp (12.5 g) of caster sugar and the cashews. Mix well.
3.  In a small saucepan over high heat, bring the water to a rolling boil. Remove from the heat and stir in the rice flour. Knead into a soft dough and cut it into 8–9 small roundels. Roll each into a small circle and place the mawa in the center. Seal the sides and roll once again into a circle.
4.  In another small saucepan over medium heat, heat the milk and cardamom.
5.  Add the balls. Once the balls begin to float on top, scoop them out of the pan and continue to reduce the milk.
6.  Add the remaining 3 Tbsp (37.5 g) of sugar to the milk and cook until it thickens and reduces by half.
7.  Add the rice flour balls back into this milk and refrigerate for 3 hours before serving.

## GULGALE

Traditional whole-wheat dessert with fennel seeds.

Cooking time: 20 minutes | Makes: 6        Origin: Chhattisgarh

### INGREDIENTS

½ cup (62.5 g) whole-wheat flour (*atta*)
½ cup (100 g) caster (superfine) sugar
1 tsp salt
Vegetable oil, for the dough and for frying
3 Tbsp (45 g) yogurt (*dahi*)
1 tsp fennel seeds (*saunf*)
5 Tbsp (60 ml) water

### METHOD

1.  In a small bowl, stir together the flour, sugar, salt, 1 tsp of vegetable oil, the yogurt, and fennel seeds. Add enough water to make a thick batter. Whisk well to combine.
2.  In a deep skillet over low-medium heat, heat the vegetable oil for frying.
3.  Carefully drop spoonfuls of the batter into the hot oil (should make 6 pieces). Deep-fry until golden. Transfer to paper towels to drain. Serve hot.

## DOODH KI BARFI
Festive milk dessert with nuts.

Cooking time: 40 minutes | Makes: 12 Origin: Madhya Pradesh

### INGREDIENTS

Ghee, for preparing the baking sheet
4 cups (960 ml) milk
2 cups (400 g) sugar
½ cup (85 g) semolina (*suji*)
1 cup (240 g) whole-milk fudge (*khoya*; available at Indian markets; page 25)
1 tsp ground cardamom
1 Tbsp (15 g) finely chopped dried fruit

### METHOD

1. Grease a baking sheet with ghee and set aside.
2. In a saucepan over medium heat, bring the milk to a boil.
3. Add the sugar. Reduce the heat to low and simmer until the sugar is completely dissolved.
4. Stir in the semolina. Cook, stirring, for 4–5 minutes.
5. Add the whole-milk fudge and cardamom. Continue to cook for 7–8 minutes more, stirring constantly to avoid lumps. Stir until all the elements of the barfi come together. Pour the mixture onto the prepared baking sheet and let cool for 4–5 hours.
6. Cut into twelve, 1-in. (2.5-cm) square pieces and sprinkle the dried fruit on top before serving.

· · · · · · · · · · · ·

## SATTU KA HALWA
Ground lentil pudding.

Cooking time: 20 minutes | Serves: 2  Origin: Madhya Pradesh

### INGREDIENTS

4 cups (960 ml) milk
1 tsp saffron threads (*kesar*)
Powdered jaggery (*gur*; unrefined cane sugar), to taste
3 Tbsp (45 g) *sattu* (available at Indian markets)
2 tsp sliced almonds (*badam*)

### METHOD

1. In a thick-bottomed saucepan over medium heat, heat the milk.
2. Stir in the saffron threads and jaggery, stirring until the jaggery dissolves completely.
3. Add the *sattu*. Continue to cook for 5–6 minutes, stirring vigorously. The milk will begin to thicken and the halwa will come together.
4. Garnish with the almonds and serve hot.

· · · · · · · · · · · ·

## GAJAK
Popular winter sweet sesame snack.

Cooking time: 20 minutes | Makes: 6  Origin: Madhya Pradesh

### INGREDIENTS

3 Tbsp (45 g) ghee, plus more for preparing the baking sheet
¾ cup (108 g) white sesame seeds (*safed til*)
1 cup (200 g) sugar
3 Tbsp (45 ml) water
¼ cup (36 g) cashews (*kaju*), coarsely chopped
¼ cup (36.25 g) peanuts (*moongphali*), coarsely chopped
1 Tbsp (1.5 g) dried food-grade rose petals

### METHOD

1. Line a baking sheet with parchment paper and grease it with ghee. Set aside.
2. In a heavy-bottomed saucepan over low heat, roast the sesame seeds until slightly toasted. Remove from the heat and transfer the seeds to a bowl. Set aside.
3. Return the pan to the heat and melt the ghee.
4. Add the sugar and water. Allow it to bubble until it turns into a thick syrup. Remove from the heat and stir in the toasted sesame seeds, cashews, peanuts, and rose petals. Using a flat spatula spread the mixture evenly on the prepared sheet. While the mixture is still warm and soft, cut it into six 1-in. (2.5-cm) squares and allow it to set for 1 hour. Once it hardens, remove from the tray and store in airtight jars.

## KULFI FALOODA

Street-style Indian ice cream with summery flavors.

Cooking time: 20 minutes | Serves: 5   Origin: Madhya Pradesh

### INGREDIENTS

1 cup (240 ml) full-fat milk

1 cup (240 ml) heavy cream

1 Tbsp (7.5 g) cornflour

½ cup (60 g) powdered sugar

1 tsp saffron threads (*kesar*)

3 Tbsp (45 g) whole-milk fudge (*khoya*; available at Indian markets; page 25)

2 Tbsp (30 g) assorted sliced dried fruits

1 cup (200 g) vermicelli, soaked in water for 10–15 minutes, drained

5 tsp (25 ml) rose syrup (available at Indian markets)

2 tsp saffron syrup (optional; available at Indian markets)

½ cup (88 g) basil seeds (*sabja*) or chia seeds, soaked in water for 10–12 minutes or until sprouted

1 Tbsp (9 g) finely chopped assorted nuts

1 silver leaf, for garnishing (*warq*; optional; page 24; available at Indian markets)

### METHOD

1. In a medium-size saucepan over medium-high heat, bring the milk to a rolling boil.
2. Add the cream and cornflour. Stir well to combine.
3. Add the powdered sugar, saffron threads, and whole-milk fudge. Add the sliced dried fruits. Mix well. Bring the milk to another boil. Remove from the heat and set aside to cool.
4. Transfer to plastic kulfi molds and freeze until set. Once set, bring it out of the freezer.
5. In a tall glass, layer one-fifth of the vermicelli and place one piece of kulfi on top.
6. Drizzle 1 tsp of rose syrup and one-fifth of the saffron syrup (if using) on top. Add 1½ tsp of *sabja* or chia seeds on top.
7. Garnish with nuts and silver leaf (if using) and serve immediately.

## KHAZA

Rustic, crispy fried sweet rolls.

Cooking time: 40 minutes | Serves: 2   Origin: Madhya Pradesh

### INGREDIENTS

1 cup (125 g) all-purpose flour (*maida*)

1 Tbsp (15 ml) vegetable oil, plus more for frying

¼ cup (60 ml) warm water

2 cups (480 ml) warm sugar syrup (page 30)

1 tsp ground cardamom

### METHOD

1. In a small bowl, combine the flour, vegetable oil, and warm water. Knead into a soft dough. Let rest for 2 hours.
2. Cut the dough into 6–7 small roundels and roll large chapattis. Cut long strips of dough. Fold each strip lengthwise, 4–5 times and seal the corners.
3. In a deep skillet over medium-high heat, heat the vegetable oil for frying.
4. Carefully add the dough packages to the hot oil and deep-fry until golden brown. Transfer to paper towels to drain.
5. Place the sugar syrup in a large bowl.
6. Sprinkle the fried dough with the cardamom and drop into the sugar syrup. Let soak for 10 minutes. Remove from the syrup and serve.

# PARWAL KA MEETHA

Unique stuffed gourd dessert.

Cooking time: 1 hour | Serves: 3    Origin: Madhya Pradesh

## INGREDIENTS

1 cup (240 g) whole-milk fudge (*khoya*; available at
  Indian markets; page 25)
1 cup (200 g) sugar
3 Tbsp (45 ml) milk
1 tsp ground cardamom
1 Tbsp (10 g) milk powder
1 tsp saffron threads (*kesar*)
1 Tbsp (15 g) finely chopped dried fruits
1 tsp baking soda
1 cup (240 g) peeled and seeded pointed gourd
  (*parwal*; available at Indian markets), slit
2 cups (480 ml) warm sugar syrup (page 30)
Silver leaves, for garnishing (*warq*; optional;
  page 24; available at Indian markets)

## METHOD

1. In a heavy-bottomed saucepan over medium
   heat, dry-roast the whole-milk fudge until it
   softens slightly.
2. Add the sugar and stir until the sugar is
   completely dissolved.
3. Stir in the milk and cardamom. Remove from
   the heat and add the milk powder, saffron
   threads, and dried fruits. Let the mixture cool
   completely.
4. Fill a medium-size pot with water and add the
   baking soda. Place it over high heat and bring
   to a boil. Add the gourd and boil for 5 minutes,
   or until it softens. Drain and transfer to a
   medium-size bowl. Add the warm sugar syrup
   and let soak for 1 hour.
5. Scoop out the gourd from the syrup and stuff
   the whole-milk fudge mixture into the slit.
   Serve warm garnished with silver leaf (if using).

# MAWA BATTI

Dense sweet dough soaked in sugar syrup.

Cooking time: 1 hour | Serves: 4    Origin: Madhya Pradesh

## INGREDIENTS

For the sugar syrup
3 cups (600 g) sugar
1½ cups (360 ml) water
2 tsp saffron threads (*kesar*)
For the baati
½ cup (72.5 g) mixed nuts, finely chopped
Pinch ground cardamom
2 cups (480 g) mawa (available at Indian markets,
  page 26)
2 Tbsp (16 g) all-purpose flour (*maida*)
3 Tbsp (30 g) milk powder
Milk, as needed
Ghee, for deep-frying

## METHOD

1. **To make the sugar syrup:** In a heavy-bottomed
   saucepan over low-medium heat, combine the
   sugar and water. Cook, stir continuously and
   bring to a boil. Boil until you achieve a two-
   thread consistency (page 30–31), also called
   soft-ball stage. Remove from heat and add the
   saffron threads. Set aside.
2. **To make the baati:** In a small bowl, mix the nuts
   with the cardamom and set aside.
3. In a medium-size bowl, combine the mawa,
   flour, and milk powder. Knead it into a smooth
   dough. Add 2–3 Tbsp (30–45 ml) of milk if it
   doesn't come together. Divide the dough into
   7–8 small disks and flatten with your fingers.
   Place some of the nut mixture in the center of
   each and roll into small balls.
4. In a deep skillet over low heat, heat the ghee for
   deep-frying.
5. Carefully add the balls to the hot ghee and
   deep-fry until brown and crispy. Drain and dip
   in the warm sugar syrup. Let soak in the liquid
   for 1 hour before serving.

ACCOMPANIMENTS

# GURMA

Bhojpuri mango dip.

Cooking time: 15 minutes | Makes: 100 grams
Origin: Madhya Pradesh

INGREDIENTS

1 Tbsp (8 g) whole-wheat flour (*atta*)
2 Tbsp (30 ml) water
2 tsp ghee
1 tsp cumin seeds (*jeera*)
1 tsp fennel seeds (*saunf*)
1 semi-ripe mango (*kairi*), peeled, pitted, and
   roughly chopped
2 Tbsp (25 g) sugar
Pinch ground cinnamon (*dalchini*)

METHOD

1. In a heavy-bottomed saucepan over medium-heat, dry-roast the flour until it turns light brown.
2. Add the water and stir continuously so no lumps form.
3. In a small skillet over low-medium heat, heat the ghee.
4. Add the cumin seeds and fennel seeds. Sauté until they begin to crackle.
5. Add the mango and cook for 4–5 minutes.
6. Stir in the flour-water mixture and stir well to combine.
7. Add the sugar and let it bubble for about 3 minutes more. Finish with cinnamon and serve hot.

# JEERAVAN MASALA

Indore's all-purpose spice mix.

Cooking time: 20 minutes | Makes: 100 grams
Origin: Madhya Pradesh

INGREDIENTS

2 black cardamom pods (*badi elaichi*)
2 whole cloves (*laung*)
1 (½-in. / 1.25-cm) piece dried ginger (*adrak*)
1 small nutmeg (*jaiphal*)
1 Tbsp (6 g) fennel seeds (*saunf*)
5 dried red chiles (*sookhi lal mirch*)
1 bay leaf (*tej patta*)
1 tsp coriander seeds (*dhaniya*)
1 Tbsp (6 g) cumin seeds (*jeera*)
1 tsp dried mango powder (*amchoor*)
1 tsp ground cinnamon (*dalchini*)
1 tsp ground turmeric (*haldi*)
1 tsp Indian black salt (*kala namak*)
½ tsp ground mace (*javitri*)
Pinch ground asafoetida (*hing*)

METHOD

1. In a heavy-bottomed skillet over medium heat, combine the black cardamom pods, cloves, ginger, nutmeg, fennel seeds, dried red chiles, bay leaf, coriander seed, and cumin seeds. Roast until slightly warm. Transfer to a blender or mortar and pestle and let cool.
2. Add the dried mango powder, cinnamon, turmeric, black salt, asafoetida, and mace. Grind to a fine powder and store in airtight jars.

## BHOPALI SEEKH KEBAB MASALA

Spice mix for kebabs.

Cooking time: 30 minutes | Makes: 30 grams
Origin: Madhya Pradesh

### INGREDIENTS

1 tsp carom seeds (*ajwain*)
1 tsp dried ginger powder (*sonth*)
1 tsp cumin seeds (*jeera*)
1 Tbsp (8 g) red chile powder
10 peppercorns (*sabut kali mirch*)
2 (1-in. / 2.5-cm) cinnamon sticks (*dalchini*)
1 star anise (*chakri ke phool*)
2 black cardamom pods (*moti elaichi*)
1 Tbsp (6 g) tailed pepper (*kabab chini*)
1 Tbsp (5 g) coriander seeds (*dhania*)
1 (2-in. / 5-cm) piece mace
1 tsp ground turmeric (*haldi*)
1 Tbsp (7 g) paprika
1 tsp garam masala
Salt, to taste

### METHOD

1. In a skillet over low-medium heat, add the carom seeds, dried ginger, cumin, red chile powder, peppercorns, cinnamon, star anise, black cardamom pods, tailed pepper, coriander, mace, turmeric, paprika, and garam masala. Season to taste with salt.
2. Dry-roast until the mixture is fragrant.
3. Remove from the skillet and allow the mixture to cool.
4. Blend the mixture in a food processor into a fine powder and stock in an airtight jar.

## GHAMANDI-STYLE LASSI

Rose- and cardamom-infused yogurt drink.

Cooking time: 10 minutes | Serves: 2   Origin: Madhya Pradesh

### INGREDIENTS

1 cup (240 g) yogurt (*dahi*)
½ cup (120 ml) cold water
½ cup (120 ml) heavy cream
1 Tbsp (15 ml) rose water
1 tsp ground cardamom
½ tsp saffron threads (*kesar*)
Sugar, to taste

### METHOD

1. In a blender, combine all the ingredients. Blitz into a thick shake.
2. Transfer to 2 tall glasses and serve chilled.

## NARIYAL SHERBAT
Coconut crush.

Cooking time: 5 minutes | Serves: 2    Origin: Madhya Pradesh

INGREDIENTS

2 cups (480 ml) coconut water (*nariyal*)
½ cup (125 g) coconut flesh (*nariyal*)
½ cup (120 ml) water
Sugar, to taste

METHOD

1.  In a blender, blitz all the ingredients together into a thick shake.
2.  Transfer into tall glasses and serve chilled.

· · · · · · · · · · · ·

## MAHUA LEMONADE
Wild honey tree lemonade.

Cooking time: 10 minutes | Serves: 4   Origin: Madhya Pradesh

INGREDIENTS

2 cups (480 ml) sugar syrup (page 30)
2 cups (480 ml) freshly squeezed lemon juice
   (*nimbu*)
5 Tbsp (75 ml) honey tree concentrate (*mahua*;
   available at Indian markets)
Water, as needed
Ice, for serving

METHOD

1.  In a medium-size bowl, stir together the sugar syrup, lemon juice, honey tree concentrate, and water as desired.
2.  Serve in tall glasses with lots of ice.

## KENTHA/BAEL CHUTNEY
Cool wood apple chutney.

Cooking time: 20 minutes | Makes: 20 grams
Origin: Madhya Pradesh

INGREDIENTS

1 wood apple (*kentha/bael*)
¼ cup (84 g) jaggery (*gur*), grated
1 tsp cumin seeds (*jeera*)
2 tsp red chile powder
Salt, to taste

METHOD

1.  Scoop the flesh out of the wood apple.
2.  In a food processor or immersion blender, add the scooped-out flesh, grated jaggery, cumin seeds, red chile powder, and salt. Blend it into a fine paste. Serve immediately.

# west india

● ● ● ● ●

RAJASTHAN . GUJARAT . MAHARASHTRA . GOA

ncluding the largest Indian state by area, Rajasthan, the colorful Gujarat, and the coastal regions Maharashtra and Goa, West India is an untapped culinary gem.

Maharashtra and Goa are both lands that seek inspiration from the availability of seafood and of tropical fruits and veggies, and yet are distinct from each other. In Maharashtra, especially in the rural region, the cuisine is a motley group of wheat-, rice-, jowar-, and bajra-based dishes (especially breads), spicy gravies loaded with vegetables, and lentils. The dishes are enriched with coconut, sugar, and dairy.

Mumbai, the capital of Maharashtra, is an extraordinary culinary hub. It was originally inhabited by a fishing community called the Kolis, and the city's food today is as diverse as its inhabitants. From Parsis to Biharis, Muslims to Catholics, the city is one of India's true metropolises. It boasts of both cutting-edge chef-owned restaurants and iconic street food staples.

Today, Mumbai is the financial capital of the country and therefore there is a constant influx of travelers and migrants from other parts of India and abroad (it has one of the largest expat communities in the country), making it a melting pot of cuisines and culture. To keep everyone satiated, the city has developed a thriving street food and cheap-eats culture that is a mix of Udupi, Lucknowi, Hyderabadi, Guajarati, and Tibetan cuisines.

Two street snacks particularly stand out—the vada pav and toastie. While the former has chickpea-batter-fried potato dumpling stuffed inside *laadi* pav (chunks of dough stuck together), the latter is spiced potato stuffed into square-shaped bread and roasted on kerosene stoves.

The city plates up other street snacks as well, like *khichiya* papad (crispy disks topped with finely chopped veggies), sev, *dosa*, and Kutchi *dabeli*—largely a result of immigrant communities settled here and young professionals in need of quick-fix meals.

Mumbai houses some of the best restaurants in the country, and typical in the city are its charming Iranian cafes. Originally started by Zoroastrian immigrants from Iran who migrated to India and Pakistan in the 19th century, Iranian cafes were perhaps Mumbai's first brush with cafe culture.

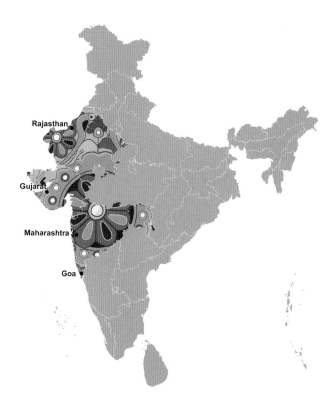

Today, these eateries serve Parsi and Iranian dishes such as berry pulao, dhansak, everyday omelets, lamb samosas, *akuri*, keema pav, mincemeat cutlets, Shrewsbury biscuits, Iranian chai, and pop-pink raspberry soda.

These spaces are usually no-frills, with wooden chairs, high ceilings, and glass tabletops. More recently, Iranian cafes have received international attention because of London's trendy Iranian-cafe-inspired restaurant Dishoom, which is now a regular feature in several top restaurant awards.

Any discussion of food and Mumbai is incomplete without mentioning the "dabbawallahs." Originating in 1890, the word "dabbawallah" literally translates to the "one who carries the box." This unionized cluster of men take charge to deliver hot food from people's homes, via a complex color-coded system, to their offices each day, and all their earnings are divided among the entire commune. The workings of dabbawallahs are so clever and unique that the Harvard Business School studied the system to understand how they work so flawlessly.

In neighboring Goa, the cuisine is heavily influenced by the 400 years of Portuguese colonization of the region. Here, matriarchs still cook using well-guarded family recipe books, passed down from one generation to another, using ingredients that the Portuguese introduced to Goa. Beef and pork were introduced to the Catholic converts by the Portuguese. They also brought with them potatoes, guavas, *sapotas*, chiles, and tomatoes, and recipes such as pork-laced vindaloo, *seradurra*, *bebinca*, guava cheese, and dishes that are now commonplace in Goan cuisine.

Goan breads are a noteworthy Portuguese import. From *poee*, to *kakkon*, to *pokshe*, to *katre*, you are likely to spot a variety of breads in Goan bakeries, most of which were introduced to them by the Portuguese, who also taught them the fine art of fermenting the dough.

Traditionally the Hindus of Goa were pescetarians, very much like the pandits of Kashmir. The Goan larder is stocked with ingredients such as *kokum*, palm jaggery, and plantains, while coconut milk and coconut cream replace dairy counterparts.

The other two states, Rajasthan and Gujarat, are predominantly vegetarian. Rajasthan is broadly divided into the Marwar and Mewar regions, which fall on either side of the Aravalli mountain range.

For centuries, Mewar was ruled by the Rajputs, who were connoisseurs of good food and good life. They were non-vegetarian and ate game meat, which led to the origin of dishes such as *laal maas*, *safed maas*, and *jungli maas*, and game dishes such as *khad khargosh*. Like royal cuisine in other parts of the country, the Rajput meal is painstakingly cooked, with hours of labor in the kitchen.

In contrast, Marwari cuisine contains an interesting range of vegetarian curries, gravies, and vegetables that play with a variety of beautiful textures. A local favorite is *kersangri*—made with *ker*, a shrub berry, and *sangri*, the bean of a flowering tree called *khejar*. According to a local saying, during summer in the Thar Desert, when all vegetation perishes, *ker* and *khejar* trees always bloom. This is because their roots run so deep that they can store water for up to seven months. When *ker* and *sangri* are cooked together with a tempering of spices, the dish is eaten as a main course. The berry and bean are also pickled to eat later.

Rajasthan is home to the largest chunk of the Thar Desert, and therefore vegetables are limited. The local cuisine has benefited from enterprising additions such as *mangodi*, *vadi*, papad, and *gattas*—

mostly flour-based dumplings or sheets boiled in hot curry, just like homemade pastas. The dishes are moderately spiced and there is abundant usage of dairy, especially yogurt, cream, ghee, and milk.

Similar flavors and ingredients are also savored in Gujarat, where the cuisine is predominantly vegetarian, and even underdog vegetables such as yams, stalks of spring onion, cluster beans, cabbage, dill leaves, and radish are used. Gujarati cuisine is known for its thali (a full-plate meal), which serves over twenty foods in one plate, with vegetables, ghee-soaked chapattis, lentil- or yogurt-based curries, milk- and *khoya*-based desserts, and *farsaan* or savories, such as *dhokla*, *patra*, and *khandvi*, along with a tall glass of buttermilk. What separates traditional Gujarati fare from vegetarian cooking in other parts of the country is the sprinkling of sugar or jaggery even in savory dishes.

The Bohri and Parsi communities of Gujarat contribute heavily to the non-vegetarian cuisine of the state. Originally a trading community, the Bohris speak Lisan ud-Dawat, a dialect of the Gujarati language, and are clustered in cities such as Baruch and Surat. Their community is known for dishes such as chicken *salan*, with a dash of vinegar, mincemeat cutlets, *malida* (a dessert of Afghani origin), and *dabba gosht*, a pasta-speckled baked dish.

The Parsis who migrated from Iran to Gujarat between the 8th and 10th centuries, to avoid persecution following the Arab conquest of Persia, brought with them Iranian dishes with heavy Middle Eastern influences.

Their basic meal was a combination of rice with meats or fish, sweets based on vermicelli, and semolina flavored with spices such as saffron, nutmeg, and cinnamon. Over time they adopted local ingredients resulting in dishes such as dhansak, which used lentils and vegetables. They also savored khichdi and chapattis, which were predominantly Indian, and made space for the "masala dabba" (box containing basic Indian spices), a mainstay in their kitchens.

As we explored the cuisine of these four states, we realized that they are quite different from each other. With the topography changing every few kilometers, the produce is varied throughout the land. And while they are geographically tight-knit, their cuisines are anything but similar.

DEBIT CARD & CREDIT CARD NOT ACCEPTED
PLEASE DO NOT ARGUE WITH MANAGEMENT
MANAGEMENT HAS GOT RIGHT TO CHECK ANY ARTICLE OR INDIVIDUAL ON SUSPICION
CUSTOMERS ARE REQUESTED TO TAKE CARE OF THEIR BELONGINGS

# APPETIZERS

# FAJETO

Sweet and tangy mango soup.

Cooking time: 30 minutes | Serves: 2    Origin: Gujarat

## INGREDIENTS

2 cups (480 ml) water
1 cup (240 g) yogurt (*dahi*)
½ cup (120 g) mango pulp (*aam*)
1 Tbsp (7.5 g) chickpea flour (*besan*)
1 Tbsp (21 g) grated jaggery (*gur*; unrefined
    cane sugar)
1 tsp ginger-chile paste (*adrak-mirch*)
1 tsp ground turmeric (*haldi*)
1 tsp vegetable oil
2 Kashmiri dried red chiles (*sookhi lal mirch*)
1 tsp mustard seeds (*rai*)
1 tsp cumin seeds (*jeera*)
2 curry leaves (*kadhi patta*)
Pinch ground asafoetida (*hing*)
1 tsp ground cinnamon (*dalchini*)
½ tsp ground cloves (*laung*)
½ tsp ground ginger (*sonth*)
Salt, to taste

## METHOD

1.  In a medium-size bowl, stir together the water, yogurt, mango pulp, chickpea flour, jaggery, ginger-chile paste, and turmeric. Use an immersion blender to blend until smooth. Alternatively, transfer to a standard blender and blend until smooth.
2.  In a skillet over medium-high heat, heat the vegetable oil.
3.  Add the dried red chiles, mustard seeds, cumin seeds, curry leaves, and asafoetida. Cook until the seeds begin to crackle.
4.  Stir in the cinnamon, cloves, and ginger.
5.  Add the mango-yogurt mixture and bring to a rolling boil. Season to taste with salt and serve hot.

# DOODHI NA MUTHIA 🍲

Steamed, spiced bottle gourd and whole-wheat rounds—a Gujarati savory.

Cooking time: 40 minutes | Serves: 2    Origin: Gujarat

## INGREDIENTS

1 cup (250 g) grated bottle gourd (calabash; *lauki*),
    water squeezed out
½ cup (62.5 g) whole-wheat flour (*atta*)
¼ cup (30 g) chickpea flour (*besan*)
1 Tbsp (10.5 g) semolina
1½ tsp ginger-chile paste (*adrak-mirch*)
1 tsp ground turmeric (*haldi*)
Juice of 1 lemon (*nimbu*)
1 tsp sugar
¼ cup (4 g) fresh cilantro leaves (*hara dhaniya*),
    finely chopped
2 pinches ground asafoetida (*hing*), divided
Salt, to taste
1 tsp baking soda
1 Tbsp (15 ml) vegetable oil, plus more for frying
1 tsp mustard seeds (*rai*)
1 tsp fenugreek seeds (*methi dana*)
1 tsp white sesame seeds (*safed til*)
2 curry leaves (*kadhi patta*)
1 green chile, finely chopped

## METHOD

1.  In a medium-size bowl, combine the bottle gourd, whole-wheat flour, chickpea flour, semolina, ginger-chile paste, turmeric, lemon juice, sugar, cilantro, a pinch of asafoetida, salt, baking soda, and vegetable oil. Add just enough water to knead the mixture into a soft dough. Roll it out into ½-in.-thick (1.25-cm) and 3-in. long (7.5-cm) cylinders.
2.  In a steamer, steam the cylinders for 30 minutes, or until cooked through. Remove and set aside.
3.  Once cool, cut into ½-in. (1.25-cm) pieces.
4.  In a skillet over low-medium heat, heat 2 Tbsp (30 ml) of vegetable oil.
5.  Add the mustard seeds, fenugreek seeds, sesame seeds, remaining pinch of asafoetida, curry leaves, and green chile. Cook until the seeds begin to crackle. Pour the tempering over the cylinders (*muthias*). Serve hot.

# CHORAFALI

Crisp golden spicy puffs.

| Cooking time: 40 minutes | Serves: 4 | Origin: Gujarat |
|---|---|---|

## INGREDIENTS

2 cups (240 g) chickpea flour (*besan*)
½ cup (60 g) split black lentil flour (*urad dal*)
2 tsp red chile powder, plus more as needed
1 tsp rice flour
1 tsp Indian black salt (*kala namak*)
½ tsp ground turmeric (*haldi*)
Pinch baking soda
Salt, to taste
¾ cup (180 ml) warm water
Vegetable oil, for frying

## METHOD

1.  In a medium-size bowl, combine the chickpea flour, black lentil flour, red chile powder, rice flour, black salt, turmeric, baking soda, and salt. Add the warm water and knead the mixture into a soft dough. Roll the dough into a thin disk, like a lasagna sheet. Cut the disk into 1½- to 2-in. (3.5- to 5-cm) strips with a sharp knife.
2.  In a wok over low-medium heat, heat the vegetable oil for frying.
3.  A few at a time, deep-fry the strips until light brown and crisp. With tongs or a slotted spoon, transfer to paper towels to drain. If you want a little more spice, sprinkle the hot chips with more red chile powder. Let cool to room temperature and store in airtight jars.

# HANDVO 🍲

Savory rice and lentil cakes.

| Cooking time: 30 minutes | Serves: 2 | Origin: Gujarat |
|---|---|---|

## INGREDIENTS

½ cup (100 g) rice
⅓ cup (34 g) split green gram (*moong dal*)
¼ cup (50 g) pigeon peas (*toor dal*)
2 Tbsp (25 g) split black lentils (*urad dal*)
2 Tbsp (25 g) Bengal gram (split chickpeas; *chana dal*)
½ cup (120 g) yogurt (*dahi*)
¼ cup (60 g) grated bottle gourd (calabash; *lauki*),
¼ cup (40 g) green peas (*hara matta*), boiled
¼ cup (27.5 g) grated carrot (*gajar*)
1 tsp red chile powder
1 tsp ground turmeric (*haldi*)
1 tsp ginger-chile (*adrak-mirch*) paste
Salt, to taste
1 Tbsp (15 ml) vegetable oil, plus more as needed
1 tsp mustard seeds (*rai*), divided
1 tsp white sesame seeds (*safed til*), divided
Pinch ground asafoetida (*hing*)
2 curry leaves (*kadhi patta*)
Juice of 1 lemon (*nimbu*)

## METHOD

1.  In a large bowl, combine the rice, green gram, pigeon peas, split black lentils, and chickpeas. Add enough water to cover and let soak for 6 hours.
2.  Drain and transfer to a blender or food processor. Process until smooth. Add the yogurt and pulse to combine. Transfer to a medium-size bowl and set aside to ferment overnight.
3.  Stir in the bottle gourd, green peas, carrot, red chile powder, turmeric, and ginger-chile paste. Season to taste with salt. Mix well.
4.  In a skillet over low-medium heat, heat the vegetable oil.
5.  Add ½ tsp of mustard seeds, ½ tsp of sesame seeds, the asafoetida, and curry leaves. Cook until the seeds begin to crackle.
6.  Pour in half of the fermented batter. Cook for 6–7 minutes, or until the handvo is crisp on the outside. Flip and cook the other side until crisp, too. Remove and repeat steps 4 through 6. Cut into squares and serve hot.

# KHAMAN 🍲

Steamed chickpea flour cakes tempered with mustard seeds.

Cooking time: 30 minutes | Serves: 2 · · · · · · · Origin: Gujarat

## INGREDIENTS

1 cup (120 g) chickpea flour (*besan*)
1 Tbsp (10.5 g) semolina
2 tsp sugar
1 tsp freshly squeezed lemon juice (*nimbu*)
Salt, to taste
1 tsp fruit salt
1 Tbsp (15 ml) vegetable oil
1 tsp mustard seeds (*rai*)
1 tsp white sesame seeds (*safed til*)
Pinch ground asafoetida (*hing*)
2 curry leaves (*kadhi patta*)
1 green chile, finely chopped
Sev (available at Indian markets), for garnishing
Grated fresh coconut (*nariyal*), for garnishing

## METHOD

1. In a medium-size bowl, combine the chickpea flour, semolina, sugar, lemon juice, salt, and fruit salt. Stir in enough water to form a thick pancake-like batter. Pour the batter onto a rimmed plate and steam in a steamer for 15 minutes, or until a toothpick inserted into the center of the cake comes out clean.

2. In a skillet over medium-high heat, heat the vegetable oil.

3. Add the mustard seeds, sesame seeds, asafoetida, curry leaves, and green chile. Cook until the seeds begin to crackle. Pour the tempering over the steamed cake. Serve garnished with sev and grated coconut.

# SABUDANA KHICHDI 🍲

Healthy sago pearls tempered with chiles and topped with crushed peanuts.

Cooking time: 30 minutes | Serves: 2 · · · · · · · Origin: Gujarat

## INGREDIENTS

1 Tbsp (15 ml) vegetable oil
1 green chile, finely chopped
1 tsp cumin seeds (*jeera*)
1 tsp red chile powder
2 curry leaves (*kadhi patta*)
1½ cups (225 g) sago (*sabu dana*), soaked in water for 2 hours, drained
½ cup (112.5 g) boiled cubed potato
Salt, to taste
¼ cup (4 g) fresh cilantro leaves (*hara dhaniya*)
Juice of 1 lemon (*nimbu*)
½ cup (72 g) roasted peanuts (*moongphali*), coarsely chopped

## METHOD

1. In a skillet over medium-high heat, heat the vegetable oil.

2. Add the green chile, cumin seeds, red chile powder, and curry leaves. Sauté for 2–3 minutes.

3. Add the sago and potato. Season to taste with salt. Cook for 9–12 minutes until the spices and oil coat the ingredients well. Serve hot, garnished with cilantro, a dash of lemon juice, and roasted peanuts.

# KHANDVI 🍲

Bite-sized chickpea and yogurt rolls tempered with sesame seeds.

| Cooking time: 30 minutes | Serves: 2 | Origin: Gujarat |
| --- | --- | --- |

INGREDIENTS

1 Tbsp (15 ml) vegetable oil, plus more for greasing the plate

1 cup (120 g) chickpea flour (*besan*)

¼ cup (60 g) yogurt (*dahi*)

1 tsp ground turmeric (*haldi*)

1 tsp red chile powder

Pinch ground asafoetida (*hing*)

3 cups (720 ml) water

Salt, to taste

1 tsp mustard seeds (*rai*)

1 tsp white sesame seeds (*safed til*)

1 green chile, finely chopped

¼ cup (4 g) fresh cilantro leaves (*hara dhaniya*), finely chopped

METHOD

1. Grease a rimmed plate with some vegetable oil and set aside.

2. In a bowl, stir together the chickpea flour, yogurt, turmeric, red chile powder, asafoetida, water, and salt, stirring continuously until you have a lump-free mixture.

3. Place a saucepan over medium heat and pour in the flour mixture. Cook, stirring continuously, until the mixture begins to thicken. Once it turns slurpy, pour a thin layer onto the prepared plate. Set aside for 10 minutes to cool, or until it hardens but is still warm. With a sharp knife, cut the hardened mixture into about 10 strips. Roll each strip like a roulade. Repeat with the remaining flour mixture, cooling, cutting, and rolling.

4. In a skillet over low-medium heat, heat the vegetable oil.

5. Add the mustard seeds, white sesame seeds, and green chile. Cook until the seeds begin to crackle. Pour the tempering over the rolled strips (*khandvi*). Serve warm or cold, garnished with cilantro.

# KUTCHI KADAK 📷

Toasts tossed with vegetables, topped with tamarind and mint relish.

| Cooking time: 30 minutes | Serves: 2 | Origin: Gujarat |
| --- | --- | --- |

INGREDIENTS

1 Tbsp (15 ml) vegetable oil

1 Tbsp (6 g) dabeli masala (available at Indian markets)

2 tsp minced garlic (*lasan*)

1½ tsp red chile powder

½ cup (120 g) grated boiled potato

¼ cup (42.5 g) finely chopped onion

¼ cup (60 g) finely chopped tomato

2 Tbsp (18 g) crushed peanuts (*moongphali*)

2 Tbsp (30 g) crunchy Indian noodles (spicy *sev*)

2 Tbsp (22 g) pomegranate seeds (*anar*)

Salt, to taste

10 pieces readymade toast (crispy crostini), available in bakeries

¼ cup (60 g) date-tamarind chutney (page 29)

¼ cup (60 g) mint chutney (page 28)

1 Tbsp (5 g) shredded dried unsweetened coconut (*nariyal*)

¼ cup (4 g) fresh cilantro leaves (*hara dhaniya*), finely chopped

METHOD

1. In a small skillet over medium heat, heat the vegetable oil.

2. Add the dabeli masala, garlic, and red chile powder. Stir well.

3. Add the potato. Cook, stirring, for 2–3 minutes.

4. In a medium-size bowl, combine the onion, tomato, peanuts, sev, and pomegranate seeds. Season to taste with salt. Toss well to mix.

5. Break the toasts in half and add to the tomato mixture. Let them rest in the mixture for a few minutes to soften a bit.

6. Add the spiced potato mixture and stir together with the toasts.

7. Drizzle the date-tamarind and mint chutneys over the toasts. Serve cold, garnished with coconut and cilantro.

## PANKI

Rice flour and yogurt pancakes cooked between banana leaves.

Cooking time: 40 minutes | Makes: 6        Origin: Gujarat

### INGREDIENTS

1 cup (160 g) rice flour
3 Tbsp (45 g) yogurt (*dahi*)
1 green chile, finely chopped
1 tsp ginger-chile paste (*adrak-mirch*)
1 tsp cumin seeds (*jeera*)
1 tsp ground turmeric (*haldi*)
Pinch ground asafoetida (*hing*)
Salt, to taste
6 banana leaves, cut into palm-size circles
1 tsp ghee

### METHOD

1. In a small bowl, stir together the rice flour and yogurt. Let rest for 2 hours.
2. Stir in the green chile, ginger-chile paste, cumin seeds, turmeric, and asafoetida. Season to taste with salt. Stir thoroughly into a thick pancake-like batter.
3. Grease the banana leaves with the ghee. Spread 1 ladle of batter on top of 3 leaves. Top each with another banana leaf.
4. Heat a griddle over medium heat.
5. Working in batches if needed, cook the banana leaf packages for 2–3 minutes per side. Repeat until all the batter is used up. Serve hot. Discard the leaves before serving.

## KOLHAPURI BHEL

Savory street snack made with vegetables and spices.

Cooking time: 10 minutes | Serves: 2        Origin: Maharashtra

### INGREDIENTS

1 cup (240 g) puffed rice (spicy *chivda*; available at Indian markets)
½ cup (120 g) farsaan mix (available at Indian markets)
½ cup (120 g) sev (available at Indian markets)
½ cup (8 g) fresh cilantro leaves (*hara dhaniya*), finely chopped
½ medium-size onion, finely chopped
½ medium-size tomato, finely chopped
6 papdi, crushed (available at Indian markets)
2 Tbsp (30 g) mint chutney (page 28)
2 Tbsp (30 g) tamarind-date chutney (page 29)
1 Tbsp (15 g) masala dal (available at Indian markets)
1 Tbsp (15 g) finely chopped mango (*kairi*)
2 tsp Maharashtrian lasan chutney (page 270)
Juice of 1 lemon (*nimbu*)

### METHOD

1. In a large bowl, mix all the ingredients and toss well to combine. Serve immediately.

# MIRCHI VADA

Deep-fried green chiles stuffed with spicy potato mash.

Cooking time: 30 minutes | Makes: 10        Origin: Rajasthan

## INGREDIENTS

1 cup (225 g) mashed potatoes
1 green chile, finely chopped
1 Tbsp (6 g) ground coriander (*dhaniya*)
2 tsp red chile powder
2 tsp dried mango powder (*amchoor*)
2 tsp fennel seeds (*saunf*)
1 tsp chaat masala
1 tsp ground cumin (*jeera*)
Salt, to taste
10 large green chiles, slit, seeded
1 cup (120 g) chickpea flour (*besan*)
Water, as needed
Vegetable oil, for deep-frying

## METHOD

1. In a medium-size bowl, stir together the mashed potatoes, chopped green chile, coriander, red chile powder, dried mango powder, fennel seeds, chaat masala, and cumin. Season to taste with salt. Stuff the large chiles with this mixture.
2. In a small bowl, mix the chickpea flour, salt to taste, and enough water to make a pancake-like batter.
3. In a deep skillet over medium-high heat, heat the vegetable oil for deep-frying.
4. Working in batches, dip the stuffed chiles into the batter and carefully add them to the hot oil. Deep-fry until golden. Transfer to paper towels to drain. Serve hot, with date-tamarind chutney (page 29).

# PAPAD CHURI

Roasted poppadum mixed with onions and spices.

Cooking time: 10 minutes | Serves: 2        Origin: Rajasthan

## INGREDIENTS

8.8 oz (250 g) poppadum (*bikaneri papad*; available at Indian markets), roasted, broken into medium-size pieces
8.8 oz (250 g) plain whole-wheat khakra (available at Indian markets), broken into medium-size pieces
½ cup (85 g) finely chopped onion
¼ cup (4 g) fresh cilantro leaves (*hara dhaniya*), finely chopped
2 Tbsp (30 g) fried onions (*birista*; page 30)
1 Tbsp (15 g) ghee
1 tsp red chile powder
1 tsp chaat masala
1 tsp ground cumin (*jeera*)
Juice of 1 lemon (*nimbu*)
Salt, to taste

## METHOD

1. In a deep bowl, combine all the ingredients. Mix well and serve as a snack.

## PITHORE

Chickpea flour squares—typical teatime snack.

Cooking time: 30 minutes | Serves: 2      Origin: Rajasthan

### INGREDIENTS

Ghee, for greasing the plate
1 cup (120 g) chickpea flour (besan)
1 cup (240 g) yogurt (dahi)
1 tsp ginger-garlic paste (adrak-lasan)
1 tsp red chile powder
1 tsp ground turmeric (haldi)
1 green chile, finely chopped
¼ cup (4 g) fresh cilantro leaves (hara dhaniya), finely chopped, plus more for garnishing
Salt, to taste
1 Tbsp (15 ml) vegetable oil, divided
1 tsp mustard seeds (rai)
1 tsp cumin seeds (jeera)
Pinch ground asafoetida (hing)
1 tsp white sesame seeds (safed til)
Juice of 1 lemon (nimbu)

### METHOD

1. Grease a plate (thali) with ghee and set aside.
2. In a medium-size bowl, combine the chickpea flour, yogurt, ginger-garlic paste, red chile powder, turmeric, green chile, cilantro, and salt.
3. In a skillet over medium heat, heat 1 tsp of vegetable oil.
4. Pour the chickpea flour mixture into the skillet and cook until it begins to leave the sides of the pan. Spread the mixture uniformly on the prepared plate. Let cool and rest for 1 hour.
5. Cut diamond-shaped squares out of the set mixture (pithore) and set aside.
6. In another skillet over medium-high heat, heat the remaining 2 tsp of vegetable oil.
7. Add the mustard seeds and cumin seeds. Cook until the seeds begin to crackle.
8. Add the asafoetida, sesame seeds, and the chickpea flour squares (pithore). Toss to ensure they are tempered well. Allow each piece to sizzle until slightly brown. Serve hot, garnished with cilantro and a dash of lemon juice.

## DAHI SAMOSA MAAS

Lamb-stuffed triangular puff pastries deep-fried and served with yogurt.

Cooking time: 40 minutes | Makes: 15      Origin: Rajasthan

### INGREDIENTS

1 Tbsp (15 ml) vegetable oil, plus for deep-frying
1 medium-size onion, finely chopped
1 Tbsp (15 g) ginger-garlic paste (adrak-lasan)
1 tsp finely chopped green chile
1 cup (240 g) minced lamb
Salt, to taste
1 Tbsp (6 g) garam masala
2 cups (480 g) yogurt (dahi), divided
¼ cup (4 g) fresh cilantro leaves (hara dhaniya), finely chopped
¼ cup (16 g) fresh mint leaves (pudina), finely chopped
2 Tbsp (30 g) fried onions (birista; page 30)
1 package samosa pastry sheets (samosa patti; available at Indian markets and online, page 33)
2 tsp sugar
1 tsp red chile powder
Ground coriander (dhaniya), for garnishing
Sev, for garnishing (available at Indian markets)

### METHOD

1. In a skillet over medium heat, heat the vegetable oil. Add the onion, ginger-garlic paste, and green chile. Sauté for 3–4 minutes.
2. Add the lamb and season to taste with salt. Cook until the lamb is thoroughly done.
3. Stir in the garam masala, ½ cup (120 g) of yogurt, the cilantro, mint, and fried onions. Remove from the heat and set aside to cool.
4. Place a spoonful of the lamb mixture on a samosa pastry sheet and wrap to enclose it in a triangular shape like spanakopita. Repeat until all the filling and pastry are used up.
5. In a deep pot over medium-high heat, heat the vegetable oil for deep-frying.
6. Working in batches if needed, carefully add the stuffed samosas to the hot oil and deep-fry until golden. Transfer to paper towels to drain.
7. In a small bowl, whisk the remaining 1½ cups (360 g) of yogurt with the sugar and red chile powder. Pour this over the fried samosas and serve garnished with coriander and sev.

# BOHRI-STYLE DRUMSTICKS

Deep-fried spicy chicken drumsticks.

| Cooking time: 40 minutes | Serves: 4 | Origin: Gujarat |
| --- | --- | --- |

INGREDIENTS

10 chicken drumsticks
1 cup (250 g) tomato purée
¼ cup (60 g) cashew paste (*kaju*)
1 Tbsp (15 g) ginger-garlic-chile paste (*adrak-lasan-mirch*)
1 Tbsp (6 g) garam masala
1 Tbsp (8 g) red chile powder
Salt, to taste
Freshly ground black pepper (*kali mirch*), to taste
1 egg yolk, whisked
1 Tbsp (15 ml) milk
Bread crumbs, for coating
Vegetable oil, for deep-frying

METHOD

1. With a fork, make 4–5 deep incisions around the fleshy part of the chicken pieces. Set aside.
2. In a small bowl, stir together the tomato purée, cashew paste, ginger-garlic-chile paste, garam masala, red chile powder, salt, and pepper. Rub this marinade into the chicken. Refrigerate to marinate for 2 hours.
3. In another small bowl, whisk the egg yolk and milk. Place the bread crumbs in a shallow dish.
4. Dip the marinated chicken in the egg yolk and then coat with bread crumbs. Repeat until all the drumsticks are coated.
5. In a deep skillet over low-medium heat, heat the vegetable oil for deep-frying.
6. Carefully add the drumsticks to the hot oil and deep-fry until golden brown and cooked through. Transfer to paper towels to drain. Serve hot.

# MURGI MINCED CUTLETS 📷

Melt-in-your-mouth chicken croquettes.

| Cooking time: 30 minutes | Makes: 10 | Origin: Gujarat |
| --- | --- | --- |

INGREDIENTS

1 cup (240 g) minced chicken
1 cup (225 g) mashed potatoes
3 Tbsp (45 ml) heavy cream
3 Tbsp (45 g) grated Cheddar cheese
2 green chiles, minced
1 Tbsp (15 g) ginger-garlic paste (*adrak-lasan*)
½ cup (62.5 g) all-purpose flour (*maida*)
Salt, to taste
Freshly ground black pepper (*kali mirch*), to taste
½ cup (57.5 g) bread crumbs
2 eggs, whisked
Vegetable oil, for deep-frying

METHOD

1. In a medium-size bowl, mix together the chicken, mashed potatoes, cream, cheese, green chiles, ginger-garlic paste, flour, salt, and pepper. Divide the mixture equally into 10 small portions. Shape each portion into a croquette.
2. Place the bread crumbs in a shallow bowl.
3. Dip the croquettes in the whisked egg and then coat them with bread crumbs. Repeat until all are coated.
4. In a deep skillet over medium-high heat, heat the vegetable oil for deep-frying.
5. A few at a time, carefully add the croquettes to the hot oil and deep-fry until golden brown and crisp. Transfer to paper towels to drain. Serve hot.

# POULTRY AND EGGS

# MURGH KI MOKUL

Shredded chicken cooked in yogurt.

Cooking time: 45 minutes | Serves: 4-6     Origin: Rajasthan

## INGREDIENTS

2 lb, 3 oz (1 kg) chicken pieces
1 cup (240 g) ghee
4 large onions, chopped
2 tsp red chile powder
2 tsp ground coriander (*dhaniya*)
1 tsp ground ginger (*adrak*)
1 tsp garlic powder (*lasan*)
1 tsp ground cumin (*jeera*)
1 cup (240 g) yogurt (*dahi*)
10 almonds (*badam*), blanched, ground
1 Tbsp (5 g) dried unsweetened coconut powder
   (*nariyal*)
Salt, to taste
½ tsp ground cardamom
4 green chiles, slit
1 Tbsp (1 g) fresh cilantro leaves (*hara dhaniya*),
   chopped
1 Tbsp (15 ml) rose water

## METHOD

1. In a large pot over high heat, boil the chicken for 15 minutes, or until tender. Remove the chicken from the water and set aside to cool. Debone and shred the chicken.
2. In a skillet over medium heat, heat the ghee.
3. Add the onions. Fry until light brown.
4. Add the red chile powder, coriander, ginger, garlic powder, and cumin. Cook until the oil separates, stirring briskly.
5. Stir in the yogurt, almonds, coconut powder, and shredded chicken. Reduce the heat to low and cook until the gravy thickens.
6. Season to taste with salt and stir in the cardamom. Serve hot, garnished with green chiles and cilantro. Add a dash of rose water just before serving.

# SABUT MURGH

Ginger-garlic flavored chicken cooked whole.

Cooking time: 45 minutes | Serves: 4-6     Origin: Rajasthan

## INGREDIENTS

1 medium-size whole chicken, cleaned
½ cup (120 ml) vegetable oil
2 medium-size onions, thinly sliced
1½ heads garlic (*lasan*), ground to a paste
1 (2-in. / 5-cm) piece peeled fresh ginger (*adrak*),
   ground to a paste
4 tsp red chile powder
4 tsp ground coriander (*dhaniya*)
½ tsp ground turmeric (*haldi*)
Salt, to taste

## METHOD

1. Prick the chicken all over with a fork.
2. In a large pot over medium heat, heat the vegetable oil.
3. Add the onions. Fry until brown.
4. Add the garlic paste and ginger paste. Fry until the oil separates.
5. Stir in the red chile powder, coriander, turmeric, and salt.
6. Add the chicken. Fry for a few minutes, turning. Cover the pot and reduce the heat to low. Cook until the chicken is tender, adding a little water, if needed, to keep the chicken from sticking to the bottom of the pot.
7. Once the chicken is done, uncover the pot and cook until the excess liquid evaporates. Serve hot.

# BOHRI-STYLE CHICKEN NU SALAN 📷

Chicken in sweet and sour curry.

Cooking time: 1 hour | Serves: 2      Origin: Gujarat

## INGREDIENTS

1 cup (240 g) chicken, bone-in pieces, chopped

1 Tbsp (15 g) ginger-garlic-chile paste (*adrak-lasan-mirch*)

1 Tbsp (15 ml) vinegar (*sirka*)

1½ cups (360 ml) water

3 Tbsp (18 g) chicken salan masala (available at Indian markets)

1 cup (240 g) yogurt (*dahi*)

½ cup (40 g) almond powder (*badam*)

½ cup (120 g) ketchup

½ cup (120 g) tomato paste

1½ tsp red chile powder

1½ tsp garam masala

Salt, to taste

Freshly ground black pepper (*kali mirch*), to taste

1 Tbsp (15 ml) vegetable oil

2 (1-in. / 2.5-cm) cinnamon sticks (*dalchini*)

2 curry leaves (*kadhi patta*)

1 medium-size onion, finely chopped

½ cup (8 g) fresh cilantro leaves (*hara dhaniya*), finely chopped

## METHOD

1. In a large pot over medium heat, combine the chicken, ginger-garlic-chile paste, vinegar, and water. Cook for 20–25 minutes, or until the meat is tender. Drain the chicken and reserve the stock. Set both aside.

2. In a blender, combine the chicken salan masala, yogurt, almond powder, ketchup, tomato paste, red chile powder, garam masala, salt, and pepper. Blend until smooth.

3. In a skillet over low-medium heat, heat the vegetable oil.

4. Add the cinnamon sticks and curry leaves. Cook until the leaves begin to crackle.

5. Add the onion. Stir-fry until golden brown.

6. Stir in the yogurt-almond mixture. Sauté until the water from the yogurt evaporates.

7. Add the cooked chicken pieces along with 1 cup (240 ml) of the cooking liquid. Let bubble for 10–12 minutes. Serve hot, garnished with cilantro. Season to taste with pepper just before serving.

## KAARI

Chicken drumsticks in coconut milk curry laced with spices.

Cooking time: 1 hour | Serves: 2       Origin: Gujarat

INGREDIENTS

2 Tbsp (30 g) ghee
1 Tbsp (15 g) whole spice mix (page 22)
2 green chiles, finely chopped
1 tsp cumin seeds (*jeera*)
1 Tbsp (15 g) ginger-garlic paste (*adrak-lasan*)
6 chicken drumsticks
2 cups (480 ml) coconut milk (*nariyal*)
7 Tbsp (42 g) kari masala (available at Indian markets)
1 Tbsp (5 g) desiccated coconut powder (*nariyal*)
1 cup (240 ml) water
1 Tbsp (15 g) tamarind paste (*imli*; page 30)
2 tsp red chile powder
Salt, to taste
¼ cup (4 g) fresh cilantro leaves (*hara dhaniya*), finely chopped

METHOD

1. In a skillet over low-medium heat, heat the ghee.
2. Add the whole spice mix, green chiles, and cumin seeds. Cook until the seeds begin to crackle.
3. Add the ginger-garlic paste. Sauté for 1 minute.
4. Add the chicken and stir well to coat in the spices. Reduce the heat to low and cook for about 20 minutes until the chicken is partially done.
5. Stir in the coconut milk, kari masala, coconut powder, and water. Reduce the heat to very low and cook for 20 minutes more, or until the meat is fully done.
6. Stir in the tamarind paste, red chile powder, and salt. Cook for 2–3 minutes. Serve hot, garnished with cilantro.

## BOHRA HARA MURGH

Coriander chicken served with assorted vegetables.

Cooking time: 30 minutes | Serves: 4       Origin: Gujarat

INGREDIENTS

1 cup (240 g) yogurt (*dahi*)
½ cup (120 g) cilantro paste (*hara dhaniya*)
2 green chiles, finely chopped
1 Tbsp (15 g) garlic paste (*lasan*)
Salt, to taste
Freshly ground black pepper (*kali mirch*), to taste
2 lb, 3 oz (1 kg) boneless chicken, cubed
1 Tbsp (15 ml) vegetable oil
1 Tbsp (15 g) whole spice mix (page 22)
½ cup (120 g) onion paste
1 tsp saffron threads (*kesar*)
1 cup (240 g) assorted cooked vegetables (optional)
1 medium-size tomato, sliced

METHOD

1. In a medium-size bowl, stir together the yogurt, cilantro paste, green chiles, garlic paste, salt, and pepper until smooth. Add the chicken and rub this spice paste into it. Refrigerate to marinate for 1 hour.
2. In a skillet over medium heat, heat the vegetable oil.
3. Add the whole spice mix. Cook until the spices begin to crackle.
4. Add the onion paste. Sauté until golden brown.
5. Add the marinated chicken. Reduce the heat to low and cook until the meat is tender and cooked through.
6. Add the saffron threads and vegetables (if using). Mix well. Taste and adjust the seasoning, if needed. Serve hot, garnished with tomato slices.

# BAFFADO DE GALINHA
Chicken in coconut gravy.

Cooking time: 35 minutes | Serves: 4-6      Origin: Goa

## INGREDIENTS

1 cup (85 g) shredded dried unsweetened coconut (*nariyal*)

Water, as needed

10 peppercorns (*sabut kali mirch*)

9 garlic cloves (*lasan*), minced

8 Kashmiri dried red chiles (*sookhi lal mirch*)

4 whole cloves (*laung*)

1 (1-in. / 2.5-cm) cinnamon stick (*dalchini*)

1 (1-in. / 2.5-cm) piece peeled fresh ginger (*adrak*), minced

1 tsp coriander seeds (*dhaniya*)

¾ tsp cumin seeds (*jeera*)

½ tsp raw rice (optional)

½ tsp ground turmeric (*haldi*)

¼ cup (60 ml) vegetable oil

2 medium-size onions, thinly sliced

2 lb, 3 oz (1 kg) chicken pieces (10–12)

2–3 green chiles, slit

2 tsp salt

3 Tbsp (45 ml) vinegar (*sirka*)

## METHOD

1. In a small bowl, soak the coconut in ½ cup (120 ml) of warm water or combine them in a blender and grind together. Strain the coconut and squeeze out the milk to extract 1 cup (240 ml) of thick coconut milk. Add 1 cup (240 ml) of warm water to the squeezed-out coconut pulp and then press it through a fine-mesh strainer to extract 1½ cups (360 ml) of thin coconut milk. Set both aside.

2. In a food processor or mortar and pestle, combine the peppercorns, garlic, dried red chiles, cloves, cinnamon stick, ginger, coriander seeds, cumin seeds, rice (if using), and turmeric. Grind into a smooth paste with just a very little water.

3. In a skillet over low-medium heat, heat the vegetable oil.

4. Add the onions. Sauté until golden.

5. Add the ground spice paste. Fry for 2 minutes.

6. Add the chicken. Increase the heat to high and fry for 3 minutes.

7. Stir in the thin coconut milk, green chiles, and salt. Bring the mixture to a boil. Partially cover the skillet. Reduce the heat as needed and simmer until the chicken is tender.

8. Stir in the vinegar and thick coconut milk. Simmer, uncovered, for 5 minutes. Remove and serve hot with rice, if desired.

# CARIL DE GALINHA 🍲

Chicken curry with coconut and tamarind.

Cooking time: 40 minutes | Serves: 6      Origin: Goa

## INGREDIENTS

2 lb, 3 oz (1 kg) boneless chicken, cubed
Salt, to taste
3 Tbsp (45 ml) coconut oil (*nariyal*)
1 medium-size onion, sliced
4 garlic cloves (*lasan*), minced
1 Tbsp (6 g) ground coriander (*dhaniya*)
1½ Tbsp (11 g) ground cumin (*jeera*)
1 tsp ground turmeric (*haldi*)
1 tsp freshly ground black pepper (*kali mirch*)
12 dried red chiles (*sookhi lal mirch*), powdered
½ cup (65 g) chopped carrot (*gajar*)
½ cup (55 g) diced potato
2 cups (480 ml) chicken broth
1½ cups (360 ml) coconut milk (*nariyal*; page 30)
3 Tbsp (45 g) tamarind paste (*imli*; page 30)

## METHOD

1. Season the chicken with salt and set aside for 30 minutes.
2. In a large pot over medium-high heat, heat the coconut oil.
3. Add the onion and garlic. Sauté until golden.
4. Meanwhile, in a small bowl, mix the coriander, cumin, turmeric, pepper, and powdered dried red chiles with enough water to make a thick paste. Add the spice paste to the onion mix and sauté for 2 minutes more.
5. Add the chicken, carrot, and potato. Cook for 2–3 minutes, stirring continuously.
6. Pour in the chicken broth and bring to a boil. Cook for about 12 minutes until the chicken and potatoes are tender.
7. Stir in the coconut milk. Boil for 2–3 minutes. Taste to adjust the seasoning with salt and stir in the tamarind paste. Serve hot.

# LAGAN NA TARKARI PER EDA 📷

Egg in a spicy tomato mixture.

Cooking time: 20 minutes | Serves: 6-8      Origin: Gujarat

## INGREDIENTS

5 Tbsp (75 ml) vegetable oil
1 tsp ginger-garlic paste (*adrak-lasan*)
4 green chiles, seeded, finely chopped
3 large tomatoes, peeled, seeded
½ cup (8 g) fresh cilantro leaves (*hara dhaniya*), finely chopped
1 Tbsp (15 ml) vinegar (*sirka*)
½ tsp red chile powder
½ tsp garam masala
Salt, to taste
3 medium-size onions, sliced, deep-fried (*birista*; page 30)
8 eggs

## METHOD

1. In a large heavy-bottomed skillet over medium heat, heat the vegetable oil.
2. Add the ginger-garlic paste. Sauté for 2 minutes.
3. Add the green chiles, tomatoes, cilantro, vinegar, red chile powder, and garam masala. Cook until the tomatoes are soft.
4. Stir in the salt and the fried onions. Flatten the mixture evenly in the pan and make 8 wells in it with the back of a spoon. Reduce the heat to low.
5. Break an egg into a saucer and slide it into one well. Repeat until all the wells are filled with eggs. Sprinkle lightly with salt. Cover the skillet and cook until the egg is set. Do not allow the eggs to become hard. Serve immediately.

# CHICKEN SAOJI 📷

Spicy chicken curry with a hint of coconut.

Cooking time: 1 hour | Serves: 4          Origin: Maharashtra

## INGREDIENTS

5 dried red chiles (*sookhi lal mirch*)

3 green cardamom pods (*choti elaichi*)

2 whole cloves (*laung*)

1 Tbsp (5g) coriander seeds (*dhaniya*)

1 tsp ground mace (*javitri*)

1 tsp fennel seeds (*saunf*)

1 tsp poppy seeds (khus khus)

1 tsp caraway seeds (*shahi jeera*)

2 Tbsp (10 g) coconut powder (*nariyal*)

2 Tbsp (16 g) sorghum flour (*jowar*)

1 Tbsp (15 ml) vegetable oil

1 tsp cumin seeds (*jeera*)

1 Tbsp (15 g) ginger-garlic paste (*adrak-lasan*)

1 tsp ground turmeric (*haldi*)

1 medium-size onion, chopped

2 lb, 3 oz (1 kg) bone-in chicken pieces

Salt, to taste

2 cups (480 ml) water

¼ cup (4 g) fresh cilantro leaves (*hara dhaniya*), chopped

## METHOD

1. In a skillet over low-medium heat, combine the dried red chiles, green cardamom pods, cloves, coriander seeds, mace, fennel seeds, poppy seeds, and caraway seeds. Dry-roast for 1–2 minutes.

2. Add the coconut powder and sorghum flour. Dry-roast for 30 seconds more. Remove from the heat, cool, and transfer to a food processor. Blend into a fine powder. Set aside.

3. In a skillet over medium-high heat, heat the vegetable oil.

4. Add the cumin seeds. Sauté until the seeds begin to crackle.

5. Stir in the ginger-garlic paste, turmeric, and dry-roasted spice powder. Mix well.

6. Add the onion. Sauté until golden.

7. Add the chicken pieces. Reduce the heat to medium and cook for 3–4 minutes.

8. Add the salt and water. Simmer the chicken for about 40 minutes, or until the meat is cooked. Serve hot, garnished with cilantro.

# MEAT AND PORK

## LAAL MAAS
Tender lamb in spicy, red-hot curry.

Cooking time: 1 hour 30 minutes | Serves: 2   Origin: Rajasthan

### INGREDIENTS

10 dried red chiles (*sookhi lal mirch*)
1 Tbsp (5 g) coriander seeds (*dhaniya*)
1 Tbsp (6 g) cumin seeds (*jeera*)
2 Tbsp (30 ml) vegetable oil
1 Tbsp (15 g) garlic paste (*lasan*)
1 tsp red chile powder
1 lb, 2 oz (500 g) bone-in lamb pieces, rinsed
5 peppercorns (*sabut kali mirch*)
2 green cardamom pods (*choti elaichi*)
1 (1-in. / 2.5-cm) cinnamon stick (*dalchini*)
1 tsp ground mace (*javitri*)
1 bay leaf (*tej patta*)
2 Tbsp (20 g) ground caper (*kachri,* optional;
   page 22)
1 medium-size onion, finely chopped
1½ cups (360 ml) water
Salt, to taste
¼ cup (4 g) fresh cilantro leaves (*hara dhaniya*),
   finely chopped

### METHOD

1. In a skillet over low-medium heat, combine the red chiles, coriander seeds, and cumin seeds. Dry-roast until fragrant. Transfer to a blender or mortar and pestle and grind the spices into a powder. Set aside.
2. Return the skillet to the heat and add the vegetable oil, garlic paste, red chile powder, and lamb. Stir-fry for 2–3 minutes, or until the meat is well coated in the oil.
3. Add the ground spice powder and mix well.
4. Add the peppercorns, green cardamom pods, cinnamon stick, mace, and bay leaf. Stir-fry for 1 minute.
5. Add the caper powder (if using) and onion. Sauté until the onion caramelizes.
6. Pour in the water, cover the skillet, and reduce the heat to low. Cook for about 30 minutes, or until the lamb is partially done. Remove the meat pieces and set aside.
7. Strain the gravy and remove the whole spices. Transfer the gravy back into the skillet and cook for 10 minutes, or until the fat begins to float on top and the gravy is reduced to 1 cup (240 ml).
8. Add the meat back to the pan and cook until the meat is cooked through and starts to leave the bones. Serve hot, seasoned to taste with salt and garnished with cilantro.

# BAJRE KA SOYTA
Millet and lamb porridge.

Cooking time: 2 hours 30 minutes | Serves: 4-6 Origin: Rajasthan

INGREDIENTS

1 lb, 2 oz (500 g) millet (*bajra*)
1 lb, 2 oz (500 g) lamb, cubed
Salt, to taste
6 cups (1.4 L) water, divided
½ cup (120 g) ghee
3 Tbsp (24 g) red chile powder
2 Tbsp (12 g) ground coriander (*dhaniya*)
1 tsp ground turmeric (*haldi*)
4 medium-size onions, sliced
1 (3-in. / 7.5-cm) piece peeled fresh ginger (*adrak*),
   ground to a paste
2–3 large garlic cloves (*lasan*), ground to a paste
15–20 green chiles, slit
2 Tbsp (2 g) fresh cilantro leaves (*hara dhaniya*),
   chopped
1 Tbsp (15 g) julienned peeled fresh ginger (*adrak*)
4–5 fresh red chiles, seeded, fried

METHOD

1. Place the millet in a medium-size bowl and sprinkle a little water on it. Set aside for 30 minutes. Pound lightly to split the grains. Pass through a sieve to remove the chaff.
2. In a medium-size saucepan over high heat, boil the lamb with salt and 1 cup (240 ml) of water until half done.
3. In a skillet over medium heat, heat the ghee.
4. Add the red chile powder, coriander, turmeric, and the millet. Sauté for 3 minutes.
5. Add the onions, ginger paste, garlic, lamb, and green chiles. Mix well.
6. Add the remaining 5 cups (1.2 L) of water. Reduce the heat to low and cook until the lamb is tender and the water is absorbed. Serve hot, garnished with cilantro, julienned ginger, and fried red chiles.

# ANJEER MAAS 📷
Robust lamb with figs.

Cooking time: 1 hour | Serves: 2                    Origin: Rajasthan

INGREDIENTS

1 Tbsp (15 g) ghee
2 dried red chiles (*sookhi lal mirch*)
1 tsp cumin seeds (*jeera*)
1 tsp fennel seeds (*saunf*)
1 (1-in. / 2.5-cm) cinnamon stick (*dalchini*)
1 medium-size onion, finely chopped
½ cup (75 g) figs (*anjeer*), soaked in water to
   soften, drained, finely chopped
1 Tbsp (15 g) finely chopped peeled fresh
   ginger (*adrak*)
1 green chile, finely chopped
1 Tbsp (6 g) ground coriander (*dhaniya*)
1½ cups (360 g) cubed boneless lamb
1 cup (240 ml) water
¼ cup (20 g) almond (*badam*)
¼ cup (20 g) cashew (*kaju*) meal
½ cup (120 g) yogurt (*dahi*)
3 Tbsp (45 ml) heavy cream
Salt, to taste

METHOD

1. On your pressure cooker, select Sauté and preheat the cooking pot.
2. Add the ghee.
3. When hot, add the dried red chiles, cumin seeds, fennel seeds, and cinnamon stick. Cook until the spices begin to crackle.
4. Add the onion, figs, and ginger. Lower the heat level to medium and sauté for 4 minutes.
5. Add the green chile and coriander. Sauté until the masalas are cooked and fragrant.
6. Add the lamb and stir well.
7. Add the water, almond powder, and cashew powder. Lock the lid in place and close the pressure release valve. Select Manual/Pressure Cook and cook for 40 minutes until the lamb is done. Release the pressure and remove the lid.
8. Stir in the yogurt and cream. Season to taste with salt. Serve hot.

# DHANSAK

Lamb cooked with mixed grams and vegetables.

Cooking time: 30 minutes | Serves: 6-8          Origin: Gujarat

## INGREDIENTS

¼ cup (50 g) split red gram (*masoor dal*)
1 cup (200 g) pigeon peas (*toor dal*)
¼ cup (50 g) green gram (*sabut moong dal*)
¼ cup (50 g) Bengal gram (*chana dal*)
3 Tbsp (45 ml) vegetable oil
3 medium-size onions, finely chopped
2 Tbsp (30 g) ginger-garlic paste (*adrak-lasan*)
2 Tbsp (20 g) dhansak masala (page 32)
2 lb, 3 oz (1 kg) lamb, cut into small pieces
¼ cup (50 g) red pumpkin (*lal kaddu*), chopped
1 eggplant (brinjal), small, chopped
2 small tomatoes, chopped
1 medium-size potato, chopped
3 cups (720 ml) water
Salt, to taste
1 tsp dried fenugreek leaves (*kasuri methi*)
For the garnish: fresh mint leaves, fresh cilantro
   leaves, green chiles, lemons

## METHOD

1. In large bowl soak the split red gram, pigeon peas, green gram, and Bengal gram for 1 hour. Drain and set aside.
2. In a skillet over medium-high heat, heat the vegetable oil.
3. Add the onions, ginger-garlic paste, and dhansak masala. Sauté until brown.
4. On your pressure cooker, select Sauté and preheat the cooking pot.
5. When hot add the meat, grams, pumpkin, eggplant, tomato, potato, the prepared onion mixture, and the water. Season to taste with salt.
6. Lock the lid in place and close the pressure release valve. Select the Manual/Pressure Cook and cook for 12 minutes. Release the pressure and remove the lid.
7. With a slotted spoon transfer the meat pieces into a bowl. Mash and strain the remaining mixture. Cook for 6 minutes.
8. Add the cooked meat pieces to the mixture. Add the dried fenugreek leaves and simmer until it becomes thick like a broth.
9. Garnish with mint leaves, lemon juice, chopped green chiles, and cilantro.

# BANJAARI GOSHT

A slow-cooked flavorful lamb prepared in yogurt.

Cooking time: 1 hour 30 minutes | Serves: 2   Origin: Rajasthan

## INGREDIENTS

1 Tbsp (15 ml) vegetable oil
¼ cup (60 g) crispy golden fried onions (*birista*;
   page 30)
2 dried red chiles (*sookhi lal mirch*)
2 Tbsp (30 g) ginger-garlic paste (*adrak-lasan*)
1 Tbsp (6 g) ground coriander (*dhaniya*)
2 tsp garam masala
1 tsp red chile powder
1 tsp ground turmeric (*haldi*)
¾ cup (180 g) yogurt (*dahi*), plus more to finish
   the gravy
9 oz (250 g) bone-in lamb pieces, rinsed
Salt, to taste
¼ cup (4 g) fresh cilantro leaves (*hara dhaniya*),
   finely chopped
1 tsp pounded dried red chiles (*sookhi lal mirch*)

## METHOD

1. In a skillet over low-medium heat, heat the vegetable oil.
2. Add the fried onions, dried red chiles, and ginger-garlic paste. Sauté for 2–3 minutes.
3. Stir in the coriander, garam masala, red chile powder, and turmeric. Stir-fry for 2 minutes.
4. Add the yogurt and lamb. Mix well. Season to taste with salt. Cover the skillet and reduce the heat to low. Cook for 1 hour, or until the meat is cooked and begins to leave the bones.
5. Stir in an additional spoonful of yogurt to give the gravy a creamy finish. Serve hot, garnished with cilantro and pounded dried red chiles.

# JARDALOO MA GOSHT

Lamb cooked with apricots.

| Cooking time: 30 minutes | Serves: 4 | Origin: Gujarat |
|---|---|---|

## INGREDIENTS

2 Tbsp (30 ml) vegetable oil

2–3 medium-size onions, chopped

6–8 garlic cloves (*lasan*), ground to a paste

1 (2-in. / 5-cm) piece peeled fresh ginger (*adrak*), ground to a paste

1 lb, 2 oz (500 g) lamb, cut into 1½–2 in. (3.75–5 cm) pieces

Salt, to taste

1 (2-in. / 5-cm) cinnamon stick (*dalchini*)

Sugar, to taste

9 oz (250 g) dried apricots (*khumani*), seeded, soaked in water for 4 hours

## METHOD:

1. In a wok over low-medium heat, heat the vegetable oil.
2. Add the onions. Sauté until golden brown.
3. Add the garlic paste and ginger paste. Sauté for 5–8 minutes.
4. Add the lamb, salt, and cinnamon stick. Sauté for about 3 minutes. Add enough water to cook the lamb until tender.
5. In a saucepan over low-medium heat, brown some sugar. Add the apricots and their soaking water and bring the mixture to the boil. Reduce the heat as needed and cook until the apricots are soft.
6. Stir the apricot stew into the cooked lamb. Cook until heated through. Serve hot.

# DABBA GOSHT

Pasta with shredded lamb cooked with vegetables in a white sauce.

| Cooking time: 1 hour | Serves: 4 | Origin: Gujarat |
|---|---|---|

## INGREDIENTS

**For the white sauce**

3 Tbsp (45 g) butter

½ cup (62.5 g) all-purpose flour (*maida*)

2 cups (480 ml) milk

¼ cup (30 g) grated Cheddar cheese

Salt, to taste

Freshly ground black pepper (*kali mirch*), to taste

**For the lamb**

⅓ cup (80 g) onion paste

1 Tbsp (15 g) ginger-garlic paste (*adrak-lasan*)

1½ tsp paprika

Salt, to taste

2 cups (480 g) boneless cubed lamb

2 Tbsp (30 g) butter

1 cup (240 g) assorted boiled vegetables

2 hardboiled eggs, peeled and chopped

2 cups (280 g) macaroni pasta, boiled

1 Tbsp (15 ml) vinegar (*sirka*)

½ cup (120 g) ketchup

¼ cup (20 g) cashew powder (*kaju*)

2 eggs, whisked

## METHOD

1. **To make the white sauce:** In a pan over medium heat, heat the butter. Add the flour. Stirring continuously, add the milk. Add the cheese and cook until it melts. Season to taste with salt and pepper. Set aside.
2. **To make the lamb:** In a medium-size bowl, combine the onion paste, ginger-garlic paste, paprika, and salt. Add the lamb and rub the marinade into it. Refrigerate to marinate overnight.
3. Preheat the oven to 400°F (200°C).
4. In a skillet over medium heat, melt the butter.
5. Add the lamb. Sauté for 35–40 minutes, or until tender. Remove the lamb pieces from the mixture and shred. Set aside.
6. In a medium-size saucepan over medium heat, combine the white sauce, cooked vegetables, hardboiled eggs, pasta, vinegar, ketchup, cashew powder, and shredded lamb. Mix well to combine. Transfer this mixture to a casserole dish and pour the whisked eggs on top. Bake for 20–30 minutes. Serve hot.

## PANDHRA RASSA

White flavorful lamb stock curry.

| Cooking time: 40 minutes | Serves: 2 | Origin: Maharashtra |
| --- | --- | --- |

INGREDIENTS

1 tsp white sesame seeds (*safed til*)
5 Tbsp (25 g) shredded dried unsweetened
   coconut (*nariyal*)
2 Tbsp (18 g) poppy seeds (*khus khus*), soaked in
   water for 20 minutes, drained
2 Tbsp (10 g) cashew powder (*kaju*)
1 cup (170 g) finely diced onion
1 Tbsp (15 ml) vegetable oil
1 Tbsp (15 g) whole spice mix (page 22)
1 bay leaf (*tej patta*)
1 Tbsp (15 g) ginger-garlic paste (*adrak-lasan*)
1 tsp white pepper (*safed mirch*)
4 cups (960 ml) lamb stock
Salt, to taste

METHOD

1.  In a food processor, combine the white sesame seeds, coconut, poppy seeds, and cashew powder. Blend into a fine powder. Set aside.
2.  In a saucepan, combine the onion with enough water to cover. Place the pan over high heat and boil the onion for 20 minutes. Drain, transfer to a blender or food processor, and grind into a fine paste.
3.  In a skillet over low-medium heat, heat the vegetable oil.
4.  Add the whole spice mix, bay leaf, and boiled onion paste. Stir-fry until the onion paste turns brown.
5.  Add the ginger-garlic paste, white pepper, and coconut-sesame powder. Mix well. Reduce the heat to low and cook for 6–7 minutes, stirring constantly.
6.  Stir in the lamb stock. Simmer for 10–15 minutes. Season to taste with salt. Serve hot.

## BALCHAOW PORK

Spicy pork curry speckled with shrimp paste.

| Cooking time: 40 minutes | Serves: 6 | Origin: Goa |
| --- | --- | --- |

INGREDIENTS

2 lb, 3 oz (1 kg) pork shoulder, cubed
Salt, to taste
15 Kashmiri dried red chiles (*sookhi lal mirch*)
¼ cup (60 g) minced peeled fresh ginger (*adrak*)
¼ cup (60 g) minced garlic (*lasan*)
1½ tsp cumin seeds (*jeera*)
1 tsp ground turmeric (*haldi*)
1 (2-in. / 5-cm) cinnamon stick (*dalchini*)
⅓ cup (80 ml) palm vinegar, plus more as needed
1 cup (240 ml) plus 3 Tbsp (45 ml) water, divided
5 Tbsp (75 ml) vegetable oil
4 large onions, sliced
4 Tbsp (60 g) dried shrimp paste

METHOD

1.  In a medium-size bowl, season the pork with salt and set aside for 30 minutes.
2.  Meanwhile, in a blender, combine the dried red chiles, ginger, garlic, cumin seeds, turmeric, cinnamon stick, vinegar, and 3 Tbsp (45 ml) of water. Purée until smooth.
3.  In a skillet over low-medium heat, heat the vegetable oil.
4.  Add the onions. Cook until golden.
5.  Add the prepared spice paste. Sauté for 5–8 minutes until fragrant.
6.  Stir in the dried shrimp paste. Cook for 3–4 minutes more.
7.  Add the seasoned pork and remaining 1 cup (240 ml) of water. Reduce the heat to low, and cook until the pork is tender. Taste and add more vinegar, if needed. Serve hot.

# CARIL DE ALMONDEGAS DE CARNE

Meatballs in spicy Goan curry.

Cooking time: 30 minutes | Serves: 6-8  Origin: Goa

## INGREDIENTS

**For the spice paste**

8 Kashmiri dried red chiles (*sookhi lal mirch*)

2 tsp coriander seeds (*dhaniya*)

½ tsp cumin seeds (*jeera*)

6 peppercorns (*sabut kali mirch*)

½ tsp poppy seeds (khus khus)

5 whole cloves (*laung*)

2 (1-in. / 2.5-cm) cinnamon sticks (*dalchini*)

½ tsp ground turmeric (*haldi*)

9 garlic cloves (*lasan*), minced

1 (1-in. / 2.5-cm) piece peeled fresh ginger (*adrak*), chopped

3½ oz (100 g) shredded dried unsweetened coconut (*nariyal*)

**For the meatballs**

1 lb, 2 oz (500 g) minced lamb or beef

1 Tbsp (7.5 g) chickpea flour (*besan*) or 2 slices bread, crumbled

3 Tbsp (3 g) fresh cilantro leaves (*hara dhaniya*), chopped

1½ tsp salt, or to taste, divided

3 Tbsp (45 ml) vegetable oil

1 medium-size onion, thinly sliced

6–8 curry leaves (*kadhi patta*)

1 large tomato, chopped

2 cups (480 ml) water

2 Tbsp (30 ml) vinegar (*sirka*)

## METHOD

1. **To make the spice paste:** In a blender or food processor, combine all the ingredients with a little water and grind into a smooth paste. Transfer to a small bowl and set aside.

2. **To make the meatballs:** In the food processor (no need to clean it), combine the minced meat with 3 Tbsp (45 g) of the spice paste. Process until smooth.

3. Add the chickpea flour or bread, cilantro, and ½ tsp of salt. Process to combine well. Divide the mixture into small balls (about 1-in. / 2.5-cm in diameter). Set aside.

4. In a large skillet over medium heat, heat the vegetable oil.

5. Add the onion. Sauté until soft and golden brown.

6. Add the curry leaves and the remaining spice paste. Stir-fry for 3 minutes.

7. Add the tomato. Sauté for 3 minutes more until soft and mushy and the oil begins to separate.

8. Add the water and bring the mixture to the boil. Reduce the heat as needed and simmer for 15 minutes.

9. Carefully place the meatballs, one by one, into the gravy. Cook gently for 10 minutes, or until just cooked. Shake the pan gently from time to time. Do not stir or the meatballs may break.

10. Add the vinegar and cook for 2 minutes more. Taste and adjust the seasoning with more salt, if needed. Remove from the heat and serve hot.

# FISH AND SEAFOOD

# GOAN PRAWN CURRY 🍲

Prawns in coconut milk curry cooked with drumsticks and raw mangoes.

Cooking time: 30 minutes | Serves: 6      Origin: Goa

## INGREDIENTS

16 Kashmiri dried red chiles (*sookhi lal mirch*)
1 medium-size onion, finely chopped
½ cup (40 g) grated fresh coconut (*nariyal*)
3 garlic cloves (*lasan*), finely chopped
1 Tbsp (5 g) coriander seeds (*dhaniya*)
1 tsp cumin seeds (*jeera*)
1 cup (240 ml) water, plus more as needed for the spice paste
3 Tbsp (45 ml) vegetable oil
2 green chiles, split
2 Tbsp (30 g) tamarind paste (*imli*; page 30)
4–5 drumsticks (*saijan ki phalli*), chopped
5 (1-in. / 2.5-cm) pieces cubed raw mango (*kairi*)
1¼ cups (300 ml) coconut milk (*nariyal*)
14 oz (400 g) medium-size prawns, shelled
Salt, to taste

## METHOD

1. In a blender, combine the dried red chiles, onion, coconut, garlic, coriander seeds, and cumin seeds. Process until smooth, adding 3–4 Tbsp (45–60 ml) of water, if needed. Set aside.
2. In a shallow pan over medium heat, heat the vegetable oil.
3. Add the coconut-spice paste and green chiles. Cook for 5–6 minutes.
4. Add the water and tamarind paste. Mix well. Reduce the heat as needed and simmer for about 4 minutes.
5. Add the drumsticks and raw mango. Cook for 6–8 minutes.
6. Add the coconut milk and prawns. Bring the mixture to a simmer again. Cook until the prawns are tender. Season to taste with salt. Serve hot.

# PAPARIS RECHEADOS

Poppadums stuffed with prawns.

Cooking time: 40 minutes | Serves: 4-6      Origin: Goa

## INGREDIENTS

2 Tbsp (30 ml) vegetable oil, plus more for deep-frying
1 medium-size onion, chopped
½ tsp garlic paste (*lasan*)
¼ tsp ginger paste (*adrak*)
2 tsp recheio spice paste (page 220)
7 oz (200 g) prawns, shelled, deveined
1½ tsp vinegar (*sirka*)
Salt to taste
10 poppadums (*pappad*), garlic flavored, 5-in. (12.5-cm) in diameter

## METHOD

1. In a skillet over medium-high heat, heat 2 Tbsp (30 ml) of vegetable oil.
2. Add the onion. Sauté for 2 minutes until soft.
3. Add the garlic paste and ginger paste. Sauté for 30 seconds.
4. Add the recheio spice paste and prawns. Stir-fry until the prawns change color.
5. Add the vinegar. Mix well to combine. Season to taste with salt. Cook, stirring, until the prawns are tender and the mixture is almost dry. Set aside to cool.
6. Dip each poppadum in water. Wipe with a clean cloth to make it pliable.
7. Spread a little filling on each poppadum. Roll up firmly by moistening the edges and pinch to seal.
8. In a skillet over medium-high heat, heat the vegetable oil for deep-frying.
9. Working in batches, carefully fry the stuffed poppadum until crisp. Remove with a slotted spoon and transfer on paper towels to drain.
10. Cut each poppadum roll into 4 pieces. Serve hot.

## AMBOT-TIK 📷

Hot and sour Goan fish curry.

Cooking time: 20 minutes | Serves: 6-8      Origin: Goa

### INGREDIENTS

For the recheio spice paste
6 Tbsp (90 ml) vinegar (*sirka*)
10–12 Kashmiri dried red chiles (*sookhi lal mirch*)
12 garlic cloves, peeled (*lasan*)
12 peppercorns (*sabut kali mirch*)
½ small onion, chopped (optional)
4 tsp (20 g) tamarind paste (*imli*; page 30)
1 (½-in. / 1.25-cm) piece peeled fresh ginger, chopped
1 tsp sugar
1 tsp salt
½ tsp cumin seeds (*jeera*)
½ tsp ground turmeric (*haldi*)
For the fish
9 oz (250 g) fish (preferably shark or catfish), rinsed, cut into 1½-in. (3.75-cm) cubes
Salt, to taste
3 Tbsp (45 ml) vegetable oil
1 medium-size onion, chopped
3 garlic cloves (*lasan*), minced
1 (½-in. / 1.25-cm) piece peeled fresh ginger (*adrak*), minced
1¼ cups (300 ml) water, plus more as needed
Pinch sugar
Vinegar (*sirka*), to taste

### METHOD

1. **To make the recheio spice paste:** In a blender or mortar and pestle, combine all the spice paste ingredients and grind into a smooth paste. Measure ¼ cup (60 g) and set aside. Refrigerate remaining paste for another use.
2. **To make the fish:** Sprinkle the fish with salt all over and set aside.
3. In a skillet over medium heat, heat the vegetable oil.
4. Add the onion. Sauté for 3 minutes until soft and transparent.
5. Add the garlic and ginger. Sauté for 30 seconds.
6. Stir in the reserved recheio spice paste. Stir-fry for 2 minutes, adding a little water, if needed.
7. Add the water and bring the mixture to the boil. Cover the skillet and reduce the heat as needed. Simmer for 10 minutes.
8. Add the fish and sugar. Season to taste with salt. Mix well. Simmer for 5 minutes more until the fish is cooked and the gravy is thick. Taste and adjust the seasoning, if needed. Stir in the vinegar. Serve hot with rice or bread, if desired.

· · · · · · · · · · · ·

## AMEIJOAS (TISRIO) COM COCO

Clams cooked with coconut.

Cooking time: 30 minutes | Serves: 4      Origin: Goa

### INGREDIENTS

4½ cups clams, medium-size, washed
5 kashmiri dried red chiles (*sookhi lal mirch*)
½ tsp cumin seeds (*jeera*)
¾ tsp coriander seeds (*dhaniya*)
6 peppercorns (*sabut kali mirch*)
½ tsp garam masala
½ tsp ground turmeric (*haldi*)
1 tsp garlic (*lasan*), minced
1 cup (80 g) coconut (*nariyal*), grated
4 Tbsp (60 ml) vegetable oil
3 medium-size onions, finely sliced
Salt, to taste
Water, as needed
15 g tamarind (*imli*), soaked in 4 Tbsp (60 ml) water

### METHOD

1. In a large pan, over medium-high heat, boil 1 cup of water. Add the clams and boil for 5 minutes, or until the clams open. Drain. Prise open with a sharp knife, and discard the empty half. Set aside.
2. In a blender or food processor, blend the dried red chile, cumin seeds, coriander seeds, peppercorns, garam masala, turmeric, and garlic. Add the grated coconut to this paste and grind coarsely.
3. In a pan over medium-high heat, heat the vegetable oil. Add the onions. Sauté until soft.
4. Add the spice-coconut paste. Sauté for 2 minutes.
5. Add the clams. Mix well. Add water and season to taste with salt. Cook for 10–15 minutes.
6. Stir in the tamarind pulp. Cook for 5 minutes more. Taste and adjust the seasoning. Cook until the mixture is almost dry. Serve hot with rice, if desired.

## CARANGUEJOS RECHEADOS 📷
Stuffed breaded crabs grilled to perfection.

Cooking time: 20 minutes | Serves: 6-8 — Origin: Goa

### INGREDIENTS

6 medium-size crabs, washed
4 Tbsp (60 g) butter, divided
1 large onion, minced
2 green chiles, minced
6 garlic cloves (*lasan*), minced
1 (1-in. / 2.5-cm) piece peeled fresh ginger (*adrak*), minced
¼ tsp ground turmeric (*haldi*; optional)
Pinch freshly ground black pepper (*kali mirch*)
Salt, to taste
2 tsp fresh cilantro leaves (*hara dhaniya*), finely chopped
1–2 tsp freshly squeezed lemon juice (*nimbu*)
1 egg, beaten
2 Tbsp (14 g) bread crumbs

### METHOD

1. Preheat the oven to 375°F (190.5°C).
2. Plunge the crabs into a pan of boiling water. Boil for a few minutes until red. Drain and cool. Remove the hard shells, wash them, and set aside. Carefully remove and discard the stomach pouch and the gills. Lift out as much meat as possible from the body. Crack the claws and remove the meat from within.
3. In a skillet over medium heat, melt 3 Tbsp (45 g) of butter.
4. Add the onion. Sauté until soft and transparent.
5. Add the green chiles, garlic, ginger, turmeric (if using), pepper, and salt. Sauté for 1 minute.
6. Add the crabmeat and cook for 2 minutes more.
7. Mix in the cilantro and lemon juice. Remove from the heat.
8. Stir in the egg. Fill the crab shells with the stuffing. Sprinkle the stuffing with bread crumbs and dot with the remaining 1 Tbsp (15 g) of butter.
9. Bake for 20–25 minutes until golden brown on top. Alternatively, grill until golden brown. Serve hot.

## NARIYAL MACHHI
Coconut fish.

Cooking time: 30 minutes | Serves: 6-8 — Origin: Maharashtra

### INGREDIENTS

2 tsp ground turmeric (*haldi*)
2 tsp salt
2 lb, 3 oz (1 kg) pomfret, kingfish, of any white fish fillets, cubed
½ cup (120 ml) mustard seed oil (page 26)
2 Tbsp (25 g) garlic (*lasan*), finely chopped
2 tsp ground turmeric (*haldi*)
1 tsp red chile powder
20 curry leaves (*kadhi patta*)
1 cup (240 ml) coconut milk (*nariyal*), thick, from 1 whole grated coconut (page 30)
50 g tamarind pulp (*imli*; page 30)
15 green chiles, seeded
Salt, to taste

### METHOD

1. In a medium-size bowl, mix the turmeric and salt. Add the fish pieces. Rub this marinade to cover the fish pieces thoroughly. Set aside for 30 minutes.
2. In a skillet over medium-high heat, heat the mustard seed oil for deep-frying. Working in batches, add the marinated fish cubes in the hot oil. Cook until golden. Remove with a slotted spoon. Transfer on paper towels to drain.
3. In the same oil, add the garlic. Sauté until light brown.
4. Add the turmeric, red chile powder, curry leaves, coconut milk, tamarind pulp, and green chiles. Season to taste with salt. Cook, stirring continuously and bring to the boil.
5. Add the fried fish cubes and let the gravy simmer for 5 minutes. Serve hot.

# TARELI MACHHI

Fried fish—Parsi-style.

Cooking time: 20 minutes | Serves: 6-8   Origin: Maharashtra

INGREDIENTS

1 tsp ground turmeric (*haldi*)
1 tsp red chile powder
1 tsp ground cumin (*jeera*; optional)
Juice of 1 lemon (*nimbu*), plus slices for serving
Salt, to taste
6 large pomfret fillets, cut into ½-in. (2.5-cm) slices
1 cup (240 ml) sesame oil (*til*)

METHOD

1. In a medium-size bowl, mix the turmeric, red chile powder, cumin (if using), lemon juice, and salt. Rub the marinade onto the fish. Set aside for 30 minutes.
2. In a skillet over low heat, heat the sesame oil. Working in batches, carefully add the fish fillets to the hot oil and deep-fry until crisp. Transfer with a slotted spoon onto paper towels to drain. Serve immediately with lemon slices.

# SAS NI MACHHI 📷

Sweet and sour Parsi fish curry.

Cooking time: 20 minutes | Serves: 6   Origin: Gujarat

INGREDIENTS

2 Tbsp (30 ml) vegetable oil
1 large onion, finely chopped
1 Tbsp (10 g) rice flour
8 green chiles, seeded, chopped
2 garlic cloves (*lasan*), finely chopped
1 tsp cumin seeds (*jeera*), coarsely ground
3 cups (720 ml) water
Salt, to taste
2 lb, 3 oz (1 kg) pomfret fillets, cut into ½-in. (1.25-cm) thick slices
½ cup (120 ml) vinegar (*sirka*), plus more as needed
1 tsp sugar, plus more as needed
3 eggs, beaten
3 Tbsp (3 g) fresh cilantro leaves (*hara dhaniya*), finely chopped

METHOD

1. In a large skillet or sauté pan over medium heat, heat the vegetable oil.
2. Add the onion. Sauté until light brown.
3. Add the rice flour. Sauté for 2 minutes.
4. Add the green chiles, garlic, and cumin seeds. Sauté for 1 minute.
5. Add the water and salt. Bring the mixture to the boil.
6. Add the fish, reduce the heat as needed, and simmer until almost done. Remove from the heat.
7. In a small bowl, whisk the vinegar, sugar, and beaten eggs. Pour the egg mixture into the skillet and swirl it around, taking care not to break the fish. Return the pan to the heat and simmer until the gravy thickens.
8. Taste and adjust the vinegar and sugar to get a sweet and sour taste. Serve hot, garnished with cilantro.

VEGETARIAN

# DAL DHOKLI 🍲
Diamond-shaped wheat flour strips in pigeon pea curry.

Cooking time: 1 hour | Serves: 4          Origin: Gujarat

## INGREDIENTS

For the wheat flour strips (*dhokli*)
1 cup (125 g) whole-wheat flour (*atta*)
2 Tbsp (15 g) chickpea flour ( *besan*)
1 tsp red chile powder
1 tsp ground turmeric (*haldi*)
Pinch carom seeds (*ajwain*)
1 Tbsp (15 ml) vegetable oil
Salt, to taste
Water, for kneading

For the dal
1 cup (200 g) pigeon peas (*toor dal*)
2 tsp ground turmeric (*haldi*), divided
2 Tbsp (42 g) jaggery (*gur*; unrefined cane sugar)
1 Tbsp (15 g) tamarind paste (*imli*; page 30)
1 tsp ginger-chile paste (*adrak-mirch*)
1 tsp red chile powder
5 Tbsp (75 g) ghee
3 curry leaves (*kadhi patta*)
1 tsp cumin seeds (*jeera*)
1 tsp mustard seeds (*rai*)
Pinch ground asafoetida (*hing*)
1 Kashmiri dried red chile (*sookhi lal mirch*)
1 (1-in. / 2.5-cm) cinnamon stick (*dalchini*)
2 whole cloves (*laung*)
Salt, to taste
¼ cup (4 g) fresh cilantro leaves (*hara dhaniya*), finely chopped
1 Tbsp (15 g) ghee
Juice of 1 lemon (*nimbu*)

## METHOD

1. **To make the wheat flour strips (*dhokli*):** In a medium-size bowl, mix all the ingredients. Gradually add enough water to knead the mixture into a soft dough. Roll the dough into 3–4 thin chapattis (disks). With a sharp knife, cut out 6–7 strips. Further cut each strip into about 6 diamond-shaped pieces and set aside.

2. **To make the dal:** In your pressure cooker cooking pot, combine the pigeon peas, 1 tsp of turmeric, and enough water to cover the peas. Lock the lid in place and close the pressure release valve. Select Manual/Pressure Cook and cook for about 12 minutes. Release the pressure and remove the lid.

3. Add 2 cups (480 ml) of warm water, the jaggery, tamarind paste, ginger-chile paste, red chile powder, and remaining 1 tsp of turmeric. Select Sauté and stir well until the dal begins to bubble.

4. In a skillet over low-medium heat, heat the ghee.

5. Add the curry leaves, cumin seeds, mustard seeds, asafoetida, dried red chile, cinnamon stick, and cloves. Cook until the seeds begin to crackle. Add this tempering to the dal. Stir well to combine. Reduce the heat as needed and simmer for 5–7 minutes. Taste and adjust the seasoning, if required.

6. Add the wheat strips to the dal and simmer for 7–8 minutes more until the strips turn al dente. Turn off the pressure cooker. Serve hot, garnished with cilantro, ghee, and lemon juice.

# LACHKO DAL 🍲

Sweet and thick yellow lentils.

Cooking time: 15 minutes | Serves: 2     Origin: Gujarat

## INGREDIENTS

1 Tbsp (15 g) ghee, plus more for serving
1 tsp cumin seeds (*jeera*)
1 tsp ground turmeric (*haldi*)
1 cup (200 g) pigeon peas (*toor dal*), boiled until soft, drained
1 Tbsp (21 g) grated jaggery (*gur*; unrefined cane sugar)
Salt, to taste

## METHOD

1. In a small saucepan over medium heat, heat the ghee.
2. Add the cumin seeds. Cook until the seeds begin to crackle.
3. Add the turmeric, boiled pigeon peas, and jaggery. Season to taste with salt. Cook, stirring well, until heated through. Serve hot, with a dollop of ghee.

# VATANA CHAUSAL

White chickpeas tempered with curry leaves and bay leaf.

Cooking time: 1 hour | Serves: 2     Origin: Maharashtra

## INGREDIENTS

2 medium-size onions, finely chopped, divided
2 dried red chiles (*sookhi lal mirch*)
½ cup (47.5 g) shredded dried unsweetened coconut (*nariyal*)
1 Tbsp (15 g) ginger-garlic paste (*adrak-lasan*)
1 Tbsp (15 ml) vegetable oil
2 curry leaves (*kadhi patta*)
1 bay leaf (*tej patta*)
1 Tbsp (6 g) goda garam masala (available at Indian markets)
1 tsp ground turmeric (*haldi*)
1 medium-size tomato, finely chopped
1 cup (200 g) white chickpeas (*kabuli chana*), soaked in water overnight, drained
2 cups (480 ml) water
Salt, to taste
¼ cup (4 g) fresh cilantro leaves (*hara dhaniya*), finely chopped

## METHOD

1. In a food processor, combine 1 chopped onion, the dried red chiles, coconut, and ginger-garlic paste. Blend into a smooth paste.
2. In a skillet over medium-high heat, heat the vegetable oil.
3. Add the curry leaves and bay leaf. Cook until the leaves begin to crackle.
4. Add the remaining chopped onion, the goda garam masala, and turmeric. Stir well to combine.
5. Add the tomato. Sauté for 4–5 minute, or until cooked.
6. Add the white chickpeas and water. Cover the skillet and reduce the heat. Cook for 30 minutes, or until the chickpeas are soft.
7. Season to taste with salt and stir well. Serve hot, garnished with cilantro.

# MISAL PAV

Spicy sprouted moth bean curry topped with yogurt and served with buttered Indian rolls.

Cooking time: 1 hour | Serves: 4      Origin: Maharashtra

## INGREDIENTS

### For the gravy paste
1 Tbsp (15 ml) vegetable oil
½ cup (47.5 g) diced fresh coconut (*nariyal*)
2 medium-size tomatoes, diced
1 medium-size onion, finely chopped
¼ cup (4 g) fresh cilantro leaves (*hara dhaniya*),
   finely chopped
1 Tbsp (15 g) minced garlic (*lasan*)
1 Tbsp (6 g) ground coriander (*dhaniya*)
1 Tbsp (6 g) goda garam masala
1 tsp ground turmeric (*haldi*)
1 tsp red chile powder
1 tsp ground cumin (*jeera*)
1 tsp mustard seeds (*rai*)
Pinch ground asafoetida (*hing*)
Salt, to taste

### For the usal
1 Tbsp (15 ml) vegetable oil
1 green chile, finely chopped
2 curry leaves (*kadhi patta*)
1 tsp cumin seeds (*jeera*)
1 tsp mustard seeds (*rai*)
Pinch ground asafoetida (*hing*)
1 medium-size onion, finely chopped
1 Tbsp (15 g) ginger-garlic paste (*adrak-lasan*)
1 tsp ground turmeric (*haldi*)
1 tsp red chile powder
1 tsp goda garam masala (available at Indian
   markets)
Salt, to taste
1 cup (200 g) moth beans (*matki*), sprouted
   (page 13)
1 medium-size potato, boiled, cubed

### For the misal
1 cup (240 g) yogurt (*dahi*; optional)
1 medium-size onion, finely chopped
1 medium-size tomato, finely chopped
¼ cup (4 g) fresh cilantro leaves (*hara dhaniya*),
   finely chopped
Juice of 1 lemon (*nimbu*)
½ cup (120 g) misal farsaan (available at Indian
   markets)
6 pavs (Indian bread rolls)
3 Tbsp (45 g) bu tter

## METHOD

1. **To make the gravy paste:** In a skillet over low-medium heat, heat the vegetable oil.
2. Add the coconut. Cook until the pieces are toasted.
3. Add the remaining gravy paste ingredients and cook for 5–6 minutes. Toss well to combine and remove from the heat. Taste and add more salt, if needed. Let cool to room temperature.
4. Transfer the gravy mixture to a blender or food processor and purée into a smooth paste. Set aside.
5. **To make the usal:** In a skillet over low-medium heat, heat the vegetable oil.
6. Add the green chile, curry leaves, cumin seeds, mustard seeds, and asafoetida. Cook until the seeds begin to crackle.
7. Add the onion and ginger-garlic paste. Sauté for 2 minutes.
8. Add the turmeric, red chile powder, and goda garam masala. Cook, stirring, for 1 minute more.
9. Add the gravy paste and 1 cup (240 ml) of water. Season to taste with salt. Bring the mixture to a rolling boil.
10. Add the sprouts and potato. Cook for 10–15 minutes.
11. **To make the misal:** Plate the sprouted gravy and top with yogurt (if using), onion, tomato, cilantro, lemon juice, and misal farsaan. Serve with buttered pav (buns).

# OSAMAN 🍲

Clear pigeon pea soup tempered with cumin and mustard seeds.

Cooking time: 40 minutes | Serves: 4          Origin: Gujarat

## INGREDIENTS

1 tsp vegetable oil
1 tsp seeds cumin (*jeera*)
1 tsp mustard seeds (*rai*)
2 whole cloves (*laung*)
1 (1-in. / 2.5-cm) cinnamon stick (*dalchini*)
1 curry leaf (*kadhi patta*)
1 tsp minced peeled fresh ginger (*adrak*)
1 tsp red chile powder
1 tsp ground turmeric (*haldi*)
1½ tsp tamarind paste (*imli*; page 30)
1 Tbsp (21 g) grated jaggery (*gur*; unrefined cane sugar)
1 cup (200 g) pigeon peas (*toor dal*), boiled in 2 cups (480 ml) water, drained, only 1½ cup (360 ml) cooking liquid reserved
Salt, to taste
¼ cup (4 g) fresh cilantro leaves (*hara dhaniya*), finely chopped
Juice of 1 lemon (*nimbu*)

## METHOD

1. In a medium-size pot over low-medium heat, heat the vegetable oil.
2. Add the cumin seeds and mustard seeds. Cook until the seeds begin to crackle.
3. Add the cloves, cinnamon stick, curry leaf, ginger, red chile powder, turmeric, tamarind paste, and jaggery. Stir well to combine.
4. Stir in the reserved pigeon pea cooking water and mix well. Reduce the heat to low and simmer for 15–20 minutes. Season to taste with salt. Serve hot, garnished with cilantro and lemon juice.

# ALOO WADI 📷

Dried potato dumplings in coconut milk curry.

Cooking time: 30 minutes | Serves: 4          Origin: Maharashtra

## INGREDIENTS

1 Tbsp (15 g) ghee
1 roll ready-made steamed aloo wadi (available at Indian markets)
1 Tbsp (15 g) whole spice mix (page 22)
1 green chile, finely chopped
2 curry leaves (*kadhi patta*)
1 tsp ground turmeric (*haldi*)
1 tsp red chile powder
1 cup (240 ml) coconut milk (*nariyal*)
2 Tbsp (30 ml) coconut cream (*nariyal*)
Salt, to taste

## METHOD

1. In a skillet over low-medium heat, heat the ghee.
2. Add the whole spice mix. Sauté until the spices begin to crackle.
3. Add the green chile and curry leaves. Stir well.
4. Add the aloo wadi and stir to coat well in the spices.
5. Add the turmeric and red chile powder. Stir well.
6. Stir in the coconut milk and coconut cream. Reduce the heat as needed and simmer the gravy for 4–5 minutes. Season to taste with salt. Serve hot.

## MACROLYUNPATATA 📷
Macaroni and potato in spicy tomato sauce.

Cooking time: 30 minutes | Serves: 2        Origin: Maharashtra

INGREDIENTS

1 Tbsp (15 ml) vegetable oil
1 tsp cumin seeds (*jeera*)
1 Tbsp (15 g) ginger-garlic paste (*adrak-lasan*)
1 medium-size onion, finely chopped
1 Tbsp (6 g) ground coriander (*dhaniya*)
1 tsp ground turmeric (*haldi*)
1 tsp red chile powder
2 medium-size tomatoes, finely chopped
2 Tbsp (30 g) tomato purée
½ cup (112.5 g) cubed boiled potatoes
1 cup (200 g) macaroni, cooked according to the
   package directions
Salt, to taste
¼ cup (4 g) fresh cilantro leaves (*hara dhaniya*),
   finely chopped

METHOD

1. In a skillet over low-medium heat, heat the
   vegetable oil.
2. Add the cumin seeds. Cook until the seeds
   begin to crackle.
3. Add the ginger-garlic paste and onion. Sauté
   for 2–3 minutes.
4. Stir in the coriander, turmeric, and red chile
   powder. Sauté for 1 minute.
5. Add the tomatoes and tomato purée. Sauté until
   the tomatoes soften.
6. Stir in the potatoes and macaroni. Season
   to taste with salt and garnish with cilantro.
   Serve hot.

## KOKUM KADHI
Kokum-laced coconut milk curry.

Cooking time: 40 minutes | Serves: 4        Origin: Maharashtra

INGREDIENTS

20 pieces kokum
2 green chiles, finely chopped
Salt, to taste
1 cup (240 ml) water
1 Tbsp (15 ml) vegetable oil
1 tsp cumin seeds (*jeera*)
2 curry leaves (*kadhi patta*)
2 dried red chiles (*sookhi lal mirch*)
1 Tbsp (15 g) minced garlic (*lasan*)
2 cups (480 ml) coconut milk (*nariyal*)
Freshly ground black pepper (*kali mirch*), to taste
¼ cup (4 g) fresh cilantro leaves (*hara dhaniya*),
   finely chopped

METHOD

1. In a medium-size bowl, combine the kokum,
   green chiles, salt, and water. Soak for 30 minutes.
2. Strain, reserving the soaking water while
   discarding the kokum and chiles.
3. In a skillet over medium-high heat, heat the
   vegetable oil.
4. Add the cumin seeds. Cook until the seeds
   begin to crackle.
5. Add the curry leaves, dried red chiles, and
   garlic. Sauté for 1 minute.
6. Add the coconut milk and reserved kokum
   water. Season to taste with salt and pepper.
   Reduce the heat as needed and simmer for
   10–12 minutes. Serve hot, with steamed rice, if
   desired, garnished with cilantro.

# SINDHI KADHI

Pigeon pea curry with assorted vegetables.

Cooking time: 40 minutes | Serves: 2    Origin: Maharashtra

## INGREDIENTS

1½ cups (300 g) pigeon peas (*toor dal*)
1 medium-size onion, finely chopped
1 medium-size tomato, chopped
1 Tbsp (15 g) minced garlic (*lasan*)
Salt, to taste
4 cups (960 ml) water
1 Tbsp (15 ml) vegetable oil
1 Tbsp (15 g) whole spice mix (page 22)
1 tsp fenugreek seeds (*methi dana*)
1 tsp mustard seeds (*rai*)
1 dried red chile (*sookhi lal mirch*)
Pinch ground asafoetida (*hing*)
1 medium-size potato, cubed
½ cup (165 g) chopped okra (*bhindi*)
½ cup (50 g) cauliflower florets (*phool gobhi*)
½ cup (120 g) chopped drumsticks (*saijan ki phalli*)
Salt, to taste
¼ cup (4 g) fresh cilantro leaves (*hara dhaniya*), finely chopped

## METHOD

1. In a pressure cooker cooking pot, combine the pigeon peas, onion, tomato, garlic, salt, and water. Lock the lid in place and close the pressure release valve. Select Manual/Pressure Cook and cook for 12 minutes. Release the pressure and remove the lid. With an immersion blender, blend the mixture until smooth. Set aside.
2. In a skillet over low-medium heat, heat the vegetable oil.
3. Add the whole spice mix, fenugreek seeds, mustard seeds, dried red chile, and asafoetida. Sauté until the seeds begin to crackle.
4. Stir in the pigeon pea mixture along with the potato, okra, cauliflower, and drumsticks. Season to taste with salt. Reduce the heat to low and let the mixture bubble for 20 minutes, or until the vegetables are cooked through. Taste and adjust the seasoning, if needed. Serve hot, garnished with cilantro.

# SINDHI SAI BHAJI

Bengal gram, spinach, and vegetables mashed into a delicious wholesome curry.

Cooking time: 40 minutes | Serves: 2    Origin: Maharashtra

## INGREDIENTS

2 cups (60 g) spinach (*palak*), finely chopped
1 medium-size potato, diced
1 medium-size onion, finely chopped
1 medium-size carrot (*gajar*), cubed
1 cup (100 g) cauliflower florets (*phool gobhi*)
½ cup (120 g) finely chopped tomato
1 Tbsp (15 g) ginger-garlic-chile paste (*adrak-lasan-mirch*)
2 tsp ground turmeric (*haldi*)
2 tsp red chile powder
Salt, to taste
1 cup (200 g) Bengal gram (split chickpeas; *chana dal*), cooked
1 Tbsp (15 g) ghee
1 tsp cumin seeds (*jeera*)
1 dried red chile (*sookhi lal mirch*)
1½ tsp minced garlic (*lasan*)
Juice of 1 lemon (*nimbu*)

## METHOD

1. In a medium-size pot over low-medium heat, combine the spinach, potato, onion, carrot, cauliflower, tomato, ginger-garlic-chile paste, turmeric, and red chile powder. Season to taste with salt. Add enough water to cover the vegetables. Bring to a boil and cook for 15–20 minutes. Drain, return the vegetables to the pot, and mash the mixture coarsely.
2. Add the cooked chickpeas and mash again. Place the pot over low-medium heat and bubble the mixture for 7–8 minutes.
3. In a small skillet over low-medium heat, heat the ghee.
4. Add the cumin seeds, dried red chile, and garlic. Heat until the seeds begin to crackle. Pour the spices into the vegetable and chickpea mixture. Stir well to combine. Serve hot with a dash of lemon juice.

# BHINDI WITH KOKUM 🍲
Mildly spiced stir-fried okra with kokum.

Cooking time: 20 minutes | Serves: 3     Origin: Maharashtra

INGREDIENTS

¼ cup (60 ml) vegetable oil
2 medium-size onions, sliced
3 garlic cloves (*lasan*), sliced
3 green chiles, split
2 cups (600 g) chopped okra (*bhindi*)
8 pieces kokum
1 tsp ground turmeric (*haldi*)
Salt, to taste
Freshly ground black pepper (*kali mirch*), to taste
2 Tbsp (30 ml) water

METHOD

1. In a skillet over medium heat, heat the vegetable oil.
2. Add the onions, garlic, and green chiles. Sauté for 5 minutes.
3. Add the okra, kokum, and turmeric. Stir well to combine.
4. Season to taste with salt and pepper. Add the water. Cover the skillet and reduce the heat to low. Cook until the vegetables are tender and the mix is dry. Serve hot.

# BADI KI SUBZI
Dried lentil dumplings in yogurt gravy.

Cooking time: 30 minutes | Serves: 2     Origin: Rajasthan

INGREDIENTS

1 cup (240 g) yogurt (*dahi*)
1 Tbsp (6 g) ground coriander (*dhaniya*)
2 tsp red chile powder
1 tsp ground turmeric (*haldi*)
1 Tbsp (15 g) ghee
1 tsp cumin seeds (*jeera*)
1 Tbsp (15 g) ginger-garlic paste (*adrak-lasan*)
1 cup (240 ml) water
½ cup (120 g) dried lentil dumplings (*badis*; available at Indian markets or online)
1 Tbsp (13.5 g) dried fenugreek leaves (*kasuri methi*)
¼ cup (4 g) fresh cilantro leaves (*hara dhaniya*), finely chopped
Salt, to taste

METHOD

1. In a medium-size bowl, whisk the yogurt, coriander, red chile powder, and turmeric until well combined.
2. In a skillet over medium heat, heat the ghee.
3. Add the cumin seeds. Cook until the seeds begin to crackle.
4. Add the ginger-garlic paste. Sauté for 2 minutes.
5. Add the yogurt mixture. Cook, stirring, until the water from the yogurt evaporates.
6. Add the water and bring the mixture to a boil. Remove the skillet from the heat and run an immersion blender through it. Return the skillet to the heat.
7. Add the dumplings. Cook until the gravy thickens and the dumplings soften.
8. Add the dried fenugreek leaves, cilantro, and salt. Mix well. Serve hot.

# CHAKKI KI SUBZI 📷
Fried crisps soaked in gravy.

Cooking time: 30 minutes | Serves: 3      Origin: Rajasthan

## INGREDIENTS

**For the fried crisps** (*chakkis*)
1 cup (125 g) whole-wheat flour
1 tsp carom seeds (*ajwain*)
1 Tbsp (15 ml) vegetable oil, plus more for
  deep-frying
Pinch salt
Water, to knead

**For the gravy**
1 Tbsp (15 g) ghee
¼ cup (37.5 g) onion, finely chopped
1 Tbsp (15 g) garlic (*lasan*), minced
1 tsp red chile powder
1 tsp ground turmeric (*haldi*)
1 tsp garam masala
1 Tbsp (15 g) ground coriander (*dhaniya*)
3 Tbsp (45 g) yogurt (*dahi*)
Salt, to taste
1 Tbsp (15 g) dried fenugreek leaves (*kasuri methi*)
¼ cup (4 g) fresh cilantro leaves (*hara dhaniya*),
  finely chopped

## METHOD

1. **To make the** *chakkis*: In a medium-size bowl, mix the whole-wheat flour, carom seeds, 1 Tbsp (15 ml) of vegetable oil, and a pinch of salt. Add just enough water to knead into stretchy dough.

2. Divide the dough into equal portions and roll each out into flat rounds. Cut into diamond-shaped squares.

3. In a deep skillet over medium-high heat, heat the vegetable oil for deep-frying.

4. Working in batches, carefully slide the chakkis in the hot oil and deep fry until golden brown. Transfer to paper towels to drain.

5. **To make the gravy:** In a skillet over low heat, heat the ghee.

6. Add the onion, garlic, red chile powder, turmeric, garam masala, and coriander. Sauté for 4 minutes.

7. Add the yogurt. Stir well to mix. Season to taste with salt.

8. Add dried fenugreek leaves and the prepared chakkis.

9. Garnish with cilantro and serve hot.

## AAMRAS KI KADHI
A refreshing summer mango drink.

Cooking time: 40 minutes | Serves: 3          Origin: Rajasthan

### METHOD

1 cup (240 ml) ripe mango purée (page 27)
5 Tbsp (75 ml) raw mango purée (page 27)
1 cup (240 ml) buttermilk (*chaach*)
2 Tbsp (15 g) chickpea flour (*besan*)
1 tsp ground turmeric (*haldi*)
1 tsp red chile powder
Pinch ground asafoetida (*hing*)
Salt, to taste
2 Tbsp (30 ml) vegetable oil, divided
1 tsp cumin seeds (*jeera*)
¼ tsp mustard seeds (*rai*)
¼ tsp fenugreek seeds (*methi dana*)
1 bay leaf (*tej patta*)
3 green chiles, finely chopped
½ cup (120 g) boondi (deep-fried chickpea flour
   pearls; available at Indian markets)
1 tsp julienned peeled fresh ginger (*adrak*)
1 dried red chile (*sookhi lal mirch*)
¼ tsp finely chopped fresh cilantro leaves (*hara
   dhaniya*), plus more for garnishing
¼ tsp baby fenugreek leaves (*methi*)

### METHOD

1. In a medium-size bowl, combine the ripe mango
   and raw mango purées, the buttermilk, and
   chickpea flour. Use an immersion blender to
   blend until smooth. Strain out any lumps.
   Transfer the strained mixture back to the bowl.
2. Stir in the turmeric, red chile powder, asafoetida,
   and salt.
3. In a skillet over low-medium heat, heat 1 Tbsp
   (15 ml) of vegetable oil.
4. Add the cumin seeds. Sauté until the seeds
   begin to crackle.
5. Add the mustard seeds, fenugreek seeds, bay
   leaf, and green chiles. Sauté well for 1 minute.
6. Add the boondi and mango-buttermilk mixture.
   Bring to a boil, adding more water if it thickens
   excessively.

7. In a small skillet over medium-high heat, heat
   the remaining 1 Tbsp (15 ml) of vegetable oil.
8. Add the ginger, dried red chile, cilantro, and
   fenugreek leaves. Cook until the spices and
   herbs crackle. Pour this into the mango curry
   and stir well to combine. Serve hot, garnished
   with cilantro.

· · · · · · · · · · · ·

## RABODI KI SUBZI
Corn poppadums in a flavorful curry.

Cooking time: 20 minutes | Serves: 2          Origin: Rajasthan

### INGREDIENTS

1 cup (250 g) rabodi (available at Indian markets)
1 Tbsp (15 ml) vegetable oil
1 tsp cumin seeds (*jeera*)
2 green chiles, finely chopped
1 Tbsp (6 g) ground coriander (*dhaniya*)
1 tsp red chile powder
1 tsp ground turmeric (*haldi*)
½ cup (120 g) yogurt (*dahi*)
Salt, to taste
¼ cup (4 g) fresh cilantro leaves (*hara dhaniya*),
   finely chopped

### METHOD

1. Fill a medium-size pot with water and bring to
   a boil over high heat. Turn off the heat and add
   the rabodi. Let soak until the rabodi is soft.
   Drain.
2. In a skillet over medium heat, heat the vegetable
   oil.
3. Add the cumin seeds and green chiles. Cook
   until the seeds begin to crackle.
4. Stir in the coriander, red chile powder, turmeric,
   yogurt, and salt. Cook until the water from the
   yogurt evaporates.
5. Add the rabodi. Cook for 5 minutes more. Serve
   hot, with hot chapattis (Indian bread), if desired,
   and garnished with cilantro.

## GATTE KI SUBZI 🍲
Chickpea dumplings in yogurt gravy.

Cooking time: 45 minutes | Serves: 2          Origin: Rajasthan

### INGREDIENTS

For the dumplings
1 cup (120 g) chickpea flour (*besan*)
1 tsp ground turmeric (*haldi*)
1 tsp red chile powder
Pinch ground asafoetida (*hing*)
1 Tbsp (15 g) ghee
Water, for kneading
Salt, to taste
For the gravy
1 Tbsp (15 g) ghee
1 tsp cumin seeds (*jeera*)
2 green chiles, finely chopped
1 Tbsp (15 g) ginger-garlic paste (*adrak-lasan*)
1 Tbsp (6 g) ground coriander (*dhaniya*)
2 tsp red chile powder
1 tsp ground turmeric (*haldi*)
1 tsp garam masala
1 cup (240 g) yogurt (*dahi*)
Salt, to taste

### METHOD

1. **To make the dumplings:** In a small bowl, combine the chickpea flour, turmeric, red chile powder, asafoetida, and ghee. Add enough water to knead the mixture into a tight dough.
2. Bring a medium-size saucepan full of water to a rolling boil over high heat.
3. Meanwhile, divide the dough equally into small roundels and roll each out into 1-in. (2.5-cm) cylindrical dumplings. Add the dumplings to the boiling water and cook for 3–4 minutes, like you would gnocchi, until they begin to float on the surface of the water. Drain and let rest.
4. **To make the gravy:** In a skillet over medium heat, heat the ghee.
5. Add the cumin seeds. Cook until the seeds begin to crackle.
6. Add the green chiles, ginger-garlic paste, coriander, red chile powder, turmeric, garam masala, and yogurt. Season to taste with salt. Stir to combine and cook for 10–12 minutes, or until the water from the yogurt evaporates. Taste and adjust the seasoning, if needed.
7. Add the dumplings and cook for a few minutes until heated through. Serve hot, with steamed rice, if desired.

## KER SANGRI

A berry and bean dish cooked dry.

| Cooking time: 40 minutes | Serves: 2 | Origin: Rajasthan |
|---|---|---|

### INGREDIENTS

4 Tbsp (60 g) ker (available at Indian markets;
    page 25)
1 cup (250 g) sangri (available at Indian markets;
    page 25)
Salt, to taste
2 cups (480 ml) water
2 Tbsp (30 ml) vegetable oil
1 tsp carom seeds (*ajwain*)
Pinch ground asafoetida (*hing*)
1 dried red chile (*sookhi lal mirch*)
1 Tbsp (30 g) dried mango powder (*amchoor*)
1 Tbsp (6 g) ground coriander (*dhaniya*)
1 tsp ground turmeric (*haldi*)
1 tsp red chile powder

### METHOD

1. In your pressure cooker cooking pot, combine
   the ker, sangri, salt, and water. Lock the lid in
   place and close the pressure release valve.
   Select Manual/Pressure Cook and cook for 9
   minutes. Release the pressure and remove the
   lid. Drain out the water.
2. In a skillet over low-medium heat, heat the
   vegetable oil.
3. Add the carom seeds and asafoetida. Cook until
   the seeds begin to crackle.
4. Add the dried red chile, dried mango powder,
   coriander, turmeric, and red chile powder. Sauté
   for 2 minutes.
5. Add the cooked ker-sangri mix. Stir well.
   Reduce the heat to low and cook for 4–5 minutes.
   Taste and adjust the seasoning, and serve hot.

## METHI MANGODI KI SUBZI

Green gram dumplings in a fenugreek gravy.

| Cooking time: 35 minutes | Serves: 2 | Origin: Rajasthan |
|---|---|---|

### INGREDIENTS

1 Tbsp (15 g) ghee
2 dried red chiles (*sookhi lal mirch*)
1 tsp cumin seeds (*jeera*)
1 tsp garlic paste (*lasan*)
1 medium-size onion, finely chopped
1 cup (250 g) moong dal mangodi (available at
    Indian markets or online)
1 Tbsp (6 g) garam masala
2 tsp red chile powder
1 tsp ground turmeric (*haldi*)
5 Tbsp (75 g) yogurt (*dahi*)
2 cups (120 g) fresh fenugreek leaves (*methi*),
    finely chopped
Salt, to taste

### METHOD

1. In a skillet over low-medium heat, heat the
   ghee.
2. Add the dried red chiles and cumin seeds. Cook
   until the seeds begin to crackle.
3. Add the garlic paste and onion. Sauté for 2–3
   minutes.
4. Add the mangodi. Stir-fry until slightly brown.
5. Stir in the garam masala, red chile powder, and
   turmeric. Sauté for 2 minutes more.
6. Add the yogurt and cook until the water from
   the yogurt evaporates.
7. Add the fenugreek leaves and cook until the
   leaves are thoroughly cooked (dark green).
   Season to taste with salt and serve hot.

# UNDHIYU

One-pot vegetable casserole with fenugreek dumplings tossed in aromatic spices.

Cooking time: 1 hour 30 minutes | Serves: 4    Origin: Gujarat

## INGREDIENTS

For the fenugreek dumplings (*muthiya*)

2 cups (120 g) fresh fenugreek leaves (*methi*),
   finely chopped

Salt, to taste

½ cup (62.5 g) whole-wheat flour (*atta*)

2 Tbsp (21 g) semolina

2 Tbsp (15 g) chickpea flour (*besan*)

1 Tbsp (15 g) ginger-chile (*adrak-mirch*) paste

2 tsp sugar

2 tsp red chile powder

1 tsp ground turmeric (*haldi*)

Vegetable oil, for deep-frying

For the undhiyu

1 cup (85 g) shredded dried unsweetened coconut
   (*nariyal*)

½ cup (8 g) fresh cilantro leaves (*hara dhaniya*),
   finely chopped

½ cup (75 g) minced green garlic (*lasan*)

1 Tbsp (6 g) ground coriander (*dhaniya*)

2 tsp red chile powder

1 tsp ground cumin (*jeera*)

1 tsp sugar

Juice of 1 lemon (*nimbu*), plus more for serving

Salt, to taste

2 Tbsp (30 ml) vegetable oil, divided

1 tsp carom seeds (*ajwain*)

Pinch ground asafoetida (*hing*)

1 cup (200 g broad beans (*surti papdi*)

3 Tbsp (4 5g) minced garlic (*lasan*)

1 cup (225 g) baby potatoes

1 cup (150 g) unripe banana, sliced

1 cup (85 g) cubed eggplant (*brinjal*)

1 cup (110 g) cubed elephant foot yam (*suran*)

½ cup (55 g) cubed peeled purple yam (*jimikand*)

## METHOD

1. **To make the fenugreek dumplings (*muthiya*):** In a large bowl, mix the fenugreek leaves with the salt and let rest for 10 minutes. Squeeze out the liquid from the leaves over the sink, return the leaves to the bowl, and add the whole-wheat flour, semolina, chickpea flour, ginger-chile paste, sugar, red chile powder, and turmeric. Mix well to combine. Divide the mixture equally into lemon-size balls.

2. In a deep skillet over medium-high heat, heat the vegetable oil for frying.

3. Carefully add the balls to the hot oil and deep-fry until golden brown. Transfer to paper towels to drain. Set the *muthiyas* aside.

4. **To make the undhiyu:** On a plate, mix together the coconut, cilantro, green garlic, coriander, red chile powder, cumin, sugar, lemon juice, and salt. Set aside.

5. In a medium-size saucepan over medium-low heat, heat 1 Tbsp (15 ml) of vegetable oil.

6. Add the carom seeds and asafoetida. Cook until the seeds begin to crackle.

7. Add the broad beans and enough water to cover. Cook for 10 minutes.

8. Meanwhile, on your pressure cooker, select Sauté to preheat the cooking pot.

9. Add the remaining 1 Tbsp (15 ml) of vegetable oil to heat, followed by the garlic, potatoes, banana, eggplant, and yams. Cook for 7–8 minutes, stirring constantly.

10. Add the broad beans along with the cooking liquid.

11. Stir in the coconut-green garlic mixture and the fried muthiyas. Lock the lid in place and close the pressure release valve. Select Manual/Pressure Cook and cook for about 15 minutes. Release the pressure and remove the lid.

12. Taste and adjust seasoning as needed and check that the root vegetables are soft. Serve hot, with a dash of lemon juice.

# KATHIYAWADI RINGAN SHAAK

Eggplant coated with spices in a yogurt gravy.

Cooking time: 30 minutes | Serves: 2        Origin: Gujarat

## INGREDIENTS

1 Tbsp (15 g) ghee
1½ tsp garlic paste (*lasan*)
1 medium-size onion, finely chopped
1 large eggplant (*brinjal*), finely chopped
1 Tbsp (6 g) ground coriander (*dhaniya*)
2 tsp red chile powder
1 tsp ground turmeric (*haldi*)
1 tsp ground cumin (*jeera*) powder
½ cup (120 g) yogurt (*dahi*)
1 tsp garam masala
Salt, to taste
¼ cup (4 g) fresh cilantro leaves (*hara dhaniya*),
    finely chopped
1 Tbsp (5 g) peanut powder

## METHOD

1.  In a skillet over medium heat, heat the ghee.
2.  Add the garlic paste. Sauté for 3 minutes.
3.  Add the onion. Cook for 3–4 minutes, stirring.
4.  Add the eggplant. Cook until it begins to soften.
5.  Stir in the coriander, red chile powder, turmeric, and cumin.
6.  Mix in the yogurt and cook until the water from the yogurt evaporates.
7.  Add the garam masala and stir well to combine. Season to taste with salt. Serve hot, garnished with cilantro and peanut powder.

# SURTI PAPADI NU SHAAK

Green beans with a hint of carom seeds.

Cooking time: 20 minutes | Serves: 2        Origin: Gujarat

## INGREDIENTS

1 cup (100 g) green beans
Salt, to taste
1 tsp vegetable oil
1 tsp carom seeds (*ajwain*)
1 Tbsp ground coriander (*dhaniya*)
1 tsp garlic paste (*lasan*)
1 tsp red chile powder
1 tsp ground cumin (*jeera*)
1 tsp ground turmeric (*haldi*)
¼ cup (4 g) fresh cilantro leaves (*hara dhaniya*),
    finely chopped

## METHOD

1.  Fill a saucepan about halfway with water, place it over high heat, and bring to a boil. Add the green beans and some salt. Boil for 8–10 minutes, or until the green beans turn soft. Drain and set aside.
2.  In a skillet over medium-high heat, heat the vegetable oil.
3.  Add the carom seeds. Sauté until the seeds begin to crackle.
4.  Add the coriander, garlic paste, red chile powder, cumin, and turmeric. Cook, stirring, for 1 minute.
5.  Add the green beans. Cook for 2–3 minutes more. Taste and adjust the seasoning, if needed. Serve hot, garnished with cilantro.

# RICE AND BREADS

# SANNA

Steamed Goan rice bread.

Cooking time: 30 min | Makes: 8       Origin: Goa

## INGREDIENTS

1 cup (200 g) rice, rinsed, soaked in water
   overnight, or for 8 hours, drained
½ cup (100 g) raw rice, rinsed, soaked in water
   overnight, or for 8 hours, drained
Heaping ½ cup (50 g) shredded dried
   unsweetened coconut (*nariyal*)
Water, as needed
¾ tsp active dry yeast or 1¼ cups (300 ml) toddy
   (optional; page 25)
3–4 Tbsp (37.5–50 g) sugar, divided
Salt, to taste
Ghee, for greasing the molds

## METHOD

1. In a food processor, combine the soaked rice,
   raw rice, coconut, and a little water or a little
   toddy (if using). Grind into a thick, smooth
   paste.
2. If using yeast, in a small bowl stir together ½
   cup (120 ml) of warm water and 1 tsp of sugar.
   Sprinkle the yeast over the water. Set aside for a
   few minutes to froth.
3. In a large bowl, mix together the rice-coconut
   paste, remaining sugar, salt to taste, and the
   yeast mixture or remaining toddy, and enough
   water to make a thick batter. Cover the bowl
   and leave to rise, undisturbed, in a warm place
   for at least 4 hours, or until the batter doubles in
   volume.
4. Grease small steaming molds (circular, 2–3-in. /
   5–7.5-cm deep remekins) with ghee and pour a
   little batter into each mold, leaving enough
   room for it to rise. In a steamer, steam for 10–15
   minutes, or until fluffy and cooked through.
   Serve hot, with sarapatel, a traditional Goan
   dish, if desired.

# BISCUIT BHAKRI

Savory whole-wheat and chickpea flour
cookies.

Cooking time: 25 min | Makes: 10       Origin: Rajasthan

## INGREDIENT

2 cups (250 g) whole-wheat flour (*atta*)
½ cup (60 g) chickpea flour (*besan*)
1 cup (240 ml) milk
2 Tbsp (30 g) ghee
1 tsp carom seeds (*ajwain*)
Salt, to taste
Hot water, for kneading

## METHOD

1. In a medium-size bowl, combine the whole-
   wheat flour, chickpea flour, milk, ghee, carom
   seeds, salt, and enough hot water to knead the
   mixture into a tight dough. Divide the dough
   equally into small roundels and roll each into a
   ½-in. (1.25-cm) thick bread.
2. Place a griddle over low heat.
3. Working in batches if needed, roast the bread
   for 7–8 minutes on both sides. Serve hot.

## BAJRA NO ROTLO

Rich Indian finger millet bread with ghee.

Cooking time: 40 min | Makes: 5      Origin: Rajasthan

### INGREDIENTS

1 cup (120 g) finger millet flour (*ragi*)
1 tsp salt
¾ cup (180 ml) water, or as needed
5 Tbsp (75 g) ghee

### METHOD

1. In a small bowl, mix the finger millet flour with the salt. Add the water and knead the mixture into a soft dough. Divide the dough equally into 5 small portions. Press each portion with your fingertips in a circular motion to make the disk larger with every press. Keep patting the bread until you get the thinnest sheet that doesn't break. It should be ¼-in. (0.6-cm) thick. Wet your palms and brush them on the breads to ensure the dough doesn't dry out.

2. Heat a griddle over low-medium heat until very hot.

3. Working in batches as needed, place the bread on the hot griddle and cook for 4–5 minutes on both sides, or until cooked. Serve hot, smeared with generous amounts of ghee.

## KHOBA ROTI 📷

Whole-wheat bread soaked in ghee.

Cooking time: 20 min | Makes: 6      Origin: Rajasthan

### INGREDIENTS

1 cup (125 g) whole-wheat flour (*atta*)
1 Tbsp (13.5 g) dried fenugreek leaves (*kasuri methi*)
1 tsp carom seeds (*ajwain*)
1 tsp salt
2 Tbsp (30 g) ghee, plus more for serving
Water, for kneading

### METHOD

1. In a medium-size bowl, combine the flour, dried fenugreek leaves, carom seeds, salt, and ghee. Rub the ingredients together with your fingertips until the mixture resembles bread crumbs. Add enough water to knead into a tight dough. Cut the dough into 6 roundels and roll each into a thick bread about the size of your palm. With your fingertips, punch indents on the bread and pinch the corners.

2. Place a griddle over low-medium heat.

3. Once hot, roast the bread on both sides until crisp. Pour warm ghee over the indents and serve hot.

# MISSI ROTI

Healthy flattened Indian bread made with a combination of flours and spices.

Cooking time: 30 min | Makes: 6     Origin: Rajasthan

INGREDIENTS

1 cup (125 g) whole-wheat flour (*atta*)
1 cup (120 g) chickpea flour (*besan*)
Salt, to taste
1 Tbsp (15 g) ghee
1 tsp carom seeds (*ajwain*)
1 tsp ground turmeric (*haldi*)
1 tsp red chile powder
1 tsp ground asafoetida (*hing*)
1 tsp ginger paste (*adrak*)
¼ cup (42.5 g) finely chopped onion
¼ cup (4 g) fresh cilantro leaves (*hara dhaniya*), finely chopped
¼ tsp finely chopped fresh fenugreek leaves (*methi*)
Water, for kneading
1 Tbsp (15 g) white butter

METHOD

1. In a medium-size bowl, combine the whole-wheat flour and chickpea flour.
2. Add the salt, ghee, carom seeds, turmeric, red chile powder, asafoetida, ginger paste, onion, cilantro, and fenugreek leaves. Rub the flour well with your fingertips and add enough water to knead the mixture into a soft dough. Divide the dough equally into 6 small roundels and roll each into a thick bread about the size of your palm.
3. Place a griddle over low-medium heat.
4. Once hot, cook the bread, one at a time, until golden brown spots appear. Serve hot, with a dollop of white butter.

# METHI THEPLA

Fenugreek-speckled Indian flatbread.

Cooking time: 30 min | Makes: 7     Origin: Gujarat

INGREDIENTS

1 cup (125 g) whole-wheat flour (*atta*)
¼ cup (15 g) fresh fenugreek leaves (*methi*), finely chopped
2 Tbsp (30 g) yogurt (*dahi*)
1 Tbsp (15 ml) vegetable oil
2 tsp ginger-chile paste (*adrak-mirch*)
1 tsp red chile powder
1 tsp ground turmeric (*haldi*)
1 tsp white sesame seeds (*safed til*)
Salt, to taste
Water, for kneading

METHOD

1. In a medium-size bowl, mix the whole-wheat flour, fenugreek leaves, yogurt, vegetable oil, ginger-chile paste, red chile powder, turmeric, white sesame seeds, salt, and enough water to knead the mixture into a soft dough. Divide the dough into about 6 roundels and roll each into a thin tortilla-like bread.
2. Heat a griddle over medium heat until hot.
3. Place the bread on the griddle and cook for 3–4 minutes on both sides. Serve hot, with chunda (page 268).

## VAGHARELI KHICHDI

One-pot meal of rice and green gram.

Cooking time: 30 minutes | Serves: 2     Origin: Maharashtra

### INGREDIENTS

1 cup (200 g) rice
1 cup (200 g) split green gram (*moong dal*)
4 Tbsp (60 g) ghee, divided
1 Tbsp (15 g) minced garlic (*lasan*)
1 tsp ginger paste (*adrak*)
2 tsp red chile powder
1 tsp ground turmeric (*haldi*)
½ cup (80 g) green peas (*hara mattar*)
1 medium-size potato, diced
1 medium-size tomato, diced
1 medium-size carrot (*gajar*), diced
1 cup (150 g) diced green bell pepper
1 cup (100 g) chopped cauliflower (*phool gobhi*)
3½ cups (840 ml) water
Salt, to taste
1 green chile, sliced
1 bay leaf (*tej patta*)
2 tsp cumin seeds (*jeera*)
2 tsp peppercorns (*sabut kali mirch*)
1 tsp ground asafoetida (*hing*)
½ cup (8 g) fresh cilantro leaves (*hara dhaniya*), finely chopped

### METHOD

1. In a medium-size bowl, combine the rice and green gram with enough water to cover. Soak for 1 hour. Drain.
2. On your pressure cooker, select Sauté and preheat the cooking pot.
3. Add 2 Tbsp (30 g) of ghee to heat.
4. Add the garlic and ginger paste. Sauté for 2–3 minutes.
5. Add the red chile powder, turmeric, green peas, potato, tomato, carrot, bell pepper, and cauliflower. Cook for 2–3 minutes more.
6. Mix in the drained rice and green gram. Cook for 2 minutes.
7. Pour in the water and season to taste with salt. Lock the lid in place and close the pressure release valve. Select Manual/Pressure Cook and cook the mixture (*khichdi*) for 15 minutes. Release the pressure and remove the lid.
8. In a small skillet over medium-high heat, heat the remaining 2 Tbsp (30 g) of ghee.
9. Add the green chile, bay leaf, cumin seeds, peppercorns, and asafoetida. Cook until the seeds begin to crackle. Pour the spices over the *khichdi* and stir well. Serve hot, garnished with cilantro.

· · · · · · · · · · · ·

## GATTE KA PULAO

Chickpea flour cubes mixed with spices and tossed in rice—a complete meal.

Cooking time: 40 minutes | Serves: 2     Origin: Rajasthan

### INGREDIENTS

1 Tbsp (15 g) ghee
1 tsp cumin seeds (*jeera*)
Pinch ground asafoetida (*hing*)
1 green chile
1 Tbsp (15 g) ginger-garlic paste (*adrak-lasan*)
1 Tbsp (15 g) whole spice mix (page 22)
1 Tbsp (6 g) garam masala
1 tsp red chile powder
½ cup (120 g) fried onions (*birista*; page 30)
1 cup (240 g) gatte ki subzi (page 239)
Salt, to taste
2 cups (400 g) basmati rice, cooked

### METHOD

1. In a medium-size saucepan over medium-high heat, heat the ghee.
2. Add the cumin seeds and asafoetida. Cook until the seeds begin to crackle.
3. Add the green chile, ginger-garlic paste, and whole spice mix. Cook, stirring, for 4–5 minutes.
4. Add the garam masala, red chile powder, and fried onions. Mix well.
5. Add the gatte. Reduce the heat to medium and cook, stirring, for 4–5 minutes. Taste and season with salt, as needed. Add ½ cup (120 ml) of water if the mixture seems too dry.
6. Add the cooked rice. Mix well to combine. Serve hot.

# BROWN CHAWAL

Parsi-style cinnamon-flavored brown rice garnished with fried onions.

Cooking time: 30 min | Serves: 6-8      Origin: Gujarat

## INGREDIENTS

3 Tbsp (45 ml) vegetable oil, divided
1 (1-in. / 2.5-cm) cinnamon stick (*dalchini*)
2 Tbsp (25 g) sugar
4 cups (960 ml) water
1 tsp salt
2 cups (400 g) basmati rice, rinsed, soaked in
    water for 30 minutes, drained
2 medium-size onions, sliced

## METHOD

1. In a heavy-bottomed pan over low heat, heat 1 Tbsp (15 ml) of vegetable oil.
2. Add the cinnamon stick and sugar. Cook, stirring, until the sugar caramelizes (ensuring that the sugar does not burn).
3. Add the water and salt. Bring the mixture to the boil.
4. Add the rice. Cover the pan and cook on low heat for 20 minutes, or until the rice is done and the water is absorbed. Remove from the heat.
5. In a skillet over medium heat, heat the remaining 2 Tbsp (30 ml) of vegetable oil.
6. Add the onions and fry until golden brown. With a slotted spoon, transfer to paper towels to drain.
7. Serve the rice hot, garnished with the fried onions.

# DAL CHAWAL

Lentil-speckled pulao.

Cooking time: 40 min | Serves: 4      Origin: Gujarat

## INGREDIENTS

½ cup (100 g) pigeon peas (*toor dal*)
1 tsp ground turmeric (*haldi*)
Salt, to taste
1 cup (200 g) rice
1 Tbsp (15 ml) vegetable oil
3 garlic cloves (*lasan*), minced
1 green chile, finely chopped
1 tsp cumin seeds (*jeera*)
1 bay leaf (*tej patta*)
1 medium-size onion, finely chopped
¼ cup (4 g) spring onion (*hara pyaz*), finely
    chopped

## METHOD

1. In a medium-size pot over low-medium heat, combine the pigeon peas, turmeric, salt, and enough water to cover. Cook until the pigeon peas are partially cooked. They should not be mushy. Drain.
2. Similarly, cook the rice with enough water to cover until partially cooked. Drain and set aside.
3. In a skillet over low-medium heat, heat the vegetable oil.
4. Add the garlic, green chile, cumin seeds, and bay leaf. Heat until the seeds begin to crackle.
5. Add the onion. Sauté for 2–3 minutes.
6. Add the partially cooked pigeon peas and rice. Stir well to combine. Add about ½ cup water and season to taste with salt. Cover the skillet and reduce the heat to low. Cook for 9–10 minutes, or until everything is soft and cooked through. Serve hot, garnished with spring onion.

## CALANGUTE CLAM PULAO 🍲

Portuguese-influenced clam pilaf.

Cooking time: 45 minutes | Serves: 6      Origin: Goa

### INGREDIENTS

1¾ lb (800 g) clams
3 cups (720 ml) water
3 Tbsp (45 ml) canola oil
1 (1-in. / 2.5-cm) cinnamon stick (*dalchini*)
3 whole cloves (*laung*)
4 spring onions (*hara pyaz*), sliced
3 Tbsp (45 g) minced garlic (*lasan*)
1 Tbsp (15 g) minced ginger (*adrak*)
1 cup (170 g) finely chopped onion
1 tsp ground turmeric (*haldi*)
2 bay leaves (*tej patta*)
2 cups (400 g) basmati rice, soaked in water for 20 minutes, drained
1½ cups (270 g) diced tomato
2 chicken bouillon cubes
Salt, to taste
1 cup (16 g) fresh cilantro leaves (*hara dhaniya*), finely chopped

### METHOD

1.  In a large pot over medium heat, combine the clams and water. Cover the pot and cook until all the clams open. One at a time, gently remove the clams. Save the liquid and carefully pour it out so all the sand remains at the bottom of the pot. Discard any unopened clams. Remove the clams from the shells and discard the shells.
2.  Rinse out the pot and return it to medium-high heat and add the canola oil to heat. Add the cinnamon stick and cloves. Cook until fragrant.
3.  Add the spring onions, garlic, ginger, and finely chopped onion. Cook for 3 minutes, stirring continuously. Add the turmeric, bay leaves, and drained rice. Cook, stirring well, for 4–6 minutes, or until the rice is well coated.
4.  Stir in the tomato, bouillon cubes, and the clam cooking water. Season to taste with salt and bring the mixture to a boil. Gently fold the rice a couple of times and cover the pot. Reduce the heat to low and cook for 15 minutes, or until most of the liquid has evaporated.
5.  Add the clams and cilantro. Remove from the heat and let the pilaf stand, covered, for 15 minutes. Discard the cinnamon stick, cloves, and bay leaves and serve hot.

## ARROZ DE CAMARÃO 📷

Prawn rice flavored with whole spices cooked in coconut milk.

Cooking time: 40 minutes | Serves: 6      Origin: Goa

### INGREDIENTS

1 lb, 2 oz (500 g) medium-size unshelled prawns, washed
3 cups (720 ml) water
2 tsp salt, plus more for sprinkling on the prawns
¼ cup (60 g) ghee
2 medium-size onions, thinly sliced
4 whole cloves (*laung*)
3 (1-in. / 2.5-cm) cinnamon sticks (*dalchini*)
3 green cardamom pods (*choti elaichi*)
12 garlic cloves (*lasan*), minced
1 (2-in. / 5-cm) piece fresh ginger (*adrak*), peeled and chopped
1 large tomato, chopped
1–2 green chiles, chopped
¼ tsp ground turmeric (*haldi*)
2 cups (400 g) long-grain rice
1 cup (240 ml) coconut milk (*nariyal*)
½ tsp sugar

### METHOD

1.  Remove the heads and shells of the prawns. Boil the prawns in the water for 20 minutes. Strain to extract 3 cups (720 ml) of stock. If you don't have 3 cups (720 ml), add enough water to make up the difference.
2.  Devein the cooked prawns, sprinkle with a little salt, and set aside.
3.  In a skillet over medium heat, heat the ghee.
4.  Add the onions. Sauté until light brown.
5.  Add the cloves, cinnamon sticks, and green cardamom pods. Sauté for 30 seconds.
6.  Add the garlic and ginger. Sauté for 1 minute.
7.  Add the tomato, green chiles, and turmeric. Stir-fry until the tomato becomes soft and pulpy.
8.  Add the prawns. Stir-fry for 2 minutes more until they change color.
9.  Add the rice. Stir-fry for 1 minute. Stir in the 3 cups (720 ml) of prawn stock, the coconut milk, salt, and sugar. Bring the mixture to a boil. Cover the skillet and reduce the heat as needed. Simmer, covered, until the rice is tender. Serve hot.

DESSERTS

# BOLO DE COCO

Baked coconut and semolina cake.

Cooking time: 40 minutes | Serves: 6      Origin: Goa

## INGREDIENTS

4 Tbsp (60 g) butter, plus more for preparing the
   cake pan
1 cup (200 g) sugar
¼ cup (60 ml) water
5 oz (140 g) shredded dried unsweetened coconut
   (*nariyal*)
1 cup plus 1 Tbsp (180 g) semolina
½ tsp vanilla extract
1 tsp baking powder
3 eggs, separated

## METHOD

1.  Preheat the oven to 350°F (180°C). Butter a 9-in.
    (22.5-cm) round cake pan and set aside.
2.  In a saucepan over low heat, combine the sugar
    and water. Cook until the sugar dissolves
    completely.
3.  Add the coconut. Cook for 2 minutes.
4.  Stir in the butter, semolina, and vanilla. Mix
    well. Remove from the heat and set aside to
    cool.
5.  Once cool, stir in the baking powder.
6.  In a small bowl, beat the egg yolks until thick
    and foamy. Add them to the semolina mixture
    and stir to combine.
7.  In a medium-size bowl, beat the egg whites
    until stiff. Gently fold into the batter mixture.
    Pour the batter into the prepared pan and bake
    for 25–30 minutes until well risen and golden.
8.  Remove from the oven and let cool in the pan
    for 10 minutes. Turn the cake onto a wire rack
    to cool completely. Cut into pieces and serve.

# PERADA

Guava cheese.

Cooking time: 40 minutes | Makes: 300 grams      Origin: Goa

## INGREDIENTS

6 medium-size guavas, peeled
1¼ cups (300 ml) water, divided
Granulated sugar, as needed
1–2 tsp lemon juice (*nimbu*)
1 tsp butter (optional)
Few drops red food color (optional)

## METHOD

1.  In a medium-size bowl cut the guavas into
    pieces and scoop out the seeds.
2.  Place a saucepan over medium-high heat. Add
    ¼ cup water and the scooped-out seeds. Boil for
    3 minutes. Strain through a sieve. Reserve the
    liquid and discard the seeds.
3.  In a pan over medium-high heat, heat the
    remaining 1 cup of water. Add the guava pieces
    and the reserved liquid. Cook until the guava
    becomes soft and pulpy. Set aside to cool.
4.  In a blender or food processor, blend the
    mixture until smooth. Weigh the pulp.
5.  Return the pulp to the pan. Add the sugar
    (which should be half the weight of the guava
    pulp). Cook, stirring continuously, until the
    mixture begins to leave the sides of the pan and
    is of soft-ball consistency. Add the lemon juice,
    butter, and red food color (if using). Stir well.
    Remove from the heat.
6.  Pour the mixture on to a greased rimmed plate
    and spread evenly with the back of a greased
    spoon. Set aside to cool. Cut into diamond
    shapes to serve.

## RAVA

Roasted semolina sweetened and garnished with dry fruits.

Cooking time: 30 minutes | Serves: 6        Origin: Maharashtra

INGREDIENTS

1 cup (240 g) ghee, divided
1 cup (144 g) blanched almonds (*badam*)
1 cup (144 g) raisins (*kishmish*)
1 cup (170 g) semolina
½ cup (120 ml) water
Sugar, to taste
4 eggs, beaten
4 cups (960 ml) full-fat milk
6 green cardamom pods (*choti elaichi*), ground
½ tsp ground nutmeg (*jaiphal*)
2 tsp rose water, plus more for garnishing

METHOD

1. In a wok over medium heat, heat ½ cup (120 g) of ghee.
2. Add the almonds and raisins. Fry until brown. With a slotted spoon, transfer to paper towels to drain.
3. Turn the heat under the wok to low. In the same ghee, roast the semolina until fragrant. Remove the wok from the heat and mix in the water. Return the wok to the heat and cook for 2–3 minutes. Remove the wok from the heat again and add sugar to taste.
4. In a medium-size bowl, whisk the eggs and milk. Add this to the semolina mixture. Return the wok to low heat and cook, stirring continuously to avoid formation of lumps.
5. Bit by bit, add the remaining ½ cup (120 g) of ghee until the mixture thickens.
6. Stir in the ground green cardamom pods, nutmeg, and rose water. Serve warm in a big bowl, garnished with fried almonds and raisins, and a dash of rose water.

## SEV BARFI

Vermicelli fudge cake.

Cooking time: 30 minutes | Makes: 6        Origin: Maharashtra

INGREDIENTS

1 cup (240 ml) milk
1 cup (200 g) caster (superfine) sugar
1 cup (240 g) whole-milk fudge (*khoya*; page 25)
1 tsp saffron threads (*kesar*)
1 tsp rose water
1 tsp ground cardamom
1 cup (200 g) vermicelli

METHOD

1. In a saucepan over medium heat, heat the milk until it reaches a rolling boil.
2. Stir in the sugar and continue to cook for 20–30 minutes more until the milk begins to reduce.
3. Stir in the whole-milk fudge, saffron threads, rose water, and cardamom. Cook until the mixture thickens further, 20–25 minutes.
4. Add the vermicelli. Cook, stirring, until it softens and the mixture begins to come together. Cook for 4–5 minutes more from this point, stirring continuously. Transfer to a baking dish and set aside for 4–5 hours to set. Refrigerate. Cut into 6 pieces before serving.

## PURAN POLI 🍲

Sweet Indian flatbread stuffed with jaggery and Bengal gram.

Cooking time: 1 hour | Makes: 6     Origin: Maharashtra

INGREDIENTS

5 Tbsp (75 g) ghee, divided, plus more for panfrying and serving
1 cup (200 g) Bengal gram (split chickpeas; *chana dal*), boiled, ground
1 cup (336 g) jaggery (*gur*; unrefined cane sugar)
2 pinches saffron threads (*kesar*)
Pinch ground green cardamom (*choti elaichi*)
Pinch ground nutmeg (*jaiphal*)
1 cup (125 g) whole-wheat flour (*atta*)
Pinch salt
Water, for kneading

METHOD

1. In a saucepan over medium heat, heat 2 Tbsp (30 g) of ghee.
2. Add the ground chickpeas, jaggery, saffron threads, cardamom, and nutmeg. Cook until the mixture comes together into a thick paste and the water has completely evaporated. This should take 15–20 minutes. Divide the mixture equally into 6 small portions.
3. In a medium-size bowl, combine the flour, salt, and remaining 3 Tbsp (45 g) of ghee. Add just enough water to knead the mixture into a soft dough. Divide the dough into small roundels and roll each out into a small disk. Place a spoonful of the filling in the center and fold the edges over to seal the filling inside like quesadilla stuffing. Flatten the stuffed balls and roll again like you would a stuffed bread.
4. Place a griddle over medium heat and add some ghee.
5. Once hot, working in batches, place the stuffed rounds on the griddle and panfry until golden brown on both sides. Serve hot with lots of warm ghee.

## CHURMA LADDOO

Fragrant ghee-laden whole-wheat jaggery balls coated with poppy seeds.

Cooking time: 1 hour | Makes: 15-20     Origin: Rajasthan

INGREDIENTS

3 cups (375 g) whole-wheat flour (*atta*)
7 Tbsp (105 ml) vegetable oil, divided
Warm water, for kneading
1 cup (240 g) ghee, warmed, plus more as needed
1 cup (336 g) finely chopped jaggery (*gur*; unrefined cane sugar)
1 tsp ground cardamom
¼ tsp ground nutmeg (*jaiphal*)
Poppy seeds (*khus khus*), for coating

METHOD

1. In a shallow bowl, combine the whole-wheat flour and 2 Tbsp (30 ml) of vegetable oil. Rub together with your fingertips until a bread crumb-like texture is achieved. Add enough warm water to the flour mixture to knead it into a tight dough. Divide the dough equally into about 10 small roundels and shape each into a *tikki* (flat cake).
2. In a skillet over medium heat, heat the remaining 5 Tbsp (75 ml) of vegetable oil.
3. Working in batches if needed, carefully add the cakes to the hot oil and fry for 5–7 minutes, or until golden-brown. Remove and set aside to cool.
4. When completely cold, grind the cakes into a fine powder and place in a medium-size bowl.
5. Add the warm ghee, jaggery, cardamom, and nutmeg. Mix well. Knead the dough again. Divide the dough equally into 15–20 small portions and shape into balls.
6. Place the poppy seeds in a small bowl. Roll the balls in the poppy seeds until well coated. Serve warm.

## MAKHANE KI KHEER

Sweet thickened rice pudding with lotus seeds.

Cooking time: 1 hour 30 minutes | Serves: 4  Origin: Rajasthan

INGREDIENTS

7 oz (200 g) puffed lotus seeds (*makhane*)
1 cup (240 ml) water
2 qt (1.9 L) milk
1 cup (200 g) sugar

METHOD

1.  In a medium saucepan over medium-high heat, combine the lotus seeds and water. Bring to a boil. Reduce the heat as needed and simmer for 30 minutes. Drain.
2.  In a wok over medium heat, bring the milk to a boil. Reduce the heat as needed and simmer for 30 minutes, or until thick.
3.  Add the lotus seeds to the milk and cook for about 5 minutes.
4.  Stir in the sugar. Cook, stirring, until the sugar dissolves completely. Pour the mixture into a serving dish and serve warm or chilled, as you prefer.

## MALIDA 📷

Sweet confection made with whole-wheat, jaggery, and dried fruits.

Cooking time: 30 minutes | Serves: 4        Origin: Gujarat

INGREDIENTS

8 whole-wheat Indian flatbreads (chapattis) (page 33)
¼ cup (45 g) Medjool dates (*khajoor*), finely chopped
2 Tbsp (18 g) almonds (*badam*)
1 tsp ground cardamom
2 Tbsp (30 g) ghee
½ cup (118 g) grated jaggery (*gur*; unrefined cane sugar)
2 Tbsp (30 g) whole-milk fudge (*khoya*; page 25)

METHOD

1.  In a food processor, blend the flatbread into a coarse powder. Transfer to a plate.
2.  In the same processor (no need to clean it), blend the dates, almonds, and cardamom into a coarse mixture.
3.  In a saucepan over medium heat, heat the ghee.
4.  Add the jaggery, whole-milk fudge, powdered flatbread, and date mixture. Stir until jaggery dissolves and the whole-milk fudge melts. Remove from the heat and cool to room temperature. Serve warm.

## DOODHPAAK
Saffron-laced rice pudding.

Cooking time: 40 minutes | Serves: 2      Origin: Gujarat

INGREDIENTS

1 Tbsp (15 g) ghee
2 Tbsp (25 g) basmati rice, soaked in water,
   drained
2 cups (480 ml) milk
½ cup (100 g) sugar
1 tsp saffron threads (*kesar*), soaked in 2 Tbsp
   (30 ml) warm milk
1 tsp ground cardamom
1 Tbsp (9 g) slivered almonds (*badam*)
1 Tbsp (9 g) slivered pistachios

METHOD

1. In a skillet over low-medium heat, heat the
   ghee.
2. Add the rice. Stir-fry for 2 minutes. Remove
   from the heat and set aside.
3. In a heavy-bottomed saucepan over medium
   heat, heat the milk and bring it to a boil.
4. Stir in the rice. Reduce the heat to low and cook
   for 15–20 minutes.
5. Stir in the sugar and saffron milk. Cook for 15
   minutes more, stirring constantly to avoid
   burning, until the rice is cooked and the milk
   has thickened slightly. Remove the pan from
   the heat and set aside to cool. Refrigerate for
   2 hours.
6. Serve chilled, garnished with cardamom, and
   almond and pistachio slivers.

## MAGAJ NA LADOO
Aromatic chickpea flour fudge.

Cooking time: 40 minutes | Makes: 12      Origin: Gujarat

INGREDIENTS

½ cup (120 g) ghee
2 cups (240 g) chickpea flour ( *besan*)
½ cup (100 g) caster (superfine) sugar
2 Tbsp (10 g) almond powder (*badam*)
1 tsp ground cardamom

METHOD

1. In a heavy-bottomed skillet over medium heat,
   heat the ghee.
2. Add the chickpea flour. Stir-fry for 2–3 minutes
   until the flour turns dark brown. Remove from
   the heat.
3. Stir in the sugar, almond powder, and cardamom.
   Continue to mix until the sugar dissolves
   completely. Divide the mixture equally into 12
   small portions. Roll each into a small ball and
   store in an airtight container. These can be
   stored safely for a week.

## LAPSI

Cracked wheat and jaggery porridge enriched with nuts.

Cooking time: 40 minutes | Serves: 3      Origin: Gujarat

### INGREDIENTS

2 Tbsp (30 g) ghee
2 cups (320 g) cracked wheat (*daliya*)
1 cup (336 g) jaggery (*gur*; unrefined cane sugar)
½ cup (120 ml) water
1 Tbsp (9 g) finely chopped cashews (*kaju*)
Pinch ground black cardamom (*badi elaichi*)
1 Tbsp (5 g) almond powder (*badam*)

### METHOD

1. In a skillet over medium heat, heat the ghee.
2. Add the cracked wheat. Fry for 10–12 minutes, or until golden brown.
3. In a small saucepan over medium heat, melt the jaggery.
4. Carefully and gradually, as the jaggery can splutter, add the water and fried cracked wheat. Stir well.
5. Add the cashews and cardamom. Reduce the heat to low and cook the porridge for about 25 minutes, stirring occasionally. Serve hot, garnished with almond powder.

## GUD PAPDI

Whole-wheat and jaggery sweet treat sprinkled with almonds.

Cooking time: 40 minutes | Serves: 4      Origin: Gujarat

### INGREDIENTS

½ cup (120 g) ghee, plus more for greasing a plate
½ cup (62.5 g) whole-wheat flour (*atta*)
½ cup (118 g) grated jaggery (*gur*; unrefined cane sugar)
2 Tbsp (18 g) sliced almonds (*badam*)
1 sheet silver leaf (*warq*; available at Indian markets; page 24)

### METHOD

1. Grease a plate with ghee and set aside.
2. In a heavy-bottomed saucepan over low heat, heat the ghee.
3. Add the flour. Toast for 10 minutes, or until the flour turns golden brown. Remove from the heat.
4. Stir in the jaggery until it completely melts into the mixture. Transfer the mixture onto the prepared plate and spread it evenly with a flat spoon. Cut the mixture into diamond-shaped pieces while still warm.
5. Sprinkle almonds and silver leaf over top. Let set for 20 minutes. Serve warm.

## MOHANTHAAL

Molten sweet chickpea flour fudge.

Cooking time: 40 minutes | Serves: 2       Origin: Gujarat

### INGREDIENTS

¾ cup (180 g) ghee, divided, plus more for greasing the container

1½ cups (180 g) chickpea flour (*besan*)

5 Tbsp (75 g) whole-milk fudge (*khoya*; available at Indian markets; page 25)

1 cup (240 ml) sugar syrup, one-thread consistency, warmed (page 30–31)

1 tsp ground cardamom

5 Tbsp (45 g) slivered almonds (*badam*)

2 Tbsp (18 g) pistachios, slivered

### METHOD

1. Grease a high-sided casserole dish or other container with ghee. Set aside.
2. In a medium-size bowl, combine 2 Tbsp (30 g) of ghee and the flour. Rub together with your fingertips until well incorporated and the mixture resembles bread crumbs.
3. In a skillet over low heat, heat the remaining 10 Tbsp (150 g) of ghee.
4. Add the flour mixture. Stir-fry for 15–20 minutes, or until dark brown in color.
5. Add the whole-milk fudge. Cook, stirring, for 5 minutes more. Remove the pan from the heat and stir in the warm sugar syrup, stirring until the syrup is well absorbed into the mixture.
6. Stir in the cardamom. Transfer to the prepared dish and spread it evenly.
7. Garnish with almond and pistachio slivers. Cut into diamond-shaped pieces and allow it to set until it comes to room temperature. Serve the pieces individually or eat it semi-soft with a spoon.

## PINEAPPLE BASUNDI

Caramelized pineapple in saffron milk.

Cooking time: 40 minutes | Serves: 2       Origin: Gujarat

### INGREDIENTS

¾ cup (180 g) grated pineapple (*ananas*)

1 cup (200 g) caster (superfine) sugar, divided

2 cups (480 ml) milk

1 tsp saffron threads (*kesar*)

1 tsp ground cardamom

### METHOD

1. Place a skillet over medium heat.
2. When hot, add the pineapple and 1 tsp of sugar. Sauté for 2 minutes, or until the sugar dissolves and the pineapple begins to burn out its water. Remove from the heat and set aside.
3. In a heavy-bottomed saucepan over medium heat, bring the milk to a rolling boil. Continue boiling the milk for 20 minutes to reduce.
4. Add the caramelized pineapple mixture along with the remaining sugar, the saffron threads, and cardamom. Cook for 10 minutes. Remove from the heat and set aside to cool. Refrigerate for 2 hours before serving.

# ACCOMPANIMENTS

## DUGARI CHAACH

Spiced, smoked yogurt buttermilk.

Cooking time: 20 minutes | Serves: 2          Origin: Rajasthan

INGREDIENTS

1 cup (240 g) yogurt (*dahi*)
1 green chile, finely chopped
1 tsp chopped peeled fresh ginger (*adrak*)
1 tsp ground cumin (*jeera*)
Sea salt, to taste
2½–3 cups (600–720 ml) water
1 Tbsp (15 g) ghee, divided
1 tsp cumin seeds (*jeera*)
½ tsp mustard seeds (*rai*)
Dungaar (page 26)

METHOD

1. In a glass pitcher, combine the yogurt, green chile, ginger, cumin, sea salt, and water. Use an immersion blender to blend until smooth. Chill in the refrigerator.
2. In a small skillet over medium-high heat, heat 1½ tsp of ghee.
3. Add the cumin seeds and mustard seeds. Cook until the seeds begin to crackle. Pour the tempering into the yogurt mixture and stir well to combine.
4. Meanwhile prepare the dungaar.
5. In a pan, heat the remaining ghee. Pour the melted ghee over the prepared dungaar and shut the lid for 2 minutes.
6. Open the lid and pull out the bowl and quickly pour the buttermilk into the big bowl.
7. Stir well to ensure the liquid catches the flavor of the smoke, shut the lid for 7–8 minutes more. Adjust the sea salt, if required and serve.

## SOL KADHI

A refreshing kokum drink with coconut milk.

Cooking time: 20 minutes | Serves: 2          Origin: Maharashtra

INGREDIENTS

8 pieces fresh kokum
1 cup (240 ml) hot water
Pinch ground asafoetida (*hing*)
Salt, to taste
1 cup (85 g) shredded dried unsweetened coconut (*nariyal*)
2 garlic cloves (*lasan*), peeled
1 green chile, finely chopped
Indian black salt (*kala namak*), to taste
2 Tbsp (2 g) fresh cilantro leaves (*hara dhaniya*), finely chopped

METHOD

1. In a small bowl, combine the kokum, hot water, asafoetida, and salt. Soak for 30 minutes. Drain, reserve the soaking water, and set aside. Discard the solids.
2. In a food processor, blend the coconut, garlic, green chile, and ½ cup (120 ml) of water. Squeeze out the coconut milk from this purée into the bowl with the kokum soaking water. Stir into a refreshing drink. Serve with a dash of black salt and a sprinkle of cilantro.

## AMALVANIYA

Tamarind drink—a perfect thirst quencher.

Cooking time: 20 minutes | Serves: 2        Origin: Rajasthan

### INGREDIENTS

1 cup (240 g) tamarind (*imli*), soaked in warm
   water for 2 hours, drained
4 cups (960 ml) water
2 cups (400 g) sugar

### METHOD

1. In a blender, blitz the tamarind. Strain to remove
   the fiber and seeds. Transfer to a medium-size
   bowl.
2. Stir in the water and sugar, stirring until the
   sugar dissolves completely. Serve chilled,
   over ice.

. . . . . . . . . . . .

## JAL JEERA

Refreshing raw mango drink.

Cooking time: 20 minutes | Serves: 2        Origin: Rajasthan

### INGREDIENTS

1 cup (175 g) finely chopped raw mango (*kairi*)
¼ cup (4 g) fresh cilantro leaves (*hara dhaniya*),
   finely chopped
¼ cup (32 g) fresh mint leaves (*pudina*),
   finely chopped
2 Tbsp (25 g) sugar
1 tsp ground cumin (*jeera*)
1 tsp Indian black salt (*kala namak*)
Salt, to taste
Cold water, as needed

### METHOD

1. In a blender, combine all the ingredients and
   blend until smooth. Add cold water to adjust
   the consistency.
2. Strain and transfer the mixture into tall glasses.
   Add ice or more cold water and stir well before
   serving.

## KOKUM SHERBET

Cool and rejuvenating kokum drink.

Cooking time: 20 minutes | Serves: 2        Origin: Maharashtra

### INGREDIENTS

1 cup (240 g) fresh kokum, soaked in 2 cups (480
   ml) water for 1 hour, drained, soaking water
   reserved
½ cup (100 g) caster (superfine) sugar
1½ tsp ground cumin (*jeera*)
1 tsp Indian black salt (*kala namak*)

### METHOD

1. In a blender or food processor, combine the
   drained kokum with half the reserved soaking
   water. Blend until smooth. Strain through a
   fine-mesh sieve and set aside.
2. In a saucepan over low heat, mix the remaining
   half of the reserved kokum water with the sugar.
   Cook, stir continuously, until the sugar dissolves
   completely. Remove the pan from the heat and
   let cool to room temperature.
3. Mix the strained kokum paste with the sugar
   syrup and stir well. Strain the mixture again
   over a bowl. Discard the remaining solids.
4. To the strained liquid, add the cumin and black
   salt. Stir well to combine.
5. Pour about 3 Tbsp (45 ml) of the kokum
   concentrate in a glass. Add ice and water.
   Serve cold.

## DOODH SHERBET 🍮

Rose syrup-spiked milk shake.

Cooking time: 10 minutes | Serves: 2      Origin: Gujarat

### INGREDIENTS

2 cups (480 ml) full-fat milk
3 Tbsp (45 ml) rose syrup
1 Tbsp (9 g) basil seeds (*subja*), soaked in water
Sugar, to taste

### METHOD

1. In a small bowl, combine all the ingredients and stir well. Serve chilled in tall glasses over ice.

. . . . . . . . . . . . .

## CHUNDA

Sweet mango relish.

Cooking time: 30 minutes | Makes: 10½ oz (300 grams)
Origin: Gujarat

### INGREDIENTS

1 cup (175 g) grated raw mango (*kairi*)
1 cup (200 g) sugar
½ tsp ground turmeric (*haldi*)
1 tsp red chile powder
½ tsp ground cumin (*jeera*)

### METHOD

1. In a medium-size bowl, combine all the ingredients and toss well. Transfer the mixture to a nonstick pan and place it over medium heat. Sauté until the sugar melts. When the mixture starts to bubble, reduce the heat to low and cook until the sugar syrup reaches a one-thread consistency (page 31). Remove from the heat and cool completely before serving.

## SURATI SALAD

Crunchy cucumber salad.

Cooking time: 5 minutes | Serves: 3-4      Origin: Gujarat

### INGREDIENTS

1 tsp vegetable oil
Pinch ground asafoetida (*hing*)
1 Tbsp (12.5 g) Bengal gram (*chana dal*), roasted
1 Tbsp (9 g) peanuts (*moongphalli*), roasted, chopped
1 Tbsp (4 g) coconut (*nariyal*), fresh, grated
1 tsp sesame seeds (*til*), roasted
2 green chiles, finely chopped
½ tsp sugar
Salt, to taste
1 cup (300 g) cucumber (*khira*), small, diced

### METHOD

1. In a skillet over medium-high heat, heat the vegetable oil.
2. Add the asafoetida and Bengal gram. Sauté for 2 minutes.
3. In a large bowl, mix the peanuts, coconut, sesame seeds, green chiles, sugar, and salt.
4. Add the Bengal gram-asafoetida mixture and cucumber. Taste to adjust the seasoning and serve.

## MARCHA NU ATHANU

Green chile pickle.

Cooking time: 15 minutes | Makes: 500 grams   Origin: Gujarat

### INGREDIENTS

1 lb, 2 oz (500 g) green chiles, thick, washed, dried
**For the filling**
¾ cup (204 g) Indian black salt (*kala namak*)
¾ tsp ground mustard (*rai*)
½ tsp ground asafoetida (*hing*)
1 tsp ground turmeric (*haldi*)
2 Tbsp (30 ml) vegetable oil
Juice of 2 lemons (*nimbu*)

### METHOD

1. In a medium-size bowl, slit each chile lengthwise. Gently tap the sides to remove the excess seeds.
2. **To make the filling:** In a small bowl, combine the black salt, mustard, asafoetida, turmeric, and the vegetable oil. Mix well.
3. Stuff the filling in each chile. Preserve the stuffed chiles in a sterilized container. Top with leftover filling, if any.
4. Add the lemon juice and shake the container well.
5. Set aside for at least 1 day before serving.

## LAGAN NU ACHAR

Wedding pickle.

Cooking time: 30-45 minutes | Makes: 500 grams
Origin: Gujarat

### INGREDIENTS

3.5 oz (100 g) dried dates (*khajoor*), finely chopped
3 cups (300 g) raisins (*kishmish*)
3 cups (300 g) dried apricots (*khumani*)
10 cups (2 kg) sugar, divided
3¼ cups (780 ml) vinegar (*sirka*), divided
4 lb, 6 oz (2 kg) carrots (*gajar*), grated
¾ cup (180 g) jaggery (*gur;* unrefined cane sugar)
½ cup (50 g) ginger (*adrak*), julienned
1 cup (100 g) garlic (*lasan*), sliced
Salt to taste
15 dried red chiles (*sookhi lal mirch*)
2 Tbsp (12 g) garam masala

### METHOD

1. In a large bowl, soak the dates, raisins, and apricots in 1 cup (200 g) sugar and 1 cup (240 ml) vinegar for 8 hours.
2. Place a heavy-bottomed pan over low heat. Add the carrots, the remaining sugar, jaggery, and the remaining vinegar. Cook until the carrots become soft.
3. Add the ginger and garlic. Season to taste with salt. Cook, stirring until the mixture becomes sticky.
4. Add the mixture of dates, raisins, and apricots. Bring to a boil.
5. Add the dried red chiles and garam masala. Set aside to cool and store in an airtight container. This pickle can be preserved for several years if handled properly and kept in a cool, dark place.

## LASAN CHUTNEY

Dry garlic chutney. Use as a spread or serve with a full-course Maharashtrian meal.

Cooking time: 10 minutes | Makes: 80 grams
Origin: Maharashtra

INGREDIENTS

8 garlic cloves (*lasan*), peeled
3 Tbsp (15 g) desiccated coconut powder (*nariyal*)
1 Tbsp (8 g) white sesame seeds (*safed til*)
1 Tbsp (9 g) peanuts
2 tsp red chile powder
1 tsp ground coriander (*dhaniya*)
1 tsp tamarind paste (*imli*; page 30)
1 tsp vegetable oil
Salt, to taste

METHOD

1. In a skillet over low-medium heat, combine the garlic, coconut powder, sesame seeds, peanuts, red chile powder, and coriander. Dry-roast until the ingredients begin to emit a nutty aroma. Transfer to a food processor and blend into a coarse powder.
2. Add the tamarind paste, vegetable oil, and salt. Mix well.

## KACHRI KI CHUTNEY

A tangy relish.

Cooking time: 30 minutes | Makes: 250 grams
Origin: Rajasthan

INGREDIENTS

1 tsp vegetable oil
½ cup (120 g) garlic cloves (*lasan*), ground
2 Tbsp (20 g) caper powder (ground *kachri*; available at some Indian markets and online; page 22)
1 tsp ground cumin (*jeera*)
1 medium-size onion, chopped
4–5 dried red chiles (*sookhi lal mirch*), ground
½ cup (120 g) yogurt (*dahi*)
Salt, to taste

METHOD

1. In skillet over medium heat, heat the vegetable oil.
2. Add the garlic, caper powder, and cumin. Sauté for a few seconds.
3. Add the onion. Fry until golden brown.
4. Add the dried red chiles, yogurt, and salt. Reduce the heat to low and cook until the oil separates. Remove from the heat. Refrigerate in an airtight jar for up to 1 month.

## PAPAYA SAMBHARO

Refreshing raw papaya salad with a hint of asafoetida.

Time: 20 minutes | Makes: 50 grams          Origin: Gujarat

### INGREDIENTS

1 tsp vegetable oil
2 green chiles, finely chopped
1 tsp mustard seeds (*rai*)
Pinch ground asafoetida (*hing*)
1 cup (175 g) grated raw papaya (*papita*)
1 tsp ground turmeric (*haldi*)
Salt, to taste

### METHOD

1. In a skillet over medium-high heat, heat the vegetable oil.
2. Add the green chiles, mustard seeds, and asafoetida. Cook until the seeds begin to crackle.
3. Add the papaya and turmeric. Season to taste with salt. Cover the skillet and cook for 5 minutes, or until the papaya is soft. Serve at room temperature.

## CHETNIM DE CAMARÕES SECOS

Dried roasted prawn relish.

Cooking time: 5 minutes | Makes: 50 grams          Origin: Goa

### INGREDIENTS

1¾ oz (50 g) dried prawns, cleaned, top part of the head and tip of the tail and legs pinched off
1 medium-size onion, minced
5 Tbsp (25 g) shredded dried unsweetened coconut (*nariyal*)
2 garlic cloves (*lasan*), minced
2 tsp tamarind pulp (*imli*; page 30)
1 tsp Kashmiri red chile powder
Pinch ground turmeric (*haldi*)
Salt, to taste

### METHOD

1. In a skillet over medium heat, dry-roast the prawns until crisp.
2. In a medium-size bowl, stir together the onion, coconut, garlic, tamarind pulp, Kashmiri red chile powder, and turmeric. Season to taste with salt. Crumble in the prawns and stir to combine. Alternatively, in a skillet over medium heat, sauté the onion and garlic in a little vegetable oil for about 3 minutes. Transfer to a blender or food processor, add the remaining ingredients, and grind to a coarse paste. Serve with rice and curry.

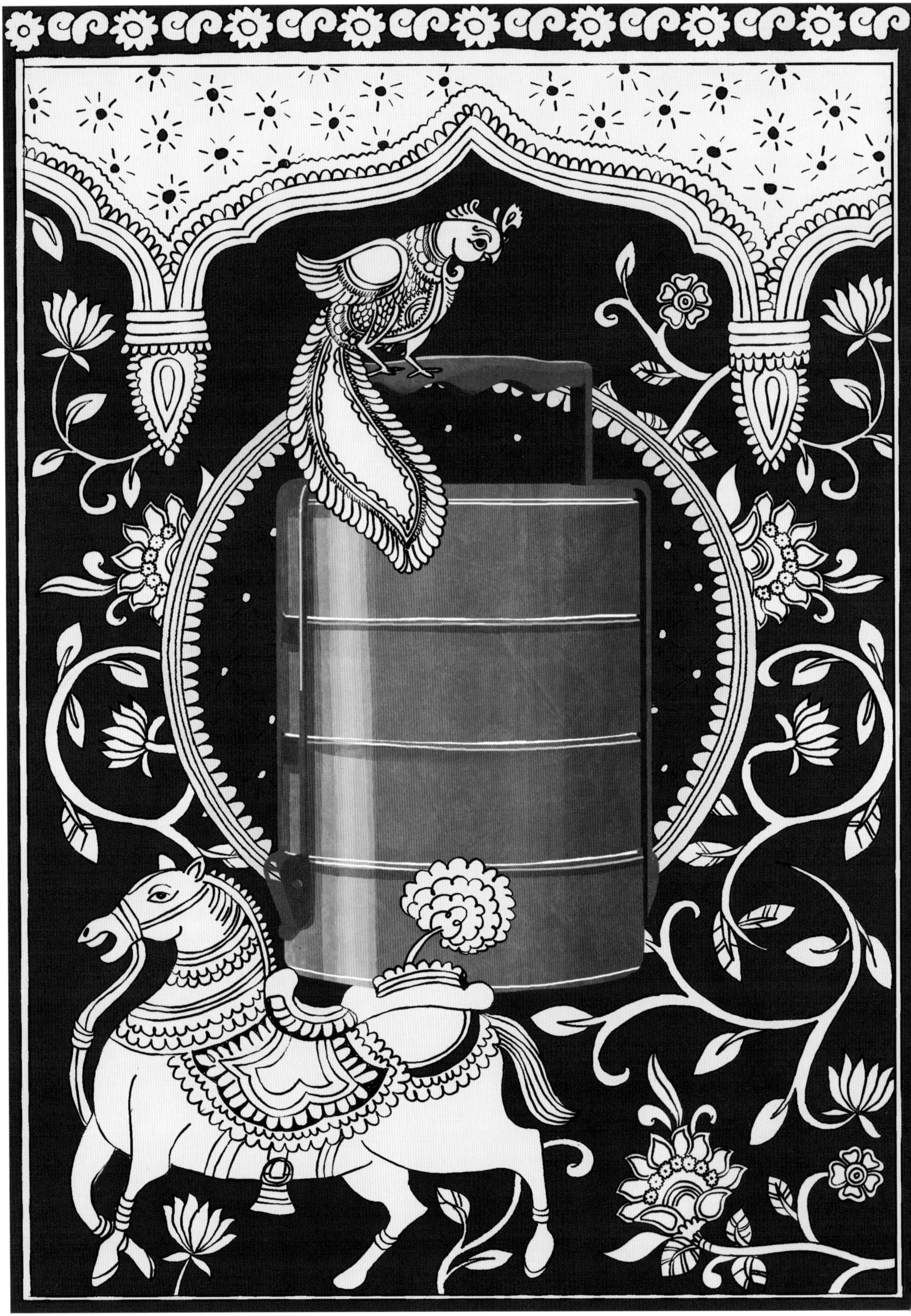

# south india

TELANGANA . KARNATAKA .
ANDHRA PRADESH . TAMIL NADU . KERALA

There is a saying: "Give a South Indian bananas, coconuts, and rice, and they'll come up with at least 100 recipes using just these three ingredients." This could well be true, as many traditional South Indian recipes have at least one of these three ingredients cleverly used to make a snack, a main course, or a dessert. This is not to say that South Indian cuisine is restricted to these ingredients. The states of Karnataka, Andhra Pradesh, Kerala, Tamil Nadu, and Telangana, with their beautiful tropical weather, use these ingredients plus a variety of rice, lentils, dried red chiles, curry leaves, *urad* dal, tamarind, fenugreek, and mustard seeds.

It is believed that in 9000 BCE, before the Indus Valley Civilization, Neolithic settlers introduced the idea of domesticating plants in the Indian subcontinent. One study claims agricultural activities, especially cultivation of cotton, pulses, millets, wheat, and seeds, to have begun in Andhra Pradesh and Karnataka, which makes South Indian cuisine the oldest in the country.

The most widely traveled and popular dishes from the southern part of the country include an assortment of idlis, dosas, chutneys, and sambhars. From the crumbly, crispy ghee-roasted dosa to the coarse, gritty coconut chutney, it is a motley of flavors and textures.

While a large part of the country consumes wheat-based breads that are used to soak up curries, dals, and gravies, here you will savor gluten-free lentil and rice-based breads as accompaniments. Indigenous grains, foxtail or *thinai*, finger millet or ragi, and little millet or *samai*, from South India, are now classified as superfoods because of their healthy qualities. Take for instance Andhra Pradesh's *pesarattu*—a combination of dals cooked on a griddle like a thin crepe. In Kerala and Tamil Nadu, you will find appams, concave crepes made of pulverized rice, which are best eaten with stews. Most South Indian breads are so refined that they can be eaten on their own, without meat or vegetables, with a side of a fiery chile or curry-leaf *podi*, or a calming coconut- and yogurt-laced chutney.

Bananas play an integral role not only as an ingredient, but as a handy kitchen tool. Throughout South India, you will find that eateries serve food on fresh, clarified plantain (raw banana) leaves,

as it is traditionally believed to be auspicious and healthy to eat off a banana leaf. Historically, food was served to deities on plantain leaves and then distributed as *prasad* (holy offering). Banana leaves contain polyphenols (natural antioxidants) that are believed to transfer to the food that is served on it.

Today, banana leaves are used mainly for weddings and festivals such as Onam. The leaves are also used for wrapping or steaming food such as marinated fish.

Tempering is an important element of dishes from this region. What separates a typical South Indian tempering from that of other parts of the country is the presence of fenugreek seeds, whole peppercorns, curry leaves, dried red chiles, mustard, lentils, and particularly *urad* dal, blistered in hot oil, though not necessarily all together.

Surrounded by the Arabian Sea, Bay of Bengal, and the Indian Ocean, South India is rich in seafood, including a variety of fish, ranging from king fish, *surmai*, sear fish, pearl spot, sardine, and shark, and to seafood such as crab, mussel, shrimp, and prawn. Here, the catch is fresh, and gravies are sprightly and served with helpings of fluffy rice, translucent *neer* dosas, appams, or flaky parathas.

A notable contributor to a unique variation of cuisine that is today ubiquitous in many parts of the country is a small town called Udupi in Karnataka. Udupi is the birthplace of the dosa, a crispy lentil- and rice-based crepe that is popular in Mumbai, Manchester, and Manhattan alike, being served at pop-ups and food trucks, and in various formats such as the dosa waffle at the hip New York cafe called Inday. It is to India what the crepe is to France.

Udupi cooks adhere to a strict *satvik* tradition of using no onions and no garlic in their daily cooking. A typical menu includes *saaru* or rasam, *huli* (coconut-based gravy), *patrode* or spicy roundels, *undala kai* (steamed rice balls), and a milky kheer-like dessert. But newer variations, available in Udupi cafes in Indian metros, have forsaken these recipes to serve more common South Indian dishes such as idli, dosa, *medu* vada, dahi vada, and uttapam.

Further down, we discovered Konkani Muslim cuisine, which takes pride in heavy coastal curries and fish- and meat-based appetizers. Here, the red and green curries are similar to their Thai namesakes. Traditional Muslim houses prefer dishes like simple seafood biryani and *salans* that are loaded with crispy, fried fish. Interestingly, the urban Konkani Muslims living in metro cities consume chic mince-lamb loaves, lentil and coconut curry, tropical cucumber pancakes, and an occasional coconut and banana cake.

Andhra dining tables shine with *pesarattu* (lentil pancake), *pappu* (spinach and tomato dal), *gongura mamsam* (gravy speckled with juicy lamb and *gongura* leaves), rasam (peppery soup), and *ullipaya karam* (fiery onion chutney). The joint capital of Andhra Pradesh and the newly formed state of Telangana is Hyderabad, a city famous for its rich royal history and for the food it inherited from this legacy. Nizami rule enriched the cuisine of Hyderabad by introducing dishes such as *haleem*, *khubani ka meetha*, *sheermal*, *paya*, and *mirchi ka salan*. The cuisine from the southernmost state in India, Kerala, is a confluence of Christian, Muslim, and Hindu culinary expressions. Historically, Kerala attracted Portuguese, Dutch, Chinese, Arab, and British traders, among others, who brought with them their own distinct cultures. As settlers made the ports of Kerala their home, their culinary

traditions combined with indigenous ones results in a most unique cuisine that is still today distinct from the rest of the country's. The Hindu population of the state serves a special meal called the *sadya* (which refers to a large meal in Malayalam) that is predominantly vegetarian, comprising sambhar, rasam, *avail*, *kaalan*, *thoran*, *pachadi*, pappadam, *uperi*, and various forms of vegetarian stews, gravies, sides, and stir-fries served in a specific order on a banana leaf.

The Syrian Christians of Kerala take pride in beautifully cooked meat stews, non-vegetarian *thorans* or stir-fries, cutlets, and *sallas* or salad with a liberal use of lamb or beef. The cuisine of the Muslims of Kerala, known as the Mappilas, is a combination of Keralite and Arab food traditions. Take for instance *alissa*, a wheat- and meat-based porridge that is similar to *harissa*. Their biryani has an Arab touch, as rice and meat are cooked separately and then layered. Here, you will also find the famous Sulaimani chai—a black tea brewed with a dash of lemon and spices—which gets its name from the Sulaymani Bohras, a community from Saudi Arabia and from Yemen that was settled here.

Tamil Nadu is rich in its culinary traditions. Here, you begin the day with pongal, a rice flour–based breakfast porridge doused in sambhar and coconut chutney, best enjoyed when eaten with your hands. This cuisine's most nuanced fare comes from Chettinad, a quaint town known for its 19th-century–style mansions, wide verandas, central courtyards, and stellar architecture. Though traditionally a vegetarian community, Chettiars turned non-vegetarian after establishing businesses in Ceylon, Burma, and Malaysia since the 18th century. What separates Chettiar cooking from other South Indian cooking is the puritanical methods of hand-pounding spices in stone grinders, chopping vegetables with an *aruamanai* or iron blade, and cooking food in different fire-woods to develop specific flavors.

The most striking feature of South Indian cuisines is its intense flavors. Be it a curry leaf and chile-flavored gravy, or a milky cardamom-laced dessert, expect pronounced flavors everywhere. We think that no cuisine in India makes a hero out of seafood and spices like South Indian cuisines.

# APPETIZERS

## ELUMICHAPAZHAM RASAM

Thin green gram soup with a hint of lemon.

Cooking time: 20 minutes | Serves: 2    Origin: Tamil Nadu

INGREDIENTS

1½ Tbsp (18.75 g) split green gram (*moong dal*)
1 Tbsp (15 ml) vegetable oil
¼ tsp mustard seeds (*rai*)
1 (1-in. / 2.5-cm) piece peeled fresh ginger (*adrak*),
   finely chopped
1 green chile, slit
1½ cups (360 ml) water
½ tsp ground turmeric (*haldi*)
Juice of 2 lemons (*nimbu*)
Salt, to taste
1 small bunch fresh cilantro leaves (*hara dhaniya*),
   finely chopped

METHOD

1. Boil the green gram in enough water to cover
   until soft. Drain and mash the green gram.
   Set aside.
2. In a skillet over low-medium heat, heat the
   vegetable oil.
3. Add the mustard seeds. Cook until the seeds
   begin to crackle.
4. Add the ginger and green chile. Sauté until the
   ginger turns brown.
5. Add the mashed green gram to the tempering.
   Pour in the water and add the turmeric. Reduce
   the heat to low and bring the mixture to a boil.
6. Stir in the lemon juice and salt. Remove from
   the heat and ladle into serving bowls. Serve hot,
   garnished with cilantro.

## KUZHI PANIYARAM 🍲

Steamed dumplings mixed with vegetables.

Cooking time: 40 minutes | Serves: 2    Origin: Karnataka

INGREDIENTS

1 cup (240 g) idli / dosa batter, available at
   Indian markets)
1 tsp vegetable oil
1 tsp mustard seeds (*rai*)
1 tsp Bengal gram (split chickpeas; *chana dal*)
1 tsp black lentils (*urad dal*)
2 tsp ginger-chile paste (*adrak-mirchi*)
2–3 curry leaves (*kadhi patta*)
1 cup (240 g) mixed chopped vegetables (carrot
   [*gajar*], beans, green peas [*hara mattar*])
2 Tbsp (10 g) finely chopped fresh coconut
   (*nariyal*)
Salt, to taste
1 Tbsp (1 g) fresh cilantro leaves (*hara dhaniya*),
   finely chopped
Ghee, for preparing the paniyaram mold (available
   online) and panfrying

METHOD

1. Place the batter in a medium-size bowl and set
   aside.
2. In a skillet over medium heat, heat the vegetable
   oil.
3. Add the mustard seeds, chickpeas, and black
   lentils. Cook until the seeds begin to crackle.
   Add the ginger-chile paste and curry leaves.
   Sauté for 2 minutes.
4. Add the mixed vegetables. Sauté for about 10
   minutes, or until semi-cooked.
5. Add the coconut and season to taste with salt.
   Mix well. Remove from the heat and sprinkle in
   the cilantro. Add this mixture to the idli / dosa
   batter and stir well to combine.
6. Grease the paniyaram mold with ghee and pour
   the batter into the wells. Cook over medium
   heat for 5–7 minutes, or until done. Flip the
   dough with the wooden spatula and cook on the
   other side until done. Serve hot, with coconut
   chutney (page 31), if desired.

# THAIR VADAIS
Black gram dumplings in spiced yogurt.

Cooking time: 1 hour | Makes: 12-15      Origin: Tamil Nadu

## INGREDIENTS

**For the vadai (dumplings)**
2 cups (400 g) split black lentils (*urad dal*), soaked
   in water overnight, drained
Salt, to taste
½ cup (32 g) curry leaves (*kadhi patta*), chopped
2 green chiles, finely chopped
1 Tbsp (15 g) crushed peeled fresh ginger (*adrak*)
1 Tbsp (15 ml) freshly squeezed lemon juice
   (*nimbu*)
½ tsp ground asafoetida (*hing*) stirred into ½ cup
   (120 ml) water

**For spice mix**
2 dried red chiles (*sookhi lal mirch*)
1 tsp cumin seeds (*jeera*)
½ tsp black mustard seeds (*rai*)

**For the yogurt**
2 tsp vegetable oil
½ cup (32 g) curry leaves (*kadhi patta*), chopped
4 green chiles
3 cups (720 g) yogurt (*dahi*)
1 cup (240 ml) water
Salt, to taste
Vegetable oil, for deep-frying

## METHOD

1. **To make the vadai:** In a blender or food processor, grind the black lentils to a paste. Add salt to taste, the curry leaves, green chiles, ginger, lemon juice, and asafoetida water. Blend into a stiff batter and set aside.

2. **To make the spice mix:** In a blender or mortar and pestle, coarsely crush the dried red chiles, cumin seeds, and mustard seeds.

3. **To make the yogurt:** In a wok over low-medium heat, heat the vegetable oil.

4. Add the coarsely crushed spice mix, curry leaves, and green chiles. Cook for a few seconds.

5. Stir in the yogurt and water. Season to taste with salt. Transfer to a bowl and set aside.

6. **To finish the vadai:** Clean the wok and return it to the heat. Heat the vegetable oil for deep-frying.

7. Have a bowl of cold water nearby. Gently lower spoonfuls of the black gram batter into the hot oil and deep-fry the dumplings until golden. Remove and drain on paper towels to remove the excess oil. Transfer the dumplings to the water for just a few seconds. Remove and gently squeeze out the excess water. Repeat with the remaining batter.

8. Add the dumplings to the spiced yogurt and serve cold.

# VAZAIPOO VADAIS 🍽

Deep-fried plantain flower fritters.

Cooking time: 40 minutes | Makes: 16      Origin: Tamil Nadu

## INGREDIENTS

¼ cup (60 ml) buttermilk (*chaach*)

1 tsp salt, plus more as needed

1 lb, 2 oz (500 g) large plantain flowers

2 cups (480 ml) vegetable oil, for frying

1 cup (200 g) Bengal gram (split chickpeas; *chana dal*), fried and ground

4 oz (120 g) dried unsweetened coconut (*nariyal*), ground to a paste

1 tsp ground cumin (*jeera*)

1 tsp ginger-garlic paste (*adrak-lasan*)

½ tsp garam masala

1 slice bread, soaked in water, squeezed

1 tsp ghee

1 medium-size onion, finely chopped

2 green chiles, finely chopped

½ cup (8 g) fresh cilantro leaves (*hara dhaniya*), chopped

## METHOD

1. In a large bowl, stir together the buttermilk and salt. Set aside.
2. Discard the outer dark leaves encasing the plantain flowers and gently remove the flowers. Discard the stamen and the outer transparent pink skin at the base of each flower. Chop the flowers into fine pieces and add them to the buttermilk. Soak for about 30 minutes. Squeeze out all the liquid, and rinse the flowers in fresh water. Pat dry.
3. In a wok over medium-high heat, heat the vegetable oil.
4. Add the flowers. Fry for 2 minutes. Transfer to paper towels to drain. Set aside to cool.
5. In a blender or mortar and pestle, grind the fried flowers into a fine powder. Transfer to a medium-size bowl.
6. Add the Bengal gram, coconut paste, cumin, ginger-garlic paste, garam masala, and bread. Knead into a smooth mixture. Mix in the ghee. The mixture should be firm yet soft and yielding. Alter the amount of ground Bengal gram and bread to achieve the consistency required to shape the mixture.
7. Add the onion, green chiles, and cilantro. Adjust the seasoning with more salt, if required. Divide the mixture equally into 16 portions and shape each into a smooth lime-size ball. Flatten each in the hollow of your hand to form a vadai (a doughnut).
8. Return the wok to medium-high heat and reheat the oil remaining in it.
9. Working in batches, gently lower the vadais into the hot oil. Deep-fry until golden brown. With a slotted spoon, transfer the vadais to paper towels to drain. Serve hot as a snack with ketchup, if desired.

# KANCHIPURAM IDLI

Idli tempered with spices and turmeric.

Cooking time: 30 minutes | Serves: 3       Origin: Tamil Nadu

INGREDIENTS

1 cup (200 g) idli rice, soaked in water for 6 hours,
    drained
¾ cup (150 g) split black lentils (*urad dal*), soaked
    in water for 6 hours, drained
Water, as needed
¼ cup (4 g) fresh cilantro leaves (*hara dhaniya*),
    finely chopped
1 tsp ground turmeric (*haldi*)
Pinch ground asafoetida (*hing*)
1 Tbsp (15 g) ghee
5 curry leaves (*kadhi patta*)
¼ cup (36 g) mixed cashews (*kaju*) and raisins
    (*kishmish*)
1 Tbsp (12.5 g) Bengal gram (split chickpeas;
    *chana dal*)
1 Tbsp (15 g) ginger-chile paste (*adrak mirch*)
1 tsp cumin seeds (*jeera*)
1 tsp mustard seeds (*rai*)
Salt, to taste

METHOD

1. In a food processor combine the rice and black
   lentils. Grind together into a coarse paste.
2. Add water to adjust the consistency—making it
   not too thick or thin, simply pourable.
3. Cover and let ferment at room temperature
   overnight.
4. Whisk the rice-lentil mixture and add the
   cilantro, turmeric, and asafoetida. Stir well to
   combine.
5. In a skillet over low-medium heat, heat the
   ghee.
6. Add the remaining ingredients. Cook until the
   seeds begin to crackle. Add the mixture to the
   idli batter.
7. Stir well. Fill an idli mold with the batter. Steam
   for 10–12 minutes and serve hot with coconut
   chutney (page 31), if desired.

# ARBI BONDA

Crispy taro root.

Cooking time: 30 minutes | Makes: 6       Origin: Karnataka

INGREDIENTS

2 cups (450 g) boiled, mashed taro root (*arbi*)
6 green chiles, chopped
1 Tbsp (1 g) fresh cilantro leaves (*hara dhaniya*),
    chopped
1 Tbsp (15 g) yogurt (*dahi*)
1 tsp chopped peeled fresh ginger (*adrak*)
Pinch ground asafoetida (*hing*)
Salt, to taste
1 cup (125 g) all-purpose flour (*maida*)
½ cup (60 g) chickpea flour (*besan*)
½ cup (80 g) rice flour
Baking soda, pinch
Water, as needed
Vegetable oil, for frying

METHOD

1. In a medium-size bowl, stir together the mashed
   taro root, green chiles, cilantro, yogurt, ginger,
   and asafoetida. Season to taste with salt. Shape
   the mixture into medium-size balls.
2. In another medium-size bowl, stir together the
   flours, baking soda, and enough water to make
   a semi-thick batter.
3. In a wok over medium heat, heat the vegetable
   oil for frying.
4. Working in small batches, dip the taro root balls
   into the batter and then carefully lower them
   into the hot oil.
5. Cook until crisp. With a slotted spoon, transfer
   to paper towels to drain. Serve hot.

## PULI VADAIS 🍽
Tamarind patties.

Cooking time: 30 minutes | Makes: 14      Origin: Tamil Nadu

### INGREDIENTS

2 cups (400 g) rice, parboiled, soaked in water for
  1 hour, drained
¼ cup (50 g) split pigeon peas (*toor dal*), soaked in
  water for 1 hour, drained
¼ cup (50 g) Bengal gram (split chickpeas; *chana
  dal*), soaked in water for 1 hour, drained
1 cup (85 g) grated dried unsweetened coconut
  (*nariyal*)
2 green chiles
2 red chiles
1 marble-size tamarind (*imli*), pulp extracted
  (page 30)
¼ tsp cumin seeds (*jeera*)
1 tsp salt, or to taste
3 medium-size onions, sliced
4 curry leaves (*kadhi patta*)
2 cups (480 ml) vegetable oil, plus more for the
  work surface

### METHOD

1. In a food processor or mortar and pestle, grind
   the rice, pigeon peas, and chickpeas without
   water into a coarse semolina-like consistency.
   Transfer to a bowl and set aside.
2. In a food processor or mortar and pestle, grind
   the coconut, green chiles, red chiles, tamarind
   pulp, cumin seeds, salt, onions, and curry leaves
   into a fine paste. Transfer to the rice paste bowl
   and mix the two pastes together thoroughly.
   Taste and add more salt if needed. The paste
   should be firm like a dough.
3. In a wok over low-medium heat, heat the
   vegetable oil.
4. Grease a work surface with a little vegetable oil.
   Take a lime-size piece of dough, pat it into a
   ball on the greased surface, and slip it into the
   hot oil. It will puff up. Flip and brown the other
   side. Transfer to paper towels to drain. Repeat
   until all the dough is fried.
5. Serve hot, with coconut chutney (page 30), if
   desired.

## GHAARI 🍽
Cucumber pancakes.

Cooking time: 30 minutes | Makes: 8      Origin: Karnataka

### INGREDIENTS

2 medium-size cucumbers, peeled and grated
1 cup (80 g) grated fresh coconut (*nariyal*)
¾ cup (93.75 g) all-purpose flour
½ cup (120 g) grated jaggery (*gur*; unrefined
  cane sugar)
¼ cup (40 g) rice flour (*maida*)
1 tsp ground cardamom
1 tsp ground nutmeg (*jaiphal*)
1 tsp salt
Water, to make the batter
1 Tbsp (15 g) butter

### METHOD

1. In a medium-size bowl, stir together the grated
   cucumber, coconut, all-purpose flour, jaggery,
   rice flour, cardamom, nutmeg, and salt. Add
   enough water to make a smooth batter.
2. In a skillet over medium heat, melt the butter.
3. Pour in a ladleful of batter. Spread it out and
   allow it to spread evenly.
4. Cook on both sides until golden brown.
5. Repeat with the remaining batter (should make
   8 pancakes). Serve hot.
6. Serve with green chutney (page 28), if desired.

## KERALA CHICKEN FRY 🍽

Spicy fried chicken tempered with mustard.

Cooking time: 30 minutes | Serves: 4     Origin: Kerala

### INGREDIENTS

1 cup (170 g) chopped onion
1 cup curry leaves (*kadhi patta*)
¼ cup (60 g) *kasundi* (Bengali mustard; available at Indian markets)
3 Tbsp (45 g) ginger paste (*adrak*)
2 Tbsp (18 g) chopped green chile
1 Tbsp (15 g) garlic paste (*lasan*)
1 Tbsp (6 g) freshly ground black pepper (*kali mirch*)
1 Tbsp (8 g) red chile powder
1 Tbsp (6 g) ground coriander (*dhaniya*)
1½ tsp ground turmeric (*haldi*)
Salt, to taste
12 pieces chicken
Vegetable oil, for deep-frying
Rice flour, for dusting

### METHOD

1. In a large bowl, stir together the onion, curry leaves, *kasundi*, ginger paste, green chile, garlic paste, pepper, red chile powder, coriander, and turmeric into a marinade. Season to taste with salt. Add the chicken, cover, and refrigerate overnight.
2. In a deep skillet over low-medium heat, heat the vegetable oil for deep-frying.
3. Remove the chicken from the marinade and dust the pieces with rice flour. Carefully add them to the hot oil and deep-fry until dark brown.
4. Serve hot.

## CHICKEN BEZULA 📷 🍽

Spicy chicken gravy with lemon juice.

Cooking time: 30 minutes | Serves: 2     Origin: Karnataka

### INGREDIENTS

1 tsp vegetable oil
1 tsp ginger-garlic paste (*adrak-lasan*)
3 green chiles, chopped
10 curry leaves (*kadhi patta*)
2 Tbsp (20 g) rice flour
2 tsp deghi chile powder
1 Tbsp (15 g) yogurt (*dahi*)
2 cups (480 g) cubed boneless chicken
Juice of 1 lemon (*nimbu*)
1 Tbsp (8 g) all-purpose flour (*maida*)
Water, as needed
Salt, to taste
Onion rings, for serving
Lemon wedges, for serving

### METHOD

1. In a saucepan over medium heat, heat the vegetable oil.
2. Add the ginger-garlic paste, green chiles, and curry leaves. Sauté for 2 minutes.
3. Stir in the rice flour, deghi chile powder, and yogurt. Cook for 5–7 minutes more.
4. Add the chicken and lemon juice. Let the gravy bubble for 30–35 minutes. Dilute the flour in water enough to give it a pancake batter–like consistency. Add it to the gravy to thicken the gravy.
5. Once the chicken is tender, season to taste with salt and serve hot with onion rings and lemon wedges.

## MYSORE CHILE CHICKEN 📷 🍲

A rustic chicken dish with robust spices.

Cooking time: 30 minutes | Serves: 2 | Origin: Karnataka

INGREDIENTS

1 medium-size fresh coconut (*nariyal*), grated
3 green chiles
3 green cardamom pods (*elaichi*)
3 whole cloves (*laung*)
2 Tbsp (18 g) cashews (*kaju*)
1 whole mace (*javitri*)
1 bay leaf (*tej patta*)
1 tsp fennel seeds (*saunf*)
1 Tbsp (15 ml) vegetable oil
1 Tbsp (15 g) whole spice mix (page 22)
1½ cups (255 g) chopped onion
2 tsp ginger-garlic paste (*adrak-lasan*)
1½ tsp ground coriander (*dhaniya*)
1 tsp red chile powder
½ tsp ground turmeric (*haldi*)
1 cup (240 g) finely chopped tomato
4 chicken legs
Salt, to taste
1 Tbsp (1 g) fresh cilantro leaves (*hara dhaniya*),
   finely chopped

METHOD

1. In a blender, blitz the coconut, green chiles, green cardamom pods, cloves, cashews, mace, bay leaf, and fennel seeds. In a skillet over medium heat, heat the vegetable oil.
2. Add the whole spice mix. Cook until the spices begin to crackle.
3. Add the onion. Sauté until golden.
4. Add the ginger-garlic paste, coriander, red chile powder, and turmeric. Cook for 3 minutes, adding a bit of water if it becomes too dry.
5. Add the tomato. Cook until it is mashed.
6. Stir in the coconut-spice paste and cook until the oil begins to float on the top.
7. Nestle in the chicken pieces and season to taste with salt. Reduce the heat to low and cook for 25–30 minutes, or until the chicken is done, stirring to ensure it doesn't burn.
8. Finish with cilantro and serve.

## CHEMEEM VADA

Coconut prawn cutlet.

Cooking time: 30 minutes | Makes: 20 | Origin: Kerala

INGREDIENTS

2 cups (480 g) fresh coconut (*nariyal*), grated
1 cup (240 g) prawns, finely chopped
1 Tbsp (9 g) cashew (*kaju*), finely chopped
1 green chile, finely chopped
2 tsp dried mango powder (*amchoor*)
2 tsp chaat masala
1 tsp red chile powder
1 Tbsp (15 g) ginger-garlic paste (*adrak-lasan*)
¼ cup (4 g) fresh cilantro leaves (*hara dhaniya*),
   finely chopped
Salt, to taste
Freshly ground black pepper (*kali mirch*), to taste
1½ cups (337.5 g) potato, boiled and mashed
Vegetable oil, for frying

METHOD

1. On a plate, stir together the coconut, chopped prawns, cashew nuts, green chile, dried mango powder, chaat masala, red chile powder, ginger-garlic paste, cilantro, and salt and pepper to taste.
2. Divide the potato mash into 20 coin-size balls.
3. Take one ball of potato mash and pat it with your fingers. Place a marble-size ball of the prawn filling in the center of the potato ball and roll it together into a ball.
4. Pat it once again in the shape of a round cutlet or a croquette (*tikki*). Repeat with the remaining mashed potato and filling.
5. In a wok over low-medium heat, heat the vegetable oil for frying.
6. Carefully add the cutlets to the hot oil and shallow-fry until golden brown. Transfer with slotted spoon to paper towels to drain. Serve hot.

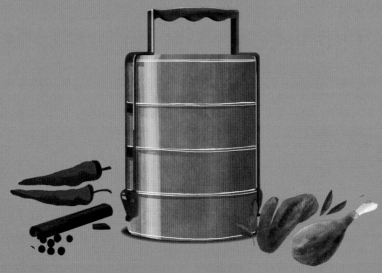

POULTRY AND EGGS

# EGG ROAST

Boiled eggs in an onion-tomato masala gravy.

Cooking time: 30 minutes | Serves: 3     Origin: Kerala

## INGREDIENTS

3 Tbsp (45 g) ghee
3 curry leaves (*kadhi patta*)
1 tsp peppercorns (*sabut kali mirch*)
1 medium-size onion, finely chopped
1 tsp red chile powder
½ tsp ground turmeric (*haldi*)
1 medium-size tomato, finely chopped
¼ cup (60 ml) water
4 eggs, boiled, peeled
Salt, to taste

## METHOD

1. In a skillet over low-medium heat, heat the ghee.
2. Add the curry leaves and peppercorns. Sauté until the leaves begin to sizzle.
3. Add the onions and sauté until translucent.
4. Add the red chile powder and turmeric. Sauté for ½ a minute.
5. Add the tomatoes. Cook for 7–8 minutes, or until they turn mushy.
6. Add the water. Simmer the gravy for 6–7 minutes.
7. Add the boiled eggs and simmer for 10 minutes more.
8. Season to taste with salt. Serve hot with rice or appams, if desired.

# EGG MASALA

Eggs in a flavorful spiced curry.

Cooking time: 10 minutes | Serves: 6     Origin: Kerala

## INGREDIENTS

**For the masala paste**
1 tsp dried red chiles (*sookhi lal mirch*), broiled, powdered
2 tsp ground coriander (*dhaniya*)
1 tsp poppy seeds (*khus khus*)
¼ tsp aniseed (*saunf*)
12 peppercorns (*sabut kali mirch*)
3 whole cloves (*laung*)
1 (1-in. / 2.5-cm) cinnamon stick (*dalchini*)
**For the gravy**
¼ cup (50 ml) vegetable oil
½ tsp mustard seeds (*rai*)
2 cups (240 g) onions, cut into thin, long slices
½ tsp ground turmeric (*haldi*)
12 garlic cloves (*lasan*), chopped
1 (½-in. / 1.25-cm) piece peeled fresh ginger (*adrak*), grated
¼ cup (60 ml) water
Salt, to taste
6 eggs, boiled, peeled with 2–3 gashes on each

## METHOD

1. **To make the masala paste:** In a food processor or grinder combine the dried red chiles, coriander, poppy seeds, aniseed, peppercorns, cloves, and cinnamon. Grind to a fine paste. Set aside.
2. **To make the gravy:** In a skillet over low-medium heat, heat the vegetable oil.
3. Add the mustard seeds. Sauté until the seeds begin to crackle. Add the onions and turmeric. Sauté for a few minutes.
4. Add the garlic, ginger, and the spice paste. Sauté for a while. Pour in the water and cook until the oil separates. Season to taste with salt. Simmer the gravy for 4–5 minutes, or until it thickens.
5. Add the eggs and mix gently. Remove from the heat.
6. Serve hot with appam, if desired.

# MUTTAI OMELET KAZHAMBU 🍲
## Omelet Curry

Cooking time: 10 minutes | Serves: 6     Origin: Tamil Nadu

## INGREDIENTS

4 eggs

½ tsp salt

1 small onion, finely chopped

1 green chile, finely chopped

1 Tbsp (1 g) fresh cilantro leaves (*hara dhaniya*), finely chopped

3 tsp vegetable oil

**For the first paste**

1 small onion

3 green chiles

1 Tbsp (5 g) coriander seeds (*dhaniya*)

4 black peppercorns (*sabut kali mich*)

1 tsp garlic paste (*lasan*)

1 tsp ginger paste (*adrak*)

½ cup (8 g) fresh cilantro leaves (*green dhaniya*), finely chopped

5 fresh mint leaves (*pudina*)

1 medium-size tomato

**For the second paste**

½ coconut (*nariyal*)

1 tsp poppy seeds (*khus khus*)

**For the tempering**

2 Tbsp (30 ml) vegetable oil

3 whole cloves (*laung*)

1 (1-in. / 2.5-cm) cinnamon stick (*dalchini*)

2 green cardamom (*choti elaichi*)

6 curry leaves (*kadhi patta*)

1 large onion, finely sliced

½ tsp ground turmeric (*haldi*)

½ cup (120 g) yogurt (*dahi*)

Water as needed

Salt, to taste

¼ cup (4 g) fresh cilantro leaves (*hara dhaniya*), finely chopped

## METHOD

1. In a medium-size bowl break the eggs. Add the salt, and whisk until creamy. Add the onions, green chiles, and cilantro.
2. In a griddle over low-medium heat, heat the vegetable oil. Pour in the egg mixture. Fold the edges when done, and flip over on the other side.
3. Remove the omelet from the griddle and cut into 12 pieces.
4. **To make the first paste:** In a food processor or spice grinder, add all the ingredients. Grind into a paste. Transfer to a small bowl and set aside.
5. **To make the second paste:** In the same food processor or spice grinder, add coconut and poppy seeds. Grind into a paste. Set aside.
6. **To make the tempering:** In a skillet over medium heat, heat the vegetable oil. Add the cloves, cinnamon, cardamom, and curry leaves. Sauté until fragrant.
7. Add the onions and fry until translucent. Reduce the heat to low and add the first spice paste. Sauté until the oil rises to the top.
8. Add the turmeric, yogurt, and enough water to form a thin gravy. Season to taste with salt.
9. Add the second spice paste and simmer till the gravy becomes thick.
10. Add the prepared omelet pieces and simmer for 5 minutes more.
11. Garnish with cilantro. Serve hot with rotis or puris, if desired.

## MUTTAI KOZHAMBU 🍽
Eggs in tamarind sauce.

Cooking time: 30 minutes | Serves: 5    Origin: Tamil Nadu

INGREDIENTS

4 tsp vegetable oil
½ tsp fenugreek seeds (*methi dana*)
1 cup shallots, sliced
½ tsp red chile powder
4 tsp curry powder
2 medium-size tomatoes, chopped
1 lime-size tamarind ball (*imli*), pulp extracted
   (page 30)
1 tsp salt. divided
2 cups (480 ml) water
1 egg, beaten

METHOD

1. In a skillet over low-medium heat, heat the vegetable oil.
2. Add the fenugreek seeds. Sauté until the seeds begin to crackle.
3. Add the shallots and fry lightly.
4. Add the red chile powder and curry powder. Cook for 1 minute.
5. Add the chopped tomatoes. Sauté until the mixture is well blended.
6. Add the tamarind extract, ¾ tsp salt, and water to make a thin gravy. Let simmer.
7. In a small bowl whisk the egg and ¼ tsp salt. Pour the beaten egg mixture into each kuzhiappam mold until three-quarters full. Steam on low heat until cooked on both the sides.
8. Add the steamed eggs into the gravy. Simmer for 3–4 minutes. Remove from the heat.
9. Serve hot.

## KOZHI MILAGU VARUVAL 🍽
Chettinad pepper chicken with roasted spices.

Cooking time: 40 minutes | Serves: 5    Origin: Tamil Nadu

INGREDIENTS

Juice of 1 lemon (*nimbu*)
1 Tbsp (15 g) ginger-garlic paste (*adrak-lasan*)
1½ tsp salt, or to taste
½ tsp ground turmeric (*haldi*)
2 lb, 3 oz (1 kg) boneless, skinless chicken pieces,
   chopped into bite-size pieces
3 whole cloves (*laung*)
2 dried red chiles (*sookhi lal mirch*)
2 (1-in. / 2.5-cm) cinnamon sticks (*dalchini*)
2 tsp peppercorns (*sabut kali mirch*)
2 tsp cumin seeds (*jeera*)
1 tsp coriander seeds (*dhaniya*)
3 Tbsp (45 ml) vegetable oil
10 curry leaves (*kadhi patta*)
2 large onions, thinly sliced
½ cup (120 ml) water
½ cup (8 g) fresh cilantro leaves (*hara dhaniya*)

METHOD

1. In a large bowl, stir together the lemon juice, ginger-garlic paste, salt, and turmeric. Add the chicken and mix thoroughly to coat. Set aside.
2. On a griddle over low-medium heat, dry-roast the cloves, dried red chiles, cinnamon sticks, peppercorns, cumin seeds, and coriander seeds until fragrant. Transfer to a spice grinder or mortar and pestle, let cool, and grind into a coarse powder.
3. In a wok over low-medium heat, heat the vegetable oil.
4. Add the curry leaves and onions. Sauté until golden brown.
5. Add the spice powder. Sauté briskly for 1 minute.
6. Add the chicken. Reduce the heat to low and cook for about 5 minutes.
7. Add the water. Cover the wok and simmer the chicken until tender and all the water is absorbed.
8. Uncover, and fry the chicken for 1–2 minutes until coated with the masala. You can make it as dry as you like.
9. Serve hot, garnished with cilantro.

# KONKANI KEEMA MURGH ♨

Chicken with mince stuffing.

| Cooking time: 50 minutes | Serves: 4 | Origin: Karnataka |
|---|---|---|

## INGREDIENTS

3 medium-size onions, finely chopped
¼ cup (60 g) yogurt (*dahi*)
Juice of 1 lemon (*nimbu*)
2 tsp red chile powder
1 tsp ground cumin (*jeera*)
1 tsp ground coriander (*dhaniya*)
1 tsp curry powder
½ tsp ground turmeric (*haldi*)
Salt, to taste
1 whole chicken
6 Tbsp (90 ml) vegetable oil, divided
7 oz (200 g) minced lamb (*keema*)
1 green chile, finely chopped
1 Tbsp (15 g) ginger-garlic paste (*adrak-lasan*)
1 medium-size tomato, chopped
½ cup (8 g) fresh cilantro leaves (*hara dhaniya*), finely chopped
2 Tbsp (8 g) fresh mint leaves (*pudina*), chopped
1 Tbsp (15 g) fried onion (*birista*; page 30)

## METHOD

1. In a large bowl, combine the onions, yogurt, lemon juice, red chile powder, cumin, coriander, curry powder, and turmeric. Season to taste with salt. Add the chicken, turn to coat, and refrigerate to marinate for 4–5 hours.
2. In a skillet over medium heat, heat 1 Tbsp (15 ml) of oil. Stir-fry the lamb with the green chile, ginger-garlic paste, and tomato. Cook until all the water from the lamb evaporates and it is cooked thoroughly. Season well with salt. Stir in the cilantro and mint.
3. Remove the chicken from the marinade and stuff this mixture inside the chicken. Tie the legs with kitchen twine.
4. In a Dutch oven over medium heat, heat the remaining 5 Tbsp (75 ml) of vegetable oil. Add the stuffed chicken. Shallow-fry for 10 minutes.
5. Cover the pot and cook for 30 minutes, or until completely done.
6. Sprinkle with *birista* and serve with fried potatoes and boiled eggs, if desired.

# KOZI PORICHATHU

Fried chicken with coconut.

| Cooking time: 40 minutes | Serves: 5 | Origin: Kerala |
|---|---|---|

## INGREDIENTS

4 Tbsp (60 ml) vegetable oil
2 (1-in. / 2.5-cm) cinnamon sticks (*dalchini*)
2 tsp aniseed (*saunf*)
3 Tbsp (36 g) garlic cloves (*lasan*), chopped
1½ cup (250 g) Madras onions, chopped
4 medium-size tomatoes, chopped
1 lb, 12 oz (800 g) chicken pieces
½ tsp ground turmeric (*haldi*)
2½ tsp red chile powder
¼ cup (60 ml) water
Salt, to taste
1 fresh coconut (*nariyal*), grated
½ tsp ginger (*adrak*), julienned

## METHOD

1. In a skillet over low-medium heat, heat the vegetable oil.
2. Add the cinnamon sticks, aniseed, and garlic. Sauté for a few seconds.
3. Add the Madras onions, tomatoes, and chicken. Sauté for 10 minutes.
4. Add the turmeric, red chile powder, water, and salt. Mix well to combine.
5. Cook the chicken until three-quarters done. Add the coconut and ginger. Cook until the chicken is thoroughly done. Serve hot.

## KOZHI VELLAI KOZHAMBU 🍛
White chicken curry.

Cooking time: 40 minutes | Serves: 6       Origin: Kerala

### INGREDIENTS

2 lb, 3 oz (1 kg) chicken

1 coconut (*nariyal*)

2 Tbsp (30 ml) plus 2 tsp vegetable oil, divided

1 large onion, chopped

1 (1½-in. / 3.75-cm) piece peeled fresh ginger
   (*adrak*)

20 flakes garlic (*lasan*)

2 (1-in. / 2.5-cm) cinnamon sticks (*dalchini*), divided

4 whole cloves (*laung*), divided

2 cardamom pods (*elaichi*)

½ tsp fennel seeds (*saunf*)

5 green chiles

1 tsp coriander seeds (*dhaniya*)

1 tsp cumin seeds (*jeera*)

3 Tbsp (27 g) cashews (*kaju*)

1 cup (240 g) yogurt (*dahi*), thick

1 bay leaf (*tej patta*)

2 small onions, sliced

Salt, to taste

Juice of 1 lemon (*nimbu*)

½ cup (8 g) fresh cilantro leaves (*hara dhaniya*),
   finely chopped

### METHOD

1.  Clean the chicken, remove the skin and extra fat. Cut into 14 pieces, and wash thoroughly.
2.  Grate the coconut, extract 1½ cups thick milk, and 1½ cups thin milk (page 203).
3.  **To make the paste:** In a skillet over medium heat, heat 2 tsp of vegetable oil. Add the chopped onion, ginger, garlic flakes, 1 cinnamon stick, 2 whole cloves, cardamom, fennel seeds, green chiles, coriander seeds, cumin seeds, and cashews and sauté. Take care not to brown the onions, and remove from the heat as soon as they turn transparent. Cool, and grind to a fine paste.
4.  Beat the yogurt lightly and blend in the prepared masala. Coat the chicken with this masala and set aside.
5.  In a heavy vessel over medium heat, heat the remaining 2 Tbsp (30 ml) of vegetable oil. Add the bay leaf, and remaining 2 cloves and cinnamon stick. Sauté until fragrant.
6.  Add the sliced onions. Cook until the onion turns translucent.
7.  Add the chicken with the masala and fry lightly.
8.  Reduce the heat to low and add the thin coconut milk. Season to taste with salt.
9.  Let the gravy simmer till the chicken is tender. Add the thick coconut milk and simmer for 3 minutes. Remove from the heat. Add the lemon juice and mix well.
10. Garnish with cilantro. Serve hot with steamed rice or chapattis, if desired.

# KORI GASSI 📷

Mangalorean-style spicy coconut chicken curry.

Cooking time: 40 minutes | Serves: 3     Origin: Karnataka

## INGREDIENTS

**For the paste**
1 tsp coconut oil (*nariyal*)
1 cup (170 g) finely chopped onion
1 Tbsp (15 g) garlic paste (*lasan*)
10 dried red chiles (*sookhi lal mirch*)
1 tsp ghee
1 Tbsp (5 g) coriander seeds (*dhaniya*)
¾ tsp cumin seeds (*jeera*)
½ tsp fenugreek seeds (*methi dana*)
1 tsp freshly ground black pepper (*kali mirch*)
Salt, to taste

**For the curry**
1 tsp coconut oil (*nariyal*)
2 curry leaves (*kadhi patta*)
1 Tbsp (15 g) whole spice mix (page 22)
2 cups (480 g) cubed chicken
1 tsp ground turmeric (*haldi*)
1 Tbsp (15 g) tamarind paste (*imli*)
3 cups (720 ml) coconut milk (*nariyal*)
1 tsp ghee, melted

## METHOD

1. **To make the paste:** In a skillet over low-medium heat, heat the coconut oil.
2. Add the onion and garlic. Cook, stirring, until the onion turns golden brown.
3. Add the dried red chiles, ghee, coriander seeds, cumin seeds, fenugreek seeds, and pepper. Season to taste with salt. Cook for 4–5 minutes, stirring well. Transfer to a food processor or mortar and pestle and blend into a smooth paste.
4. **To make the curry:** In another skillet over medium-high heat, heat the coconut oil.
5. Add the curry leaves and whole spice mix. Cook until the seeds begin to crackle.
6. Add the chicken and the dried chile paste. Reduce the heat to medium and stir-fry for 3–4 minutes.
7. Stir in the turmeric, tamarind paste, and coconut milk. Reduce the heat to low and cook for 30–40 minutes, or until the chicken is thoroughly done.
8. Season to taste with salt and pour the ghee over the top. Serve hot.

# KUNDAPURAKOLISAARU

A delicious and rustic chicken curry.

Cooking time: 40 minutes | Serves: 3     Origin: Karnataka

## INGREDIENTS

**For the paste**
6 whole cloves (*laung*)
5 small cinnamon sticks (*dalchini*)
5 dried red chiles (*sookhi lal mirch*)
½ cup (40 g) grated fresh coconut (*nariyal*)
2 tsp coriander seeds (*dhaniya*)
1 tsp peppercorns (*sabut kali mirch*)
1 tsp cumin seeds (*jeera*)
1 cup (240 ml) water, or as needed

**For the curry**
1 Tbsp (15 ml) coconut oil (*nariyal*)
1 tsp cumin seeds (*jeera*)
3 curry leaves (*kadhi patta*)
1 medium-size onion, finely chopped
1 medium-size tomato, finely chopped
2 cups (480 g) cubed chicken
2 cups (480 ml) water
Salt, to taste
¼ cup (4 g) fresh cilantro leaves (hara dhaniya), finely chopped

## METHOD

1. **To make the paste:** In a skillet over medium-high heat, combine the cloves, cinnamon sticks, dried red chiles, coconut, coriander seeds, peppercorns, and cumin seeds. Dry-roast for 4–5 minutes. Transfer to a blender or mortar and pestle and blend into a coarse paste, adding the water as needed.
2. **To make the curry:** In another skillet over medium heat, heat the coconut oil.
3. Add the cumin seeds and curry leaves. Cook until the seeds begin to crackle.
4. Add the onion and tomato. Sauté for 4–5 minutes.
5. Add the chicken and the paste you just made. Toss well to coat the chicken.
6. Add the water and season to taste with salt. Cover the skillet and cook for 30–35 minutes until the chicken is done.
7. Garnish with cilantro and serve hot.

# MEAT AND PORK

# CHUPPAL KARI KOZHAMBU 🍲
Skewered lamb in a spiced curry.

Cooking time: 1 hour 30 minutes | Serves: 5  Origin: Tamil Nadu

## INGREDIENTS

**For the lamb**

1 cup (240 g) cubed lamb, rinsed

3 medium-size onions, peeled, quartered, layers separated

2 large heads garlic (*lasan*), peeled

3 Tbsp (45 g) sliced peeled fresh ginger (*adrak*)

8 green chiles, stemmed, each cut into 3 pieces

**For the spice powder**

6 dried red chiles (*sabut lal mirch*)

2 Tbsp (10 g) coriander seeds (*dhaniya*)

2 (1-in. / 2.5-cm) cinnamon sticks (*dalchini*)

2 whole cloves (*laung*)

1 tsp cumin seeds (*jeera*)

1 tsp peppercorns (*sabut kali mirch*)

1 tsp mustard seeds (*rai*)

½ tsp vegetable oil

¼ tsp fenugreek seeds (*methi dana*)

**For the onion paste**

1 small onion

2 green chiles

½ cup (8 g) fresh cilantro leaves (*hara dhaniya*), chopped

**For the curry**

¼ cup (60 ml) vegetable oil

1 (1-in. / 2.5-cm) cinnamon stick (*dalchini*)

2 whole cloves (*laung*)

2 large onions, thinly sliced

1 green chile, slit

2 tsp ginger paste (*adrak*)

2 tsp garlic paste (*lasan*)

1 large tomato

½ tsp ground turmeric (*haldi*)

1 cup (240 ml) water

Salt, to taste

2 Tbsp (30 g) tamarind pulp (*imli*), juice extracted (page 30)

## METHOD

1. **To make the skewers:** Alternating, thread the lamb cubes, onion, garlic cloves, ginger slices, and green chiles onto 6-in. (15-cm) metal skewers. Tightly pack the ingredients to cover 5-in. (12.5-cm) of the skewer. Set aside.

2. **To make the spice powder:** On a griddle over low-medium heat, working with one spice at a time, dry-roast the dried red chiles, coriander seeds, cinnamon sticks, cloves, cumin seeds, peppercorns, and mustard seeds, each until fragrant. Remove from the heat, cool, and transfer to a spice grinder or mortar and pestle.

3. In a small skillet over low-medium heat, heat the vegetable oil.

4. Add the fenugreek seeds. Fry until brown. Remove from the heat, cool, and add to the other spices. Grind them all into a powder. This spice powder can be kept for a month or more, if refrigerated.

5. **To make the onion paste:** In a blender or food processor, grind the onion, green chiles, and cilantro into a smooth paste. Set aside.

6. **To make the curry:** In a wide-bottomed pan over medium-high heat, heat the vegetable oil.

7. Add the cinnamon stick, cloves, onions, and green chile. Sauté until the onions turn a rich brown color.

8. Stir in the ginger paste and garlic paste. Fry for 2–3 minutes.

9. Add the onion-cilantro paste, tomato, and turmeric. Reduce the heat to low and cook for 5–7 minutes, until the tomato is cooked and well blended with the rest of the masala. Stir in the spice powder.

10. Pour in the water and bring the mixture to a boil. Gently lower the skewers into the curry and cook. When the lamb is nearly cooked, season to taste with salt, and add tamarind juice. Simmer the curry until fairly thick, and the lamb is tender.

# KADAMBA CURRY 📷 🍲

A coconut milk laced lamb dish.

Cooking time: 40 minutes | Serves: 2     Origin: Karnataka

## INGREDIENTS

5 (2-in. / 5-cm) pieces lamb, cubed
1 Tbsp (15 g) whole spice mix (page 22)
1 tsp salt, plus more for seasoning
1 tsp ground turmeric (*haldi*), divided
Water, as needed
1 Tbsp (15 ml) vegetable oil
1½ cups (255 g) chopped onion
1½ tsp ground coriander (*dhaniya*)
1 tsp red chile powder
½ tsp fennel seeds (*saunf*)
½ cup (120 g) yogurt (*dahi*)
2 cups (480 g) assorted chopped vegetables
   (beans, potato, cauliflower [*phool gobhi*],
   shredded spinach [*palak*])
½ cup (120 ml) coconut milk (*nariyal*; page 30)

## METHOD

1. In a saucepan, combine the lamb, whole spice mix, salt, ½ tsp of turmeric, and enough water to cover. Bring to a boil. Cook until the lamb is tender. Drain and set aside.
2. In a skillet over medium heat, combine the vegetable oil, onion, coriander, red chile powder, fennel seeds, and remaining ½ tsp of turmeric.
3. Sauté for 2 minutes.
4. Add the boiled lamb. Stir to coat the lamb well with the spices.
5. Stir in the yogurt. Cook for 4–5 minutes.
6. Add the vegetables and coconut milk. Let the dish bubble until the vegetables are cooked. Season to taste with salt and serve hot.

# HYDERABADI MUTTON CURRY

Spicy mutton curry.

Cooking time: 55 minutes | Serves: 3     Origin: Telengana

## INGREDIENTS

2 Tbsp (30 ml) vegetable oil
1 tsp cumin seeds (*jeera*)
1 medium-size onion, finely chopped
2 Tbsp (30 g) ginger-garlic paste (*adrak-lasan*)
1 Tbsp (8 g) red chile powder
1 Tbsp (6 g) ground coriander (*dhaniya*)
1 tsp ground turmeric (*haldi*)
2 medium-size tomatoes, finely chopped
2 cups (480 g) cubed mutton
1 cup (240 g) yogurt (dahi)
Juice of 1 lemon (*nimbu*)
1 tsp Hyderabadi mutton masala (available online)
1 tsp garam masala
2 Tbsp (2 g) fresh cilantro leaves (*hara dhaniya*),
   finely chopped
Salt, to taste

## METHOD

1. In a skillet over low-medium heat, heat the vegetable oil.
2. Add the cumin seeds and onion. Sauté until the onion is golden brown.
3. Stir in the ginger-garlic paste, red chile powder, coriander, and turmeric. Sauté for 6–7 minutes.
4. Add the tomatoes and cook until they soften.
5. Add the mutton. Stir well until the masala coats the meat.
6. Add the yogurt. Reduce the heat to low and cover the skillet. Cook the mutton for 40–45 minutes, or until done.
7. Finish with the lemon juice, Hyderabadi masala, garam masla, and cilantro. Season to taste with salt.

## KNOLKOL KARIKOZHAMBU 🍲
Lamb with knolkol in thick onion-tomato curry.

Cooking time: 1 hour 30 minutes | Serves: 6  Origin: Tamil Nadu

INGREDIENTS

For the lamb
½ cup (120 g) yogurt (*dahi*), whisked
1 lb, 2 oz (500 g) lamb, cut into medium-size pieces
1 cup (85 g) grated dried unsweetened coconut
  (*nariyal*)
2 tsp poppy seeds (*khus khus*)
For the curry
1 Tbsp (15 g) ghee
8 curry leaves (*kadhi patta*)
2 (1-in. / 2.5-cm) cinnamon sticks (*dalchini*)
3 whole cloves (*laung*)
2 green cardamom pods (*choti elaichi*)
2 medium-size onions, chopped
1 medium-size tomato, chopped
1½ tsp red chile powder
1½ tsp ground coriander (*dhaniya*)
½ tsp ground turmeric (*haldi*)
2 tsp ginger-garlic paste (*adrak-lasan*)
4 cups (960 ml) plus 2 Tbsp (30 ml) water, divided
2 small knolkols (*kohlrabi*), peeled, halved, sliced
  into 3-in. (7.5-cm) pieces
3 small potatoes, peeled, cut into 4 pieces each
  (optional)
1½ tsp salt, or to taste
1 tsp tamarind pulp (*imli*; page 30)

METHOD

1. **To make the lamb:** In a large bowl, mix the yogurt with the lamb. Set aside.
2. In a food processor or mortar and pestle, grind the coconut and poppy seeds into a fine paste.
3. **To make the curry:** In a skillet over low-medium heat, heat the ghee and temper with the curry leaves.
4. Add the cinnamon sticks, cloves, and green cardamom pods. Cook until the spices begin to crackle. Add the onions. Fry until brown. Add the tomato. Fry until well blended.
5. Add the red chile powder, coriander, turmeric, ginger-garlic paste, and 2 Tbsp (30 ml) of water. Sauté for 2 minutes.
6. Add the lamb, knolkol, and potatoes (if using). Continue to fry, stirring continuously, until the oil rises to the surface.
7. Add 2 cups (480 ml) of water and salt. Transfer

to a pressure cooker. Lock the lid in place and close the pressure valve. Select Manual/ Pressure Cook and cook for 15 minutes. Release the pressure and remove the lid.
8. In a small bowl, stir together the coconut and poppy seed paste with the remaining 2 cups (480 ml) of water and add this to the lamb. Mix well.
9. Add the tamarind pulp. On your pressure cooker, select Sauté and simmer the curry for 5 minutes. serve hot.

· · · · · · · · · · · ·

## UPPU CURRY 📷 🍲
Succulent lamb dish cooked with whole spices.

Cooking time: 1 hour 30 minutes | Serves: 2  Origin: Tamil Nadu

INGREDIENTS

1 cup (240 g) cubed lamb
1 tsp minced garlic (*lasan*)
1 tsp minced peeled fresh ginger (*adrak*)
Salt, to taste
1 Tbsp (15 ml) vegetable oil
1 bay leaf (*tej patta*)
4 whole cloves (*laung*)
2 green cardamom pods (*choti elaichi*)
1 black cardamom pod (*badi elaichi*)
1 cinnamon stick (*dalchini*)
1 tsp fennel seeds (*saunf*)
1 cup (170 g) chopped onion
½ cup (85 g) chopped pearl onion
10 fresh curry leaves (*kadhi patta*)
1 Tbsp (5 g) grated fresh coconut (*nariyal*)

METHOD

1. In a medium-size saucepan over medium heat, mix the lamb with enough water to cover it fully. Add the garlic, ginger, and season to taste with salt. Bring to a boil and let it boil for 40 minutes, or until the lamb is thoroughly cooked.
2. In a skillet over low-medium heat, heat the vegetable oil.
3. Add the bay leaf, cloves, green and black cardamom pods, the cinnamon stick, and fennel seeds. Cook until the seeds begin to crackle.
4. Add both onions. Sauté until golden.
5. Add the curry leaves and drained cooked lamb.
6. Finish with salt to taste and coconut. Serve hot.

# GOSHT KEEMA KOZHAMBU 🍲
Cabbage rolls with minced meat in a curry.

Cooking time: 1 hour | Serves: 5  Origin: Tamil Nadu

## INGREDIENTS

**For the cabbage**

½ tsp salt

1 medium-size cabbage (*bandh gobhi*)

**For the stuffing**

1 cup (240 g) minced lamb, rinsed

½ cup (120 ml) water

½ tsp ground turmeric (*haldi*)

1½ tsp ginger-garlic paste (*adrak-lasan*)

¾ tsp salt, plus more as needed

2 Tbsp (30 ml) vegetable oil

2 whole cloves (*laung*)

1 (1-in. / 2.5-cm) cinnamon stick (*dalchini*)

3 medium-size onions, finely chopped

3 green chiles, finely chopped

½ tsp red chile powder

¾ tsp ground coriander (*dhaniya*)

**For the gravy**

2 Tbsp (30 ml) vegetable oil

2 whole cloves

2 (1-in. / (2.5-cm) cinnamon sticks (*dalchini*)

2 green cardamom pods (*choti elaichi*)

1 medium-size onion, sliced

1½ tsp red chile powder

¾ tsp ground coriander (*dhaniya*)

½ tsp ground turmeric (*haldi*)

1½ tsp ginger-garlic paste (*adrak-lasan*)

2 medium-size tomatoes, chopped

½ cup (42.5 g) grated dried unsweetened coconut
  (*nariyal*)

2 tsp poppy seeds (*khus khus*)

2 cups (480 ml) water

1½ tsp salt

3 sprigs fresh cilantro leaves (*hara dhaniya*), finely
  chopped, for garnishing

## METHOD

1. **To prepare the cabbage:** Bring a large pot of water with the salt to a boil over high heat.
2. Carefully remove 10 leaves from the cabbage, making sure they are fresh and green. Slice off part of the thick central stem, taking care to keep the leaves whole without any tears or gashes. Rinse thoroughly. Submerge the cabbage leaves in the boiling water. Reduce the heat to low and simmer for 2 minutes. Remove from the water and pat dry with paper towels.
3. **To make the stuffing:** In your pressure cook cooking pot, combine the minced meat, water, turmeric, ginger-garlic paste, and salt. Lock the lid in place and close the pressure release valve. Select Manual/Pressure Cook and cook for 12 minutes. Release the pressure and remove the lid.
4. In a wok over medium-high heat, heat the vegetable oil.
5. Add the cloves, cinnamon stick, onions, and green chiles. Sauté until the onions brown.
6. Stir in the red chile powder and coriander. Fry for 2 minutes.
7. Add the cooked minced meat along with the cooking liquid and fry until the mixture turns dry.
8. Place 1 Tbsp (15 g) of the minced meat in a cabbage leaf and roll inward, tightly. Set aside on a plate, seam-side down, or tie with kitchen string, if desired. Repeat the process until all the cabbage leaves are filled and rolled.
9. **To make the gravy:** In a heavy-bottomed pot over medium-high heat, heat the vegetable oil.
10. Add the cloves, cinnamon sticks, green cardamom pods, and onion. Cook until the onion is slightly browned.
11. Stir in the red chile powder, coriander, and turmeric.
12. Add the ginger-garlic paste and tomatoes. Reduce the heat to low and cook for 3 minutes.
13. In a blender or mortar and pestle, grind the coconut and poppy seeds into a fine paste. Mix this paste into the onion-tomato mixture. Add the water and salt. Simmer until the raw smell disappears and the curry thickens.
14. Gently slip in the cabbage rolls, one at a time, and simmer for 5 minutes, or until the cabbage leaves are fully cooked. Serve hot, garnished with cilantro.

## GONGURA MAMSAM
Juicy lamb gravy with gongura leaves.

Cooking time: 1 hour | Serves: 3          Origin: Andhra Pradesh

INGREDIENTS

5 Tbsp (75 ml) vegetable oil, divided
1 lb, 2 oz (500 g) lamb, cubed
1 Tbsp (15 g) ginger-garlic paste (*adrak-lasan*)
2 tsp red chile powder
1 tsp ground turmeric (*haldi*)
1½ cups (360 ml) water, divided
½ cup (85 g) finely chopped onion
2 cup (35 g) gongura leaves, chopped
1 tsp mustard seeds (*rai*)
2 tsp black lentils (*urad dal*)
5 curry leaves (*kadhi patta*)
3 dried red chiles (*sookhi lal mirch*)
1 Tbsp (15 g) minced garlic (*lasan*)
1 tsp ground cumin (*jeera*)
1 tsp ground coriander (*dhaniya*)
Salt, to taste

METHOD

1. On your pressure cooker, select Sauté and preheat the cooking pot.
2. Add 1 Tbsp (15 ml) of vegetable oil to the pot along with the lamb. Sauté for 4–5 minutes.
3. Stir in the ginger-garlic paste, red chile powder, turmeric, and 1 cup (240 ml) of water. Lock the lid in place and close the pressure release valve. Select Manual/Pressure Cook and cook for 21 minutes. Release the pressure and remove the lid. Transfer the lamb to a bowl and set aside.
4. In a skillet over low-medium heat, heat 1 tsp of vegetable oil.
5. Add the onion. Sauté until golden.
6. Add the gongura leaves. Cook, stirring, until the leaves wilt completely. Remove from the heat and let cool. Transfer to food processor and blend until smooth.
7. Return the skillet to the heat and heat the remaining 3 Tbsp (45 ml) plus 2 tsp vegetable oil.
8. Add the mustard seeds, black lentils, curry leaves, and dried red chiles. Cook until the seeds begin to crackle.
9. Add the garlic, cumin, and coriander. Mix well.
10. Add the lamb and the gongura paste. Stir to combine. Reduce the heat to low and simmer for 20 minutes. Add the remaining ½ cup (120 ml) of water if the gravy seems dry. Season to taste with salt and serve hot.

· · · · · · · · · · · · · · · · ·

## NADAN PORK ULARTHIYATHU
Spicy pork cooked dry.

Cooking time: 35 minutes | Serves: 6          Origin: Kerala

INGREDIENTS

1½ Tbsp red chile powder
1½ Tbsp (7 g) ground coriander (*dhaniya*)
½ tsp ground turmeric (*haldi*)
1 tsp black peppercorns (*sabut kali mirch*), coarsely powdered
½ tsp ginger paste (*adrak*)
3 Tbsp (45 g) yogurt (*dahi*)
Salt, to taste
1 lb, 2 oz (500 g) pork with a little fat, cubed
1 tsp vegetable oil
½ tsp mustard seeds (*rai*)
4 curry leaves (*kadhi patta*)
½ cup (60 g) Madras onions (pearl onions), chopped

METHOD

1. In a medium-size bowl, combine the red chile powder, coriander, turmeric, peppercorns, ginger paste, and yogurt. Add the pork and stir well to coat. Set aside for about 4 hours.
2. In a skillet over medium heat, cook the pork without any water. Keep the skillet covered.
3. In a saucepan over medium heat, heat the vegetable oil. Add the mustard seeds and curry leaves. Sauté until the seeds begin to crackle. Add onions and fry until brown. Season to taste with salt.
4. Add the pork and cook for another 5 minutes. Serve hot.

# FISH AND SEAFOOD

## SORRA PUTTU 🍲

Protein-rich fish dish given to feeding mothers.

Cooking time: 40 minutes | Serves: 5-6      Origin: Tamil Nadu

### INGREDIENTS

6 cups (1.4 L) water plus 5 Tbsp for the puttu
1 tsp ground turmeric (*haldi*), divided
1 lb, 2 oz (500 g) *sora* fish or shark, cut into large
   pieces, rinsed
½ cup (120 g) green peas (*hara mattar*; optional)
2 Tbsp (30 ml) vegetable oil
4 medium-size onions, finely chopped
4 green chiles, finely chopped
20 garlic cloves (*lasan*), minced
2 tsp ginger paste (*adrak*)
1½ tsp salt, or to taste
Juice of ½ lemon (*nimbu*)
1 large bunch fresh cilantro leaves (*hara dhaniya*),
   finely chopped

### METHOD

1. Fill a large pan with the water and bring to a boil over high heat. Add ½ tsp of turmeric and the fish. Let boil for 3–5 minutes, or until the fish is tender. Remove the pan from the heat and drain the water. Peel off the fish skin and discard it. Wash the fish gently again to remove any grit sticking to the surface. Cool.

2. Crumble the cooled fish flesh into a mixture that resembles bread crumbs. The backbone of the fish may be retained, cut into 1½-in. (3.75-cm) pieces, and add to the crumble or puttu.

3. In a small saucepan, boil the peas in salted water until soft. Remove from the heat, drain the water out completely, and set aside.

4. In a heavy-bottomed pan over low-medium heat, heat the vegetable oil.

5. Add the onions and green chiles. Sauté until the onions turn transparent. Stir in the remaining ½ tsp of turmeric. Sauté until the raw smell disappears.

6. Add the garlic. Sauté until light brown. Stir in the ginger paste. Sauté for 1 minute.

7. Add the crumbled fish and salt. Stir briskly so the ingredients are evenly distributed. Reduce the heat to low.

8. Add the peas and 5 Tbsp of water. Cook until the water is absorbed. The mixture should be moist, not dry.

9. Remove from the heat, squeeze in the lemon juice, and mix well.

10. Serve hot, garnished with cilantro and accompanied with steamed rice and a dash of ghee, if desired.

## MACHHI KA HARA SALAN 🍲

A unique Konkani-style fish curry.

Cooking time: 30 minutes | Serves: 4          Origin: Karnataka

INGREDIENTS

½ cup (72 g) roasted peanuts
½ cup (8 g) fresh cilantro leaves (*hara dhaniya*),
   finely chopped
6–8 green chiles, finely chopped
4 garlic cloves, minced (*lasan*)
1½ tsp cumin seeds (*jeera*)
½ cup (120 g) yogurt (*dahi*)
¼ cup (60 ml) vegetable oil
2 spring onions (*hara pyaz*), finely chopped
6 curry leaves (*kadhi patta*)
1 cup (240 ml) water
½ tsp ground turmeric (*haldi*)
2 pieces mango (*kairi*), chopped
5 pomfret fillets
2 cups (480 ml) coconut milk (*nariyal*)
Salt, to taste

METHOD

1. In a food processor, combine the peanuts, cilantro, green chiles, garlic, cumin seeds, and yogurt. Process until smooth.
2. In a skillet over medium heat, heat the vegetable oil.
3. Add the spring onions and curry leaves. Sauté for 2 minutes.
4. Stir in the yogurt paste, water, turmeric, and mango. Reduce the heat to low and simmer for 5 minutes.
5. Add the fish. Cook for 10 minutes.
6. Pour in the coconut milk and simmer until heated through.
7. Season to taste with salt and serve.

## CHEPALA PULUSU 📷🍲

Coconut-based fish gravy.

Cooking time: 40 minutes | Serves: 2   Origin: Andhra Pradesh

INGREDIENTS

8 pieces rohu fish, carp, or other white-fleshed fish
   (available at some Indian markets), cubed
Salt, to taste
½ tsp ground turmeric (*haldi*)
1 tsp garlic paste (*lasan*)
1 Tbsp (5 g) coriander seeds (*dhaniya*)
1 Tbsp (8 g) white sesame seeds (*safed til*)
1 tsp cumin seeds (*jeera*)
1 Tbsp (15 ml) vegetable oil
½ tsp mustard seeds (*rai*)
3 fresh red chiles
½ cup (87.5 g) chopped onion
10 curry leaves (*kadhi patta*)
1 tsp red chile powder
½ tsp ground turmeric (*haldi*)
¼ cup (60 g) finely chopped tomato
1½ Tbsp (23 ml) coconut milk (*nariyal*)

METHOD

1. Sprinkle the fish with salt and turmeric and rub with the garlic paste. Set aside to marinate.
2. In a small skillet over medium-high heat, individually dry-roast the coriander seeds, and set aside; the sesame seeds, and set aside; and the cumin seeds, and set aside. Let cool. Transfer to a spice grinder or mortar and pestle and blend into a fine powder.
3. In a skillet over medium-high heat, heat the vegetable oil.
4. Add the mustard seeds and fresh red chiles. Cook until they begin to crackle.
5. Add the onion. Sauté until golden.
6. Add the curry leaves and stir to combine.
7. Add the red chile powder, turmeric, and roasted spice powder. Cook for 3 minutes. Add a bit of water if it's too dry.
8. Add the marinated fish along with the paste. Cook for 3 minutes.
9. Add the tomato and cook until broken down.
10. Finish with the coconut milk, bringing the mixture to a boil. Taste and adjust the seasoning and serve hot.

## MEEN POLLICHATHU 🍲

Fish with karimeen wrapped in banana leaf.

Cooking time: 40 minutes | Serves: 2     Origin: Kerala

### INGREDIENTS

3 Tbsp (45 ml) coconut oil (*nariyal*), plus more for
  cooking the fish
6 Tbsp (24 g) curry leaves (*kadhi patta*)
3 cups (720 g) sliced onion
2 Tbsp (30 g) ginger paste (*adrak*)
1 Tbsp (15 g) garlic paste (*lasan*)
1½ tsp chopped green chile
1½ Tbsp (9 g) ground coriander (*dhaniya*)
1 Tbsp (6 g) garam masala
1½ tsp red chile powder
¾ tsp ground turmeric (*haldi*)
¾ tsp freshly ground black pepper (*kali mirch*),
  plus more for the fish
3 cups (720 g) sliced tomato
4–6 Tbsp (60–90 ml) coconut milk (*nariyal*)
Sugar, to taste
4 boneless white fish fillets (red snapper, sea bass,
  barramundi)
Salt, to taste
4 banana leaves
Freshly squeezed lemon juice (*nimbu*), to taste

### METHOD

1. In a skillet over medium heat, heat the coconut
   oil.
2. Add the curry leaves and sliced onion. Cook
   until the onion is golden.
3. Add the ginger paste and garlic paste. Sauté for
   2–3 minutes.
4. Add green chile, coriander, garam masala, red
   chile powder, turmeric, and pepper. Cook for
   2–3 minutes.
5. Add the tomato. Sauté until it turns into a mash.
6. Stir in the coconut milk and a little sugar. Cook
   until the gravy begins to thicken. Remove from
   the heat and cool to room temperature.
7. Season the fish with salt and pepper.

8. On a banana leaf, place a fish fillet and about
   3–4 Tbsp (45–60 ml) of gravy. Wrap the banana
   leaf tightly. Repeat with the remaining fillets and
   gravy.
9. Place a tawa or large griddle over medium heat
   and add a little coconut oil. Place the banana
   leaf-wrapped fish bundles on the pan. Cook for
   10 minutes, turning the fish every 2–3 minutes,
   until cooked through. Finish with lemon juice
   just before serving.

· · · · · · · · · · · ·

## MACHHI KA LAAL SALAN 🍲

Red fish curry.

Cooking time: 30 minutes | Serves: 4     Origin: Karnataka

### INGREDIENTS

5–6 dried red chiles (*sookhi lal mirch*)
½ cup (40 g) fresh coconut, grated
3–4 garlic cloves (*lasan*), grated
1 Tbsp (6 g) ground coriander (*dhaniya*)
1 tsp tamarind pulp (*imli;* page 30)
4 Tbsp (60 ml) vegetable oil
5–6 curry leaves (*kadhi patta*)
2 cups (480 ml) water
Salt, to taste
5 king fish (*surmai*) fillets

### METHOD

1. In a food processor or grinder, combine the
   dried red chiles, coconut, garlic, coriander, and
   tamarind pulp. Blend into a smooth paste.
2. In a skillet over medium heat, heat the vegetable
   oil.
3. Add the curry leaves. Cook unil they begin to
   crackle.
4. Stir in the prepared chile-coconut paste and the
   water. Cook until it reaches a boil.
5. Season to taste with salt and add the fish. Cook
   thoroughly until the fish is done. Serve hot.

# KONGUNADU PACHAI PULI MEEN KOZHAMBU

Fish in onion-tomato curry.

Cooking time: 40 minutes | Serves: 5          Origin: Tamil Nadu

## INGREDIENTS

**For the fish**

2 cups (480 g) river fish chunks, cleaned and
   rinsed thoroughly

1 Tbsp (8 g) red chile powder

1½ tsp salt

1 tsp freshly squeezed lemon juice (*nimbu*)

2 Tbsp (30 ml) sesame oil (*til*)

7 dried red chiles (*sookhi lal mirch*)

2 Tbsp (12 g) cumin seeds (*jeera*)

1 Tbsp (5 g) coriander seeds (*dhaniya*)

1 tsp peppercorns (*sabut kali mirch*)

1 head garlic (*lasan*), peeled

2 Tbsp (16 g) chopped peeled fresh ginger (*adrak*)

4 Tbsp (60 g) grated dried unsweetened coconut
   (*nariyal*)

**For the tempering**

½ cup (120 ml) sesame oil (*til*)

1 tsp mustard seeds (*rai*)

½ tsp fennel seeds (*saunf*)

4 sprigs curry leaves (*kadhi patta*), leaves removed

1¾ cups (297.5 g) chopped onion

3 medium-size tomatoes, chopped

½ tsp ground turmeric (*haldi*)

1 lime-size tamarind (*imli*), soaked in water, juice
   extracted (page 30)

Salt, to taste

½ cup (8 g) fresh cilantro leaves (*hara dhaniya*),
   chopped

## METHOD

1. **To make the fish:** In a medium-size bowl combine the fish with the red chile powder, salt, and lemon juice. Refrigerate for 1 hour to marinate.

2. In a wok over low-medium heat, heat the sesame oil.

3. Add the dried red chiles, cumin seeds, coriander seeds, and peppercorns. Sauté until the seeds change color.

4. Add the garlic and ginger. Stir-fry for 2 minutes.

5. Add the coconut. Mix well. Transfer the spices to a blender or mortar and pestle. Grind into a smooth paste.

6. **To make the tempering:** In a skillet over low-medium heat, heat the sesame oil.

7. Add the mustard seeds, fennel seeds, and curry leaves. Cook until the seeds begin to crackle.

8. Add the onion. Brown slightly.

9. Add the tomatoes. Sauté until soft.

10. Mix in the spice paste. Sauté for 2 minutes.

11. Add the turmeric and tamarind extract, and season to taste with salt. Reduce the heat to low and simmer for 15 minutes, or until the masala is well blended. Add 1 cup (240 ml) of water if the gravy is too thick.

12. Add the fish pieces. Simmer gently for about 7 minutes, or until the fish is cooked through.

13. Add the cilantro. Stir and remove from the heat. Serve hot.

# KERALA FISH PARCELS
Fish cooked in banana leaves.

Cooking time: 30 minutes | Serves: 6      Origin: Kerala

## INGREDIENTS

2 cups (170 g) grated dried unsweetened coconut (*nariyal*)

8 garlic cloves (*lasan*), peeled

6 green chiles

3 sprigs curry leaves (*kadhi patta*), leaves removed

½ tsp cumin seeds (*jeera*)

2 whole cloves (*laung*)

1 lemon-size tamarind (*imli*)

Salt, to taste

½ tsp sugar

2 lb, 3 oz (1 kg) fish of choice, cleaned, cut into pieces

Banana leaves, for cooking, cleaned

5 Tbsp (75 ml) coconut oil (*nariyal*), divided, plus more for greasing the banana leaves

## METHOD

1. In a food processor or mortar and pestle, grind the coconut, garlic, green chiles, curry leaves, cumin seeds, cloves, tamarind, and salt to taste into a smooth paste. Transfer to a small bowl and stir in the sugar.

2. Rub the paste over the fish pieces.

3. Cut 2 banana leaves into pieces large enough to wrap each piece of fish. Grease each leaf with ½ tsp coconut oil. Place the fish over the oil and wrap it in the leaf like a parcel. Secure with kitchen string.

4. In a skillet over low heat, heat 2 Tbsp (30 g) of coconut oil.

5. Working in batches, add the banana leaf parcels. Panfry until one side is brown. Add the remaining 3 Tbsp (45 g) of coconut oil and cook the other side until crisp. Remove and repeat until all the parcels are panfried.

6. Before serving remove the string, unwrap the fish, and serve hot.

# CHETTINAD NANDURASAM
Tomato-based sauce with bits of crabmeat.

Cooking time: 40 minutes | Serves: 4      Origin: Tamil Nadu

## INGREDIENTS

For the rasam paste

3 dried red chiles (*sookhi lal mirch*)

1 Tbsp (5 g) coriander seeds (*dhaniya*)

1 tsp cumin seeds (*jeera*)

1 tsp peppercorns (*sabut kali mirch*)

1 medium-size onion, diced

1 Tbsp (15 g) minced garlic (*lasan*)

For the sauce

1 Tbsp (15 ml) vegetable oil

1 tsp fennel seeds (*saunf*)

3 curry leaves (*kadhi patta*)

1 medium-size onion, finely chopped

1 medium-size tomato, finely chopped

1 tsp ground turmeric (*haldi*)

1 cup (240 ml) water

2 lb, 3 oz (1 kg) crabmeat

Salt, to taste

## METHOD

1. **To make the rasam paste:** In a skillet over low-medium heat, dry-roast the dried red chiles, coriander seeds, cumin seeds, peppercorns, onion, and garlic until fragrant. Transfer to a blender or mortar and pestle and grind into a fine paste, adding water if needed. Set aside.

2. **To make the sauce:** Return the skillet to low heat and heat the vegetable oil.

3. Add the fennel seeds and curry leaves. Cook until the seeds begin to crackle.

4. Add the onion and tomato. Sauté for 5 minutes.

5. Stir in the rasam paste and turmeric. Reduce the heat to low and cook for 4–5 minutes more.

6. Add the water and bring the mixture to a boil.

7. Stir in the crabmeat. Cook for 7–8 minutes until the crab turns orange-red in color. Season to taste with salt and serve hot.

# GONGURA NEYYULU IGUROOS

Prawns fried with gongura.

Cooking time: 35 minutes | Serves: 5   Origin: Andhra Pradesh

## INGREDIENTS

1 lb, 2 oz (500 g) medium-size prawns, cleaned and deveined
½ tsp ground turmeric (*haldi*)
2 Tbsp (30 ml) vegetable oil
3 medium-size onions, chopped
1 green chile
2 sprigs curry leaves (*kadhi patta*), leaves removed
1 tsp ginger-garlic paste (*adrak-lasan*)
¾ tsp salt
2 tsp red chile powder
1 tsp ground coriander (*dhaniya*)
1 cup gongura leaves, chopped
½ cup water
½ cup (8 g) fresh cilantro leaves (*hara dhaniya*), finely chopped

## METHOD

1.  In a medium-size bowl combine the prawns and turmeric. Set aside.
2.  In a skillet over medium heat, heat the vegetable oil.
3.  Add the onions. Sauté until they turn light brown.
4.  Add green chiles and curry leaves. Cook until the leaves turn crisp.
5.  Add ginger-garlic paste, salt, red chile powder, and coriander. Sauté until the oil surfaces and the masala is nicely blended.
6.  Reduce the heat to low. Add the gongura and prawns. Add the water and cover the pan. Cook for a few minutes, or until the prawns shrink and are soft. Overcooking will make them tough.
7.  Remove from the heat and garnish with cilantro.

# CHEMEEN CURRY

Shrimp in coconut milk.

Cooking time: 35 minutes | Serves: 3-4   Origin: Kerala

## INGREDIENTS

6 Tbsp (90 ml) vegetable oil
1 tsp mustard seeds (*rai*)
2 curry leaves (*kadhi patta*)
2 tsp garlic (*lasan*), slivered
4 medium-size onions, chopped
1 green chile, chopped
1 tsp ground coriander (*dhaniya*)
1 tsp red chile powder
1 tsp ground turmeric (*haldi*)
1 coconut (*nariyal*), fresh, grated
2 tsp cumin seeds (*jeera*)
Salt, to taste
Water, as needed
1 cup (240 ml) coconut milk
1 lb, 5 oz (600 g) shrimp, peeled

## METHOD

1.  In a skillet over medium heat, heat the vegetable oil.
2.  Add the mustard seeds. Sauté until the seeds begin to crackle. Add the curry leaves, garlic, and onions. Stir-fry until the onions turn transparent.
3.  Add the green chile, coriander, red chile powder, turmeric, coconut, and cumin. Season to taste with salt. Cook until the oil separates and appears on the surface. Add water as and when necessary to cook the curry.
4.  Stir in the coconut milk and shrimp. Fry until the shrimp are cooked and the curry thickens. Remove from the heat.
5.  Serve hot.

# CRAB MAPPAS 🍲
Crab cooked in tamarind.

Cooking time: 30 minutes | Serves: 4      Origin: Kerala

## INGREDIENTS

¼ cup (60 ml) vegetable oil
2 cups (340 g) chopped onion
½ cup (32 g) curry leaves (*kadhi patta*)
1 Tbsp (8 g) red chile powder
1 Tbsp (6 g) ground coriander (*dhaniya*)
2 tsp freshly ground black pepper (*kali mirch*)
½ tsp ground turmeric (*haldi*)
2 Tbsp (30 g) chopped peeled fresh ginger (*adrak*)
4 green chiles, slit
10 pot Malabar tamarind (*kudampuli*), soaked in
   ¼ cup (60 ml) water for 1 hour, drained
3 cups (720 ml) coconut milk (*nariyal*)
Salt, to taste
4 large crabs, cleaned and cracked
Sugar, to taste

## METHOD

1. In a large pot over low heat, heat the vegetable oil.
2. Add the onion. Cook until translucent (do not brown).
3. Add the curry leaves, red chile powder, coriander, pepper, and turmeric. Sauté until fragrant.
4. Add the ginger, green chiles, pot tamarind, and coconut milk. Season to taste with salt. Simmer for 8–10 minutes until the curry thickens.
5. Add the crabs. Increase the heat to medium, cover the pot, and cook for 8–10 minutes (without boiling).
6. Adjust the seasoning with salt and sugar. Serve hot.

# CHEMEEN MANGA CURRY
Prawn and mango in coconut-flavored curry.

Cooking time: 20 minutes | Serves: 4      Original: Kerala

## INGREDIENTS

3 Tbsp (24 g) red chile powder
1¼ tsp ground coriander (*dhaniya*)
1 tsp ground turmeric (*haldi*)
1 lb, 2 oz (500 g) fresh prawns
1 medium-size mango (*kairi*), peeled, pitted, and chopped
½ cup (120 g) sliced (lengthwise) onion
6 green chiles
1 (1-in. / 2.5-cm) piece peeled fresh ginger (*adrak*), julienned
1½ Tbsp (23 g) minced garlic (*lasan*)
3 curry leaves (*kadhi patta*)
Salt, to taste
½ cup (42.5 g) grated dried unsweetened coconut (*nariyal*)
¼ cup (60 ml) coconut oil (*nariyal*)

## METHOD

1. In a small bowl, combine the red chile powder, coriander, and turmeric. Stir in a little water to make a smooth paste.
2. In a medium-size saucepan over low-medium heat, combine the prawns, mango, spice paste, onion, green chiles, ginger, garlic, and curry leaves. Season to taste with salt. Reduce the heat to low and simmer until the prawns are cooked and the gravy is thick.
3. Gently stir in the coconut and pour in the coconut oil.
4. Serve hot.

VEGETARIAN

## VAZHATHANDU KOOTU 🍲
Plantain stems cooked with split chickpeas.

Cooking time: 40 minutes | Serves: 4-6     Origin: Tamil Nadu

### INGREDIENTS

For the plantain stems
1 cup (250 g) plantain stems, cut into 1-in. (2.5-cm) cubes
1 cup (200 g) Bengal gram (split chickpeas; *chana dal*)
¼ tsp ground turmeric (*haldi*)
¼ tsp ground asafoetida (*hing*)
½ tsp vegetable oil
1 tsp cumin seeds (*jeera*)
2 green chiles
2 Tbsp (10 g) grated dried unsweetened coconut (*nariyal*)

For the tempering
2 Tbsp (30 ml) vegetable oil
1 tsp mustard seeds (*rai*)
1 tsp black lentils (*urad dal*)
10 curry leaves (*kadhi patta*)
4 dried red chiles (*sookhi lal mirch*), broken
1 medium-size onion, chopped
1 medium-size tomato, chopped
1½ tsp salt, or to taste
¼ cup (4 g) fresh cilantro leaves (*hara dhaniya*), finely chopped

### METHOD

1. **To make the plantain stems:** Put the cut plantain in a pan of water. Using a fork, swirl the vegetable around in the water. The fiber will twirl itself around the fork. Discard the fiber.
2. In your pressure cooker cooking pot, combine the chickpeas with enough water to cover. Add the turmeric, asafoetida, and vegetable oil. Lock the lid in place and close the pressure release valve. Select Manual/Pressure Cook and cook for 15 minutes, or until the lentils are firm to the bite, and not too soft. Release the pressure and remove the lid.
3. In a blender or mortar and pestle, grind the cumin seeds, green chiles, and coconut into a smooth paste with some water.
4. **To make the tempering:** In a heavy-bottomed skillet over low-medium heat, heat the vegetable oil.
5. Add the mustard seeds, black lentils, curry leaves, and dried red chiles. Cook until the seeds begin to crackle.
6. Add the onion. Sauté until transparent.
7. Add the tomato. Sauté for 3 minutes.
8. Add the spice paste and the prepared plantain stems. Cook for 3 minutes more.
9. Add the cooked chickpeas along with the cooking water. Season to taste with salt. Simmer until the plantain stems are soft and tender.
10. Sprinkle with cilantro. Stir well to combine and remove from the heat.
11. Serve hot, with steamed rice, if desired.

## KEERAI MASIYAL

Mashed amaranth and green gram tempered with mustard seeds.

Cooking time: 15 minutes | Serves: 4     Origin: Tamil Nadu

### INGREDIENTS

**For the amaranth**
1 cup (200 g) green gram (*moong dal*)
2 cups (480 ml) water, divided
Salt, to taste
2 bunches amaranth leaves, washed, finely
  chopped
**For the tempering**
1 Tbsp (15 ml) vegetable oil
½ tsp mustard seeds (*rai*)
1 tsp split black lentils (*urad dal*)
1 dried red chile (*sookhi lal mirch*)
1 tsp cumin seeds (*jeera*)
¼ tsp ground asafoetida (*hing*)

### METHOD

1. **To make the amaranth:** In your pressure cooker cooking pot, combine the green gram with 1½ cups (360 ml) of water. Lock the lid in place and close the pressure release valve. Select Manual/Pressure Cook and cook for 9 minutes. Release the pressure, remove the lid, drain, and set aside.
2. In a saucepan, combine the remaining ½ cup (120 ml) of water with salt to taste. Bring to a boil over high heat.
3. Add the amaranth leaves. Cook until soft. Drain and mash lightly.
4. Stir the boiled green gram into the mashed amaranth leaves.
5. **To make the tempering:** In a skillet over low-medium heat, heat the vegetable oil.
6. Add the mustard seeds. Cook until the seeds begin to crackle.
7. Add the black lentils, dried red chile, cumin seeds, and asafoetida. Sauté until the black gram turns golden and crispy.
8. Mix the amaranth-green gram mix with the tempering.
9. Serve hot.

## NARELI DAL

Lentils in coconut milk.

Cooking time: 30 minutes | Serves: 2     Origin: Karnataka

### INGREDIENTS

1 Tbsp (15 ml) vegetable oil
1 medium-size onion, grated
1 tsp red chile powder
1 tsp ground coriander (*dhaniya*)
1 tsp ground fennel seeds (*saunf*)
½ tsp ground turmeric (*haldi*)
Salt, to taste
1 cup (200 g) green gram (*moong dal*), soaked in
  water for 2 hours, drained
2 cups (480 ml) water
1 cup (240 ml) coconut milk (*nariyal*)

### METHOD

1. On your pressure cooker, select Sauté and preheat the cooking pot.
2. Add the vegetable oil to heat.
3. Add the onion. Cook, stirring, for 3–4 minutes.
4. Stir in the red chile powder, coriander, fennel seeds, and turmeric. Season to taste with salt.
5. Add the green gram and water. Lock the lid in place and close the pressure release valve. Select Manual/Pressure Cook and cook for 9 minutes. Release the pressure and remove the lid.
6. Add the coconut milk to finish and allow it to bubble gently on low for 3–4 minutes, ensuring it doesn't curdle. Remove from the heat and serve hot.

# HYDERABADI MIRCHI KA SALAN
Hyderabadi chile curry.

Cooking time: 1 hour | Serves: 4-5      Origin: Telengana

## INGREDIENTS

½ cup (40 g) grated fresh coconut (*nariyal*)

½ cup (72 g) peanuts

¼ cup (36 g) white sesame seeds (*safed til*)

4 tsp (6 g) coriander seeds (*dhaniya*), roasted

4 tsp (8 g) ground cumin (*jeera*)

2 tsp red chile powder

1 tsp ground turmeric (*haldi*)

2 lb, 3 oz (1 kg) brown onion paste (deep-fry onions until brown and blitz into a paste)

1 Tbsp (15 g) ginger paste (*adrak*)

1 Tbsp (15 g) garlic paste (*lasan*)

Salt, to taste

7 oz (200 g) large green chiles, slit lengthwise, seeded

2 cups (480 ml) vegetable oil

1 tsp mustard seeds (*rai*)

1 tsp nigella seeds (*kalonji*)

20 curry leaves (*kadhi patta*)

2 tsp cumin seeds (*jeera*)

4 Tbsp (60 g) tamarind (*imli*), soaked in warm water (page 30)

## METHOD

1. On a sheet pan, combine the coconut, peanuts, and sesame seeds. Dry-roast for 4–5 minutes, or until golden brown. Transfer to a food processor and grind into a fine paste. Mix in the coriander seeds, cumin, red chile powder, turmeric, brown onion paste, ginger paste, garlic paste, and salt to taste. Pulse to combine.

2. Fill the slit green chiles with this paste. Set aside.

3. In a wok over medium-high heat, heat the vegetable oil.

4. Carefully add the stuffed green chiles to the hot oil and fry until golden brown. With a slotted spoon, transfer to paper towels to drain.

5. In the same oil, sauté the mustard seeds, nigella seeds, curry leaves, and cumin seeds. Stir in any leftover ground paste and the tamarind pulp. Cook on low heat for 10 minutes. Add the fried green chiles and simmer 10 minutes more. Serve hot.

# PETHA OLAN
A dish of winter melon and red lobia beans.

Cooking time: 30 minutes | Serves: 4      Origin: Kerala

## INGREDIENTS

2 Tbsp (30 ml) coconut oil (*nariyal*)

3 green chiles, slit

¼ cup (16 g) curry leaves (*kadhi patta*)

¼ cup (42.5 g) finely chopped onion

2 cups (340 g) cubed winter melon

1½ cups (360 ml) coconut milk (*nariyal*)

Salt, to taste

Sugar, to taste

½ cup (100 g) cowpeas (*red lobia*), soaked in water overnight, boiled until tender

## METHOD

1. In a skillet over medium heat, heat the coconut oil.

2. Add the green chiles, curry leaves, and onion. Cook until the onion is translucent.

3. Add the winter melon and coconut milk.

4. Season to taste with salt and sugar. Cook for 15–20 minutes until the petha is thoroughly cooked.

5. Stir in the cowpeas and simmer for another 3–4 minutes. Serve hot.

## KADALA CURRY

Horse gram cooked in coconut milk.

Cooking time: 20 minutes | Serves: 4-6      Origin: Kerala

INGREDIENTS

1 cup (200 g) horse gram (*kala chana*), soaked in
   water overnight, drained
3 Tbsp (45 ml) vegetable oil
12 garlic cloves (*lasan*), chopped
½ cup (120 g) sliced onion
4 green chiles, slit
8 whole cloves (*laung*)
4 green cardamom pods (*choti elaichi*)
4 (1-in. / 2.5-cm) cinnamon sticks (*dalchini*)
1 Tbsp (8 g) chopped peeled fresh ginger (*adrak*)
½ tsp ground turmeric (*haldi*)
1 cup (240 ml) water
¼ cup (21.25 g) dried unsweetened coconut
   (*nariyal*), sliced into small thin pieces
1½ Tbsp (23 ml) vinegar (*sirka*)
3 curry leaves (*kadhi patta*)
Salt, to taste
½ cup (120 ml) coconut milk (*nariyal*)

METHOD

1.  In a medium-size saucepan, combine the horse
    gram with enough water to cover. Boil until
    only ½ cup (120 ml) of water remains and the
    horse gram is soft. Do not drain.
2.  In a skillet over low-medium heat, heat the
    vegetable oil.
3.  Add the garlic, onion, green chiles, cloves,
    green cardamom pods, cinnamon sticks, ginger,
    and turmeric. Sauté until the oil separates.
4.  Pour in the water and bring to a boil.
5.  Add the cooked gram with the cooking water,
    the coconut, vinegar, and curry leaves. Season
    to taste with salt. Bring to a boil again.
6.  Stir in the coconut milk and mix well. Cook
    until the gravy thickens.
7.  Serve hot.

## KALAN CURRY

A delicious motley of raw banana and yam.

Cooking time: 40 minutes | Serves: 2      Origin: Kerala

INGREDIENTS

1 cup (110 g) cubed peeled yam
1 cup (150 g) cubed unripe banana
1 tsp freshly ground black pepper (*kali mirch*)
½ tsp ground turmeric (*haldi*)
Salt, to taste
1 cup (80 g) grated fresh coconut (*nariyal*)
3 green chiles, finely chopped
1 tsp cumin seeds (*jeera*)
½ cup (120 g) yogurt (*dahi*), whisked
1 Tbsp (15 ml) coconut oil (*nariyal*)
1 tsp mustard seeds (*rai*)
½ tsp fenugreek seeds (*methi dana*), crushed
4 dried red chiles (*sookhi lal mirch*)
10 curry leaves (*kadhi patta*)

METHOD

1.  In a medium-size saucepan over medium heat,
    combine the yam, banana, pepper, turmeric,
    and enough water to cover everything. Season
    to taste with salt.
2.  Bring to a boil and cook for 30–35 minutes until
    the yam and banana are thoroughly soft.
    Remove from the water and set aside.
3.  In a food processor, combine the coconut,
    green chiles, and cumin seeds. Blend into a
    paste. Transfer to a skillet and add the boiled
    yam and banana. Place the skillet over medium
    heat. Stir in the yogurt and adjust the seasoning.
4.  Let the curry bubble well for 10–15 minutes.
5.  In a small skillet over low-medium heat, heat
    the coconut oil.
6.  Add the mustard seeds, fenugreek seeds, dried
    red chiles, and curry leaves. Cook until the
    seeds begin to crackle. Pour the tempering over
    the curry.
7.  Serve hot.

# CHAKKA KURU MANGA CURRY

Jackfruit seeds and mango in coconut curry.

Cooking time: 20 minutes | Serves: 4 — Origin: Kerala

## INGREDIENTS

For the jackfruit seed curry

1 cup (150 g) jackfruit seeds (*kathal*), skinned, halved lengthwise
4 green chiles, slit
½ tsp ground turmeric (*haldi*)
Salt, to taste
3 baby onions
Pinch cumin seeds (*jeera*)
½ tsp red chile powder
½ cup (82.5 g) sliced mango (*kairi*)
1 cup (85 g) grated dried unsweetened coconut (*nariyal*)
3 curry leaves (*kadhi patta*)

For the tempering

¼ cup (60 ml) vegetable oil
½ tsp mustard seeds (*rai*)
Pinch fenugreek seeds (*methi dana*)
3 Tbsp (30 g) chopped onion
2 dried red chiles (*sookhi lal mirch*), quartered

## METHOD

1. **To make the jackfruit seed curry:** In a medium-size saucepan, combine the jackfruit seeds with enough water to cover. Add the green chiles and turmeric. Season to taste with salt. Bring to a boil over high heat and cook for about 15 minutes until soft.
2. Meanwhile, in a blender or mortar and pestle, grind the baby onions, cumin seeds, and red chile powder into a paste.
3. When the jackfruit seeds are about three-fourths cooked (after about 10 minutes), add the mango and the onion-chile paste. Mix well.
4. Return the mixture to a boil. Add the coconut and curry leaves. Cook until the gravy thickens.
5. **To make the tempering:** In a skillet over low-medium heat, heat the vegetable oil.
6. Add the mustard seeds, fenugreek seeds, onion, and dried red chiles. Sauté until the onion turns brown. Pour the tempering into the curry and mix well. Serve hot.

# KAPPA PURATIYATHU

Tapioca with mustard seeds and coconut.

Cooking time: 25 minutes | Serves: 6 — Origin: Kerala

## INGREDIENTS

For the tapioca

2 lb, 3 oz (1 kg) fresh tapioca (cassava) root, peeled and diced
½ tsp red chile powder
¼ tsp ground turmeric (*haldi*)
½ cup (42.5 g) grated dried unsweetened coconut (*nariyal*)
2 baby onions
Pinch cumin seeds (*jeera*)
Salt, to taste

For the tempering

3 Tbsp (45 ml) vegetable oil
½ tsp mustard seeds (*rai*)
3 Tbsp (30 g) chopped onion
3 sprigs curry leaves (*kadhi patta*), leaves removed
2 dried red chiles (*sookhi lal mirch*), halved
3 Tbsp (15 g) grated dried unsweetened coconut (*nariyal*)

## METHOD

1. **To make the tapioca:** In a saucepan, combine the tapioca with enough water to cover. Place it over high heat and boil until tender. Remove from the heat, drain, and set aside to cool. When cool enough to handle, mash the tapioca into a smooth paste.
2. In a small bowl, mix together the red chile powder and turmeric.
3. In a blender or mortar and pestle, crush the coconut, baby onions, and cumin seeds together. Stir in the spice mix.
4. Add this paste to the mashed tapioca. Stir to combine and season to taste with salt. Place the pan over low heat.
5. **To make the tempering:** In a wok over low-medium heat, heat the vegetable oil.
6. Add the mustard seeds, onion, curry leaves, dried red chiles, and coconut. Sauté until the ingredients turn brown. Transfer to the tapioca. Mix well and serve hot.

# KOOTU THEEYAL

Tangy vegetables with coconut.

Cooking time: 20 minutes | Serves: 6      Origin: Kerala

## INGREDIENTS

¼ cup (60 ml) coconut oil (*nariyal*), divided
12 dried red chiles (*sookhi lal mirch*), divided
1 cup (85 g) grated dried unsweetened coconut
  (*nariyal*)
¾ tsp fenugreek seeds (*methi dana*)
3 cups (910 g) diced okra (*bhindi*)
3 cups (250 g) diced eggplant (*brinjal*)
3 cups (405 g) diced cucumber
3 cups (330 g) diced potato
½ cup (85 g) pearl onions, slit, cut into small slices
½ tsp mustard seeds (*rai*)
2 medium-size onions, sliced
1 lemon-size tamarind (*imli*), dissolved in 2 cups
  water, strained (page 30 )
Salt, to taste

## METHOD

1. In a wok over low-medium heat, heat 1 tsp of coconut oil.
2. Add 8 dried red chiles, the coconut, and fenugreek seeds. Sauté until the coconut turns brown. Remove from the heat. Set aside to cool.
3. Transfer the fried ingredients to a food processor or mortar and pestle. Add a little water and grind them into a fine paste.
4. Return the wok to the heat and add 3 Tbsp (45 ml) of coconut oil.
5. Add the okra, eggplant, cucumber, potato, and pearl onions. Cook until the vegetables are tender. Remove the vegetables and set aside.
6. In the same wok, add the remaining 2 tsp of coconut oil.
7. When hot, add the mustard seeds. Sauté until the seeds begin to crackle.
8. Add the sliced onions and the remaining 4 dried red chiles. Cook until the onions turn brown.
9. Add the okra, eggplant, cucumber, potato, and pearl onions back to the wok. Stir well to combine.
10. Mix in the tamarind extract and spice paste. Season to taste with salt. Cook until the mixture is heated through. Remove from the heat and serve hot.

# STUFFED BAIGAN

Eggplant stuffed with coconut.

Cooking time: 35 minutes | Serves: 2      Origin: Karnataka

## INGREDIENTS

2 green chiles, finely chopped
1 medium-size onion, sliced
½ medium-size fresh coconut (*nariyal*), grated
¼ cup (4 g) fresh cilantro leaves (*hara dhaniya*),
  finely chopped
2 tsp red chile powder
1 tsp ground cumin (*jeera*)
½ tsp ground turmeric (*haldi*)
Salt, to taste
1 medium-size eggplant (brinjal), stem end
  removed, halved lengthwise, and slit with a
  knife making a deep incision on top to stuff the
  mixture
3 Tbsp (45 ml) vegetable oil

## METHOD

1. Preheat the oven to 400°F (200°C).
2. In a medium-size bowl, combine the green chiles, onion, coconut, cilantro, red chile powder, cumin, and turmeric. Season to taste with salt. Stuff this mixture inside the eggplant halves.
3. Grease a large ovenproof skillet with the vegetable oil and place it over low heat.
4. Put the stuffed eggplant halves in the skillet. Cover the pan and cook for 8–10 minutes.
5. Remove the cover and transfer the skillet to the oven. Finish cooking there for 10 minutes.

## VAREKA UPERI

Stir-fried raw banana with black-eyed peas flavored with coconut and curry leaves.

Cooking time: 35 minutes | Serves: 3-4     Origin: Kerala

### INGREDIENTS

¼ cup (50 g) black-eyed peas (*lobia*)
2 green chiles
4 garlic cloves (*lasan*)
½ tsp ground turmeric (*haldi*)
Pinch cumin seeds (*jeera*)
4 oz (120 g) grated dried unsweetened coconut (*nariyal*)
2 raw medium-size bananas, sliced
2 Tbsp (30 ml) vegetable oil
1 tsp mustard seeds (*rai*)
2 dried red chiles (*sookhi lal mirch*), quartered
1 Tbsp (10 g) finely chopped baby onion
3 curry leaves (*kadhi patta*)
Salt, to taste

### METHOD

1. In your pressure cooker cooking pot, combine the black-eyed beans with enough water to cover. Lock the lid in place and close the pressure release valve. Select Manual/Pressure Cook and cook for 9 minutes. Release the pressure, drain the beans, transfer to a saucepan, and set aside to cool.
2. In a blender or mortar and pestle, grind the green chiles, garlic, turmeric, and cumin seeds into a paste.
3. Add the coconut and grind again until smooth.
4. Stir the bananas into the black-eyed peas.
5. Add the coconut-spice paste in the center. Cover the pan and cook for about 3 minutes. Uncover and mix well once before removing from the heat.
6. In a skillet over medium-high heat, heat the vegetable oil.
7. Add the mustard seeds, dried red chiles, baby onion, and curry leaves. Sauté until the seeds begin to crackle and the leaves turn brown. Add the black-eyed pea mixture and stir well. Season to taste with salt. Remove from the heat and transfer to a serving dish.

## KALAN PATTANI MILAGUE

Mushroom and green peas cooked with onions, tomato, and pepper.

Cooking time: 30 minutes | Serves: 2     Origin: Tamil Nadu

### INGREDIENTS

2 tsp vegetable oil
¾ cup (127.5 g) chopped onion
1 tsp ginger paste (*adrak*)
1 tsp garlic paste (*lasan*)
1 tsp red chile powder
1 tsp ground coriander (*dhaniya*)
½ tsp ground turmeric (*haldi*)
Salt, to taste
½ cup (120 g) chopped tomato
2 cups (192 g) button mushrooms, chopped and blanched
½ cup (80 g) green peas (*hara mattar*)
2 tsp peppercorns (*sabut kali mirch*), crushed
¼ cup (4 g) fresh cilantro leaves (*hara dhaniya*), finely chopped
1 tsp ghee

### METHOD

1. In a skillet over medium heat, heat the vegetable oil.
2. Add the onion. Sauté until golden.
3. Add the ginger paste and garlic paste. Sauté for 1 minute more.
4. Add the red chile powder, coriander, turmeric, and salt to taste. Sauté until the oil floats on the top.
5. Add the tomato. Cook for 4–5 minutes.
6. Add mushrooms and green peas. Sauté until the vegetables are cooked thoroughly.
7. Season with salt as needed and the crushed peppercorns. Garnish with cilantro and the ghee just before serving.

# ARAITHA SAMBHAR

Tangy pigeon peas cooked with vegetables.

Cooking time: 40 minutes | Serves: 2    Origin: Tamil Nadu

## INGREDIENTS

**For the pigeon peas**

½ cup (100 g) pigeon peas (*toor dal*), soaked in water for 5 minutes, drained

2 cups (480 ml) water

3¼ Tbsp (40 g) chopped small baby onion

½ tsp ground turmeric (*haldi*)

Salt, to taste

1¾ oz (50 g) diced eggplant (*brinjal*)

½ medium-size green bell pepper, diced

1 long drumstick (*saijan ki phalli*), diced

1 medium-size potato, diced

3 Tbsp (30 g) grated dried unsweetened coconut (*nariyal*)

2 dried red chiles (*sookhi lal mirch*)

2½ tsp coriander seeds (*dhaniya*)

¾ tsp fenugreek seeds (*methi dana*)

½ tsp ground asafoetida (*hing*)

2 tsp Bengal gram (split chickpeas; *chana dal*)

¾ tsp cumin seeds (*jeera*)

2 tsp vegetable oil

½ tsp tamarind extract (*imli*; page 30)

**For the tempering**

1 tsp vegetable oil

¾ tsp mustard seeds (*rai*)

½ tsp cumin seeds (*jeera*)

½ tsp aniseed (*saunf*)

2 dried red chiles (*sookhi lal mirch*)

3 curry leaves (*kadhi patta*)

Salt, to taste

2 Tbsp (2 g) fresh cilantro leaves (*hara dhaniya*), finely chopped

## METHOD

1. **To make the pigeon peas:** In a saucepan over high heat, combine the pigeon peas and water and bring to a boil. Cook until tender.

2. Add the onion and turmeric. Season to taste with salt. Continue to cook until everything is soft. Remove the pot from the heat and set aside. Discard the water.

3. In a steamer basket, combine the eggplant, green bell pepper, drumstick, and potato. Steam until soft. Remove and set aside.

4. In a blender or mortar and pestle, grind the coconut, dried red chiles, coriander seeds, fenugreek seeds, asafoetida, chickpeas, cumin seeds, and vegetable oil into a smooth paste.

5. Add the steamed vegetables to the pigeon pea mix. Stir to combine, place the pan over low heat, and cook for 10–12 minutes.

6. Stir in the ground paste and tamarind extract. Cook for 5 minutes more.

7. **To make the tempering:** In a wok over medium-high heat, heat the vegetable oil

8. Add the mustard seeds, cumin seeds, aniseed, dried red chiles, and curry leaves. Sauté until the seeds begin to crackle and the curry leaves turn crisp. Pour the tempering into the pigeon peas and mix well. Season to taste with salt. Serve hot, garnished with cilantro.

## PARUPPU URUNDAI KOZHAMBHU

Steamed dumplings in tamarind gravy.

Cooking time: 30 minutes | Serves: 4     Origin: Tamil Nadu

### INGREDIENTS

For the dumplings

1 cup (200 g) pigeon peas (*toor dal*)
3 dried red chiles (*sookhi lal mirch*)
Pinch ground asafoetida (*hing*)
Salt, to taste

For the tamarind gravy

1 Tbsp (15 ml) vegetable oil
½ tsp mustard seeds (*rai*)
2 dried red chiles
¼ tsp fenugreek seeds (*methi dana*)
Pinch ground asafoetida (*hing*)
1½ tsp Bengal gram (split chickpeas; *chana dal*)
½ tsp sambhar powder (available at Indian markets)
Pinch ground turmeric (*haldi*)
1 lemon-size tamarind (*imli*), dissolved in 2 cups hot water, juice and pulp extracted, separated (page 30)
1 Tbsp (10 g) rice flour mixed with ¼ cup (60 ml) water to make a paste
1½ tsp powdered jaggery (*gur*; unrefined cane sugar)

### METHOD

1.  **To make the dumplings:** In a medium-size bowl, combine the pigeon peas, dried red chiles, and asafoetida. Season to taste with salt and add enough water to cover. Soak for 2 hours.
2.  Drain the pigeon peas. Transfer to a blender or mortar and pestle and grind into a thick paste. Divide the paste into lime-size portions and shape each into a ball.
3.  Place the dumplings in a greased idli stand (available at Indian markets and online) and steam in a steamer for 8 minutes. Remove and set aside.
4.  **To make the tamarind gravy:** In a skillet over low-medium heat, heat the vegetable oil.
5.  Add the mustard seeds. Sauté until the seeds begin to crackle.
6.  Add the dried red chiles, fenugreek seeds, and asafoetida. Stir-fry for 1 minute.
7.  Add the chickpeas and cook until golden.
8.  Stir in the sambhar powder, turmeric, and tamarind juice. Reduce the heat to low and simmer for 10 minutes.
9.  While the gravy simmers, coat the dumplings with the rice flour paste (this prevents the dumplings from dissolving) and lower them into the gravy. Simmer for 10 minutes more.
10. Add the jaggery and mix well. Serve hot, with steamed rice, if desired.

## VAZHAKAI KOZHSAL CURRY

Sticky banana curry.

Cooking time: 40 minutes | Serves: 3     Origin: Tamil Nadu

### INGREDIENTS

2 large or 3 medium unripe bananas, peeled
3 Tbsp (45 ml) vegetable oil
¼ tsp mustard seeds (*rai*)
1 tsp split black lentils (*urad dal*)
1 dried red chile (*sookhi lal mirch*)
Pinch ground asafoetida
½ tsp ground turmeric (*haldi*)
Salt, to taste

### METHOD

1. Cook the bananas in a steamer or shallow vessel with enough water to cover until soft. Remove and dice into small pieces. Set aside.
2. In a small skillet over medium-high heat, heat the vegetable oil.
3. Add the mustard seeds. Cook until they begin to crackle.
4. Add the black lentils, dried red chile, and asafoetida. Sauté until fragrant.
5. Add the diced bananas and turmeric. Season to taste with salt. Cooking, stirring, until the mixture forms a sticky mass. Remove from the heat and serve hot.

## URULAIKIZHANGHU PALIYA

Potatoes in onion-tomato masala.

Cooking time: 20 minutes | Serves: 4-6     Origin: Tamil Nadu

### INGREDIENTS

1 lb, 2 oz (500 g) medium-size potatoes, unpeeled
1½ cups (360 ml) water, plus more for cooking the potatoes
2 Tbsp (30 ml) vegetable oil
½ tsp mustard seeds (*rai*)
1 dried red chile (*sookhi lal mirch*)
1 (1-in. / 2.5-cm) piece fresh ginger (*adrak*), peeled and finely chopped
1 green chile, slit
1 medium-size onion, finely chopped
1 medium-size tomato, diced
¼ tsp ground turmeric (*haldi*)
Pinch ground asafoetida (*hing*)
Salt, to taste
Juice of 1–2 lemons (*nimbu*)
1 small bunch fresh cilantro leaves (*hara dhaniya*), finely chopped

### METHOD

1. In your pressure cooker cooking pot, combine the potatoes with enough water to cover. Lock the lid in place and close the pressure valve. Select Manual/Pressure Cook and cook for 2–3 minutes, until soft. Release the pressure and remove the lid. When cool enough to handle, peel the potatoes and cut them into chunks. Set aside.
2. In a skillet over medium-high heat, heat the vegetable oil.
3. Add the mustard seeds. Sauté until the seeds begin to crackle.
4. Add the dried red chile, ginger, green chile, and onion. Sauté until the onions turn light brown.
5. Add the tomato and turmeric. Sauté for 2 minutes.
6. Add the water, asafoetida, and season to taste with salt. Cover the skillet and reduce the heat to low. Simmer the mixture for 5 minutes.
7. Add the potatoes. Stir to combine and cook for 3 minutes more. Remove the skillet from the heat and set aside to cool a bit.
8. Add the lemon juice and serve garnished with cilantro.

## KOZHAMBU

Eggplant and Bengal gram in a tangy curry.

Cooking time: 30 minutes | Serves: 6     Origin: Tamil Nadu

### INGREDIENTS

¾ cup (150 g) Bengal gram (split chickpeas; *chana dal*)

2 cups (480 ml) water, plus additional to make the gravy

2 Tbsp (30 ml) vegetable oil

12 curry leaves (*kadhi patta*)

2 (1-in. / 2.5-cm) cinnamon sticks (*dalchini*)

2 whole cloves (*laung*)

2 medium-size onions, sliced

2 cups (170 g) cubed eggplant (*brinjal*)

2 tsp red chile powder

2 tsp ground coriander (*dhaniya*)

1 tsp ginger-garlic paste (*adrak-lasan*)

½ tsp ground turmeric (*haldi*)

1½ tsp salt

1 marble-size tamarind (*imli*), juice extracted (page 30)

½ medium-size dried unsweetened coconut (*nariyal*)

2 tsp poppy seeds (*khus khus*)

2 medium-size tomatoes

¼ cup (4 g) fresh cilantro leaves (*hara dhaniya*), finely chopped

### METHOD

1. In your pressure cooker cooking pot, combine the chickpeas and water. Lock the lid in place and close the pressure release valve. Select Manual/Pressure Cook and cook for 10 minutes, or until the lentils are firm to the bite, and not too soft. Release the pressure and remove the lid.

2. In a wok over low-medium heat, heat the vegetable oil.

3. Add the curry leaves, cinnamon sticks, cloves, and onions. Sauté until the onions turn light brown.

4. Add the eggplant. Cook until it discolors and softens.

5. Add the red chile powder, coriander, ginger-garlic paste, and turmeric. Sauté for 3 minutes.

6. Add the cooked chickpeas, salt, and enough water to make a gravy. Boil until the chickpeas and eggplant are cooked through.

7. Stir in the tamarind extract. Reduce the heat and simmer the gravy for 5 minutes.

8. In a blender or mortar and pestle, grind the coconut, poppy seeds, and tomatoes into a smooth paste. Mix this paste with the chickpea mixture and cook until all ingredients are well blended. Simmer for about 3 minutes. Serve hot, garnished with cilantro.

RICE AND BREADS

## NAIDU LAMB BIRYANI
Naidu-style lamb rice.

Cooking time: 1 hour 30 minutes | Serves: 6
Origin: Andhra Pradesh

### INGREDIENTS

½ cup (120 g) yogurt (*dahi*)

3 Tbsp (45 g) freshly ground ginger paste (*adrak*)

1 lb, 2 oz (500 g) lamb, rinsed and cubed

6 almonds (*badam*), blanched, or 8 cashews (*kaju*)

6 Tbsp (90 ml) vegetable oil

4 (1-in. / 2.5-cm) cinnamon sticks (*dalchini*)

4 whole cloves (*laung*)

4 green cardamom pods (*choti elaichi*)

4 medium-size onions, chopped

5 green chiles, slit

3 Tbsp (45 g) fresh garlic paste (*lasan*)

2 medium-size tomatoes, chopped

1 cup (64 g) fresh mint leaves (*pudina*), washed

1 cup (16 g) fresh cilantro leaves (*hara dhaniya*), chopped

1 Tbsp (8 g) red chile powder

Salt, to taste

7 cups (1.7 L) water, divided

Juice of 1 lemon (*nimbu*)

3 cups (600 g) rice, rinsed, soaked in water for 30 minutes, drained

### METHOD

1. In a large bowl, whisk the yogurt and ginger paste. Add the lamb and stir to coat. Refrigerate to marinate for 1 hour.
2. In a mortar and pestle, grind the almonds into a smooth paste.
3. In a large heavy-bottomed skillet over low-medium heat, heat the vegetable oil.
4. Add the cinnamon sticks, cloves, and green cardamom pods. Sauté for about 30 seconds.
5. Add the onions and fry until translucent.
6. Add the green chiles and garlic paste. Reduce the heat to low and sauté for 2 minutes.
7. Add the lamb and the marinade. Sauté for 2 minutes.
8. Stir in the tomatoes, mint, cilantro, red chile powder, and almond paste. Season to taste with salt. Sauté for 2–3 minutes, or until the oil rises to the top.
9. Add 2 cups (480 ml) of water and cook until the lamb is done and all the water is absorbed and the mixture is dry.
10. Pour in the remaining 5 cups (1.2 L) of water. Add the lemon juice and rice. Increase the heat to high. Cook for 10 minutes.
11. Reduce the heat to low and stir gently, cooking until the rice is done. Remove from the heat but keep the vessel covered until serving.

# YEL ADAI

Coconut and rice pancakes.

Cooking time: 40 minutes | Makes: 8     Origin: Tamil Nadu

## INGREDIENTS

2 cups (480 ml) water
1¼ cups (300 g) jaggery (*gur*; unrefined cane
    sugar)
1¼ cups (250 g) fresh coconut (*nariyal*), grated
¾ cup (150 g) ghee, divided
2½ cups (500 g) rice, washed, soaked for
    10–15 minutes, drained
Salt, to taste
1 tsp green cardamom seeds (*choti elaichi*)
4 banana leaves, cut into 4-in. (10-cm) squares

## METHOD

1. To prepare the jaggery syrup, boil the water, add the jaggery, and stir well. Remove the scum from time to time. Cook until the syrup is reduced to a quarter.

2. Add the coconut and cook for 5-8 minutes more. Stir in the ghee, reserving about 2 Tbsp (25 g).

3. In a food processor or grinder, combine the rice with enough water to make a batter of pouring consistency. Add salt to taste and the green cardamom seeds.

4. Smear the remaining ghee over the banana leaves. Pour the rice batter over the banana leaves (should make 8 pancakes), spread on the jaggery mixture, and fold in the shape of an envelope.

5. In a steamer, steam them for 18–20 minutes. Serve hot or cold.

# SEAFOOD BIRYANI 📷

A coastal spicy rice dish topped with yogurt.

Cooking time: 40 minutes | Serves: 4     Origin: Karnataka

## INGREDIENTS

2 Tbsp (16 g) red chile powder
1½ tsp ground turmeric (*haldi*)
1 Tbsp (15 ml) vinegar (*sirka*)
Salt, to taste
5 rawas fillets (Indian salmon) or mackerel
1 Tbsp (15 ml) vegetable oil, plus more for
    deep-frying
2 spring onions (*hara pyaz*), finely chopped
1 Tbsp (6 g) ground coriander (*dhaniya*)
1 Tbsp (8 g) fennel seed powder (*saunf*)
1 cup (240 g) yogurt (*dahi*)
1 cup (240 g) prawns, shells removed
2 cups (480 g) fried onion (*birista*; page 30)
2 medium-size potatoes, sliced and deep-fried
4 cups (800 g) long-grain rice, parboiled
Juice of 1 lemon (*nimbu*)
½ cup (8 g) fresh cilantro leaves (*hara dhaniya*),
    finely chopped
½ cup (32 g) fresh mint leaves (*pudina*), finely
    chopped

## METHOD

1. In a shallow dish, stir together the red chile powder, turmeric, and vinegar. Season to taste with salt. Add the fish, turn to coat, and set aside for 10 minutes to marinate.

2. In a deep skillet over low-medium heat, heat the vegetable oil for frying.

3. Carefully add the fish and deep-fry until golden and cooked through. Remove and set aside.

4. In a skillet over medium heat, heat 1 Tbsp (15 ml) of vegetable oil.

5. Add the spring onions, coriander, and fennel seed powder. Cook until the onions soften. Add the yogurt and prawns. Cook for 5 minutes.

6. Add the lemon juice and fried onion. Toss well to combine. Cook until the prawns are done.

7. Place the fried potatoes on top. Layer on the rice and fried fish. Cover the skillet, adjust the heat as needed, and simmer for about 20 minutes until the rice is thoroughly cooked. Finish with the lemon juice and garnish with cilantro and mint. Serve hot.

## RAGI RAVA DOSA

A breakfast staple made of millet.

Cooking time: 30 minutes | Makes: 6     Origin: Karnataka

### INGREDIENTS

½ cup (60 g) millet flour (*ragi*)
5 Tbsp (50 g) rice flour
5 Tbsp (52.5 g) semolina (*suji*)
1 green chile, finely chopped
½ spring onion (*hara pyaz*), finely chopped
1 tsp freshly ground black pepper (*kali mirch*)
2 cups (480 ml) water
Salt, to taste
5 Tbsp (75 g) ghee

### METHOD

1. In a medium-size bowl, combine the flours, semolina, green chile, spring onion, pepper, and water. Season to taste with salt. Stir well to combine.
2. Add more water to get a crepe-like consistency.
3. In a skillet over medium heat, heat the ghee.
4. Pour one ladle of the batter into the skillet. Spread it in a circular motion. Cook on both sides until golden.
5. Repeat for the remaining batter.
6. Serve hot with coconut chutney (page 31), if desired.

## AKKI ROTI

Rice flour flatbread cooked in banana leaf.

Cooking time: 30 minutes | Makes: 5     Origin: Karnataka

### INGREDIENTS

1 cup (160 g) rice flour
1 medium-size onion, finely chopped
½ cup (55 g) grated carrot (*gajar*)
¼ cup (4 g) fresh cilantro leaves (*hara dhaniya*), finely chopped
1 tsp ginger paste (*adrak*)
1 tsp red chile paste
1 tsp cumin seeds (*jeera*)
Salt, to taste
Water, for kneading
Banana leaves, for cooking the dough
1 Tbsp (15 ml) vegetable oil

### METHOD

1. In a medium-size bowl, combine the rice flour, onion, carrot, cilantro, ginger paste, red chile paste, and cumin seeds. Season to taste with salt.
2. Add enough water so you can knead the ingredients into a soft dough. Divide the dough equally into 5 small disks.
3. Grease a square sheet of banana leaf with the vegetable oil and place 1 dough disk on the banana leaf. Pat it with your fingers, as thinly as possible.
4. Puncture the disk with the tip of your finger so the holes can absorb some oil.
5. Cover it with another banana leaf.
6. Heat a griddle over low-medium heat.
7. Add the banana leaf packet and cook on both sides until done—the banana leaves turn slightly brown and the roti inside is cooked. Peel the flatbread off the banana leaf and serve hot. Repeat until all flatbreads are cooked.

## NEER DOSA 📷

A light dosa, literally translating to "water dosa."

Cooking time: 30 minutes | Makes: 8      Origin: Karnataka

### INGREDIENTS

1 cup (200 g) rice, soaked in water for 2 hours, drained
½ cup (40 g) grated fresh coconut (*nariyal*)
3 cups (720 ml) water
5 Tbsp (75 g) ghee

### METHOD

1. In a food processor, grind the rice into a fine paste.
2. Add the coconut and water. Blend into a thin batter.
3. In a skillet over medium heat, heat the ghee.
4. Pour in one ladleful of the batter. Swirl the pan in a circular motion and allow the batter to spread evenly and thinly, like a crepe.
5. Cook on both sides until golden.
6. Serve hot with coconut chutney (page 31), if desired.

• • • • • • • • • • • •

## PESARATTU

Green gram dosa.

Cooking time: 30 minutes | Makes: 14   Origin: Andhra Pradesh

### INGREDIENTS

2 cups (400 g) green gram (*moong dal*), soaked in water for 2 hours, drained
½ cup (100 g) rice, soaked in water for 2 hours, drained
¼ cup (4 g) fresh cilantro leaves (*hara dhaniya*), finely chopped
¼ cup (42.5 g) finely chopped onion
1 Tbsp (15 g) ginger-chile paste (*adrak-mirch*)
Pinch ground asafoetida (*hing*)
Salt, to taste
5–6 Tbsp (75–90 g) ghee

### METHOD

1. In a food processor, combine the green gram and rice. Blend into a fine paste. Transfer to a medium-size bowl.
2. Add the cilantro, onion, chile-ginger paste, and asafoetida. Season to taste with salt. Mix well.
3. Add water to get a thick pancake consistency.
4. In a skillet over medium heat, heat the ghee.
5. Using a ladle, pour in one ladleful of the batter. Spread in circular motion and cook on both sides until the dosa is golden-brown and slightly crispy. Repeat with the remaining batter.
6. Serve hot with coconut chutney (page 31), if desired.

• • • • • • • • • • • •

## POOTU

Steamed rice flour and coconut mixture.

Cooking time: 20 minutes | Serves: 3      Origin: Kerala

### INGREDIENTS

2 cups (320 g) rice flour
Salt, to taste
¼ cup (60 ml) water
¼ cup (20 g) fresh coconut (*nariyal*), grated

### METHOD

1. In a medium-size bowl mix the flour with salt. Sprinkle some water and mix lightly with the fingers to form a slightly damp and powdery mixture, but not lumpy.
2. In a *pootu* maker, put a layer of coconut and rice powder. Do this alternately with coconut on the top layer.
3. Attach the *pootu* maker with its perforated lid to a pressure cooker cooking pot half filled with boiling water; increase the heat so that the steam rushes through the *pootu* maker and comes out of the perforated lid, cooking the *pootu* in the process.
4. Open the lid and push the *pootu* out onto a plate.
5. Repeat the process with the rest of the rice powder.

## PATHRI

Malabar rice bread.

| Cooking time: 30 minutes | Makes: 8 | Origin: Kerala |
| --- | --- | --- |

INGREDIENTS

2 cups (320 g) rice flour
½ tsp ground cumin (*jeera*)
½ tsp red chile powder
Salt, to taste
Water, for kneading
2 Tbsp (30 g) ghee

METHOD

1. In a pan over medium heat, dry-roast the rice flour, cumin, and red chile powder for 4–5 minutes. Remove the pan from the heat. Add salt to taste and a little water and knead into a soft dough.
2. Divide the dough into 8 balls. Roll each out into thin disks.
3. In a frying pan on low-medium heat, place the disk flat. Add 1 tsp ghee and panfry the bread until slightly brown on both sides.
4. Repeat until all are done.
5. Serve hot, smeared with ghee and accompanied with any curry of your choice.

## APPAM

Lacy rice pancakes.

| Cooking time: 30 minutes | Makes: 8 | Origin: Kerala |
| --- | --- | --- |

INGREDIENTS

2 cups (400 g) raw rice
1 cup (200 g) rice, cooked
1 cup (80 g) grated fresh coconut (*nariyal*)
2 Tbsp (25 g) sugar
Water, as needed
½ tsp yeast
Vegetable oil, for shallow-frying

METHOD

1. In a blender or food processor, combine the raw and cooked rice, coconut, and sugar. Grind together with enough water to make a pourable batter.
2. Add the yeast. Pulse to combine. Transfer the batter to a bowl, cover, and leave the batter to ferment overnight at room temperature.
3. Heat a heavy-bottomed skillet over medium heat.
4. Rub the skillet with a little vegetable oil and pour in 2 Tbsp (30 ml) of batter. Tilt the vessel around until the batter coats it. Sprinkle in some oil, cover the skillet, and cook for 2 minutes, or until the base is golden and the top is soft and pale. Remove and repeat with the remaining batter (should make 8 appams).
5. Serve hot with Elumichapazham Rasam (page 278), Chettinad Nandurasam (page 310), or Araitha Sambhar (page 324), if desired.

# MALABAR PAROTTA
Crisp panfried layered bread.

Cooking time: 30 minutes | Makes: 7      Origin: Kerala

## INGREDIENTS

¾ cup (93.75 g) all-purpose flour (*maida*)
1 tsp baking powder
6 Tbsp (90 g) ghee, divided, plus more as needed
Salt, to taste
Water, as needed

## METHOD

1. Sift the flour and baking powder together into a small bowl.
2. Add 1½ Tbsp (23 g) of ghee and rub it into the flour mixture until well incorporated. Season to taste with salt and add enough water (about ¾ cup / 180 ml) to form a soft dough.
3. Knead well. Divide the dough into 7 portions. Roll each portion into a thin disk and, using the remaining 4½ Tbsp (67 g) of ghee, smear some over the surface of each. Roll each disk from one end to the other and form it into a coil. Set aside for 15 minutes.
4. Roll the coils again into thin disks.
5. Heat a griddle over low heat. Place the flat disk on the griddle and cook for about 3 minutes. Turn the disk over and smear some ghee over and around it. Flip it again and do the same on the other side. Panfry until both sides are golden brown. Remove and repeat with all the disks. Serve hot.

# IDIAPPAM
String hoppers.

Cooking time: 30 minutes | Makes: 4      Origin: Tamil Nadu

## INGREDIENTS

1 cup (240 ml) water
Salt, to taste
1½ Tbsp (23 ml) vegetable oil
1 cup (160 g) rice flour

## METHOD

1. In a small pot with a lid over high heat, combine the water, salt, and vegetable oil. Cover the pot and bring to a boil.
2. Reduce the heat to low and slowly stir in the rice flour, mixing continuously so the mixture is lump free.
3. Remove from the heat. Knead the mixture. Working in batches, pass the dough through a vermicelli press, pressing it onto a clean kitchen cloth.
4. In a steamer, steam for 3 minutes, or until cooked.
5. Serve hot with Elumichapazham Rasam (page 279), Chettinad Nandurasam (page 310), or Araitha Sambhar (page 324), if desired.

## THIKKADI

Madurai-style rice cake biryani.

Cooking time: 30 minutes | Serves: 4     Origin: Tamil Nadu

### INGREDIENTS

**For the rice cakes**

1 cup (200 g) rice, soaked in water for 30 minutes, drained and dried

1 cup (240 ml) boiling water

½ tsp salt

Vegetable oil, for greasing your palms

**For the gravy**

3½ oz (100 g) boneless lamb pieces

½ tsp salt

½ tsp red chile powder, divided

1 cup (240 ml) water, plus additional if needed

1 Tbsp (15 ml) vegetable oil

1 (1-in. / 2.5-cm) cinnamon stick (*dalchini*)

2 whole cloves (*laung*)

1 green cardamom pod (*choti elaichi*)

1 small onion, sliced

1 green chile, slit

1 medium-size tomato, chopped

½ tsp ginger-garlic paste (*adrak-lasan*)

1 Tbsp (4 g) fresh mint leaves (*pudina*), finely chopped

1 Tbsp (1 g) fresh cilantro leaves (*hara dhaniya*), finely chopped

2 Tbsp (10 g) grated dried unsweetened coconut (*nariyal*)

### METHOD

1. **To make the rice cakes:** Make sure the rice is completely dry and place it in a blender or food processor, or mortar and pestle, and grind into a fine powder.

2. Gradually add the hot water to the rice powder and knead to make a very soft, pliable dough.

3. Divide the dough into marble-size portions. With greased palms, shape each portion into a ball and press down lightly to make a small 1-in. (2.5-cm) cake.

4. **To make the gravy:** In your pressure cooker cooking pot, combine the lamb, salt, and ¼ tsp of red chile powder. Add the water. Lock the lid in place and close the pressure valve. Select Manual/Pressure Cook and cook for 40 minutes. Release the pressure and turn off the cooker.

5. In a skillet over medium-high heat, heat the vegetable oil.

6. Add the cinnamon stick, cloves, green cardamom pod, and onion. Fry until the onion is lightly browned.

7. Add the green chile, tomato, ginger-garlic paste, the remaining ¼ tsp of red chile powder, the mint, and cilantro. Cook for 5–7 minutes.

8. Stir in the cooked lamb and cooking water. Cook for 5 minutes more.

9. Add the coconut and measure the liquid content. The ratio should be 1:2—double the quantity of gravy to the quantity of rice used. In this case, the gravy needs to be 2 cups (480 ml). If it is less, add enough water. Pour the gravy into a rice cooker and check the seasoning. Bring the mixture to a boil.

10. Add the rice cakes and close the cooker (do not add the cakes before the liquid comes to a boil, as they will dissolve and become gooey).

11. When it is done, the switch will move to Keep Warm and the liquid will be absorbed by the rice cakes. The finished dish will resemble a porridge.

## VENPONGAL

Rice and green gram tempered with cashew nuts.

Cooking time: 35 minutes | Serves: 2     Origin: Tamil Nadu

### INGREDIENTS

4 Tbsp (60 g) ghee, divided
½ cup (100 g) rice
¼ cup (50 g) split green gram (*moong dal*)
1 cup (240 ml) water
Salt, to taste
1 Tbsp (15 g) cashews (*kaju*)
1 tsp peppercorns (*sabut kali mirch*)
1 tsp cumin seeds (*jeera*)
2 curry leaves (*kadhi patta*)
1 green chile, finely chopped
1 tsp minced peeled fresh ginger (*adrak*)

### METHOD

1. On your pressure cooker, select Sauté and preheat the cooking pot.
2. Add 2 Tbsp (30 g) of ghee, the rice, and green gram. Sauté for 2 minutes.
3. Add the water and season to taste with salt. Lock the lid in place and close the pressure release valve. Select Manual/Pressure Cook and cook for 9 minutes.
4. In a skillet over low-medium heat, heat the remaining 2 Tbsp (30 g) of ghee.
5. Add the cashews, peppercorns, cumin seeds, curry leaves, green chile, and ginger. Cook, stirring, until the spices begin to crackle.
6. Season to taste with salt and pour the tempering on the rice and lentil mixture.
7. Serve hot, with coconut chutney (page 31) and sambhar (page 324), if desired.

## THENGAI SAADHAM

Coconut rice.

Cooking time: 40 minutes | Serves: 3-4     Origin: Tamil Nadu

### INGREDIENTS

4½ cups (1 L) water
2¼ cup (450 g) rice, rinsed
1 Tbsp (15 ml) coconut oil (*nariyal*)
½ tsp mustard seeds (*rai*)
½ tsp Bengal gram (split chickpeas; *chana dal*)
½ tsp split black lentils (*urad dal*)
¼ tsp cumin seeds (*jeera*)
Pinch ground asafoetida (*hing*)
Few curry leaves (*kadhi patta*)
3 Tbsp (15 g) grated fresh coconut (*nariyal*), divided
1 Tbsp (9 g) white sesame seeds (*safed til*), roasted, ground into a powder
1 tsp chopped green chile
1 tsp chopped peeled fresh ginger (*adrak*)
12 cashews (*kaju*), fried
Salt, to taste

### METHOD

1. In a medium-size pot over high heat, bring the water to a boil.
2. Add the rice and cook according to the package directions until done. Drain and set aside.
3. In a wok over medium-high heat, heat the coconut oil.
4. Add the mustard seeds. Cook until the seeds begin to crackle.
5. Add the Bengal grams, black lentils, and cumin seeds. Fry for 2–3 seconds.
6. Add the asafoetida, curry leaves, 2 Tbsp (10 g) of coconut, the sesame seeds, green chile, ginger, cashews, and salt to taste. Cook for 3 minutes until fragrant. Transfer to a large bowl and stir in the rice, the remaining 1 Tbsp (5 g) of coconut. Serve hot.

DESSERTS

## ADHIRASAMS 🍮
Deepavali jaggery cookies.

Cooking time: 40 minutes | Makes: 15     Origin: Tamil Nadu

### INGREDIENTS

1½ cups (300 g) rice, rinsed, soaked in water for
  3 hours
1 tsp ground ginger (*sonth*)
Pinch ground black cardamom (*badi elaichi*)
½ cup (120 ml) water
1 cup (240 g) powdered jaggery (*gur*; unrefined
  cane sugar)
Vegetable oil, for greasing the work surface
  and frying

### METHOD

1. Drain the rice and spread it out to dry on an absorbent kitchen towel until most of the water is drained off, but the rice is still slightly damp. In a food processor, grind the rice into a fine powder. Mix in the ginger and cardamom powder. Using a fine-mesh sieve, sift the rice flour. Set aside.

2. In a heavy-bottomed pot over high heat, combine the water and jaggery. Bring to a boil. Ladle off a thin layer from the top of the mixture. Test the syrup for a one-thread consistency (page 31).

3. Stir in the rice flour gradually, mixing vigorously. Remove from the heat and continue stirring until the dough thickens. It should resemble a soft chapatti dough. Cover the pot with a damp cloth; let sit for 10 minutes.

4. Divide the dough equally into 15 lime-size portions. Grease a work surface with vegetable oil and pat each portion into a flat cake on the greased surface.

5. In a deep pot over low-medium heat, heat the vegetable oil for frying. Working in batches, gently ease the cakes into the hot oil and cook until brown. Flip and cook the other side until brown. Transfer to paper towels to drain. Repeat until all the cakes are fried.

## ARISITENGAAY PAYASAM
Rice pudding with poppy seeds and jaggery.

Cooking time: 1 hour | Serves: 2     Origin: Tamil Nadu

### INGREDIENTS

1½ cups (300 g) rice
3 Tbsp (27 g) poppy seeds (*khus khus*)
1 cup (85 g) grated dried unsweetened coconut
  (*nariyal*)
1 cup (240 ml) milk
½ cup (120 g) grated jaggery (*gur*; unrefined cane
  sugar)
Pinch ground green cardamom (*choti elaichi*)

### METHOD

1. In a medium-size bowl, combine the rice and poppy seeds with enough water to cover for 5 hours.

2. Drain and transfer to a blender. Add the coconut. Blend the rice mixture into a thick paste.

3. Transfer to a heavy-bottomed pot and place it over low-medium heat on the stove. Pour in the milk. Mix well. Bring to a simmer and cook until the milk begins to bubble.

4. Add the jaggery. Cook, stirring, until it dissolves completely. Keep stirring until the mixture comes to a porridge-like consistency. Remove from the heat. Sprinkle with cardamom and serve.

## THIRATIPAL 📷

Slow-cooked condensed milk with cardamom.

Cooking time: 1 hour | Serves: 4     Origin: Tamil Nadu

INGREDIENTS

2 tsp ghee
4 cups (960 ml) milk
¼ cup (50 g) sugar
2 tsp ground green cardamom (*choti elaichi*)

METHOD

1. Heat a heavy-bottomed pot over medium heat.
2. Add the ghee to melt.
3. Add the milk and bring to a boil. Cook, stirring, until the milk is reduced by half. This should take about 20 minutes.
4. Once it thickens and condenses, stir in the sugar and cardamom. Continue to cook for 20–25 minutes more to thicken the milk further. Serve warm.

## VELAI DOSAI

Wheat and rice pancakes sweetened with jaggery

Cooking time: 30 minutes | Makes: 10     Origin: Tamil Nadu

INGREDIENTS

½ cup (120 ml) water, plus more for the batter
¾ cup (252 g) jaggery (*gur*; unrefined cane sugar)
½ cup (62.5 g) whole-wheat flour (*atta*)
½ cup (80 g) rice flour
2 Tbsp (10 g) grated coconut (*nariyal*)
¼ tsp ground green cardamom (*choti elaichi*)
Ghee, for frying

METHOD

1. In a small saucepan over medium heat, heat the water.
2. Add the jaggery and cook until it melts. Remove and strain to remove all impurities.
3. In a small bowl, mix together the wheat flour, rice flour, coconut, cardamom, and enough water to make a pancake-like batter.
4. In a skillet over medium heat, heat the ghee.
5. Pour a ladleful of batter in the skillet and swirl in a circular motion allowing the batter to spread evenly and thinly, like a crepe. Cook on both sides until golden brown. Repeat until all the batter is used up. Serve hot with the jaggery syrup.

# KOZHUKATTA

Steamed rolls stuffed with coconut.

| Cooking time: 25 minutes | Makes: 9 | Origin: Kerala |
|---|---|---|

## INGREDIENTS

2 cups (400 ml) water
Salt, to taste
1½ Tbsp (22 ml) vegetable oil
1 cup (160 g) rice flour, sifted
1 cup (80 g) coconut (*nariyal*), grated
¼ cup (60 g) grated jaggery (*gur*; unrefined cane sugar)

## METHOD

1. In a vessel over medium heat combine the water, salt, and oil. Cover the vessel with a lid and bring to a boil.
2. Reduce the heat to low and add the rice flour gradually; mixing continuously so that no lumps are formed.
3. Remove from the heat and when cool, knead into a smooth dough.
4. Divide the dough equally into 9 balls.
5. Roll each ball into a thin disk. Put a small amount of coconut and jaggery in the center and fold over into a crescent-shape, pressing the end with a fork. Repeat till all are done.
6. Steam them in a steam cooker until done (insert a toothpick in the center; if it comes out clean, the kozhukatta are done).

• • • • • • • • • • • •

# THENGAI POLI 🍽

Stuffed sweet bread.

| Cooking time: 30 minutes | Makes: 12 | Origin: Karnataka |
|---|---|---|

## INGREDIENTS

1 cup (200 g) Bengal gram (split chickpea; *chana dal*), rinsed and drained
3 cups (720 ml) water, divided
¼ cup (20 g) coconut, grated
1 cup (240 g) powdered jaggery (*gur*; unrefined cane suger)
7 green cardamom pods
1 tsp sugar
⅛ tsp salt, plus more to taste
1½ cups (187.5 g) whole-wheat flour (*atta*)
½ cup (62.5 g) all-purpose refined flour (*maida*)
½ tsp ground turmeric (*haldi*)
½ cup (120 g) ghee, divided
Rice flour for dusting

## METHOD

1. In your pressure cooker cooking pot combine the Bengal gram with 2 cups (480 ml) of water. Lock the lid and close the pressure release valve. Select Manual/Pressure Cook and cook for 8 minutes. Let the pressure release. Remove the lid and using a slotted spoon transfer the dal to a bowl; reserve the excess water for another dish. Mash the dal to a smooth paste.
2. Toast the grated coconut in a small pan.
3. Boil the jaggery with the remaining 1 cup (240 ml) of water, along with the cardamom pods, coconut, sugar, and salt, and simmer until the jaggery is dissolved. Use cheesecloth to filter the mixture and remove impurities. Add the dal paste and cook until the moisture is absorbed and the mixture is semi-solid.
4. Mix the whole-wheat flour, all-purpose flour, salt to taste, turmeric, and 1 Tbsp (15 ml) of ghee to make a soft pliable dough, and use a little cold water to knead it. Make smooth lime-size balls. Flatten each ball into disk 4 in. (10 cm) in diameter.
5. Place 2 teaspoons of filling in the center of each disk and bring one edge to cover the other, pressing the edges to seal them completely. Gently form into a ball. Using the rice flour for dusting, roll out each ball into a thin chapatti of 6 in. (15 cm) in diameter.
6. Fry each chapatti on a tawa or griddle using the remaining ghee, spooning a little at a time around the edges till light brown. Flip over and brown. Repeat for the remaining chapattis.

## BADAM PURIS 🍲
Deep-fried bread stuffed with sweet almonds.

Cooking time: 40 minutes | Makes: 15-20     Origin: Karnataka

## INGREDIENTS

**For the dough**

2 cups (250 g) all-purpose flour (*maida*), plus more
   for the work surface as needed

½ cup (85 g) fine semolina (*suji*)

¼ tsp salt

6 Tbsp (90 g) ghee

Water, as needed

**For the filling**

½ cup (72.5 g) almonds (*badam*), soaked in warm
   water for 30 minutes, drained, peeled

1 Tbsp (15 ml) milk, plus more as needed

1½ cups (300 g) caster (superfine) sugar

Few drops almond extract (*badam*)

1 cups (240 ml) vegetable oil, plus more for the
   work surface as needed

## METHOD

1. **To make the dough:** In a medium-size bowl,
   combine the flour, semolina, salt, and ghee.
   Using as little water as possible, knead the
   mixture into a stiff dough. Cover the dough
   with a damp cloth and set aside for 2–3 hours.

2. **To make the filling:** In a blender or mortar and
   pestle, grind the almonds into a fine paste,
   using as little milk as possible. Transfer to a
   small bowl.

3. Add the caster sugar and almond extract. Stir to
   combine. If the filling is a little runny, place it in
   a heavy-bottomed pot and cook over medium
   heat, stirring the mixture briskly until it hardens.
   Divide the mixture equally into 15–20 lime-size
   balls. Set aside.

4. Knead the dough again and divide it equally
   into 15–20 balls.

5. On a lightly floured or oiled surface, flatten the
   balls with a rolling pin into thin disks like
   pancakes. Place the filling in the center of each.
   Fold the edges over to seal the filling inside.
   Roll the stuffed balls in your palm to even out
   the wrinkles. Press down firmly and roll out
   again into a thin disk, sprinkling more oil or
   flour to keep the disks from sticking to the
   surface. Repeat with all the dough and filling.

6. In a heavy-bottomed skillet over low-medium
   heat, heat the oil.

7. Working in batches, carefully slide the disks
   into the hot oil. Fry evenly until golden on both
   sides. With a slotted spoon, transfer to paper
   towels to drain. Serve hot.

## POORNALU

Deep-fried rice and lentil balls with jaggery.

Cooking time: 40 minutes | Makes: 10 Origin: Andhra Pradesh

INGREDIENTS

½ cup (100 g) black lentils (*urad dal*), soaked in water for 2 hours, drained
1 cup (200 g) rice, soaked in water for 2 hours, drained
Salt, to taste
1 cup (200 g) Bengal gram (split chickpeas; *chana dal*), boiled
1 cup (336 g) grated jaggery (*gur*; unrefined cane sugar)
½ cup (40 g) grated fresh coconut (*nariyal*)
¾ cup (72 g) ground cardamom
Vegetable oil, for frying

METHOD

1. In a food processor or blender, combine the drained black lentils and rice. Add enough water to process into a thick batter. Season to taste with salt, transfer to a small bowl, and set aside.
2. In another small bowl, combine the boiled chickpeas and jaggery. With a potato masher, mash into a soft paste.
3. Transfer to a small heavy-bottomed pot and place it over medium heat. Cook, stirring, for 10–15 minutes, or until a thick paste-like mixture forms. Remove from the heat and set aside to cool.
4. Stir in the coconut and cardamom.
5. In a deep skillet over low-medium heat, heat the vegetable oil for frying.
6. Cut the chickpea mixture into 10 balls. Dip each ball into the black gram and rice batter and, working in batches, deep-fry in hot oil, on low heat, until golden brown. Transfer to paper towels to drain. Repeat until all the balls are fried.
7. Serve hot or store in an airtight container.

## BANANA COCONUT BAKE

Breakfast favorite from Konkan coast.

Cooking time: 35 minutes | Serves: 2     Origin: Karnataka

INGREDIENTS

2 Tbsp (30 g) butter
½ tsp vanilla extract
2 cups (160 g) grated fresh coconut (*nariyal*)
¼ cup (50 g) sugar
½ tsp ground cardamom
3 medium-size bananas, halved lengthwise
½ cup (120 ml) milk
Few saffron threads (*kesar*)

METHOD

1. Preheat the oven to 400°F (200°C).
2. In a skillet over medium heat, melt the butter.
3. Add the vanilla and coconut. Cook, stirring, until lightly browned.
4. Stir in the sugar and cardamom. Remove from the heat.
5. In a baking dish, layer one-third of the coconut mixture. Top with half the banana pieces. Cover with another one-third of the coconut, and layer the remaining banana pieces on top. Top with the remaining one-third of the coconut.
6. In a small bowl, combine the milk and saffron threads. Pour this over the coconut mixture. Bake for 10–15 minutes until golden. Serve hot.

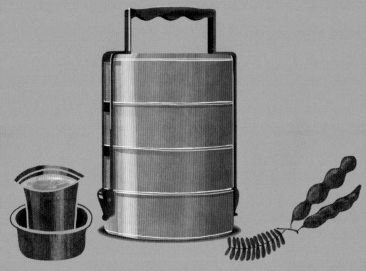

ACCOMPANIMENTS

## DOODHI PACHADI

A cooling bottle gourd-based side dish.

Cooking time: 40 minutes | Serves: 2          Origin: Kerala

INGREDIENTS

3 tsp (15 ml) coconut oil (*nariyal*), divided
1 cup (240 g) chopped (peeled and seeded) bottle
   gourd (*doodhi / lauki*)
2 Tbsp (21.25 g) finely chopped onion
1 green chile, finely chopped
1 tsp ginger paste (*adrak*)
1 cup (240 g) yogurt (*dahi*)
5 curry leaves (*kadhi patta*)
1 tsp mustard seeds (*rai*)
1 dried red chile (*sookhi lal mirch*)
3 Tbsp (45 g) sliced onion
Salt, to taste

METHOD

1. In a skillet over low heat, combine 1 tsp of
   coconut oil, the bottle gourd, chopped onion,
   green chile, and ginger paste. Cook for 10
   minutes until the bottle gourd is tender.
   Transfer to a bowl and cool to room temperature.
2. Stir in the yogurt.
3. Place the skillet over low-medium heat and add
   the remaining 2 tsp of coconut oil.
4. Add the curry leaves, mustard seeds, and dried
   red chile. Sauté until the spices begin to crackle.
5. Add the sliced onion. Sauté until golden.
6. Pour the spices and onion onto the yogurt.
   Season to taste with salt and serve.

## KACHIA MORU

Buttermilk tempered with mustard seeds.

Cooking time: 10 minutes | Serves: 2          Origin: Kerala

INGREDIENTS

2 cups (480 ml) buttermilk (*chaach*)
1 tsp ground turmeric (*haldi*)
3 curry leaves (*kadhi patta*)
Salt, to taste
1 Tbsp (5 g) grated dried unsweetened coconut
   (*nariyal*; optional)
2 pinches red chile powder
1 large pearl onion
Pinch cumin seeds (*jeera*)
1 Tbsp (15 ml) vegetable oil
¼ tsp mustard seeds (*rai*)
Pinch fenugreek seeds (*methi dana*)
1 dried red chile (*sookhi lal mirch*), halved

METHOD

1. In a medium-size saucepan, stir together the
   buttermilk, turmeric, and curry leaves. Season
   to taste with salt.
2. In a blender or mortar and pestle, grind the
   coconut (if using), red chile powder, onion, and
   cumin seeds into a smooth paste.
3. Stir this paste into the buttermilk mixture and
   place the pan over low heat. Cook, stirring
   continuously, until the mixture is just about to
   come to a boil. Remove from the heat. Stir
   continuously until it cools.
4. In a skillet over low-medium heat, heat the
   vegetable oil.
5. Add the mustard seeds, fenugreek seeds, and
   dried red chile. Cook until the seeds begin to
   crackle. Remove the skillet from the heat and
   set aside to cool.
6. When cool, add the spices to the buttermilk, stir
   to combine, and serve.

## ELANEER MILKSHAKE
Tender coconut creamy milkshake.

Cooking time: 30 minutes | Serves: 2     Origin: Tamil Nadu

INGREDIENTS

½ cup (40 g) grated fresh coconut (*nariyal*)
1 cup (240 ml) coconut water (*nariyal*)
¾ cup (180 ml) milk
2 Tbsp (30 g) honey

METHOD

1. In a blender, combine the coconut, coconut water, milk, and honey. Blend until smooth. Refrigerate.
2. Serve chilled.

## JIL JIL JIGARTHANDA
Nannari syrup-infused brown milk smoothie.

Cooking time: 1 hour | Serves: 4     Origin: Tamil Nadu

INGREDIENTS

3 cups (720 ml) milk, divided
½ cup (120 ml) heavy cream
¾ cup (150 g) sugar
5 milk pedas or any milk-based sweet, crumbled (available at Indian markets)
1 tsp vanilla extract
2 Tbsp (30 ml) nannari syrup
1 Tbsp (15 g) assorted dried fruits, finely chopped

METHOD

1. In a small saucepan over low-medium heat, combine 1½ cups (360 ml) of milk, the cream, sugar, milk sweet, and vanilla. Heat, stirring well, until the sugar dissolves completely.
2. Reduce the heat to medium and simmer, stirring constantly for 20–25 minutes, or until the mixture thickens. Remove the pan from the heat. Set aside to cool.
3. When cool, transfer the contents into an airtight container and freeze it.
4. When ready to serve, transfer the frozen mixture to a blender or food processor. Add the remaining 1½ cups (360 ml) of milk and nannari syrup. Process into a smoothie.
5. Serve chilled, garnished with dried fruits.

# KARUPATTI COFFEE

Traditional village-style black coffee.

Cooking time: 5 minutes | Serves: 2     Origin: Tamil Nadu

## INGREDIENT

¼ cup (60 ml) hot water
7 tsp (35 g) palm sugar
1 cup (240 ml) brewed coffee
½ cup (120 ml) milk (optional)

## METHOD

1. In a small saucepan over medium heat, combine the water and palm sugar. Cook, stirring, to dissolve the sugar.
2. Add the coffee and milk (if using). Reduce the heat to low and simmer until it reaches a rolling boil.
3. Serve hot.

# NANNARI SHERBET

A popular and healthy summer drink.

Cooking time: 30 minutes | Serves: 2     Origin: Tamil Nadu

## INGREDIENTS

**For the syrup**
3½ oz (100 g) nannari roots (available at Indian markets and online)
4 cups (960 ml) water
2 cups (400 g) sugar
Juice of 1 lemon (*nimbu*)
**For the sherbet**
2 cups (480 ml) water
Juice of 2 lemons (*nimbu*)
Ice, for serving

## METHOD

1. **To make the syrup:** Crush the nannari roots and discard the thick interior. Break the bark and grind it into a fine powder.
2. In a saucepan over high heat, bring the water to a boil. Add the nannari powder. Remove from the heat and let rest overnight.
3. Strain the mixture into a saucepan and stir in the sugar and lemon juice. Place the pan over medium heat and cook for 20–25 minutes until the sugar dissolves completely.
4. Once it thickens, remove it from the heat and cool to room temperature.
5. **To make the sherbet:** In a small pitcher, combine 7 Tbsp (105 ml) of the nannari syrup with the water and lemon juice. Add ice and serve chilled. Refrigerate the remaining syrup in an airtight container for later use.

# NEER MORE

Yogurt drink with mustard seeds and asafoetida.

Cooking time: 5 minsute | Serves: 4          Origin: Tamil Nadu

## INGREDIENTS

1 cup (240 g) yogurt (*dahi*)

4 cups (960 ml) water

2 green chiles, finely chopped

1 Tbsp (8 g) finely chopped peeled fresh ginger (*adrak*)

1 Tbsp (1 g) fresh cilantro leaves (*hara dhaniya*), finely chopped

Salt, to taste

1 tsp vegetable oil

1 tsp mustard seeds (*rai*)

1 curry leaf (*kadhi patta*)

Pinch ground asafoetida (*hing*)

## METHOD

1. In a pitcher, combine the yogurt, water, green chiles, ginger, cilantro, and salt. Stir well.
2. In a small skillet over low-medium heat, heat the vegetable oil.
3. Add the mustard seeds, curry leaf, and asafoetida. Cook until the seeds begin to crackle. Remove the skillet from the heat and pour the spices into the yogurt mixture. Stir well and refrigerate for 2 hours. Serve cold.

# PANAKAM

A cooling drink with jaggery, cardamom, and basil.

Cooking time: 10 minutes | Serves: 2          Origin: Tamil Nadu

## INGREDIENTS

½ cup (120 g) powdered jaggery (*gur*; unrefined cane sugar)

2 cups (480 ml) water

Juice of 1 lemon

1 tsp ground cardamom

Pinch ground ginger (*sonth*)

Pinch edible camphor

Pinch salt

¼ cup (10 g) finely chopped fresh basil leaves (*tulsi*)

## METHOD

1. In a small bowl, combine the jaggery, water, lemon juice, cardamom, ginger, camphor, and salt. Stir well and strain.
2. Mix the basil leaves into the strained liquid. Serve cold.

## VASANTHA NEER

Coconut lemonade flavored with mango.

Cooking time: 15 minutes | Serves: 2     Origin: Tamil Nadu

### INGREDIENTS

½ cup (32 g) fresh mint leaves (*pudina*)
1 Tbsp (15 g) honey
Warm water, as needed
2 cups (480 ml) coconut water (*nariyal*)
Juice of 1 lemon (*nimbu*)
¼ cup (60 g) mango pulp (*aam*)

### METHOD

1.  In a small bowl, mix the mint leaves with the honey and just enough warm water to dilute the honey and submerge the leaves fully. Let rest for 10 minutes.
2.  Add the coconut water, lemon juice, and mango. Mix well and refrigerate for 2–3 hours.
3.  Serve chilled.

## VATHAL KOZHAMBHU

Sweet and sour tamarind sauce.

Cooking time: 20 minutes | Serves: 4     Origin: Tamil Nadu

### INGREDIENTS

1 lemon-size tamarind (*imli*), dissolved in 2 cups (480 ml) hot water (page 30)
1 Tbsp (15 ml) vegetable oil
¼ tsp mustard seeds (*rai*)
2 dried red chiles (*sookhi lal mirch*)
¼ tsp fenugreek seeds (*methi dana*)
Pinch ground asafoetida (*hing*)
1½ tsp Bengal gram (split chickpeas; *chana dal*)
½ tsp sambhar powder (available at Indian markets)
Pinch ground turmeric (*haldi*)
1½ tsp rice flour, mixed with a little water into a smooth, thick paste without any lumps
1½ tsp powdered jaggery (*gur*; unrefined cane sugar)

### METHOD

1.  Extract the tamarind pulp. Set aside. Discard any juice.
2.  In a skillet over low-medium heat, heat the vegetable oil.
3.  Add the mustard seeds. Sauté until the seeds begin to crackle.
4.  Add the dried red chiles, fenugreek seeds, and asafoetida. Sauté for 1 minute.
5.  Add the Bengal gram. Sauté until golden.
6.  Stir in the sambhar powder, turmeric, and tamarind pulp. Reduce the heat to low and simmer for 10 minutes.
7.  Stir in the rice flour paste. Bring the mixture to a boil.
8.  Add the jaggery and mix well. Serve hot, with rice and fried appalam (poppadum), if desired.

# MILAGUTHUVAIYAL

A zesty pepper chutney.

Cooking time: 30 minutes | Makes: 20 grams Origin: Tamil Nadu

INGREDIENTS

1 Tbsp (15 ml) sesame oil (*til*), divided
2 tsp split pigeon peas (*toor dal*)
2 tsp split black lentils (*urad dal*)
2 tsp Bengal gram (split chickpeas; *chana dal*)
5 dried red chiles (*sookhi lal mirch*)
2 tsp peppercorns (*sabut kali mirch*)
Pinch ground asafoetida (*hing*)
Water, as needed
1 small tamarind ball (*imli*)
1 tsp ground ginger (*sonth*)
1 tsp mustard seeds (*rai*)
2 curry leaves (*kadhi patta*)
Salt, to taste

METHOD

1. In a skillet over low-medium heat, heat 1 tsp of sesame oil.
2. Add the pigeon peas, black lentils, Bengal gram, dried red chiles, peppercorns, and asafoetida.
3. Toast for 4–5 minutes until the pigeon peas, black lentils, and chickpeas turn pleasantly brown.
4. Remove from the heat and let cool. Take out the dried red chiles and set aside. Transfer the rest of the ingredients to a blender or mortar and pestle. Add a little water and blend into a paste. Transfer to a small bowl and clean out the blender.
5. In the small skillet over low-medium heat, dry-roast the tamarind. Transfer to a blender and add the reserved dried red chiles and ginger. Add a little water and blend into a smooth paste. Transfer to the bowl with the chickpea paste. Mix the pastes together.
6. Return your skillet to low-medium heat and add the remaining 2 tsp of sesame oil.
7. Add the mustard seeds and curry leaves. Cook until the seeds begin to crackle. Pour the mixture onto the pastes.
8. Season to taste with salt and serve.

# THENGAI CHUTNEY

Red coconut chutney.

Cooking time: 20 minutes | Makes: 20 grams    Origin: Kerala

INGREDIENTS

2 Tbsp (30 ml) coconut oil (*nariyal*), divided
½ cup (85 g) finely chopped onion
1 tsp garlic paste (*lasan*)
1 tsp ginger paste (*adrak*)
2 cups (300 g) chopped fresh coconut (*nariyal*)
6 dried red chiles (*sookhi lal mirch*)
2 Tbsp (25 g) Bengal gram (split chickpeas; *chana dal*), roasted
Salt, to taste
1 tsp mustard seeds (*rai*)
5 curry leaves (*kadhi patta*)
1 tsp split black lentils (*urad dal*)

METHOD

1. In a skillet over medium-high heat, heat 1 Tbsp (15 ml) of coconut oil.
2. Add the onion, garlic paste, and ginger paste. Sauté until the onion softens. Transfer to a blender or food processor and add the coconut, dried red chiles, and Bengal gram. Season to taste with salt. Blend into a smooth paste.
3. Return the skillet to the heat and add the remaining 1 Tbsp (15 ml) of coconut oil to heat.
4. Add the mustard seeds, curry leaves, and black lentils. Cook until the seeds begin to crackle. Pour this mixture over the chutney and serve.

## THAKKALI PACHADI
A cooling yogurt-based dish with tomato.

Cooking time: 20 minutes | Serves: 2     Origin: Kerala

### INGREDIENTS

1 Tbsp (15 ml) sesame oil (*til*)
1 tsp mustard seeds (*rai*)
Pinch ground asafoetida (*hing*)
1 tsp split black lentils (*urad dal*)
1 tsp Bengal gram (split chickpeas; *chana dal*)
1 medium-size tomato, finely chopped
1 tsp red chile powder
Salt, to taste
1 cup (240 g) yogurt (*dahi*)

### METHOD

1. In a skillet over low-medium heat, heat the sesame oil.
2. Add the mustard seeds and asafoetida. Cook until the seeds begin to crackle.
3. Add the black lentils and Bengal gram.
4. Sauté until they turn pleasantly brown.
5. Stir in the tomato and red chile powder. Season to taste with salt. Sauté until the tomato is thoroughly cooked.
6. Stir in the yogurt, adjust the seasoning as needed, and serve cold.

## ANDHRA ONION CHUTNEY
Fiery onion relish.

Cooking time: 20 minutes | Makes: 10 grams
Origin: Andhra Pradesh

### INGREDIENTS

1 Tbsp (15 ml) vegetable oil, divided
2 fresh red chiles, finely chopped
2 tsp tamarind paste (*imli*; page 30)
1 cup (240 g) sliced onion
Salt, to taste
2 dried red chiles (*sookhi lal mirch*), soaked in water for 1 hour
1 tsp mustard seeds (*rai*)
3 curry leaves (*kadhi patta*)
1 tsp split black lentils (*urad dal*)

### METHOD

1. In a skillet over low-medium heat, heat 1½ tsp of vegetable oil.
2. Add the fresh red chiles. Cook, stirring, for 1 minute. Add the tamarind paste and onion. Sauté until the onion turns golden brown. Season to taste with salt and remove from the heat. Set aside to cool.
3. Drain the dried red chiles, transfer to a blender or mortar and pestle, and grind to a smooth paste.
4. In a clean skillet over low-medium heat, heat the remaining 1½ tsp of vegetable oil.
5. Add the mustard seeds, curry leaves, and split black lentils. Cook until the seeds begin to crackle. Remove from the heat and pour over the onion paste.
6. Serve as an accompaniment with idli or dosa (page 335).

# CHETTINAD GARLIC PICKLE
Fried garlic pickle.

Cooking time: 10 minutes | Makes: 20 grams  Origin: Tamil Nadu

## INGREDIENTS

½ cup (120 ml) vegetable oil
1 Tbsp (11 g) mustard seeds (*rai*)
1 Tbsp (11 g) fenugreek seeds (*methi dana*)
2 cups (272 g) garlic cloves (*lasan*), peeled
1½ cups (360 ml) freshly squeezed lemon juice
    (*nimbu*)
½ cup (64 g) red chile powder
¼ cup (24 g) ground coriander (*dhaniya*)
5 tsp ground asafoetida (*hing*)
5 Tbsp (35 g) ground cumin (*jeera*)
1 Tbsp (21 g) grated jaggery (*gur*; unrefined cane
    sugar)
½ cup (120 g) salt

## METHOD

1. In a skillet over low-medium heat, heat the
   vegetable oil.
2. Add the mustard seeds and fenugreek seeds.
   Cook until the seeds begin to crackle.
3. Add the garlic. Fry for 30 seconds.
4. Stir in the lemon juice, red chile powder,
   coriander, asafoetida, cumin, and jaggery. Mix
   well. Cook for precisely 4 minutes.
5. Add the salt. Mix. Remove from the heat and set
   aside to cool.
6. Refrigerate in a sterilized airtight jar.

# TOMATO MASIYAL

A side dish with proteins of dals with
tomatoes.

Cooking time: 30 minutes | Serves: 2        Origin: Tamil Nadu

## INGREDIENTS

1 tsp vegetable oil
½ tsp mustard seeds (*rai*)
2 curry leaves (*kadhi patta*)
2 green chiles
Pinch ground asafoetida (*hing*)
1 tsp split black lentils (*urad dal*)
1 tsp Bengal gram (split chickpeas; *chana dal*)
½ tsp fenugreek seeds (*methi dana*)
1 Tbsp (15 g) tamarind paste (*imli*; page 30)
2 medium-size tomatoes, finely chopped
½ cup (100 g) split pigeon peas (*toor dal*), cooked
½ cup (100 g) green gram (*moong dal*), cooked
1 tsp red chile powder
Water, as needed
Salt, taste
¾ tsp finely chopped fresh cilantro leaves
    (*hara dhaniya*)

## METHOD

1. In a skillet over medium heat, heat the vegetable
   oil.
2. Add the mustard seeds, curry leaves, green
   chiles, and asafoetida. Cook until the seeds
   begin to crackle.
3. Add the black lentils, chickpeas, and fenugreek
   seeds. Stir well to combine.
4. Stir in the tamarind paste. Cook the mixture for
   3 minutes.
5. Add the tomatoes, pigeon peas, green gram,
   and red chile powder. Stir well to combine.
   Reduce the heat to low and simmer for
   10 minutes. Add water if it becomes too thick.
6. Season to taste with salt and garnish with
   cilantro. Serve hot.

## VARDENENGA ACHAR

Eggplant pickle, South-Indian-style.

Cooking time: 30 minutes | Makes: 50 grams    Origin: Kerala

### INGREDIENTS

1¼ cups (300 ml) vinegar (*sirka*), divided
40 dried red chiles (*sookhi lal mirch*), skins only
   (stems and seeds discarded or saved for
   another use)
4½ Tbsp (68 g) minced garlic (*lasan*)
¾ tsp mustard seeds (*rai*)
¾ tsp fenugreek seeds (*methi dana*)
¾ tsp cumin seeds (*jeera*)
2 cups (164 g) 2-in. (5-cm) fingers eggplant
   (*brinjal*), immersed in salted water
Salt, to taste
1 cup (240 ml) sesame oil (*til*)
3 Tbsp (45 g) sliced peeled fresh ginger (*adrak*)
3 Tbsp (45 g) sliced garlic (*lasan*)
2 sprigs curry leaves (*kadhi patta*), leaves removed
¼ cup (50 g) sugar

### METHOD

1. In a blender or food processor, combine ¼ cup
   (60 ml) of vinegar, the dried red chile skins,
   garlic, mustard seeds, fenugreek seeds, and
   cumin seeds. Blend into a paste. Set aside.
2. Drain the eggplant and rub the pieces with salt.
   Set in the sun to dry for 4–5 hours.
3. In a skillet over medium heat, heat the sesame
   oil.
4. Add the ginger and garlic. Sauté until golden
   brown. With a slotted spoon, remove from the
   skillet and set aside.
5. Return the skillet to the heat and add the curry
   leaves, red chile–spice paste, sugar, and
   remaining 1 cup (240 ml) of vinegar. Mix well.
6. Add the eggplant. Reduce the heat to low and
   simmer until the eggplant is tender.
7. Stir in the fried garlic and ginger. Season to
   taste with salt.
8. Store in a bottle in the refrigerator for up to two
   weeks.

## GOSHT KA ACHAR

Pickled mutton, a gem from the Hyderabadi
kitchen.

Cooking time: 1 hour | Makes: 400 grams    Origin: Telengana

### INGREDIENTS

2 cups (480 g) finely cubed boneless mutton
2 cups (480 ml) mustard seed oil (page 26), divided
Pinch ground asafoetida (*hing*)
¼ cup (32 g) red chile powder
1 Tbsp (15 g) minced peeled fresh ginger (*adrak*)
1 Tbsp (7 g) ground turmeric (*haldi*)
1 Tbsp (10 g) nigella seeds (*kalonji*), powdered
1½ Tbsp (23 g) minced garlic (*lasan*)
1 tsp fenugreek seeds (*methi dana*), soaked in
   water, drained, and ground to a paste
1 tsp garam masala
1 cup (240 ml) vinegar (*sirka*)
Salt, to taste

### METHOD

1. In your pressure cooker cooking pot, combine
   the mutton with just enough water to cover the
   meat. Lock the lid in place and close the
   pressure release valve. Select Manual/Pressure
   Cook and cook for 30 minutes until the mutton
   is done.
2. Release the pressure and remove the lid.
   Transfer the mutton pieces to a clean kitchen
   towel and allow the water to evaporate.
3. In a skillet over medium heat, heat 1 tsp of
   mustard seed oil.
4. Add the asafoetida and cooked mutton pieces.
   Cook, stirring, until any leftover water from the
   mutton dries out. Transfer to a bowl and cool
   the mutton to room temperature.
5. Stir in the red chile powder, ginger, turmeric,
   powdered nigella seeds, garlic, fenugreek seed
   paste, and garam masala. Toss well to combine.
6. Return the skillet to medium-high heat. Once
   hot, add the mutton mixture and give the meat
   a quick stir-fry for 2–3 minutes. Remove from
   the heat. Allow it to cool.
7. Add the vinegar, remaining mustard seed oil,
   and salt to taste. Transfer to an airtight
   container. Refrigerate for up to 1 week.

## EERICHI ACHAR
Lamb pickle.

| Cooking time: 40 minutes | Makes: 1 kg | Origin: Kerala |
| --- | --- | --- |

### INGREDIENTS

4 lb, 6 oz (2 kg) lamb, cut into very small pieces
9 Tbsp (105 ml) vinegar (*sirka*), divided
2 Tbsp (12 g) finely chopped peeled fresh
   ginger (*adrak*)
Salt, to taste
½ cup (120 ml) sesame oil (*til*)
¼ cup (32 g) red chile powder
¼ cup (34 g) plus 6 garlic cloves (*lasan*),
   peeled, divided
2 tsp mustard seeds (*rai*), divided
1 Tbsp (27 g) thinly sliced peeled fresh ginger (*adrak*)
¼ tsp fenugreek seeds (*methi dana*)
¼ tsp cumin seeds (*jeera*)
Water, as needed
½ tsp ground turmeric (*haldi*)
1 cup (170 g) finely chopped onion
12 whole cloves (*laung*), peeled
6 (1-in. / 2.5-cm) cinnamon sticks (*dalchini*)
6 green cardamom pods (*choti elaichi*)
1 cup (240 g) chopped tomato
1 cup (240 ml) boiling water
¼ tsp sugar

### METHOD

1. In a skillet over medium heat, combine the lamb, 3 Tbsp (45 ml) of vinegar, and the chopped ginger. Season to taste with salt. Cook until tender and dry.
2. In a wok over low-medium heat, heat the sesame oil.
3. Add the cooked lamb, a few pieces at a time, and deep-fry. Do not allow the lamb to harden. With a slotted spoon, transfer the cooked lamb to a bowl.
4. In a blender or mortar and pestle, grind the red chile powder, 6 garlic cloves, 1 tsp of mustard seeds, sliced ginger, the fenugreek seeds, and cumin seeds with enough water to make a smooth paste.
5. Reheat the oil remaining in the wok over medium-high heat. Add the remaining 1 tsp of mustard seeds. Cook until the seeds begin to crackle. Add the turmeric and onion. Sauté until crisp. With a slotted spoon, transfer the onion mixture to paper towels to drain.
6. Return the wok to the heat and to the same oil add the cloves, cinnamon sticks, and green cardamom pods. Sauté until the spices change color slightly.
7. Add the tomato. Cook, stirring, until the oil separates. Add the spice paste and mix well.
8. Stir in 3 Tbsp (45 ml) of vinegar and the boiling water. Season to taste with salt. Bring the mixture to a boil.
9. Add the fried lamb, and ¼ cup (34 g) of garlic cloves.
10. In a small bowl, stir together the sugar and the remaining 3 Tbsp (45 ml) of vinegar and add this to the lamb mixture. Bring everything to a boil and remove from the heat.
11. Cool and refrigerate in airtight jars.

• • • • • • • • • • • •

## CHAMMANTHI PODI
A condiment made from coconut and chiles.

| Cooking time: 30 minutes | Makes: 100 grams | Origin: Kerala |
| --- | --- | --- |

### INGREDIENTS

1 tsp coconut oil (*nariyal*)
1 cup (80 g) grated fresh coconut, (*nariyal*)
8 curry leaves (*kadhi patta*)
4 dried red chiles (*sookhi lal mirch*)
1 tsp cumin seeds (*jeera*)
1 tsp red chile powder
1 tsp split black lentils (*urad dal*)
1 tsp sliced peeled fresh ginger (*adrak*)
½ tsp ground turmeric (*haldi*)
Pinch ground asafoetida (*hing*)
1 tsp tamarind paste (*imli*; page 30)
Salt, to taste

### METHOD

1. In a skillet over medium heat, heat the coconut oil.
2. Add the remaining ingredients except the tamarind paste and salt. Toast for 15–17 minutes, stirring, until the coconut turns dark brown. Remove from the heat. Stir in the tamarind paste and season to taste with salt. Transfer the mixture to a food processor or mortar and pestle and blend into a coarse powder.
3. Cool and store it in an airtight container.

# east india

• • • • • •

JHARKHAND . ODISHA . BIHAR . WEST BENGAL

There is an old saying among Bengalis—the way to judge the character of a man is through the way he buys fish. Bengali men take pride in selecting the best catch at the local fish market for their families and can spend hours bragging about their choice. The rivers and waterbodies in Bengal are considered its lifeline, and seafood is relished. This is also true for the neighboring state of Odisha, whose cuisine is very similar to that of West Bengal.

The cuisine profiles of the four states in East India—West Bengal, Odisha, Bihar, and Jharkhand—can be clubbed into pairs, owing to their symbiotic relationships, shared history, cultural similarities, and geographical proximity.

Odisha and West Bengal have a lot in common, so much so that they have waged a famous battle over the origin of the *roshogulla* (which was recently won by West Bengal, after several commissions of inquiry looked into the matter). While Odisha, famous for its *chhena*-based treats, has a mythological explanation that claims *kheer mohana* (*roshogulla*'s former name) was invented by Lord Jagannath as an offering to an angry Goddess Lakshmi, West Bengal asserts that it was invented by Nobin Chandra Das, a famous sweet maker in Kolkata's Bagbazar in 1868. Literally translating to "juice-filled balls," *roshogulla* is just one dessert in a long list of *chhena*, or indigenous cheese curd–based sweetmeats, made in these two states.

Being coastal states, Odisha and West Bengal have cuisines that are dominated by seafood, especially freshwater river fish, prawns, and crabs, cooked in a number of ways. The curries and gravies are flavored with many spices, including the *Panch Phoran* spice mix—a blend of cumin, mustard, fennel, fenugreek, and nigella seeds, giving a unique, sprightly flavor.

Bengali cuisine is a mix of basic meat and vegetable gravies, breads, achars, kebabs, rice, and dal. It is the only traditional Indian menu that is served in a multi-course style instead of all at once.

The hallmark of this cuisine, however, is its fish-based dishes. Fish is such an important part of Bengali culture that at least one meal of the day is certain to have a fish course and almost every village in West Bengal practices pisciculture. The

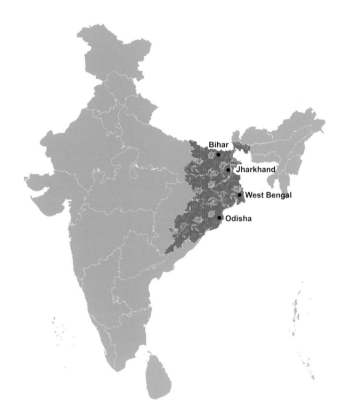

community savors the fish (except scales, fins, and innards) and the head is particularly preferred.

The region is also known for a type of mustard sauce called *kasundi*, made by fermenting mustard seeds. Strong, with a kick of umami, *kasundi* is India's answer to wasabi. Traditionally the *kasundi*-making process was restricted to the "upper" (and affluent) Hindu castes and used to begin on the day of Akshaya Tritiya (the day of prosperity), which fell at the cusp of spring–summer (April–May). This period is best in terms of weather for the fermentation of the mustard to take place. Today, *kasundi* is eaten with fish cutlets, and used to marinate fish or meats, or as a dipping sauce.

West Bengal is home to Kolkata, a buzzing metro city that represents modern Bengali food. It is famous for its street food, such as *jhal muri*, a mustard seed oil–laced puffed-rice snack, and *puchkas*, crispy globes filled with flavored water. A standout dish, however, is the Kolkata *kathi* roll. It is as characteristic to the city as its colonial buildings and pop yellow taxis. It is believed that the *kathi* roll was first served at Nizam's Restaurant, a popular eatery founded in 1932. Some say that the kebabs wrapped in parathas were invented for hurried office commuters, while others say it was for the British babus, who were fussy about touching the kebab. While Nizam's Restaurant enjoyed a monopoly over the dish for years, soon other eateries in Kolkata started serving the *kathi* roll, and now it has become a part of the city's culinary scene.

Kolkata's fascinating culinary history begins much before the arrival of the British, and reveals the emergence of Indo–Chinese cuisine around the late 19th and early 20th centuries. It was during this time that immigrant Chinese traders, settled in large numbers in Madras and southern Calcutta (Kolkata's old name), contributed to the social and culinary life of the cities. The Hakka-speaking group came to work in tanneries, ports, and railways, and soon established the country's only Chinatown in Calcutta. While this cuisine was Chinese at the core, hybrid dishes such as gobi Manchurian soon became popular with the locals and Chinese recipes were manipulated to suit the Indian palate.

The British also heavily influenced the cuisine and eating habits of the city. Kolkata was a colonial city, developed by the British East India Company and then by the British Empire, and was the capital of the Empire until 1911 (when it shifted to Delhi). The British presence was the cause of a number of clubs established in the city. These clubs became the epicenter of social activity for the British, and this is where the sahibs went to unwind, network, and socialize. Today, the remains of Raj cuisine can be experienced at the tony clubs of Kolkata. Savoring British favorites—from jam tarts and pork chops at the Tollygunge Club, to rosemary potatoes and chicken roast at the Calcutta Cricket & Football Club, to roast mutton steak and the revered orange soufflé at the nearly two-century old Bengal Club—the city still basks in its colonial charm.

In neighboring Odisha, the daily meal is similar, with a mix of rice, breads, vegetarian gravies, and fish-laced curries. But it is the elaborate temple cuisine that stands out here. The state houses one of India's most popular temples, the Jagannath Temple of Puri, which is known for its rich culinary heritage. Historically, Odisha was revered for supremely skilled chefs who worked in the temple's kitchens. These chefs were known as *swara*, the head

chef, *jouginas*, the sous-chefs, and *tunias*, the prep masters—the temple had its unique line of culinary hierarchy. They worked tirelessly to prepare the *mahaprasada*, the meal offered to Lord Jagannath. Broadly divided into *sankudi*—wet preparations such as rice, dals, veggies, and curries—and *sukhila*—dry sweetmeats—it is a feast that is doled out to 10 million people each year.

In comparison, Jharkhandi and Bihari fare is rustic. There are a lot of similarities between the two states, since Jharkhand was carved out of southern Bihar only eighteen years ago. So you will find commonalities in the usage of *litti*, whole-wheat dough balls that are a meal staple, *sattu*, roasted lentil flour, *malpuas* for dessert, and *thekua*, indigenous Indian cookies eaten on celebratory occasions.

Jharkhandi cuisine also includes tribal recipes. The state houses several tribes, including Santhal, Gond, Munda, and Kanwav, that cook using ample forest produce. Noteworthy are dishes made out of foraged veggies such as *rugra* and *photo*, rare indigenous mushrooms, bamboo shoots, and a delicious snail curry.

Comparatively, Bihari cuisine offers more vegetarian fare. Religion has impacted Bihari cuisine deeply, owing to the advent of Buddhism and Jainism in Magadha (former name for southern Bihar) around the 5th century BCE. The influence can still be seen in the vegetarianism practiced in traditional Bihari homes, especially in regions such as Bodh Gaya and Nalanda.

A traditional Bihari thali changes seasonally, with constants such as rice, roti, achar, chutney, dal, and a variety of milk-based products. In summer, you will see Bihari people savoring hydrating drinks, sherbets made of fresh fruits, including unique ones like wood apple, and *matha*, a yogurt-based buttermilk. Winter is for hot stews, curries, and soups.

From Buddhist culinary influences to food inspired by the Chinese immigrant community, from street treats to rustic desserts made with Indian superfoods—cuisine from East India is varied and steeped in tradition. These recipes will give you a glimpse of one of the most rooted Indian cuisines that has stood the test of time.

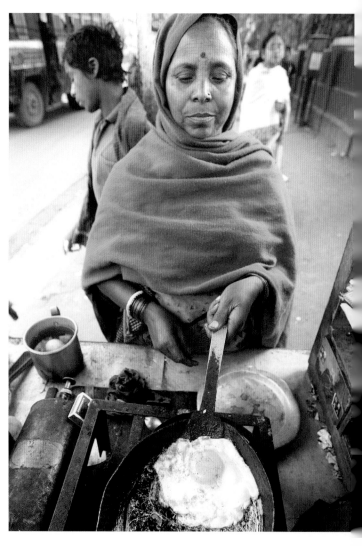

APPETIZERS

# NARKEL POSHTO BORA
Coconut poppy fritters.

Cooking time: 30 minutes | Makes: 8　　Origin: West Bengal

## INGREDIENTS

3 Tbsp (27 g) poppy seeds (*khus khus*)
1 cup (80 g) grated fresh coconut (*nariyal*)
1 Tbsp (10 g) rice flour
1 Tbsp (8 g) all-purpose flour (*maida*)
1 tsp red chile paste
1 tsp vegetable oil, plus more for frying
Salt, to taste

## METHOD

1. Fill a small saucepan with water and place it over high heat. Add the poppy seeds and bring to a boil. In a fine-mesh strainer, strain the seeds. Transfer to a blender or mortar and pestle and process into a smooth paste. Transfer the paste to small bowl.
2. Add the coconut, rice flour, all-purpose flour, red chile paste, and 1 tsp of vegetable oil. Season to taste with salt and stir the mixture well to combine.
3. Roll the mixture into 8 flat cutlets.
4. In a deep skillet over medium-high heat, heat the vegetable oil for frying.
5. Carefully add the cutlets and deep-fry until crispy. Transfer to paper towels to drain. Serve hot.

# ALOO CHOP
Potato cutlets.

Cooking time: 30 minutes | Makes: 6　　Origin: West Bengal

## INGREDIENTS

For the tikki
1 cup (225 g) mashed potatoes
2 tsp red chile powder
1 tsp ground turmeric (*haldi*)
½ cup (8 g) fresh cilantro leaves (*hara dhaniya*), finely chopped
1 Tbsp (6 g) garam masala
Salt, to taste
For the masala
1 tsp cumin seeds (*jeera*)
1 tsp coriander seeds (*dhaniya*)
1 dried red chile (*sookhi lal mirch*)
For the batter
½ cup (60 g) chickpea flour (*besan*)
Salt, to taste
Water, to dilute
Vegetable oil, for deep-frying

## METHOD

1. **To make the tikki:** In a small bowl, stir together the mashed potatoes, chile powder, turmeric, cilantro, and garam masala. Season to taste with salt. Divide into 6 roundels.
2. Flatten the roundels and set aside.
3. **To make the masala:** In a spice grinder or mortar and pestle, grind the cumin seeds, coriander seeds, and dry chile. Set aside.
4. **To make the batter:** In a small bowl, combine the chickpea flour, masala, salt to taste, and water as needed. Whisk into a thick batter.
5. In a deep skillet over low-medium heat, heat the vegetable oil for frying.
6. Take 1 flattened potato tikki and dip it into the chickpea batter. Carefully place it in the hot oil and deep-fry until golden. Transfer to paper towels to drain. Repeat with the remaining tikkis. Serve hot.

## BIRI CHOP

Deep-fried potato cutlet with lentils.

Cooking time: 30 minutes | Makes: 8-10    Origin: West Bengal

INGREDIENTS

1 cup (200 g) split black lentils (*urad dal*),
   soaked for 2 hours, drained
2 curry leaves (*kadhi patta*)
Salt, to taste
1 Tbsp (15 ml) vegetable oil, plus more for frying
1 tsp mustard seeds (*rai*)
1 green chile, finely chopped
1 medium-size onion, finely chopped
1 Tbsp (15 g) minced garlic (*lasan*)
1 cup (225 g) mashed potatoes
1 tsp ground cumin (*jeera*)

METHOD

1.  In a blender, process the black lentils into a fine paste. Add the curry leaves and season to taste with salt. Process to combine and transfer to a small bowl.
2.  In a skillet over medium-high heat, heat 1 Tbsp (15 ml) of vegetable oil.
3.  Add the mustard seeds. Cook until the seeds begin to crackle.
4.  Add the green chile, onion, and garlic. Sauté for 3–4 minutes.
5.  Add the mashed potatoes and cumin. Stir well to combine. Cook the mixture thoroughly until it comes together into one mass. Set aside to cool to room temperature.
6.  In a deep skillet over medium-high heat, heat the vegetable oil for frying.
7.  Roll the potato mixture into 8-10 coin-size balls.
8.  Dip the balls into the lentil paste and deep-fry until golden.
9.  Serve hot with Bengali-style tomato chutney (page 432 ).

## BAJKA 📷

Vegetable fritters with coriander and spices.

Cooking time: 30 minutes | Makes: 3-4    Origin: Bihar

INGREDIENTS

1 cup (120 g) chickpea flour (*besan*)
1 tsp ground turmeric (*haldi*)
1 tsp garlic paste (*lasan*)
1 tsp red chile powder
1 tsp ground cumin (*jeera*)
1 Tbsp (1 g) fresh cilantro leaves (*hara dhaniya*),
   finely chopped
Vegetable oil, for deep-frying
Pinch baking soda
Salt, to taste
1 medium-size potato, sliced
1 medium-size onion, sliced
1 medium-size eggplant (*brinjal*), sliced

METHOD

1.  In a small bowl, stir together the chickpea flour, turmeric, garlic paste, red chile powder, cumin, and cilantro with enough water to form a thick pancake-like batter.
2.  In a skillet over medium-high heat, heat the vegetable oil for frying.
3.  Add the baking soda and salt to the batter. Stir to combine.
4.  Working in batches as needed, dip each potato, onion, and eggplant slice in the batter and deep-fry until golden. Transfer to papers towels to drain. Serve hot.

## ODIYA KANCHA KADALI BARA

Raw banana cutlets.

Cooking time: 30 minutes | Makes: 12 pieces    Origin: Odisha

INGREDIENTS

4 unripe bananas, boiled
2 green chiles, finely chopped
1 Tbsp (7.5 g) chickpea flour (*besan*)
1 tsp minced peeled fresh ginger
1 tsp red chile powder
1 tsp ground cumin (*jeera*)
1 tsp chaat masala
¼ cup (4 g) fresh cilantro leaves (*hara dhaniya*),
    finely chopped
Salt, to taste
1 Tbsp (15 ml) vegetable oil

METHOD

1.  In a bowl, combine the boiled bananas, green
    chiles, chickpea flour, ginger, red chile powder,
    cumin, chaat masala, and cilantro. Season to
    taste with salt.
2.  With a potato masher, mash the mixture. Roll it
    into 12 small roundels that are the size of table-
    tennis balls.
3.  Flatten the balls with your palms.
4.  In a skillet over medium-high heat, heat the
    vegetable oil.
5.  Carefully add the cutlets to the hot oil and
    shallow-fry on both sides until golden. Serve
    warm.

## BHOJPURI ALOO

Baked potatoes stuffed with cottage cheese.

Cooking time: 40 minutes | Serves: 2    Origin: Bihar

INGREDIENTS

Vegetable oil, for frying
4 medium-size potatoes, boiled and halved
½ cup (112.5 g) cottage cheese
¼ cup (30 g) cheese
2 green chiles, finely chopped
¼ cup (4 g) fresh cilantro leaves (*hara dhaniya*),
    finely chopped
½ tsp freshly ground black pepper (*kali mirch*)
2 tsp ginger-garlic paste (*adrak-lasan*)
1 tsp dried mango powder (*amchoor*)
Salt, to taste
2 roasted papadum, crushed (available at Indian
    markets)

METHOD

1.  Preheat the oven to 400°F (200°C).
2.  In a deep skillet over medium-high heat, heat
    the vegetable oil for frying.
3.  Scoop the flesh of the potato halves into a
    medium-size bowl. Deep-fry the potato shells in
    hot oil until golden. Set aside.
4.  To the potato flesh, add the cottage cheese,
    cheese, green chiles, cilantro, pepper, ginger-
    garlic paste, and dried mango powder. Season
    to taste with salt. Mix well.
5.  Add the crushed papadum and stir to combine.
    Fill the hollowed-out fried potato shells with the
    mixture and place on a rimmed baking sheet.
    Bake for 10 minutes until the filling melts.
6.  Serve hot.

## THEKUA

Deep-fried cookies for teatime or breakfast.

Cooking time: 40 minutes | Makes: 8      Origin: Jharkhand

INGREDIENTS

½ cup (120 ml) water
½ cup (100 g) sugar
½ cup (47.5 g) ground almonds (*badam*)
½ cup (75 g) ground cashews (*kaju*)
¼ cup (60 g) ghee
¾ cup (93.75 g) all-purpose flour (*maida*)
Vegetable oil, for frying

METHOD

1. In a saucepan over high heat, boil the water. Add the sugar and cook until it dissolves. Remove from the heat and cool to room temperature.
2. In a medium-size bowl, combine the almonds, cashews, and ghee. Mix with your fingertips until it resembles crumbs.
3. Add the flour and mix again. Add the sugar-water and knead the mixture into a tight dough.
4. Roll the dough into 8 coin-size roundels.
5. In a deep skillet over low-medium heat, heat the vegetable oil for frying.
6. Working in batches as needed, carefully add the roundels to the hot oil and deep-fry until golden brown. Serve hot.

## BIHARI KEBAB

Caramelized-flavored kebab.

Cooking time: 1 hour | Makes: 5-6      Origin: Bihar

INGREDIENTS

¼ (60 g) fried onion paste
5 Tbsp (75 g) hung curd (page 28)
1 Tbsp (15 g) ginger-garlic paste (*adrak-lasan*)
1 Tbsp (6 g) ground coriander (*dhaniya*)
2 tsp ground cumin (*jeera*)
2 tsp red chile powder
½ tsp ground mace (*javitri*)
Pinch ground star anise (*chakri ke phool*)
Salt, to taste
1 cup (240 g) cubed boneless chicken
2 Tbsp (30 g) ghee

METHOD

1. In a medium-size bowl, whisk the onion paste, hung curd, ginger-garlic paste, coriander, cumin, red chile powder, mace, and star anise. Season to taste with salt. Add the chicken pieces. Stir to combine and refrigerate for 4–5 hours.
2. Heat a grill to medium heat or place a grill pan over medium heat.
3. Skewer the chicken and cook for 25–30 minutes, or until done, basting occasionally with ghee to keep it from burning.
4. Serve hot.

# CHUNGAI MALAI 📷
Cocktail party prawns.

Cooking time: 30 minutes | Serves: 4          Origin: Odisha

## INGREDIENTS

2 lb, 3 oz (1 kg) prawns, shelled and deveined
1½ tsp ground turmeric (*haldi*), divided
Salt, to taste
1 Tbsp (15 ml) vegetable oil
1 Tbsp (15 g) whole spice mix (page 22)
1 medium-size onion, finely chopped
1 tsp ginger paste (*adrak*)
2 tsp ground cumin (*jeera*)
1 tsp red chile powder
1 cup (240 ml) coconut milk (*nariyal*)
2 Tbsp (30 g) yogurt (*dahi*)
1 Tbsp (15 g) ghee
¼ cup (4 g) fresh cilantro leaves (*hara dhaniya*),
  finely chopped

## METHOD

1. In a large bowl, mix the prawns with ½ tsp of turmeric and salt to taste. Let marinate for 15 minutes.
2. In a skillet over medium-high heat, heat the vegetable oil.
3. Add the prawns. Cook for 2–3 minutes and remove from the pan.
4. Return the skillet to the heat and add the whole spice mix, onion, ginger paste, remaining 1 tsp of turmeric, the cumin, and red chile powder. Cook until the onion softens.
5. Add the prawns, coconut milk, and yogurt. Season to taste with salt and stir to combine. Simmer for 5–6 minutes.
6. Add the ghee and allow the prawns to finish cooking. Garnish with cilantro and serve hot.

# CHINGRI CUTLET
Deep-fried prawn cutlet.

Cooking time: 30 minutes | Makes: 6          Origin: West Bengal

## INGREDIENTS

6 prawns, cleaned
1 egg
1 medium-size onion, ground to a fine paste
1 Tbsp (15 g) garlic paste (*lasan*)
2 tsp red chile powder
1 tsp garam masala
Salt, to taste
Vegetable oil, for frying
1 cup (120 g) chickpea flour (*besan*)
1 cup (115 g) bread crumbs

## METHOD

1. Place the prawns between 2 sheets of plastic wrap and flatten with a meat pounder.
2. In a small bowl, stir together the egg, onion paste, garlic paste, red chile powder, and garam masala. Season to taste with salt. Stir well and add the prawns. Stir again to combine. Refrigerate to marinate for 1 hour.
3. In a deep skillet over low-medium heat, heat the vegetable oil for frying.
4. In a shallow bowl, combine the chickpea flour and bread crumbs. Season to taste with salt. Dip the marinated prawns in the flour–bread crumb mixture.
5. Carefully add the prawns to the hot oil and deep-fry until golden.
6. Serve hot.

## MANGSHER GHUGNI

Dried yellow peas with mince meat.

| Cooking time: 1 hour \| Serves: 2 | Origin: West Bengal |
|---|---|

### INGREDIENTS

2 Tbsp (30 ml) mustard seed oil (page 26), divided

2 Tbsp (30 g) ginger-garlic paste (*adrak-lasan*), divided

1 bay leaf (*tej patta*)

1 medium-size onion, finely chopped

1 cup (240 g) minced mutton (*keema*), washed and squeezed of any water

1 medium-size tomato, finely chopped

2 tsp red chile powder

1 tsp ground turmeric (*haldi*)

Pinch dried fenugreek leaves (*kasuri methi*)

1 cup (240 ml) water

Salt, to taste

½ cup (120 g) ghugni (available at Indian markets)

Juice of 1 lemon (*nimbu*)

¼ cup (4 g) fresh cilantro leaves (*hara dhaniya*), finely chopped

1 Tbsp (6 g) garam masala

### METHOD

1. In a skillet over low-medium heat, heat 1 Tbsp (15 ml) of mustard seed oil.
2. Add 1 Tbsp (15 g) of ginger-garlic paste and the bay leaf. Cook, stirring, for 2 minutes.
3. Add the onion. Sauté until golden.
4. Add the mutton and continue cooking until the water from the minced meat dries up.
5. Add the remaining 1 Tbsp (15 ml) of mustard seed oil, the remaining 1 Tbsp (15 g) of ginger-garlic paste, the tomato, red chile powder, turmeric, and fenugreek leaves. Cook, stirring, for 2–3 minutes.
6. Add the water and salt to taste. Reduce the heat to low, cover the skillet, and cook for 30 minutes.
7. Add the ghugni. Cook until softened.
8. Finish the dish with lemon juice, cilantro, and garam masala.
9. Serve hot.

## MANGSHO CUTLET

Bengali-style lamb cutlets.

| Cooking time: 40 minutes \| Makes: 10 | Origin: West Bengal |
|---|---|

### INGREDIENTS

2 white bread slices

1 lb, 2 oz (500 g) lamb (*keema*), minced

½ tsp garam masala

1 medium-size onion, finely chopped

4 green chiles, finely chopped

1 tsp fresh mint (*pudina*) leaves

Salt, to taste

8 eggs, whisked

½ cup (60 g) bread crumbs

1¼ cups (280 g) ghee

### METHOD

1. Dip the bread slices in water, soaking them well. Remove and squeeze out all the water.
2. In a medium-size bowl, combine the lamb mince, bread slices, garam masala, onion, green chiles, and mint leaves. Season to taste with salt. Set aside for 1 hour.
3. Divide the mixture into 10 portions; shape each portion into flat cutlets. Set aside on a tray.
4. In a small bowl, whisk together the eggs with salt to taste.
5. Set out the bread crumbs on a tray or shallow dish.
6. In a wok over medium-high heat, heat the ghee.
7. Dip the cutlets in the egg mixture, then roll in the bread crumbs.
8. Fry each cutlet in the wok until golden brown. Transfer to paper towels to drain and serve.

# CALCUTTA CHILE CHICKEN

Chinese influence on Calcutta shows in this dish.

Cooking time: 30 minutes | Serves: 2      Origin: West Bengal

## INGREDIENTS

¼ cup (32 g) cornstarch

1 egg

1 tsp garlic powder (*lasan*)

Salt, to taste

Freshly ground black pepper (*kali mirch*), to taste

1 cup (240 g) cubed boneless chicken

Vegetable oil, for frying

1 Tbsp (15 g) minced garlic (*lasan*)

2 green chiles, minced

½ cup (85 g) diced onion

½ cup (75 g) diced green bell pepper

3 Tbsp (45 ml) tomato sauce

1 Tbsp (15 ml) chile sauce

2 tsp white vinegar (*sirka*)

2 tsp soy sauce

¼ cup (15 g) finely chopped spring onion (*hara pyaz*)

2 tsp white sesame seeds (*safed til*)

## METHOD

1. In a medium-size bowl, whisk the cornstarch, egg, and garlic powder. Season to taste with salt and pepper.
2. Add the chicken and stir well to coat.
3. Refrigerate to marinate for 2 hours.
4. In a deep skillet over medium heat, heat the vegetable oil for frying.
5. Carefully add the chicken to the hot oil and deep-fry until golden. Remove and set aside.
6. In another skillet over low-medium heat, heat some vegetable oil.
7. Add the garlic and green chiles. Sauté for 1 minute.
8. Add the onion and green bell pepper. Stir-fry for 4–5 minutes.
9. Stir in the tomato sauce, chile sauce, vinegar, and soy sauce. Season to taste with salt and pepper.
10. Finish by adding the chicken cubes and spring onion.
11. Garnish with sesame seeds and serve hot.

# POULTRY AND EGGS

## MURGIR JHOL

Chicken in Bengali-style curry.

Cooking time: 40 minutes | Serves: 2     Origin: West Bengal

### INGREDIENTS

½ cup (120 g) yogurt (*dahi*)
1 Tbsp (15 g) ginger-garlic paste (*adrak-lasan*)
1 Tbsp (6 g) ground coriander (*dhaniya*)
1½ tsp ground cumin (*jeera*)
2 tsp ground turmeric (*haldi*), divided
1½ tsp mustard seed oil (page 26)
Salt, to taste
1 cup (240 g) cubed chicken
2 Tbsp (30 ml) vegetable oil
1 bay leaf (*tej patta*)
1 tsp cumin seeds (*jeera*)
2 dried red chiles (*sookhi lal mirch*)
½ medium-size onion, finely chopped
1 tsp red chile powder
1 tsp garam masala
1 tsp sugar
¾ tsp finely chopped fresh cilantro leaves
    (*hara dhaniya*)

### METHOD

1.  In a medium-size bowl, stir together the yogurt, ginger-garlic paste, coriander, cumin, 1 tsp of turmeric, and the mustard seed oil. Season to taste with salt. Add the chicken. Stir to coat and refrigerate to marinate for 6–7 hours.
2.  In a skillet over low-medium heat, heat the vegetable oil.
3.  Add the bay leaf, cumin seeds, and dried red chiles. Cook until the seeds begin to crackle.
4.  Add the onion. Sauté until golden brown.
5.  Add the remaining 1 tsp of turmeric, the red chile powder, garam masala, sugar, and the marinated chicken. Reduce the heat to low and cook for 30–40 minutes, or until the meat is thoroughly cooked.
6.  Garnish with cilantro and serve hot.

## KANCHA LONKA CHICKEN

Chicken dish with fiery green chiles.

Cooking time: 40 minutes | Serves: 3     Origin: West Bengal

### INGREDIENTS

10 green chiles, washed and seeded
½ cup (8 g) fresh cilantro leaves (*hara dhaniya*),
    finely chopped
½ cup (120 g) sour curd
1 Tbsp (15 g) ginger-garlic paste (*adrak-lasan*)
1 tsp garam masala
Salt, to taste
1 lb (454 g) bone-in chicken pieces
1 Tbsp (15 ml) mustard seed oil (page 26)
1 Tbsp (15 g) whole spice mix (page 22)
1 bay leaf (*tej patta*)
2 medium-size onions, finely chopped
½ cup (120 ml) water
Juice of 1 lemon (*nimbu*)

### METHOD

1.  In a food processor, blend together the green chiles and cilantro. Transfer to a medium-size bowl and stir in the sour curd, ginger-garlic paste, and garam masala. Season to taste with salt. Add the chicken to the marinade. Stir to combine, and refrigerate for 3–4 hours.
2.  In a skillet over low-medium heat, heat the mustard seed oil.
3.  Add the whole spice mix and bay leaf. Cook until the seeds begin to crackle.
4.  Add the onions. Stir-fry until golden.
5.  Add the chicken along with the marinade and the water. Reduce the heat to low and cook for 20–25 minutes, or until the chicken is fully done.
6.  Finish with the lemon juice and serve hot.

# CHICKEN CHAAP
Chicken cooked in a rich poppy seed curry.

Cooking time: 40 minutes | Serves: 3     Origin: Jharkhand

## INGREDIENTS

For the chicken chaap
2 cups (480 g) chicken, leg pieces, bone-in
1 Tbsp (15 g) ghee
1 Tbsp (15 g) whole spice mix (page 22)
1 tsp vetivier water (*kewra*; available at Indian
   markets)
1 medium-size onion, cut into rings

For the marinade
1½ cups (360 g) hung curd (page 28)
2 Tbsp (30 g) ginger-garlic paste (*adrak-lasan*)
1 Tbsp (6 g) garam masala
2 tsp red chile powder
Salt, to taste

For the cashew–poppy seed paste
2 Tbsp (18 g) poppy seeds (*khus khus*), soaked in
   warm water for 20 minutes, drained
¼ cup (35 g) cashews (*kaju*)
1 medium-size onion, diced

## METHOD

1. **To make the chicken chaap:** Prick the chicken
   all over with a fork and set aside.
2. **To make the marinade:** In a large bowl, whisk
   the hung curd, ginger-garlic paste, garam
   masala, and red chile powder. Season to taste
   with salt. Whisk well and add the chicken
   pieces to it. Stir to coat and refrigerate for 4–5
   hours minimum, or overnight, to marinate.
3. **To make the cashew–poppy seed paste:** In a
   food processor, combine the poppy seeds,
   cashews, and onion. Blitz into a paste and set
   aside.
4. **To finish the chicken chaap:** In a skillet over
   medium-high heat, heat the ghee.
5. Add the whole spice mix. Cook until the spices
   begin to crackle.
6. Add the chicken pieces with the marinade and
   stir well. Reduce the heat to medium and cook

for 15–20 minutes, stirring continuously, until
the meat is semi-done.
7. Stir in the cashew–poppy seed paste. Continue
   to cook until the chicken is fully done.
8. Finish with the vetivier water, onion rings, and
   salt to taste.

. . . . . . . . . . . . .

# CHICKEN AAM KASUNDI 📷
Mustard-coated chicken.

Cooking time: 40 minutes | Serves: 2     Origin: West Bengal

## INGREDIENTS

1 cup (240 g) cubed chicken
Juice of 1 lemon (*nimbu*)
3 Tbsp (45 g) *kasundi* (Bengali mustard; available
   at Indian markets, page 24)
1 tsp ground turmeric (*haldi*)
2 Tbsp (30 ml) mustard seed oil (page 26)
1 medium-size onion, finely chopped
1 Tbsp (15 g) ginger-garlic paste (*adrak-lasan*)
2 tsp red chile powder
Salt, to taste

## METHOD

1. In a medium-size bowl, combine the chicken,
   lemon juice, *kasundi*, and turmeric. Refrigerate
   to marinate for 2–3 hours.
2. In a skillet over medium heat, heat the mustard
   seed oil.
3. Add the onion, ginger-garlic paste, and red
   chile powder. Sauté for 2–3 minutes, stirring,
   until the onion turns golden.
4. Add the marinated chicken and stir well to
   combine. Cook for 20–30 minutes, until the
   chicken is cooked thoroughly.
5. Season to taste with salt and serve hot.

## DOI MURGI 📷
Chicken in yogurt gravy.

Cooking time: 40 minutes | Serves: 2      Origin: West Bengal

### INGREDIENTS

**For the marinade**

¼ cup (60 g) yogurt (*dahi*)

1 Tbsp (15 g) ginger-garlic paste (*adrak-lasan*)

1 Tbsp (6 g) garam masala

1 tsp ground coriander (*dhaniya*)

1 tsp ground cumin (*jeera*)

1 tsp ground turmeric (*haldi*)

Salt, to taste

**For the gravy**

2 cups (480 g) cubed chicken

1 Tbsp (15 ml) vegetable oil

1 Tbsp (15 g) whole spice mix (page 22)

1 medium-size onion, finely chopped

1 Tbsp (15 g) ginger-garlic paste (*adrak-lasan*)

½ cup (120 g) yogurt (*dahi*)

1 Tbsp (15 ml) heavy cream

1 tsp dried fenugreek leaves (*kasuri methi*)

1 tsp red chile powder

Salt, to taste

### METHOD

1. **To make the marinade:** In a medium-size bowl, combine all the marinade ingredients. Whisk well to combine.

2. **To make the gravy:** Add the chicken to the marinade and refrigerate to marinate for 4–5 hours.

3. In a skillet over low-medium heat, heat the vegetable oil.

4. Add the whole spice mix. Cook until the seeds begin to crackle.

5. Add the onion. Sauté for 3–4 minutes.

6. Add the ginger-garlic paste and the chicken along with the marinade. Reduce the heat to medium and cook for 10 minutes until the spices coat the chicken well.

7. Stir in the yogurt and cook for 20–25 minutes, or until the chicken is cooked thoroughly, is tender, and the water from the yogurt evaporates.

8. Stir in the cream, fenugreek leaves, and red chile powder. Season to taste with salt.

9. Cook for 5 minutes more. Serve hot.

# KOLKATA EGG ROLL
Street-side egg roll with a dash of mustard.

Cooking time: 40 minutes | Makes: 5       Origin: West Bengal

## INGREDIENTS

**For the paratha**
1 cup (125 g) whole-wheat flour (*atta*)
1 Tbsp (15 ml) olive oil
**For the omelet**
2 eggs
2 Tbsp (21.25 g) finely chopped onion
1 green chile, finely chopped
Salt, to taste
**For the rolls**
1 medium-size onion, sliced
1 medium-size green bell pepper, sliced
1 medium-size carrot (*gajar*), sliced
5 Tbsp (75 g) mustard sauce (page 24)

## METHOD

1. **To make the paratha:** In a small bowl, combine the flour and olive oil. Knead into a soft dough and cut the dough into 5 small balls.
2. Roll out the parathas and cook them on both sides.
3. **To make the omelet:** Preheat a griddle over medium heat.
4. In another small bowl, whisk the eggs, onion, and green chile. Season to taste with salt. Pour the egg mixture onto the hot griddle and cook the omelet to your desired doneness.
5. Place the omelet on the paratha.
6. **To finish the rolls:** Top the omelet with onion, bell pepper, and carrot.
7. Season each with 1 Tbsp (15 ml) of mustard sauce, or any hot sauce, and roll up. Serve immediately.

# EGG ROLL FROM RANCHI
Omelet in a paratha with cucumber and tomato.

Cooking time: 30 minutes | Makes: 4       Origin: Jharkhand

## INGREDIENTS

1 medium-size onion, finely chopped
1 medium-size cucumber, peeled and diced
Juice of 1 lemon (*nimbu*)
1 green chile, finely chopped
4 eggs
1 Tbsp (15 ml) milk
Salt, to taste
2 tsp vegetable oil
4 parathas (type of flatbread; page 33)
1 medium-size tomato, sliced
1 Tbsp (15 ml) green chile sauce

## METHOD

1. In a small bowl, stir together the onion and cucumber. Season with lemon juice and chopped green chile. Stir to combine.
2. In a medium-size bowl, whisk the eggs and milk. Season to taste with salt. Divide the egg batter into four portions.
3. In a skillet over medium heat, heat the vegetable oil. Pour in one portion of the egg batter. Cook the omelet well. Flip it and cook it face-side down. Place it on the paratha.
4. Place the cucumber-onion filling in the center of the omelet along with the tomato and green chile sauce. Wrap and cut before serving.
5. Repeat this process for each of the four egg rolls.

# MAACHER CHOP

Fried fish and potato cakes.

Cooking time: 20 minutes | Makes: 6-8    Origin: West Bengal

INGREDIENTS

1 tsp ghee
0.65 lb (300 g) fish, rohu, boiled, deboned
1 cup (225 g) potato, boiled, peeled
1 tsp milk
½ tsp salt, plus more to taste
2 green chiles, chopped
1 tsp ginger paste (*adrak*)
1 tsp lemon juice (*nimbu*)
1 egg, white only
Vegetable oil, for deep-frying
Bread crumbs, to coat

METHOD

1. In a skillet over medium-high heat, heat the ghee.
2. Add the fish, potato, and milk.
3. Sauté for a few minutes, stirring continuously. Remove from the heat.
4. Add salt to taste, the green chiles, ginger paste, and lemon juice. Mix well.
5. In a medium-size bowl, whisk the egg white with ½ tsp of salt. Set aside.
6. Divide the fish-spice mixture equally into 6–8 small balls.
7. In a wok over high heat, heat the vegetable oil for deep-frying.
8. Dip the balls in the whisked egg white, roll in bread crumbs. Working in batches, carefully put the balls in hot oil. Deep-fry until golden brown. Transfer on paper towels to drain. Serve hot.

# MAACHER DIM BORA

Fish fritters.

Cooking time: 20 minutes | Makes: 6    Origin: West Bengal

INGREDIENTS

0.65 lb (300 g) fish, rohu, deboned, shredded
½ cup (75 g) onion, chopped
2 green chiles, chopped
2 tsp red chile powder
Salt, to taste
¼ cup (35 g) rice powder
¾ cup (112 g) Bengal gram flour (*besan*)
½ cup (120 ml) mustard seed oil (page 26)

METHOD

1. In a medium-size bowl, combine the fish, onions, green chiles, and red chile powder. Season to taste with salt.
2. Add the rice powder and Bengal gram flour.
3. Mix well and set aside for half an hour.
4. Divide this mixture into 6 equal portions and shape each portion into flat round patties.
5. In a medium-size skillet over low-medium heat, heat the mustard seed oil. Shallow-fry the patties till golden brown.
6. Remove and drain excess oil on paper towels. Serve hot.

# MEAT AND PORK

## PISH PASH 🍲

One-pot dish of rice, lentils, and minced meat.

Cooking time: 30 minutes | Serves: 4 — Origin: West Bengal

INGREDIENTS

1 cup (240 g) minced lamb

2 tsp salt

½ tsp red chile powder

½ tsp ground coriander (*dhaniya*)

½ tsp ground turmeric (*haldi*)

3 cups (720 ml) water

1 Tbsp (15 g) ghee

1 (1-in. / 2.5-cm) cinnamon stick (*dalchini*)

1 whole clove (*laung*)

1 small onion, finely chopped

½ tsp ginger-garlic paste (*adrak-lasan*)

1 medium-size tomato, chopped

1 cup (200 g) rice, rinsed

¼ cup (50 g) split pigeon peas (*toor dal*), rinsed

¼ cup (4 g) fresh cilantro leaves (*hara dhaniya*), chopped

METHOD

1. In a large saucepan over medium heat, combine the minced lamb, salt, red chile, coriander, turmeric, and water. Cook for about 10 minutes, until cooked through. Mash the cooked meat with a wooden mallet or potato masher. Transfer to a bowl and set aside.
2. Return the pan to the heat and add the ghee, cinnamon stick, and clove. Sauté for 30 seconds.
3. Add the onion. Cook until translucent.
4. Stir in the ginger-garlic paste and tomato. Sauté for 1 minute until the tomato softens.
5. Add the rice and split pigeon peas. Mix well. Cover the pan and cook for 15 minutes, or until the rice and lentils are cooked through, the water is absorbed, and the dish resembles a soft porridge. If water still remains, cook until the water is absorbed. Stir continuously to avoid burning.
6. Stir in the cooked lamb. Serve hot, garnished with cilantro.

## BIHARI MUTTON CURRY

Basic and rustic mutton curry from Bihar.

Cooking time: 1 hour | Serves: 4 — Origin: Bihar

INGREDIENTS

½ cup (112.5 g) yogurt (*dahi*)

1 tsp freshly ground black pepper (*kali mirch*)

½ tsp ground turmeric (*haldi*), divided

1 tsp ground cumin (*jeera*)

1½ Tbsp (25 g) ginger-garlic paste (*adrak-lasan*)

2 lb, 3 oz (1 kg) mutton, chopped

3 Tbsp (45 ml) vegetable oil

1 tsp black and green cardamom powder

1 bay leaf (*tej patta*)

3 dried red chiles (*sookhi lal mirch*)

6 large onions, chopped

2 cups (480 ml) water

Salt, to taste

1 tsp garam masala

¼ cup (4 g) fresh cilantro leaves (*hara dhaniya*), finely chopped

METHOD

1. In a medium-size bowl, combine the yogurt, freshly ground black pepper, turmeric, cumin, and ginger-garlic paste. Season to taste with salt. Whisk well. Add the mutton pieces and marinate for 3–4 hours.
2. On your pressure cooker, select Sauté and preheat the cooking pot.
3. Add the vegetable oil to heat.
4. Add the cardamom powder, bay leaf and dried red chiles.
5. Cook until the spices begin to crackle.
6. Add the onion and cook until translucent.
7. Add the marinated mutton. Sauté the meat for 4-5 minutes.
8. Reduce the heat. Add the water, salt, and garam masala. Lock the lid in place and close the pressure release valve. Select Manual/Pressure Cook and cook for 20 minutes. Release the pressure and remove the lid.
9. Finish with cilantro and serve hot.

## KOSHA MANGSHO

Satisfying mutton curry.

| Cooking time: 1 hour \| Serves: 2 | Origin: West Bengal |
|---|---|

INGREDIENTS

5 Tbsp (75 g) ginger-garlic paste (*adrak-lasan*),
  divided
5 Tbsp (75 g) onion paste, divided
2 Tbsp (12 g) ground coriander (*dhaniya*)
2 tsp red chile powder
1 tsp ground turmeric (*haldi*)
½ cup (120 g) yogurt (*dahi*)
½ cup (120 ml) mustard seed oil (page 26), divided
Salt, to taste
1 lb, 2 oz (500 g) cubed mutton
1 cup (110 g) cubed potato
1 Tbsp (15 g) whole spice mix (page 22)
1 Tbsp (6 g) garam masala
¼ cup (4 g) fresh cilantro leaves (*hara dhaniya*),
  finely chopped

METHOD

1. In a large bowl, stir together half the ginger-
   garlic paste and half the onion paste.
2. Add the coriander, red chile powder, turmeric,
   yogurt, and ¼ cup (60 ml) of mustard seed oil.
   Season to taste with salt and stir to combine.
3. Add the mutton pieces and stir to coat.
   Refrigerate to marinate for 6–7 hours.
4. In a skillet over low-medium heat, heat the
   remaining ¼ cup (60 ml) of mustard seed oil.
5. Add the potato and fry until golden brown.
   With a slotted spoon, transfer to paper towels to
   drain. Set aside.
6. Return the skillet to the heat and add the whole
   spice mix. Cook until the seeds begin to crackle.
7. Stir in the remaining ginger-garlic paste and
   onion paste. Sauté until fragrant.
8. Add the mutton pieces along with the marinade
   and stir to combine. Reduce the heat to low and
   cook the mutton for 45–60 minutes, or until
   thoroughly cooked.
9. Finish the dish by sprinkling it with garam
   masala. Season to taste with salt and add the
   fried potatoes. Garnish with cilantro and serve
   hot.

## BHUNAL GOSHT

Aromatic roasted lamb gravy.

| Cooking time: 1 hour \| Serves: 2 | Origin: Bihar |
|---|---|

INGREDIENTS

4 Tbsp (60 ml) vegetable oil
1 cup (240 g) sliced onion
½ tsp ground nutmeg
1 Tbsp (15 g) ginger-garlic paste (*adrak-lasan*)
1 lb (454 g) cubed mutton
2 Tbsp (12 g) ground coriander (*dhaniya*)
1 Tbsp (15 g) whole spice mix (page 22)
1 tsp ground turmeric (*haldi*)
1 tsp red chile powder
1 dried red chile (*sookhi lal mirch*)
Freshly ground black pepper (*kali mirch*), to taste
Water, as needed
1 tsp vetivier water (*kewra*; available at Indian
  markets)
Salt, to taste

METHOD

1. In a skillet over medium heat, heat the vegetable
   oil.
2. Add the onion. Fry until golden brown. With a
   slotted spoon, transfer to a food processor, add
   the nutmeg, and blend into a smooth paste.
3. Return the skillet and any remaining oil to the
   heat. Add the ginger-garlic paste and mutton.
   Cook for 5 minutes, stirring well.
4. Add the coriander, whole spice mix, turmeric,
   red chile powder, and dried red chile. Season to
   taste with pepper. Cook for 5 minutes more.
5. Stir in the nutmeg-spiced onion paste. Reduce
   the heat to low and continue to cook the mutton
   for 40–50 minutes until done. Add water as
   needed if the dish begins to dry up.
6. Finish with the vetivier water and salt.
7. Serve hot.

# KOLKATA MUTTON CHAAP 📷

Fragrant mutton chops in a nutty sauce.

Cooking time: 3 hours | Serves: 4      Origin: West Bengal

## INGREDIENTS

1 cup (240 g) yogurt (*dahi*)
½ cup (120 g) raw papaya paste
3 Tbsp (45 g) ginger-garlic paste (*adrak-lasan*)
2 Tbsp (30 g) poppy seed paste (*khus khus*)
1 Tbsp (15 g) cashew paste (*kaju*)
2 tsp dried red chile paste (*sookhi lal mirch*)
1 Tbsp (6 g) garam masala
1 tsp ground turmeric (*haldi*)
Salt, to taste
1 lb (454 g) mutton chops
13 Tbsp plus 1 tsp (200 g) ghee
1 tsp rose water

## METHOD

1. In a medium-size bowl, stir together the yogurt, raw papaya paste, ginger-garlic paste, poppy seed paste, cashew paste, dried red chile paste, garam masala, and turmeric. Season to taste with salt. Add the mutton and turn to coat. Refrigerate to marinate for 5 hours.
2. In a skillet over low heat, heat the ghee.
3. Arrange the mutton chops in the pan. Cover and cook the chops for 2 hours, checking occasionally to ensure the chops do not burn, until golden on both sides.
4. Flip the chops halfway through the cooking time. Finish with rose water and serve with laccha parathas, if desired.

# MANGSHOR JHOL 🍲

Spicy mutton curry cooked with potato chunks.

Cooking time: 1 hour | Serves: 4      Origin: West Bengal

## INGREDIENTS

¼ cup (60 ml) vegetable oil
1 Tbsp (15 g) whole spice mix (page 22)
4 medium-size onions, finely chopped
2 green chiles, finely chopped
1 Tbsp (15 g) ginger paste (*adrak*)
1 tsp garlic paste (*lasan*)
1 Tbsp (6 g) ground coriander (*dhaniya*)
½ tsp ground turmeric (*haldi*)
½ tsp red chile powder
1 lb (454 g) cubed mutton
Salt, to taste
5 cups (1.2 L) water
4 medium-size potatoes, halved

## METHOD

1. On your pressure cooker, select Sauté and preheat the cooking pot.
2. Add the vegetable oil once the base becomes very hot.
3. Add the whole spice mix and cook until the seeds begin to crackle.
4. Add onions and green chiles. Sauté until the onions turn golden brown.
5. Stir in the ginger paste, garlic paste, coriander, turmeric, and red chile powder. Cook, stirring, for 2 minutes.
6. Add the mutton and season to taste with salt. Select Less to lower the heat and cook for 3–4 minutes.
7. When the oil begins to separate, add the water. Lock the lid in place and close the pressure release valve. Select Manual/Pressure Cook and cook for 9 minutes.
8. Release the pressure and remove the lid. Add the potatoes. Re-lock the lid in place and close the pressure release valve. Select Manual/Pressure Cook and cook for 3 minutes.
9. Release the pressure and remove the lid.

## MANGSHO GHUGNI

Lamb with chickpeas.

Cooking time: 1 hour | Serves: 2-4    Origin: West Bengal

INGREDIENTS

½ cup (100 g) chickpeas (*kabuli chana*)
5 Tbsp (75 ml) vegetable oil
¼ cup (30 g) onions, chopped
1 tsp ginger paste (*adrak*)
1 tsp garlic paste (*lasan*)
¼ cup (50 g) tomato, chopped
1 cup (200 g) lamb, boneless pieces
½ tsp red chile powder
½ tsp ground coriander (*dhaniya*)
½ tsp ground cumin (*jeera*)
1 cup (240 ml) water, plus more for soaking and
  boiling chickpeas
Salt, to taste
1 Tbsp (4 g) fresh cilantro leaves (*hara dhaniya*),
  finely chopped

METHOD

1. Soak the chickpeas in water overnight. Drain
   and discard water. In a saucepan over medium
   heat, boil the chickpeas in 1½ cups (360 ml)
   water until soft. Without draining, set aside.

2. In a skillet over low-medium heat, heat the
   vegetable oil. Add the onions, ginger paste,
   garlic paste, tomato, and lamb. Mix well.

3. Add the red chile powder, coriander, cumin, and
   1 cup of water. Season to taste with salt. Cook
   until the lamb is tender.

4. Add the boiled chickpeas along with the water
   in which they were boiled. Bring the mixture to
   a boil. Remove from the heat and serve hot,
   garnished with cilantro.

## RAILWAY MUTTON CURRY 📷

A culinary legacy of the British Raj.

Cooking time: 1 hour | Serves: 4    Origin: West Bengal

INGREDIENTS

1 Tbsp (15 ml) vegetable oil
3 dried red chiles (*sookhi lal mirch*)
2 Tbsp (12 g) ground coriander (*dhaniya*)
1 Tbsp (5 g) coriander seeds (*dhaniya*)
1 Tbsp (8 g) red chile powder
1 tsp ground turmeric (*haldi*)
1 tsp cumin seeds (*jeera*)
2 medium-size onions, finely chopped
2 cups (480 g) cubed mutton
1 cup (240 ml) water
1 cup (240 g) tomato purée
1 Tbsp (15 g) tamarind paste (*imli*; page 30)
2 medium-size potatoes, cubed and fried
1 cup (240 ml) coconut milk (*nariyal*)
Salt, to taste
¼ cup (4 g) fresh cilantro leaves (*hara dhaniya*),
  finely chopped

METHOD

1. On your pressure cooker, select Sauté and
   preheat the cooking pot.

2. Add the vegetable oil to heat.

3. Add the dried red chiles, coriander, coriander
   seeds, red chile powder, turmeric, and cumin
   seeds. Cook until the seeds begin to crackle.

4. Add the onions. Sauté for 2–3 minutes.

5. Add the mutton. Sauté until the spices coat the
   meat well.

6. Add the water, tomato purée, and tamarind
   paste. Lock the lid in place and close the
   pressure release valve. Select Manual/Pressure
   Cook and cook for 12 minutes. Release the
   pressure and remove the lid. Stir in the potatoes
   and coconut milk. Select Sauté and simmer the
   curry for 10 minutes more.

7. Season to taste with salt and finish with cilantro.
   Serve hot.

# FISH AND SEAFOOD

## SHORSHE MACH

Traditional Bengali mustard seed oil–flavored fish.

Cooking time: 30 minutes | Serves: 2      Origin: West Bengal

### INGREDIENTS

4 pieces rohu fish, carp, or other white-fleshed fish
    (available at some Indian markets)
Salt, to taste
1 tsp ground turmeric (*haldi*), divided
½ cup mustard seed oil (page 26)
2 tsp *kasundi* (Bengali mustard; available at
    Indian markets, page 24 )
1 tsp nigella seeds (*kalonji*)
1 green chile, finely chopped
1 tsp red chile powder

### METHOD

1.  Sprinkle the fish with salt and ½ tsp of turmeric. Place in a medium-size bowl and let marinate for 10 minutes.
2.  In a skillet over medium heat, heat the mustard seed oil.
3.  Add the fish and fry until golden brown. Remove the fish from the pan and discard some of the oil, leaving about 1 Tbsp (15 ml).
4.  Place the skillet over low-medium heat and add the *kasundi*, nigella seeds, and green chile. Cook until the seeds begin to crackle.
5.  Add the remaining ½ tsp of turmeric and the red chile powder. Season to taste with salt and stir well to combine.
6.  Finish with the fried fish. Cover the skillet and cook for 5 minutes before serving.

## BHETKI FISH FRY

Light fish cutlets, Bengali-style.

Cooking time: 1 hour | Serves: 2      Origin: West Bengal

### INGREDIENTS

2 Tbsp (30 g) mint leaf paste (*pudina*)
2 Tbsp (30 g) cilantro paste (*hara dhaniya*)
1 Tbsp (15 g) onion paste
1 Tbsp (15 g) ginger-garlic paste (*adrak-lasan*)
1 tsp green chile paste
Salt, to taste
Freshly ground black pepper (*kali mirch*), to taste
Juice of 1 lemon (*nimbu*)
6 pieces Bhetki fish or cod or other white flaky fish
Vegetable oil, for frying
 2 eggs
¾ cup (90 g) bread crumbs

### METHOD

1.  In a bowl, stir together the mint paste, cilantro paste, onion paste, ginger-garlic paste, and green chile paste.
2.  Season to taste with salt and pepper. Stir in the lemon juice. Apply this mix to both sides of the fish with your fingertips.
3.  Marinate for 30 minutes.
4.  In a deep skillet over low-medium heat, heat the vegetable oil for frying.
5.  In a shallow bowl, whisk the eggs and season to taste with salt.
6.  Place the bread crumbs in another shallow bowl.
7.  Dip the marinated fish in the egg, shaking off any excess, and into the bread crumbs to coat.
8.  Carefully add to the hot oil and deep-fry until cooked through. Serve hot.

# CHINGUDI JHOLA

Potato and prawn spice-rich curry.

Cooking time: 30 minutes | Serves: 2      Origin: Odisha

## INGREDIENTS

2 Tbsp (30 ml) vegetable oil, divided

1 cup (240 g) onion, sliced

½ cup (120 g) tomato, finely chopped

1 Tbsp (16 g) ginger-garlic paste (*adrak-lasan*)

½ tsp ground turmeric (*haldi*)

2 bay leaves (*tej patta*)

1 tsp red chile powder

1 tsp ground cumin (*jeera*)

1 tsp ground coriander (*dhaniya*)

1 tsp garam masala

½ cup (55 g) potato, parboiled and cubed

1 lb, 6 oz (650 g) prawns, cleaned

1 cup (240 ml) water, warm

Salt, to taste

¼ cup (4 g) fresh cilantro leaves (*hara dhaniya*), finely chopped

## METHOD

1. In a skillet, over medium-high heat, heat 1 Tbsp (15 ml) of vegetable oil. Sauté the onions until brown.

2. Add the tomato and sauté for 7-8 minutes. Once the tomato has softened, remove from the heat.

3. In a food processor, blitz the onion-tomato mixture and ginger-garlic paste into a fine purée.

4. In a skillet over medium-high heat, heat the remaining 1 Tbsp (15 ml) of vegetable oil. Add the purée. Stir and add the turmeric, bay leaves, red chile powder, cumin, and coriander. Sauté for 2–3 minutes. Add the garam masala.

5. Add the potato, prawns, and warm water.

6. Cook until the prawns are thoroughly cooked. This should take 7–9 minutes.

7. Season to taste with salt. Finish with cilantro before serving.

# CRAB KALIA

A motley of crab, potatoes, onions, and spices.

Cooking time: 1 hour | Serves: 4      Origin: West Bengal

## INGREDIENTS

1 Tbsp (15 ml) vegetable oil

½ cup (85 g) finely chopped onion

2 Tbsp (30 g) minced garlic (*lasan*)

1 Tbsp (15 g) grated peeled fresh ginger (*adrak*)

1 cup (110 g) cubed potato

1 tsp ground turmeric (*haldi*)

1 Tbsp (15 g) whole spice mix (page 22)

1 tsp cumin seeds (*jeera*)

2 dried red chiles (*sookhi lal mirch*)

2 green chiles

1 bay leaf (*tej patta*)

2 cups (480 ml) water

4 crabs

1 tsp ground cinnamon (*dalchini*)

Salt, to taste

## METHOD

1. In a skillet over low-medium heat, heat the vegetable oil.

2. Add the onion, garlic, ginger, potato, and turmeric. Fry together for 1 minute.

3. Meanwhile, in a blender or mortar and pestle, grind the whole spice mix, cumin seeds, dried red chiles, green chiles, and bay leaf into a coarse paste. Add the paste to the potato mixture.

4. Stir in the water and bring the mixture to a rolling boil.

5. Add the crabs to the gravy and finish with a sprinkle of cinnamon. Reduce the heat to low and simmer until the crabs are thoroughly cooked. Season to taste with salt.

6. Serve hot.

## GONDHORAJ MAACH

Fish cooked with fragrant makrut lime.

Cooking time: 30 minutes | Serves: 2 | Origin: West Bengal

### INGREDIENTS

1 medium-size onion, finely chopped
2 Tbsp (30 g) cashew paste (*kaju*)
1 tsp ginger-chile paste (*adrak-mirchi*)
1 tsp vegetable oil
1 tsp ground cumin (*jeera*)
½ tsp ground turmeric (*haldi*)
2 catla fish fillets, cubed
1 cup (240 ml) coconut milk (*nariyal*)
2 gondhoraj lebu (makrut lime) leaves
Salt, to taste
Freshly ground black pepper (*kali mirch*), to taste

### METHOD

1. In a food processor, combine the onion, cashew paste, and ginger-chile paste. Blend into a smooth paste.
2. In a skillet over medium heat, heat the vegetable oil.
3. Add the onion-cashew paste and cook, stirring, for 2–3 minutes.
4. Stir in the cumin and turmeric. Add the fish and stir well to combine.
5. Stir in the coconut milk and gondhoraj lebu leaves. Cook until the gravy thickens and the fish is cooked through.
6. Season with salt and pepper to taste. Serve hot.

## ILISH BHAPA

Steamed hilsa dish with Bengali-style mustard.

Cooking time: 40 minutes | Serves: 2 | Origin: West Bengal

### INGREDIENTS

2 tsp black mustard seeds (*rai*), soaked in warm water for 20 minutes, drained
2 tsp yellow mustard seeds (*rai*), soaked in warm water for 20 minutes, drained
2 green chiles, finely chopped
1 tsp *kasundi* (Bengali mustard; available at Indian markets; page 24)
Salt, to taste
1 Tbsp (9 g) poppy seeds (*khus khus*)
5 pieces hilsa fish or American shad
1 tsp ground turmeric (*haldi*)
1 tsp red chile powder
½ cup (120 g) sour yogurt (*dahi*; let regular yogurt rest for 2 days in the refrigerator until it turns sour)
3 Tbsp (15 g) grated fresh coconut (*nariyal*)
2 Tbsp (30 ml) mustard seed oil (page 26)

### METHOD

1. In a blender or mortar and pestle, combine the black and yellow mustard seeds, green chiles, and *kasundi*. Season to taste with salt. Blend into a paste and set aside.
2. In a spice grinder or mortar and pestle, grind the poppy seeds into a powder and set aside.
3. Sprinkle the fish with the turmeric, red chile powder, and salt to taste. Transfer to a plate and let marinate for 10 minutes.
4. In a small bowl, stir together the poppy seed powder, mustard seed paste, sour yogurt, coconut, and salt to taste.
5. Coat the bottom of a medium-size bowl with the mustard seed oil and add the marinated fish.
6. Place the mustard-poppy seed mixture on top.
7. In a steamer, cook the fish for 20 minutes and serve hot.

# KAKRAR JHAL

Bengali crab curry with potatoes.

Cooking time: 1 hour | Serves: 4      Origin: West Bengal

## INGREDIENTS

1 Tbsp (30 ml) vegetable oil,
  plus more for deep-frying
2 potatoes, medium-size, cubed
4 (about 1 kg) crabs, separated and cleaned
1 Tbsp (6 g) garam masala
1 tsp water, plus additional to boil the crabs
2 tsp ground turmeric (*haldi*)
1 Tbsp (15 g) whole spice mix (page 22)
1 dried red chile (*sookhi lal mirch*)
2 Tbsp (15 g) onion paste
2 Tbsp ginger-garlic (*adrak-lasan*) paste
2 cup (400 g) tomato, finely chopped
Salt, to taste

## METHOD

1.  In a wok over medium-high heat, heat the vegetable oil for deep-frying.
2.  Deep-fry the potato. Set aside.
3.  Fry the crab pieces for 1–2 minutes. Set aside.
4.  In a medium-size bowl, combine the garam masala with the water. Stir to make a thick paste.
5.  In a pan over medium-high heat, cook the crab pieces with water and the turmeric. Boil for 5 minutes.
6.  Drain and set the crab pieces aside. Allow them to dry.
7.  In a skillet over medium-high heat, heat the vegetable oil. Add the whole spice mix and dried red chile. Cook until the spices begin to crackle.
8.  Add the onion paste and ginger-garlic paste. Sauté until well-browned.
9.  Add the chopped tomato and cook until the oil begins to leave the side of the pan. Season to taste with salt.
10. Add the garam masala paste and stir well. Cook the gravy for 7–8 minutes more.
11. Add the fried potato pieces and fried crabs and cover the pan. Cook for 7–8 minutes more.
12. Give it a final stir and serve the curry with rice, if desired.

# MACHER JHOL

A traditional fish stew with vegetables.

Cooking time: 40 minutes | Serves: 3      Origin: Odisha

## INGREDIENTS

13 Tbsp plus 1 tsp (200 ml) vegetable oil
4 pieces rohu fish, carp, or other white-fleshed fish
  (available at some Indian markets)
½ cup (125 g) potato batons
1 Tbsp (15 ml) mustard seed oil (page 26)
1 medium-size onion, finely chopped
1 tsp ground turmeric (*haldi*)
1 tsp red chile powder
1 bay leaf (*tej patta*)
1 cup (240 ml) water
Salt, to taste

## METHOD

1.  In a skillet over medium heat, heat the vegetable oil.
2.  Add the fish and fry until halfway done. Remove from the skillet and set aside.
3.  Add the potatoes to the remaining oil and fry until half cooked.
4.  In another skillet over low-medium heat, heat the mustard seed oil.
5.  Add the onion. Sauté until golden.
6.  Add the turmeric, red chile powder, and bay leaf. Stir to combine with the onion.
7.  Add the partially cooked potatoes and the water. Reduce the heat to low. Simmer the gravy for 10 minutes.
8.  Finish with salt to taste and the partially cooked fish. Simmer until the fish is fully cooked. Serve hot.

## POTOLER DORMA

Bengali-style stuffed pointed gourd curry.

Cooking time: 40 minutes | Serves: 2-4    Origin: West Bengal

### INGREDIENTS

2 cups (480 g) pointed gourd (*parwal*)
¼ cup (55 ml) vegetable oil
**For the gravy**
5 cups (850 g) onions, chopped
½ tsp ground coriander (*dhaniya*)
½ tsp ground cumin (*jeera*)
½ tsp ground turmeric (*haldi*)
1 tsp red chile powder
2 tsp ginger-garlic paste (*adrak-lasan*)
¾ cup (150 g) tomato, chopped
2 tsp salt
1 cup (240 ml) water
**For the filling**
5½ Tbsp (80 ml) vegetable oil
2 Tbsp (30 g) ginger-garlic paste (*adrak-lasan*)
2 tsp red chile powder
8 oz (250 g) rohu fish, deboned
1 Tbsp salt

### METHOD

1. Without peeling the pointed gourd, scoop out the inner fleshy portion.
2. In a skillet over medium-high heat, heat the vegetable oil. Blanch the shells of the pointed gourd in hot oil. Drain the excess oil. Set aside.
3. **To make the gravy:** In a skillet over medium-high heat, heat the reserved excess oil. Sauté the onions until they turn brown. Add all the dry spices and ginger-garlic paste. Cook for 2 minutes.
4. Add the tomato, salt, and water. Cook for 12–15 minutes, stirring continuously, until a smooth gravy is obtained. Remove from the heat.
5. **To make the filling:** In a medium-size skillet over medium-high heat, heat the vegtable oil.
6. Add the ginger-garlic paste, red chile powder, and fish. Season to taste with salt. Cook for 10 minutes over low heat.
7. Remove the pan from the heat; spoon the fish mixture inside the fried pointed gourd shells.
8. Place 1-2 stuffed shells in each serving dish. Top them with the onion-tomato gravy and serve.

## MACH GHANTA 📷

Healthy fish dish with vegetables.

Cooking time: 30 minutes | Serves: 2    Origin: Odisha

### INGREDIENTS

2 tsp ground turmeric (*haldi*)
Salt to taste
1 lb, 2 oz (500 g) rohu fish, carp, or other white-fleshed fish (available at some Indian markets)
2 Tbsp (30 ml) vegetable oil, plus more for frying
1 tsp cumin seeds (*jeera*)
1 bay leaf (*tej patta*)
1 dried red chile (*sookhi lal mirch*)
1 medium-size onion, ground to a paste
1 Tbsp (15 g) ginger-garlic paste (*adrak-lasan*)
2 medium-size potatoes, cubed
1 medium-size tomato, finely chopped
1 medium-size eggplant (*brinjal*), cubed
7 oz (200 g) pumpkin, cubed
2 cups (480 ml) water
Coriander seeds, for garnishing

### METHOD

1. In a large bowl, combine the turmeric and salt to taste. Add the fish, toss to coat, and let marinate for 10–15 minutes.
2. In a skillet over medium heat, heat the vegetable oil for frying.
3. Add the fish pieces. Fry until cooked through.
4. In another skillet over medium-high heat, heat 2 Tbsp (30 ml) of vegetable oil.
5. Add the cumin seeds, bay leaf, and dried red chile. Cook until the seeds begin to crackle.
6. Stir in the onion paste and ginger-garlic paste. Sauté until golden.
7. Add the potatoes, tomato, eggplant, and pumpkin. Stir well to combine.
8. Add the water and cook the dish until the vegetables are soft.
9. Season to taste with salt and garnish with the coriander seeds. Top the vegetables with the fried fish before serving.

VEGETARIAN

# BIHARI GHUGNI

Tasteful medley of black chickpeas and spices.

| Cooking time: 40 minutes | Serves: 2 | Origin: Bihar |
| --- | --- | --- |

## INGREDIENTS

1 cup (240 g) sliced onions, divided
2 Tbsp (15 g) chickpea flour (*besan*)
1 Tbsp (15 ml) vegetable oil
1 bay leaf (*tej patta*)
1 tsp cumin seeds (*jeera*)
1 green chile, finely chopped
1 Tbsp (15 g) ginger-garlic paste (*adrak-lasan*)
1 Tbsp (6 g) ground coriander (*dhaniya*)
1 tsp red chile powder
1 tsp freshly ground black pepper (*kali mirch*)
1 tsp ground cumin (*jeera*)
Salt, to taste
¼ cup (60 ml) water
1 cup (200 g) horse gram (*kala chana*), boiled
2 Tbsp (2 g) fresh cilantro leaves (*hara dhaniya*), finely chopped
1 Tbsp (5 g) grated fresh coconut (*nariyal*)

## METHOD

1. In a food processor, combine ¼ cup (60 g) of sliced onion and the chickpea flour. Process until a paste forms.
2. In a skillet over low-medium heat, heat the vegetable oil.
3. Add the bay leaf, cumin seeds, and green chile. Cook until the seeds begin to crackle.
4. Add the remaining ¾ cup (180 g) of sliced onion and the ginger-garlic paste. Cook until the onion softens.
5. Add the coriander, red chile powder, pepper, cumin, and ground onion–chickpea flour paste. Season well with salt.
6. Stir in the water, reduce the heat to low, and bring the gravy to a simmer.
7. Add the horse gram and cook the dish for 20 minutes.
8. Finish with the cilantro and grated coconut. Serve hot.

# KALMI SAAG

Water spinach cooked in garlic and onions.

| Cooking time: 30 minutes | Serves: 2 | Origin: Bihar |
| --- | --- | --- |

## INGREDIENTS

2 Tbsp (30 ml) mustard seed oil (page 26)
2 tsp minced garlic (*lasan*)
1 green chile, finely chopped
½ medium-size onion, finely chopped
2 cups (112 g) water spinach (*kalmi saag*), finely chopped
Salt, to taste

## METHOD

1. In a skillet over medium heat, heat the mustard seed oil.
2. Add the garlic and green chile. Cook until fragrant.
3. Add the onion. Cook, stirring, until golden.
4. Add the water spinach and season to taste with salt. Cover the skillet and cook for 10–15 minutes until it begins to release its water.
5. Remove the lid and continue to cook, stirring, until all the water evaporates.
6. Serve hot.

## PITHA

Rice flour dumplings with a mild dal filling.

Cooking time: 30 minutes | Makes: 8     Origin: Jharkhand

### INGREDIENTS

1½ cups (360 ml) water
Salt, to taste
1 cup (160 g) rice flour
1 cup (200 g) Bengal gram (split chickpeas; *chana dal*)
1 green chile, finely chopped
1 Tbsp (15 g) minced garlic (*lasan*)
2 tsp cumin seeds (*jeera*)
1 tsp vegetable oil

### METHOD

1. In a saucepan over low-medium heat, combine the water and a pinch of salt. Bring to a boil, add the rice flour, and stir well and vigorously so no lumps remain.
2. Set aside to cool.
3. In a blender or mortar and pestle, combine the chickpeas, green chile, garlic, cumin seeds, and salt to taste. Grind into a coarse paste.
4. In a small skillet over low-medium heat, heat the vegetable oil.
5. Add the chickpea paste. Cook for 4–5 minutes. Remove from the heat and set aside.
6. Cut the rice flour dough into 8 small balls. Flatten the balls with your fingertips. Place a spoonful of the chickpea mixture in the center of each. Roll each again into a ball, closing any gaps.
7. Place the balls in a steamer basket.
8. Steam for 20 minutes, or until fully done. Serve hot.

## DHUSKA

Deep-fried rice and dal dumplings.

Cooking time: 40 minutes | Makes: 10-15     Origin: Jharkhand

### INGREDIENTS

2 cups (400 g) basmati rice
1 cup (200 g) Bengal gram (split chickpeas; *chana dal*), soaked in water for 2 hours, drained
2 green chiles, finely chopped
1 Tbsp (15 g) finely chopped garlic (*lasan*)
½ cup (120 ml) water
1 tsp ground turmeric (*haldi*)
4 curry leaves (*kadhi patta*)
¼ cup (4 g) fresh cilantro leaves (*hara dhaniya*), finely chopped
1 medium-size onion, finely chopped
Salt, to taste
Vegetable oil, for frying

### METHOD

1. In a food processor, combine the rice, chickpeas, green chiles, garlic, and water. Process into a thick paste.
2. Add the turmeric, curry leaves, cilantro, and onion. Season to taste with salt. Pulse to combine.
3. In a skillet over medium heat, heat the vegetable oil. Add the paste and fry until golden brown.
4. Serve hot with Bihari Ghugni (page 401), if desired.

## PURI MITTHA DALI

Hearty lentil soup served at Jagganath Temple.

Cooking time: 30 minutes | Serves: 2      Origin: Odisha

INGREDIENTS

1 Tbsp (15 g) ghee
1 Tbsp (15 g) whole spice mix (page 22)
1 tsp cumin seeds (*jeera*)
1 tsp coriander seeds (*dhaniya*)
1 tsp mustard seeds (*rai*)
¼ cup (21.25 g) sliced fresh coconut (*nariyal*)
1 tsp ground turmeric (*haldi*)
1 tsp jaggery (*gur*; unrefined cane sugar)
1 cup (200 g) split pigeon peas (*toor dal*), cooked
½ cup (120 ml) water
¾ tsp finely chopped fresh cilantro leaves (*hara dhaniya*)
Salt, to taste
Freshly ground black pepper (*kali mirch*), to taste
Shredded coconut (*nariyal*), for garnishing

METHOD

1. In a skillet over low-medium heat, heat the ghee.
2. Add the whole spice mix, cumin seeds, coriander seeds, and mustard seeds. Cook until the seeds begin to crackle.
3. Add the sliced coconut, turmeric, and jaggery. Stir well to combine.
4. Add the pigeon peas and water. Mix everything well. Cook until heated through.
5. Finish with salt, pepper, and cilantro. Garnish with shredded coconut before serving.

## DALMA

A popular lentil dish with vegetables.

Cooking time: 30 minutes | Serves: 2      Origin: Odisha

INGREDIENTS

½ cup (100 g) split pigeon peas (*toor dal*)
½ cup (150 g) mixed vegetables
1 Tbsp (5 g) grated fresh coconut (*nariyal*)
1 cup (240 ml) water
1 tsp ground turmeric (*haldi*), divided
Salt, to taste
1 tsp cumin seeds (*jeera*)
1 dried red chile (*sookhi lal mirch*)
1 Tbsp (15 g) ghee
1 tsp mustard seeds (*rai*)
1 green chile, finely chopped
1 tsp minced peeled fresh ginger (*adrak*)
1 tsp ground cumin (*jeera*)
1 medium-size onion, finely chopped

METHOD

1. In your pressure cooker cooking pot, combine the pigeon peas, mixed vegetables, coconut, water, and a pinch turmeric. Season to taste with salt. Lock the lid in place and close the pressure release valve. Select Manual/Pressure Cook and cook for 6 minutes. Release the pressure and remove the lid.
2. In a skillet over low-medium heat, dry-roast the cumin seeds and dried red chile. Transfer to a spice grinder or mortar and pestle, let cool, and grind into a fine powder.
3. Return the skillet to the heat and add the ghee to melt.
4. Add the mustard seeds, green chile, ginger, and cumin. Cook until the seeds begin to crackle.
5. Add the onion. Sauté until golden.
6. Add the pigeon pea mixture, cumin-red chile powder, and the remaining turmeric.
7. Stir well, season to taste with salt, and serve hot.

## DHOKAR DALNA
Deep-fried lentil cakes in tomato sauce.

Cooking time: 40 minutes | Serves: 2    Origin: West Bengal

INGREDIENTS

For the dhokar
1¼ cups (250 g) Bengal gram (split chickpeas;
   *chana dal)*, soaked in water overnight, drained
2 Tbsp ghee
1 tsp cumin seeds (*jeera*)
1 tsp ginger paste (*adrak*)
1 tsp ground turmeric (*haldi*)
Pinch ground asafoetida (*hing*)
Salt, to taste
Vegetable oil, for frying
For the dalna
1 cup (240 g) diced tomato
1 green chile, chopped
1 Tbsp (6 g) ground coriander (*dhaniya*)
2 tsp ginger paste (*adrak*)
1 tsp ground cumin (*jeera*)
1 tsp red chile powder
1 tsp ground turmeric (*haldi*)
1 Tbsp (15 ml) vegetable oil
1 tsp cumin seeds (*jeera*)
1 cup (240 ml) water
Salt, to taste

METHOD

1. **To make the dhoka:** In a food processor, grind the chickpeas into a smooth paste.
2. In a skillet over low-medium heat, heat the ghee.
3. Add the cumin seeds, ginger paste, turmeric, and asafoetida. Cook until the seeds begin to crackle.
4. Add the chickpea paste and season to taste with salt. Stir vigorously until the mixture comes together, but don't let it dry out, remove from the heat and transfer to a plate. Let rest for 30 minutes.
5. Cut the dhoka into cubes and set aside.
6. In a deep skillet over medium heat, heat the vegetable oil for frying.
7. Carefully add the dhokas to the hot oil and fry until golden and crispy. Transfer to paper towels to drain.
8. **To make the dalna:** In the food processor, purée

the tomato, green chile, coriander, ginger paste, cumin, red chile powder, and turmeric.
9. In a small skillet over medium-high heat, heat the vegetable oil.
10. Add the cumin seeds. Cook until they begin to crackle.
11. Add the tomato-green chile mixture and the water.
12. Reduce the heat to low and simmer for 7–9 minutes.
13. Season to taste with salt and add the fried dhokas. Cook for 5 minutes more and serve hot.

. . . . . . . . . . . .

## CHOLAR DAL
The famous Bengali dal with sliced coconut

Cooking time: 30 minutes | Serves: 2    Origin: West Bengal

INGREDIENTS

2 Tbsp (30 g) ghee, divided
1 Tbsp (15 g) whole spice mix (page 22)
2 dried red chiles (*sookhi lal mirch*)
1 tsp cumin seeds (*jeera*)
2 green chiles, chopped
1 tsp ginger paste (*adrak*)
1 tsp ground turmeric (*haldi*)
1 cup (200 g) Bengal gram (split chickpeas;
   *chana dal)*, cooked
Salt, to taste
½ cup (42.5 g) sliced coconut (*nariyal*), fried

METHOD

1. In a skillet over low-medium heat, heat 1 Tbsp (15 g) of ghee.
2. Add the whole spice mix, dried red chiles, and cumin seeds. Cook until the seeds begin to crackle.
3. Add the green chiles, ginger paste, and turmeric. Cook, stirring, for 2 minutes.
4. Add the chickpeas and reduce the heat to low. If the dal seems to dry, add about ¼ cup (60 ml) of water.
5. Season to taste with salt and simmer for 1 minute.
6. Finish with the remaining 1 Tbsp (15 g) of ghee and coconut slices. Serve hot.

## ALOO DUM

Fried baby potatoes in a smooth, creamy gravy.

Cooking time: 30 minutes | Serves: 2     Origin: West Bengal

### INGREDIENTS

1 tsp coriander seeds (*dhaniya*)
1 tsp cumin seeds (*jeera*)
1 dried red chile (*sookhi lal mirch*)
13 oz (375 g) baby potatoes
3 Tbsp (45 ml) water, plus more for cooking
   the potatoes
Salt, to taste
1 tsp ground turmeric (*haldi*)
1 Tbsp (15 ml) vegetable oil, plus more for frying
1 bay leaf (*tej patta*)
½ cup (85 g) finely chopped onion
1 Tbsp (15 g) ginger-garlic paste (*adrak-lasan*)
½ cup (120 g) finely chopped tomato
1 Tbsp (6 g) garam masala
¼ cup (4 g) fresh cilantro leaves (*hara dhaniya*),
   finely chopped

### METHOD

1. In a blender, blitz the coriander seeds, cumin seeds, and dried red chile. Set aside.
2. In a medium-size saucepan over high heat, combine the potatoes with enough water to cover and season to taste with salt. Bring to a boil and cook until the potatoes are parboiled. Drain.
3. Sprinkle the turmeric on the potatoes and toss to coat.
4. In a deep skillet over low-medium heat, heat the vegetable oil for frying.
5. Carefully add the potatoes to the hot oil and deep-fry until cooked through.
6. In another skillet, heat 1 Tbsp (15 ml) of vegetable oil.
7. Add the bay leaf and onion. Sauté for 2–3 minutes.
8. Add the ginger-garlic paste and tomato. Sauté for 5 minutes.
9. Add the fried potatoes and cumin-red chile powder and stir well to combine.
10. Add 3 Tbsp (45 ml) of water and bring the dish to a gentle simmer.
11. Finish with the garam masala, salt to taste, and cilantro. Serve hot.

## BHAPA ALOO

Mustard potatoes cooked in banana leaves.

Cooking time: 40 minutes | Serves: 2     Origin: West Bengal

### INGREDIENTS

Salt, to taste
1 cup (110 g) cubed potatoes
1 tsp mustard seed oil (page 26)
1½ tsp Panch Phoran spice mix (available at
   Indian markets and online; page 32)
2 dried red chiles (*sookhi lal mirch*)
¼ cup (60 g) hung curd (*dahi*; page 28)
1 Tbsp (5 g) desiccated coconut (*nariyal*)
1 tsp *kasundi* (Bengali mustard; available at Indian
   markets; page 24)
1 tsp ground turmeric (*haldi*)
1 tsp red chile paste
2 banana leaves
Juice of 1 lemon (*nimbu*)

### METHOD

1. Fill a saucepan with water, salt it, and place it over high heat. Bring to a boil and add the potatoes. Parboil the potatoes, drain, and set aside.
2. In a skillet over low-medium heat, heat the mustard seed oil.
3. Add the Panch Phoran. Cook until the spices begin to crackle.
4. Add the dried red chiles and potatoes. Stir well and remove from the heat.
5. In a medium-size bowl stir together the yogurt, coconut, *kasundi*, turmeric, and red chile paste. Season to taste with salt.
6. Stir the potatoes into the yogurt mixture and mix well. Set aside for 1 hour.
7. Place the potatoes in a steamer and cover with the banana leaves. Steam for 15 minutes.
8. Finish with lemon juice and serve hot.

# ALOO POSHTO

Potato stir-fry with ground poppy paste.

Cooking time: 40 minutes | Serves: 2    Origin: West Bengal

## INGREDIENTS

3 Tbsp (27 g) poppy seeds (*khus khus*), soaked in
  water for 1 hour, drained
1 Tbsp (15 ml) mustard seed oil (page 26)
1 Tbsp (10 g) nigella seeds (*kalonji*)
2 medium-size potatoes, cubed
1 green chile, finely chopped
1 Tbsp (15 ml) water
1 Tbsp (15 g) ghee
Salt, to taste

## METHOD

1. In a spice grinder or mortar and pestle, grind
   the poppy seeds into a paste and set aside.
2. In a skillet over low-medium heat, heat the
   mustard seed oil.
3. Add the nigella seeds. Cook until the seeds
   begin to crackle.
4. Add the potatoes. Stir until the nigella seeds
   coat the potatoes well.
5. Stir in the poppy seed paste and green chiles.
6. Reduce the heat to low and add the water to
   moisten the dish. Cover the skillet and cook the
   potatoes for 30–35 minutes until fully done.
7. Finish with the ghee and season to taste with
   salt. Serve hot.

# CHANAR KALIA

Spiced cheese balls in a smooth yogurt curry.

Cooking time: 40 minutes | Serves: 2    Origin: West Bengal

## INGREDIENTS

1 cup (240 g) *chhena* (available at Indian markets)
¼ cup (30 g) grated Cheddar cheese
2 Tbsp (16 g) all-purpose flour (*maida*)
2 tsp ground turmeric (*haldi*), divided
3 tsp red chile powder, divided
1½ tsp garam masala
1 tsp sugar
Salt, to taste
1 Tbsp (15 ml) vegetable oil, plus more for frying
1 medium-size tomato, diced
1 green chile, finely chopped
2 Tbsp (18 g) cashews (*kaju*)
1½ tsp minced peeled fresh ginger (*adrak*)
1 tsp cumin seeds (*jeera*)
¼ cup (60 g) yogurt (*dahi*)

## METHOD

1. In a medium-size bowl, combine the *chhena*,
   Cheddar cheese, flour, 1 tsp of turmeric, 1 tsp of
   red chile powder, the garam masala, and sugar.
   Season to taste with salt. Mash together well
   and knead into a soft dough.
2. Cut the dough into 6 small balls.
3. In a deep skillet over low-medium heat, heat the
   vegetable oil for frying.
4. Carefully add the dough balls to the hot oil and
   deep-fry until golden. Transfer to paper towels
   to drain.
5. In a food processor, blend the tomato, green
   chile, cashews, and ginger into a smooth paste.
6. In a small skillet over low-medium heat, heat
   1 Tbsp (15 ml) of vegetable oil.
7. Add the cumin seeds. Cook until the seeds
   begin to crackle.
8. Add the tomato paste and the remaining 1 tsp of
   turmeric, 2 tsp of chile powder, and the yogurt.
   Stir well.
9. Season to taste with salt and add the cheese
   balls. Reduce the heat to medium and cook for
   4–5 minutes so the balls soak up the gravy.
10. Serve hot.

## MOCHAR GHONTO

Banana flower cooked with potato and spices.

Cooking time: 30 minutes | Serves: 2     Origin: West Bengal

### INGREDIENTS

½ cup (85 g) banana flower (*mochar*; available at Indian markets), washed
1 tsp cumin seeds (*jeera*)
1 tsp coriander seeds (*dhaniya*)
1 tsp minced peeled fresh ginger (*adrak*)
½ tsp green cardamom pods (*elaichi*)
1 tsp ground turmeric (*haldi*)
5 Tbsp (75 ml) water
2 Tbsp (30 ml) mustard seed oil (page 26)
1 bay leaf (*tej patta*)
2 tsp sugar
¼ cup (20 g) grated fresh coconut (*nariyal*)
2 Tbsp (25 g) Bengal gram (split chickpeas; *chana dal*), soaked in water for 1 hour, drained
½ cup (55 g) cubed potato, fried
1½ tsp garam masala
Salt, to taste

### METHOD

1. Peel the banana flower and separate the florets. Remove the black stigma and the light white covering. Once these two components are removed, separate out the usable banana flower and use it for this dish. The larger pink petals or outer covering have to be discarded.
2. In a food processor or mortar and pestle, combine the cumin seeds, coriander seeds, ginger, and cardamom pods. Grind into a paste.
3. In a medium-size bowl, stir together the turmeric and water. Add the banana flower pieces and soak for 1 hour. Drain.
4. Bring a pot of water to a boil over high heat. Add the banana flower pieces and boil for 10–15 minutes until soft. Drain.
5. In a skillet over low-medium heat, heat the mustard seed oil.
6. Add the bay leaf and sugar. Cook until the sugar melts.
7. Add the coconut. Stir-fry for 1 minute.
8. Add the Bengal gram and the prepared spice paste. Stir to combine.
9. Add the fried potatoes and banana flower. Reduce the heat to low and allow the dish to simmer for 10 minutes.
10. Finish with the garam masala, season to taste with salt, and serve hot.

· · · · · · · · · · · ·

## YELLOW PUMPKIN, TURAI, AND POTATO CHENCHKI 🍲

Potato and pumpkin stir-fried with Panch Phoran.

Cooking time: 30 minutes | Serves: 2     Origin: West Bengal

### INGREDIENTS

1 Tbsp (15 ml) vegetable oil
1 Tbsp (11 g) Panch Phoran spice mix (available at Indian markets and online; page 32)
2 green chiles, finely chopped
2 cups (480 g) chopped peeled snake gourd (*turai*)
2 medium-size potatoes, cubed
1 cup (140 g) cubed yellow pumpkin
Salt, to taste

### METHOD

1. In a skillet over low-medium heat, heat the vegetable oil.
2. Add the Panch Phoran and green chiles. Cook until the spices begin to crackle.
3. Add the snake gourd, potatoes, and yellow pumpkin. Sauté for 2 minutes.
4. Season to taste with salt.
5. Reduce the heat to low and cover the skillet. Cook for 15 minutes until the vegetables are thoroughly cooked. Do not stir too much.
6. Serve hot.

## LITTI CHOKHA

Rustic dish of *sattu*-stuffed whole-wheat balls.

Cooking time: 2 hours | Serves: 2      Origin: Bihar

### INGREDIENTS

For the tomato and potato chokha
1 medium-size tomato, finely chopped
1 cup (225 g) coarsely mashed potato
Juice of 1 lemon (*nimbu*)
2 Tbsp (2 g) fresh cilantro leaves (*hara dhaniya*),
    finely chopped
1 Tbsp (15 ml) mustard seed oil (page 26)
1 tsp freshly ground black pepper (*kali mirch*)
1 tsp ginger paste (*adrak*)
1 green chile, finely chopped
Salt, to taste
For the (litti) filling
¾ cup (95 g) *sattu* (available at Indian markets)
½ cup (120 ml) water
1 Tbsp (15 g) ghee
1 tsp ground turmeric (*haldi*)
1 tsp red chile powder
1 tsp dried mango powder (*amchoor*)
1 tsp grated peeled fresh ginger (*adrak*)
1 tsp finely chopped green chile
Pinch ground asafoetida (*hing*)
For the dough
1 cup (125 g) whole-wheat flour (*atta*)
3 Tbsp (45 g) ghee, plus more for serving
Salt, to taste
Water, for kneading

### METHOD

1. Preheat the oven to 300°F (150°C).
2. **To make the tomato and potato chokha:** Using 2 small bowls, put the tomato in one bowl and the potato in the other. Divide each of the remaining chokha ingredients evenly between the two bowls. Season each to taste with salt. Stir each bowl to combine its ingredients. Your tomato and potato chokha are ready. Set aside.
3. **To make the (litti) filling:** In a medium-size bowl, stir together all the filling ingredients. Set aside.

4. **To make the dough:** In a small bowl, stir together all the dough ingredients with enough water to form a smooth dough. Cut the dough into 6 table tennis ball-size balls.
5. Flatten the dough balls with your finger.
6. Place a spoonful of the filling in the center of each.

Roll the balls back into shape and place on a baking sheet. Bake for 30 minutes at 150⁰ C (300⁰ F).

7. Serve the litti with the chokhas and lots of ghee.

· · · · · · · · · · · ·

## BEGUN BHAJA 🍛

Pan fried marinated slices of eggplants.

Cooking time: 40 minutes | Serves: 4      Origin: West Bengal

### INGREDIENTS

1 Tbsp (8 g) red chile powder
1 tsp ground turmeric (*haldi*)
Juice of 1 lemon (*nimbu*)
Salt, to taste
2 medium-size eggplants (*brinjal*), thickly sliced
Vegetable oil, for frying
2 Tbsp (18 g) poppy seeds (*khus khus*)

### METHOD

1. In a large bowl, stir together the red chile powder, turmeric, and lemon juice. Season to taste with salt and mix well.
2. Add the eggplant slices, toss to combine, and let marinate for 20–30 minutes.
3. In a deep skillet over medium-high heat, heat the vegetable oil for frying.
4. Place the poppy seeds in a shallow dish. Coat the eggplant slices in the poppy seeds and fry in hot oil until golden on both sides and cooked through.

## PARWAL CHOKHA

This mushed vegetable dish is truly comforting.

| Cooking time: 20 minutes | Serves: 2 | Origin: Bihar |
| --- | --- | --- |

INGREDIENTS

½ cup (120 g) peeled pointed gourd (*parwal*; available at Indian markets)
1 tsp mustard seed oil (page 26)
1 Tbsp (15 g ) minced garlic (*lasan*)
1 green chile, finely chopped
Salt, to taste

METHOD

1. Fill a small pot with water and bring to a boil over high heat.
2. Add the pointed gourd and cook until soft. Drain, transfer to a small bowl, and mash with a potato masher. Set aside.
3. In a small skillet over low-medium heat, heat the mustard seed oil.
4. Add the garlic and green chile. Cook until fragrant. Stir in the mashed parwal and finish with salt to taste.
5. Serve hot.

## PARIBA GHANTA 📷

A rich, typical vegetable curry.

| Cooking time: 30 minutes | Serves: 2 | Origin: Odisha |
| --- | --- | --- |

INGREDIENTS

2 tsp cumin seeds (*jeera*)
2 Tbsp (18 g) cashews (*kaju*)
1 Tbsp (15 ml) vegetable oil
1 head cauliflower (*phool gobhi*), chopped
1 carrot (*gajar*), diced
1 medium-size potato, cubed
1 medium-size tomato, chopped
¼ cup (40 g) green peas (*hara mattar*), boiled
1 Tbsp (11 g) Panch Phoran spice mix (available at Indian markets and online; page 32)
1 medium-size onion, chopped
1 Tbsp (15 g) ginger-garlic paste (*adrak-lasan*)
1 Tbsp (8 g) red chile powder
1 cup (240 ml) water
Salt, to taste
¼ cup (4 g) fresh cilantro leaves (hara dhaniya), finely chopped

METHOD

1. In a blender, blitz the cumin seeds and cashews. Set aside.
2. In a skillet over medium heat, heat the vegetable oil.
3. Add the cauliflower, carrot, potato, tomato, and peas. Fry until they are semi-cooked.
4. Add the Panch Phoran, onion, ginger-garlic paste, red chile powder, cashew nut–cumin powder, and water. Reduce the heat to low and cook for 6–7 minutes until the vegetables are cooked. Season to taste with salt.
5. Finish with the cilantro and serve hot.

# RUGRA KI SUBZI

An indigenous mushroom in a tomato curry.

Cooking time: 30 minutes | Serves: 2 — Origin: Jharkhand

## INGREDIENTS

1 Tbsp (15 ml) vegetable oil
1 cup (96 g) rugra mushrooms or button
   mushrooms
1 Tbsp (15 g) whole spice mix (page 22)
1 medium-size onion, finely chopped
1 Tbsp (15 g) ginger-garlic paste (*adrak-lasan*)
1 green chile, finely chopped
1 tsp red chile powder
1 tsp ground cumin (*jeera*)
1 tsp ground turmeric (*haldi*)
1 Tbsp (6 g) ground coriander (*dhaniya*)
½ cup (120 g) tomato paste
Salt, to taste
Juice of 1 lemon (*nimbu*)
¼ cup (4 g) fresh cilantro leaves (*hara dhaniya*),
   finely chopped

## METHOD

1. In a skillet over medium heat, heat the vegetable oil.
2. Add the mushrooms. Fry until deep brown in color. Transfer to a plate, leaving 1 tsp of oil in the skillet.
3. Return the skillet to the heat and add the whole spice mix and onion. Sauté until golden.
4. Stir in the ginger-garlic paste, green chile, red chile powder, cumin, turmeric, and coriander. Cook until fragrant.
5. Add the tomato paste and season to taste with salt. Simmer the gravy for 10 minutes.
6. Add the mushrooms and stir well to combine. Cook for 5–7 minutes. Finish with the lemon juice and cilantro.

# SIMBA RAI

Fleshy broad beans with mustard seeds.

Cooking time: 30 minutes | Serves: 2 — Origin: Odisha

## INGREDIENTS

1½ tsp cumin seeds (*jeera*)
1 tsp mustard seeds (*rai*)
2 dried red chiles (*sookhi lal mirch*)
3 garlic cloves (*lasan*), peeled
1 Tbsp (15 ml) mustard seed oil (page 26 )
1 cup (126 g) broad (fava) beans (*simba*), boiled
¼ cup (60 g) finely chopped tomato
1 tsp ground turmeric (*haldi*)
1 cup (240 ml) water
Salt, to taste

## METHOD

1. In a food processor, combine the cumin seeds, mustard seeds, dried red chiles, and garlic. Blend into a paste. In a skillet over medium heat, heat the mustard seed oil.
2. Add the spice paste. Cook until fragrant.
3. Stir in the broad beans, tomato, and turmeric. Sauté for 5 minutes.
4. Add the water.
5. Cook the simba rai for 10 minutes. Season to taste with salt. Serve hot.

# RICE AND BREADS

# CHILKA ROTI

Healthy pancake made of rice and lentil.

Cooking time: 30 minutes | Makes: 7-8       Origin: Jharkhand

## INGREDIENTS

1 cup (200 g) Bengal gram (split chickpeas; *chana dal*), soaked in water for 2 hours, drained
1 cup (200 g) rice, soaked in water for 2 hours, drained
Salt, to taste
Water, as needed
1 tsp vegetable oil

## METHOD

1. In a food processor, combine the chickpeas and rice. Grind together into a smooth paste.
2. Season to taste with salt and add a little water to loosen the thick paste into a pancake-like batter.
3. Heat a griddle over low-medium heat. Oil the hot griddle and add a ladleful of batter to it, spreading it evenly in a circular motion.
4. Cook on both the sides until light brown. Repeat with the remaining batter (should make 7–8 pancakes). Serve the chilka roti with mint-cilantro chutney (page 28), if desired.

# DHUSKA WITH GREEN PEAS AND SPRING ONION

A variation of the simple dhuska.

Cooking time: 30 minutes | Makes: 10-15       Origin: Jharkhand

## INGREDIENTS

2 cup (400 g) basmati rice
1 cup (200 g) Bengal gram (split chickpeas; *chana dal*), soaked in water for 2 hours, drained
2 green chiles, finely chopped
1 Tbsp (15 g) finely chopped garlic (*lasan*)
½ cup (120 ml) water
1 tsp ground turmeric (*haldi*)
4 curry leaves (*kadhi patta*)
¼ cup (4 g) fresh cilantro leaves (*hara dhaniya*), finely chopped
1 medium-size onion, finely chopped
Salt, to taste
2 Tbsp (30 ml) vegetable oil

## METHOD

1. In a food processor, combine the rice, chickpeas, green chiles, garlic, and water. Process into a thick paste.
2. Add the turmeric, curry leaves, cilantro, and onion. Season to taste with salt. Pulse to combine.
3. Heat a griddle over low-medium heat. Oil the hot griddle and add a ladleful of batter to it, spreading it evenly in a circular motion.
4. This has to be cooked like a mini dosa.

## RAGI AND SPRING ONION ROTIS

Millet bread with pepper and spring onions.

Cooking time: 30 minutes | Makes: 5            Origin: Bihar

INGREDIENTS

1 cup (120 g) finger millet flour (*ragi*)
5 Tbsp (75 g) ghee
2 Tbsp (7.5 g) sliced spring onion (*hara pyaz*)
1 tsp black sesame seeds
Salt, to taste
Freshly ground black pepper (*kali mirch*), to taste
Water, for kneading

METHOD

1. In a medium-size bowl, combine the flour, ghee, spring onion, and black sesame seeds. Season to taste with salt and pepper.
2. Add enough water to be able to mix all the ingredients into a tight dough.
3. Cut the dough into 5 small roundels.
4. Wet your palms and lightly pat the dough with your fingertips. Roll it with a rolling pin.
5. Heat a griddle over low-medium heat.
6. Cook the rotis on both sides until light brown and serve hot.

· · · · · · · · · · · · ·

## MARUA ROTI

Finger millet rotis, rich in calcium and protein.

Cooking time: 30 minutes | Makes: 4            Origin: Jharkhand

INGREDIENTS

¼ cup (180 ml) water
½ cup (60 g) finger millet flour (*ragi*)
3 Tbsp (45 g) ghee

METHOD

1. In a saucepan over medium heat, heat the water. Once it becomes warm, add the millet flour. Stir well to incorporate until all the water is absorbed by the flour.
2. Knead it into a tight dough.
3. Cut the dough into 4 small roundels and roll each into chapattis (page 33).
4. Heat a griddle over medium-high heat.
5. Cook the chapattis on the hot griddle on both sides. Finish with the ghee. Serve hot.

## LUCHI 📷

Deep-fried, all-purpose flour flatbread.

Cooking time: 30 minutes | Makes: 10            Origin: West Bengal

INGREDIENTS

2 cups (250 g) all-purpose flour (*maida*)
1 tsp salt
3 Tbsp (45 g) ghee
Water, for kneading
Vegetable oil, for frying

METHOD

1. Into a medium-size bowl, sift the flour with the salt.
2. Add the ghee and use your fingertips to rub it into the flour. Add enough water to knead the mixture into a tight dough.
3. Cover with a wet kitchen cloth and let rest for 15–20 minutes.
4. Cut the dough into 10 small balls and roll each into puris.
5. In a deep skillet over medium-high heat, heat the vegetable oil for frying
6. Add the puris and deep-fry until golden. Serve hot.

## SATTU PARATHA

A flatbread made with the superfood *sattu*.

Cooking time: 30 minutes | Makes: 6 | Origin: Bihar

INGREDIENTS

1 cup (120 g) *sattu* (available at Indian markets)
1 Tbsp (15 g) ginger-garlic paste (*adrak-lasan*)
1 green chile, finely chopped
1 Tbsp (1 g) fresh cilantro leaves (*hara dhaniya*),
    finely chopped
Juice of 1 lemon (*nimbu*)
1 tsp carom seeds (*ajwain*)
1 tsp dried mango powder (*amchoor*)
1 tsp mustard seed oil (page 26)
Salt, to taste
1 cup (125 g) whole-wheat flour (*atta*) dough
    (page 33)
Ghee, for frying

METHOD

1. In a medium-size bowl, combine the *sattu*,
   ginger-garlic paste, green chile, cilantro, lemon
   juice, carom seeds, dried mango powder, and
   mustard seed oil. Season to taste with salt.
   Stir well to combine. You may need 1–2 Tbsp
   (15–30 ml) of water to make it slightly moist.
2. Cut the dough into 6 table tennis-ball size balls
   and flatten each with your palms. Fill each with
   the *sattu* mixture and mold again into a ball.
   Flatten and roll into stuffed parathas (looks like
   a stuffed quesadilla).
3. In a skillet over medium-high heat, heat the
   ghee for frying.
4. Carefully add the stuffed parathas to the hot
   oil and shallow-fry both sides until golden.
   Serve hot.

## BIHARI KHICHDI

One-pot medley of rice, lentils, and vegetables.

Cooking time: 40 minutes | Serves: 2 | Origin: Bihar

INGREDIENTS

2 Tbsp (30 g) ghee
1 dried red chile (*sookhi lal mirch*)
1 bay leaf (*tej patta*)
2 tsp ground coriander (*dhaniya*)
1 tsp red chile powder
1 tsp ground turmeric (*haldi*)
1 tsp cumin seeds (*jeera*)
1 cup (200 g) rice, soaked in water for 2 hours,
    drained
½ cup (100 g) green gram (*moong dal*), soaked in
    water for 2 hours, drained
½ cup (100 g) split red lentils (*masoor dal*), soaked
    in water for 2 hours, drained
2½ cups (600 ml) water
1 cup (150 g) chopped mixed vegetables
1 Tbsp (6 g) garam masala
Salt, to taste

METHOD

1. On your pressure cooker, select Sauté and
   preheat the cooking pot.
2. Add the ghee to melt.
3. Add the dried red chile, bay leaf, coriander, red
   chile powder, turmeric, and cumin seeds. Stir
   well to combine.
4. Add the rice, green gram, red lentils, and water.
   Let the water bubble.
5. Add the vegetables. Lock the lid in place and
   close the pressure release valve. Select Manual/
   Pressure Cook and cook for 9 minutes. Release
   the pressure, remove the lid, and finish with the
   garam masala and salt to taste. Serve hot.

DESSERTS

## BHAPA DOI

Steamed yogurt rice pudding.

Cooking time: 40 minutes | Serves: 2     Origin: West Bengal

### INGREDIENTS

1 cup (240 g) hung curd (*dahi*; page 28)
¾ cup (225 g) sweetened condensed milk
Pinch ground cardamom
1 cup (240 ml) milk
¼ cup (36.25 g) almonds (*badam*), blanched,
    peeled, and sliced
½ cup (72.5 g) strawberries, halved

### METHOD

1. In a medium-size bowl, whisk the hung curd with the condensed milk.
2. Add the cardamom and gradually add the milk while continuing to whisk.
3. Pour the mixture into 2 ramekins and top each with the almonds.
4. Place a rack into a steamer and add 1 cup (240 ml) water (or the quantity in your steamer's user's manual). Add the ramekins. Steam for 20–25 minutes.
5. Remove and refrigerate for 4–5 hours. Garnish with the strawberries and serve cold.

## PATISHAPTA

Milky pancakes with sweetened coconut filling.

Cooking time: 30 minutes | Makes: 6     Origin: West Bengal

### INGREDIENTS

For the batter
½ cup (62.5 g) all-purpose flour (*maida*)
¼ cup (42 g) semolina (*suji*)
2 Tbsp (20 g) rice flour
1 Tbsp (12.5 g) caster (superfine) sugar
Pinch baking soda
Milk, for diluting
4–5 Tbsp (60–75 g) ghee
For the filling
1 cup (240 g) whole-milk fudge (*khoya*; available at Indian markets; page 25)
¾ cup (120 g) coconut powder (*nariyal*)
½ cup (100 g) sugar
Pinch ground cardamom
1 tsp saffron threads (*kesar*)

### METHOD

1. **To make the batter:** In a medium-size bowl, combine all the dry batter ingredients. Whisk in enough milk to form a pancake-like batter. Set aside for 30 minutes.
2. **To make the filling:** In a skillet over low heat, heat the whole-milk fudge.
3. Add the remaining filling ingredients. Mix well until the whole-milk fudge begins to cook, about 10 minutes.
4. **To finish the patishapta:** In another skillet over medium heat, heat the ghee.
5. Pour in a ladleful of batter. Cook the pancake on both sides until golden and transfer to a plate. Repeat with the remaining batter.
6. Stuff the pancakes with the filling and serve warm.

## SANDESH

Classic Bengali dessert made with milk.

Cooking time: 35 minutes | Makes: 10 pieces Origin: West Bengal

INGREDIENTS

4 cups (960 ml) milk
Juice of 2 lemons (*nimbu*)
¼ cup (50 g) caster (superfine) sugar
Pinch ground cardamom
1 Tbsp (8 g) chopped pistachios

METHOD

1. In a saucepan over medium heat, heat the milk and add the lemon juice. Allow the milk to curdle. Remove from the heat and strain out the *chhena* (curds).
2. Transfer the *chhena* to a plate and knead it well with the heel of your hand.
3. Add the caster sugar and cardamom. Knead for 2 minutes, mixing all the ingredients well. Transfer to a saucepan and place it over low heat.
4. Cook the *chhena* mixture for 7–8 minutes, stirring the mixture well until it comes together. Remove from the heat and cool.
5. Roll the mixture into 10 small coin-size balls. Make a dent on top of each ball and insert the chopped pistachio pieces. Serve at room temperature.

## DADHAURI

Deep-fried milky rice balls.

Cooking time: 1 hour | Makes: 6-7　　　Origin: Jharkhand

INGREDIENTS

4 cups (960 ml) milk
1½ cups (300 g) sugar
1 cup (200 g) rice
Vegetable oil, for frying
2 cups (480 ml) sugar syrup (page 30)
Pinch ground cardamom

METHOD

1. In a saucepan over medium heat, combine the milk and sugar and let it warm.
2. Add the rice. Cook until the milk thickens and is reduced by half.
3. Remove from the heat and let sit to thicken. Roll palm-size amounts of the mixture into small balls.
4. In a deep skillet over low-medium heat, heat the vegetable oil for frying.
5. Carefully add the balls to the hot oil and deep-fry until golden.
6. Dip them in sugar syrup and sprinkle with cardamom. Serve hot.

## DHAKKAN DABBA

A thick pancake doused in a milky emulsion.

Cooking time: 1 hour | Serves: 2      Origin: Jharkhand

### INGREDIENTS

4 cups (960 ml) milk
Pinch ground cardamom
½ cup (100 g) sugar
½ cup (100 g) rice, soaked in water for 4 hours, drained
¼ cup (50 g) Bengal gram (split chickpeas; *chana dal*), soaked in water for 4 hours, drained
2 heaping Tbsp (30 g) split black lentils (*urad dal*), soaked in water for 4 hours, drained

### METHOD

1. In a saucepan over medium heat, bring the milk to a boil.
2. Stir in the cardamom and sugar. Reduce the heat to low and simmer for 30–40 minutes to thicken. Transfer the milk into a dabba and set aside.
3. In a blender or food processor, combine the rice, chickpeas, and black lentils. Grind into a thick batter.
4. Place a griddle over low-medium heat.
5. Pour the batter onto the hot griddle and cook for 3–4 minutes on each side.
6. Place the pancake in the lid of the dabba and pour the milk mixture on top. Let soak for 4–5 hours in the refrigerator and serve. You can also do this on a plate.

## BUNIYA

Fried chickpea granules in sugar syrup.

Cooking time: 1 hour | Serves: 2      Origin: Jharkhand

### INGREDIENTS

1 cup (125 g) chickpea flour (*besan*)
1 Tbsp (11 g) semolina (*suji*)
1 tsp saffron threads (*kesar*)
¾ cup (180 ml) water
Vegetable oil, for frying and blending
1 cup (240 ml) sugar syrup (page 30), warmed slightly
1 tsp ground cardamom (*choti elaichi*)

### METHOD

1. In a medium-size bowl, combine the chickpea flour, semolina, and saffron threads. Gradually add the water, stirring continuously, so no lumps form.
2. Stir in in 1 tsp of vegetable oil. Set aside.
3. In a deep skillet over medium-high heat, heat the vegetable oil for frying. Hold a skimmer 2 in. (5-cm) above the skillet and pour the batter through it. The batter will start dropping through the holes and will begin to fry.
4. When the granules turn golden, remove them from the oil and add them to the slightly warm sugar syrup. Repeat until all the batter is fried.
5. Stir in the cardamom. Let the fried granules soak in the syrup for a few minutes. Drain and allow it to come to room temperature.

# KANIKA

A popular spice-infused rice dessert.

Cooking time: 40 minutes | Serves: 2          Origin: Odisha

INGREDIENTS

1 cup (200 g) Gobindobhog rice, soaked in water
   for 1 hour, drained, and air-dried for 20 minutes
3 Tbsp (45 g) ghee, divided
½ tsp ground turmeric (*haldi*)
¼ cup (60 g) cashew paste (*kaju*)
1 Tbsp (9 g) raisins (*kishmish*)
1 tsp whole spice mix (page 22)
2 cups (480 ml) water
Salt, to taste
3 Tbsp (37.5 g) sugar

METHOD

1. In a small bowl, combine the rice, 1½ Tbsp
   (22.5 g) of ghee, and the turmeric.
2. In a skillet over medium heat, heat the
   remaining 1½ Tbsp (22.5 g) of ghee.
3. Add the cashew paste and raisins. Fry until
   fragrant. Transfer to another small bowl.
4. Return the skillet to the heat and add the whole
   spice mix. Cook until the seeds begin to crackle.
5. Add the rice and water. Season to taste with salt.
   Cook for 10–15 minutes, until the rice is
   parboiled.
6. Stir in the sugar and raisin-cashew paste. Cook
   until the rice is done. Serve hot.

# KHIRA GAINTHA

Milk and rice flour dough porridge.

Cooking time: 40 minutes | Serves: 2          Origin: Odisha

INGREDIENTS

1 cup (200 g) rice, soaked in water for 4 hours,
   drained
½ cup (100 g) sugar, divided
Pinch salt
3 Tbsp (45 g) ghee
4 cups (960 ml) milk
¼ cup (21.25 g) chopped fresh coconut (*nariyal*)
½ tsp ground cardamom

METHOD

1. In a food processor, blend the rice into a thick
   paste. Measure the amount of paste you have.
2. In a saucepan over high heat, fill with water
   equal to the amount of rice paste.
3. Add ¼ cup (50 g) of sugar and the salt. Bring to
   a boil.
4. Reduce the heat to low and stir in the rice paste.
   Cook, stirring, until the mixture comes together
   into a dough.
5. Remove from the heat and cool to room
   temperature.
6. Add the ghee and knead into a soft dough.
7. In a clean saucepan over low-medium heat,
   combine the milk, remaining ¼ cup (50 g) of
   sugar, the coconut, and cardamom. Stir well to
   combine.
8. Make 8 small balls out of the rice flour dough
   and plonk them in the milk mixture. Bring to a
   rolling boil. This should take 10–15 minutes.
   Once the balls firm up, serve warm with the
   milk.

# RASA BALI

Milk-based dessert—a hallmark of temple cuisine across India.

Cooking time: 40 minutes | Makes: 5-6        Origin: Odisha

## INGREDIENTS

1 cup (225 g) cottage cheese (*chhena*)
1 cup (200 g) caster (superfine) sugar, divided
1 Tbsp (8 g) all-purpose flour (*maida*)
1 tsp semolina (*suji*)
½ tsp baking powder
Pinch ground cardamom
Vegetable oil, for deep-frying
4 cups (960 ml) milk
1 tsp saffron threads (*kesar*)

## METHOD

1. In a bowl, combine the cottage cheese, 3 Tbsp (37.5 g) of sugar, the flour, semolina, baking powder, and cardamom. Mash the mixture thoroughly and make 8 table tennis ball-size balls out of the dough.
2. Flatten the balls with your palm.
3. In a deep skillet over medium-high heat, heat the vegetable oil for frying.
4. Carefully add the dough balls to the hot oil and deep-fry until golden.
5. In a saucepan over low heat, bring the milk to a rolling boil.
6. Stir in the remaining sugar and the saffron threads. Add the fried balls to the milk and simmer for 2–3 minutes. Cool and serve.

# SARAPULI

A caradamom syrup–drenched cream pancake.

Cooking time: 1 hour | Makes: 12-15        Origin: Odisha

## INGREDIENTS

4 cups (960 ml) milk
Pinch ground cardamom
2 Tbsp (16 g) all-purpose flour (*maida*)
¼ cup (75 g) sweetened condensed milk
Ghee, for frying
1 cup (240 ml) water
½ cup (100 g) sugar

## METHOD

1. In a saucepan over medium heat, bring the milk to a boil and let it bubble for 20 minutes.
2. Once a layer of cream starts forming on top, skim it from the top into a bowl and set aside. Continue to do this until you have 1 cup (240 ml) of milk cream.
3. Remove the leftover milk from the heat and whisk in the cardamom, flour, milk cream, and sweetened condensed milk.
4. Whisk well so no lumps remain. It should resemble pancake batter.
5. In a skillet over medium heat, heat the ghee.
6. Drop pancake-size portions of batter into the skillet. Cook on both sides until done.
7. In another saucepan over medium heat, mix the water with the sugar and cook to form a syrup.
8. Dip the pancakes in the sugar syrup for 2 minutes and serve warm.

# BALUSHAHI

Simply described, India's glazed doughnut.

Cooking time: 1 hour | Makes: 8          Origin: Bihar

INGREDIENTS

1 cup (125 g) all-purpose flour (*maida*)
¼ cup (60 g) ghee, plus more for deep-frying
¾ cup (180 ml) water
1 tsp baking powder
Pinch salt
2 cups (480 ml) sugar syrup (page 30)
Pinch saffron threads (*kesar*)
Pinch ground cardamom
¼ cup (31 g) pistachios, sliced

METHOD

1. In a medium-size bowl, combine the flour and ghee. Rub together with your fingertips until the mixture resembles bread crumbs.
2. Add the water, baking powder, and salt. Knead into a medium-soft dough.
3. Cut the dough into 8 coin-size pieces and roll each into a circle. Flatten slightly with your palm.
4. In a deep skillet over medium heat, heat the ghee for deep-frying.
5. Carefully add the dough balls to the hot ghee and deep-fry until golden.
6. In a small saucepan over low heat, slightly warm the sugar syrup.
7. Stir in the saffron threads and cardamom. Remove from the heat.
8. Soak the balushahi in the warm syrup for 1 hour. Drain. Garnish with pistachio slices and serve.

# CHHENA PODA 📷

Fresh paneer-based sweet dish.

Cooking time: 40 minutes | Serves: 2          Origin: Odisha

INGREDIENTS

1 Tbsp (15 g) ghee, plus more for preparing the ramekins
1 Tbsp (9 g) cashews (*kaju*)
1½ cups (360 g) paneer (page 28)
3 Tbsp (31.5 g) semolina (*suji*)
Pinch ground cardamom
½ cup (100 g) sugar, plus more for the ramekins

METHOD

1. Preheat the oven to 350°F (180°C).
2. In a skillet over medium heat, heat the ghee.
3. Add the cashews. Fry until golden brown.
4. In a small bowl, mix the paneer with the semolina and cardamom.
5. Add the sugar and cashews. Knead again.
6. Grease 2 individual-size ramekins or 1 larger ramekin and coat with sugar. Place on a baking sheet and into the oven to heat for 15 minutes.
7. Spoon the paneer mixture in the ramekins and press it with the back of a spoon to even the surface.
8. Bake for 20–25 minutes and serve warm.

## GULGULE PUA

Traditional sweet jaggery dumplings.

Cooking time: 1 hour 30 minutes | Serves: 2     Origin: Bihar

INGREDIENTS

1 cup (240 ml) milk
½ cup (100 g) sugar
1 cup (125 g) whole-wheat flour (*atta*)
¼ cup (42.5 g) semolina (*suji*)
1 Tbsp (9 g) poppy seeds (*khus khus*)
Ghee, for frying

METHOD

1. In a small sauce pan over low heat, heat the milk and sugar until the sugar dissolves. Remove from the heat.
2. Add the flour and semolina. Stir until it turns into a thick batter.
3. With a handheld electric mixer, mix until slightly airy.
4. Add poppy seeds and mix once again. Let ferment for 1 hour.
5. In a skillet over low-medium heat, heat the ghee.
6. Pour a ladleful of batter into the ghee—do not stir or touch it. Allow the pancake-like pua to cook for 2–3 minutes, flip and cook the other side.
7. Once it turns golden-brown, remove. Repeat with the remaining batter. Serve hot.

## DAHI CHURA

Your very own Indian yogurt parfait.

Cooking time: 10 minutes | Serves: 2     Origin: Bihar

INGREDIENTS

½ cup (100 g) flattened rice (*poha/chura*)
¼ cup (60 ml) milk
1 cup (240 g) yogurt (*dahi*)
½ cup (120 g) assorted diced fruits, dried or fresh
Honey, to taste

METHOD

1. In a small bowl, combine the rice and milk. Soak for 25 minutes.
2. Add the yogurt, fruit, and honey. Mix well to combine and serve immediately.

# ACCOMPANIMENTS

## AMER ACHAR
Tart raw mango pickled in mustard oil.

Cooking time: 30 minutes | Makes: 700 grams
Origin: West Bengal

INGREDIENTS

2 cups (330 g) sliced raw mango (*kairi*)
1 tsp ground turmeric (*haldi*)
Salt, to taste
1 tsp fenugreek seeds (*methi dana*)
1 tsp fennel seeds (*saunf*)
5 Tbsp (75 ml) mustard seed oil (page 26)
3 dried red chiles (*sookhi lal mirch*)
1 cup (336 g) grated jaggery (*gur*; unrefined
  cane sugar)
½ cup (100 g) sugar

METHOD

1. Fill a small saucepan with water and place it
   over high heat. Bring to a boil, add the mango
   slices, and parboil.
2. Drain and allow the slices to dry thoroughly.
3. Sprinkle the mango with turmeric and season
   to taste with salt. Thoroughly rub the spices
   into the mango.
4. In a skillet over low-medium heat, dry-roast the
   fenugreek seeds and fennel seeds. Transfer to a
   spice grinder or mortar and pestle. Let cool.
   Grind into a fine powder.
5. Return the skillet to medium heat, and heat the
   mustard seed oil.
6. Add the mango slices. Shallow-fry for 5 minutes,
   until the mango slices appear cooked. Remove
   with a slotted spoon and set aside.
7. Return the skillet to the heat and add the dried
   red chiles, jaggery, and sugar to the leftover
   mustard seed oil. Cook until the jaggery and
   sugar have melted thoroughly.
8. Add the mango slices along with the fennel-
   fenugreek powder. Cook, stirring, for 10 minutes.
9. Finish with salt and take the pickles off the
   heat.
10. Spread the pickles on a wide-rimmed plate and
    expose it to sunlight for 4–5 days, covered with
    cheesecloth.
11. Store in a sterilized jar at room temperature.

## BEL SHERBET
Wood apple–infused refreshing drink.

Cooking time: 20 minutes | Serves: 2          Origin: Bihar

INGREDIENTS

2 wood apples (*bael*)
3 Tbsp (45 g) organic powdered jaggery (*gur*;
  unrefined cane sugar)
1 tsp Himalayan pink salt
1 tsp ground cumin (*jeera*)
2 cups (480 ml) water

METHOD

1. Break open the wood apples and scoop out the
   pulp. Run it through a fine-mesh sieve and
   discard all the seeds. Transfer to a small bowl.
2. Add the jaggery, pink salt, cumin, and water.
   Stir well to combine. Refrigerate for 2–3 hours
   and serve.

## BENGALI AAM SHOTTOR CHUTNEY

Tomato, date, and mango chutney.

Cooking time: 20 minutes | Makes: 400 grams
Origin: West Bengal

### INGREDIENTS

1 Tbsp (15 ml) vegetable oil
1 tsp Panch Phoran spice mix (available at Indian markets and online; page 32)
2 fresh red chiles, finely chopped
1 cup (240 g) chopped tomato
2 Tbsp (30 g) finely chopped mango fruit leather (*aam shottor*)
2 Tbsp (22.5 g) finely chopped dates
1 Tbsp (9 g) raisins (*kishmish*), finely chopped
1 tsp ground turmeric (*haldi*)
2 Tbsp (30 ml) water
Salt, to taste

### METHOD

1. In a saucepan over low-medium heat, heat the vegetable oil.
2. Add the Panch Phoran. Cook until the seeds begin to crackle.
3. Add the red chiles. Sauté for 2 minutes.
4. Add the tomato. Cook for 2–3 minutes.
5. Stir in the fruit leather, dates, raisins, turmeric, and water.
6. Cook the chutney until the tomato is cooked thoroughly, the dates and raisins have softened, and the water has evaporated.
7. Finish with salt to taste. Cool to room temperature before serving.

## BENGALI-STYLE TOMATO CHUTNEY 🔔

Sweet tomato chutney.

Cooking time: 20 minutes | Makes: 300 grams
Origin: West Bengal

### INGREDIENTS

1 Tbsp (15 ml) mustard seed oil (page 26)
1 tsp Panch Phoran spice mix (available at Indian markets and online; page 32)
1½ tsp minced peeled fresh ginger
1 cup (240 g) chopped tomato
1 Tbsp (12.5 g) sugar
Salt, to taste
1 tsp red pepper flakes

### METHOD

1. In a skillet over medium-high heat, heat the mustard seed oil.
2. Add the Panch Phoran. Cook until the seeds begin to crackle.
3. Add the ginger. Sauté for 2 minutes.
4. Stir in the tomato and sugar. Season to taste with salt. Cook until the tomato softens, mashing slightly with the back of your spoon. Reduce the heat to low, stir, and cook the chutney for 4–5 minutes until the tomato is cooked well and the moisture evaporates.
5. Add red pepper flakes and mix well. Serve at room temperature.

## MAKHANE KA RAITA

An easy accompaniment of yogurt with foxnut.

Cooking time: 10 minutes | Serves: 2          Origin: Bihar

INGREDIENTS

1 cup (240 g) yogurt (*dahi*)
½ cup (120 g) roasted, puffed lotus seeds
    (*makhana;* available at Indian markets)
1 tsp red chile powder
1 tsp ground cumin (*jeera*)
Pinch garam masala
Pinch chaat masala
¼ cup (4 g) fresh cilantro leaves (*hara dhaniya*),
    finely chopped
Salt, to taste

METHOD

1.  In a small bowl, combine the yogurt, lotus
    seeds, spices, and cilantro. Season to taste with
    salt. Stir to combine and refrigerate. Serve
    chilled.

## OLE KI CHUTNEY

Mustard-flavored yam chutney.

Cooking time: 10 minutes | Makes: 500 grams
Origin: Jharkhand

INGREDIENTS

3 Tbsp (45 ml) mustard seed oil (page 26)
2 green chiles, finely chopped
Juice of 1 lemon (*nimbu*)
1 Tbsp (15 g) ginger-garlic paste (*adrak-lasan*)
1 tsp yellow mustard seeds (*rai*)
1 tsp red chile powder
½ tsp ground turmeric (*haldi*)
2 cups (400 g) mashed yam
Salt, to taste

METHOD

1.  In a medium-size bowl, stir together the mustard
    seed oil, green chiles, lemon juice, ginger-garlic
    paste, mustard seeds, red chile powder, and
    turmeric.
2.  Add the mashed yam, stir to combine, and
    finish with salt before serving.

# SATTU DALIA

A refreshing and nourishing porridge.

Cooking time: 15 minutes | Serves: 1      Origin: Bihar

## INGREDIENTS

2 Tbsp (30 g) *chana sattu* (available at Indian markets)
1 cup (240 ml) milk
2 Tbsp (25 g) sugar
Dried fruits, for garnish

## METHOD

1. In a small skillet over medium heat, dry-roast the *sattu* until lightly browned. Set aside to cool.
2. In a tall glass, mix the toasted *sattu* with the milk and sugar. Stir it into a thick porridge.
3. Garnish with dried fruits and serve at room temperature.

# NAMKEEN SATTU SHERBET 📷

Lemonade to cure your summer woes.

Cooking time: 10 minutes | Serves: 2      Origin: Jharkhand

## INGREDIENTS

5 Tbsp (37.5 g) *chana sattu* (available at Indian markets)
4 cups (960 ml) water
Juice of 1 lemon (*nimbu*)
1 tsp ground cumin (*jeera*)
1 tsp Indian black salt (*kala namak*)
2 tsp grated mango (*kairi*)

## METHOD

1. In a large bowl, mix all the ingredients well.
2. Fill 2 tall glasses with ice and divide the drink between them.

## PALAKHA BHATAA 📷
Cooling yogurt-rice.

Cooking time: 10 minutes | Serves: 2          Origin: Odisha

INGREDIENTS

1 cup (200 g) rice, cooked
½ cup (120 ml) cold water
½ cup (120 g) yogurt (*dahi*)
2 Tbsp (30 ml) freshly squeezed juice of lemon
  (*nimbu*)
½ tsp minced peeled fresh ginger (*adrak*)
5 curry leaves (*kadhi patta*)
Salt, to taste

METHOD

1.  In a small bowl, combine the rice, cold water, yogurt, lemon juice, ginger, and curry leaf. Season to taste with salt,
2.  Stir well to combine, and serve cold.

## TISI CHUTNEY
Flaxseed chutney.

Cooking time: 15 minutes | Makes: 250 grams          Origin: Bihar

INGREDIENTS

1 cup (168 g) flaxseed
5 dried red chiles (*sookhi lal mirch*)
2 bay leaves (*tej patta*)
2 Tbsp (10 g) coriander seeds (*dhaniya*)
Salt, to taste

METHOD

1.  In a skillet over medium heat, dry-roast the flaxseed until they begin to crackle and are fragrant. Transfer to a bowl and set aside.
2.  Return the skillet to the heat and add the dried red chiles, bay leaves, coriander seeds. Dry-roast until fragrant. Combine with the flaxseed. Let cool.
3.  Transfer the spice mixture to a food processor or mortar and pestle and grind into a paste. Season to taste with salt.
4.  Store at room temperature in an airtight jar.

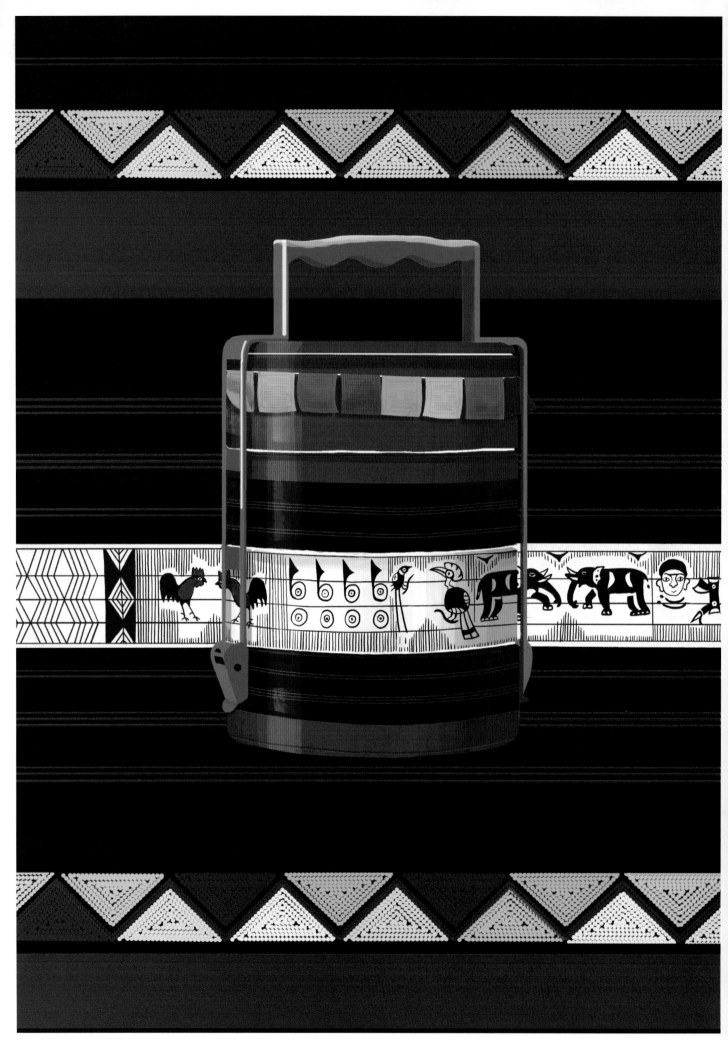

# northeast india

••••

SIKKIM . MEGHALAYA . ARUNACHAL PRADESH .
TRIPURA . NAGALAND . MIZORAM . MANIPUR . ASSAM

Northeast India is an intriguing amalgamation of cultural and tribal influences, which is evident in the culinary traditions of each state comprising this region—Nagaland, Manipur, Tripura, Mizoram, Assam, Arunachal Pradesh, Sikkim, and Meghalaya. Smoked meat, fermented cheeses, pickled treats, and unique foraged vegetables are found in abundance.

The Brahmaputra River, which flows through Assam and Arunachal Pradesh, is loaded with freshwater fish and other seafood, while the Barak, Brahmaputra, and Imphal Valleys provide a variety of greens, beans, shoots, and fungi used for cooking.

A typical meal includes steamed rice, fresh stir-fried and herb-flavored vegetables, minimally spiced fish, meat curries, salads, and lentils.

Sometimes meats and veggies are served plain boiled, without salt, to retain their pure flavors and nutrients. Other times, they are flavored with off-beat spices such as Lakadong turmeric, raja mirchi, prickly ash, dried long pepper, bird's eye chile flakes, and aromatics such as dried yam leaves, lemongrass, red poppy, and darun kesom stalks, giving it a distinct flavor profile.

While the Northeast uses methods such as steaming, blanching, and shallow-frying, its most unique feature is preparing dishes that are cooked inside bamboo barks or charred over charcoal. The cuisine is heavy on non-vegetarian food, though it would be unfair to say that there is not ample vegetarian representation.

This is especially true for Assam, which serves an array of greens, beans, and vegetables. During the traditional festival of Bihu, around 100 different types of vegetarian dishes are cooked using local produce. Assamese cuisine plays with unique ingredients such as brahmi, modhusaleng, fiddlehead ferns, fresh bamboo shoots, akhuni or fermented soy paste, pipoli, and the bhut jolokia chile, which for a time held the title of the world's spiciest chile pepper.

Assam produces an array of crops with a Geographical Identification tag (like cheese from Parma or Roquefort)—for instance, Assamese tea, Karbi Anglong ginger, Tezpur litchi, and joha rice. A short-grain aromatic rice, joha is an important ingredient because of its sweet scent. The heirloom grain is rich in antioxidants and considered to have

comparatively higher nutrition than other varieties of rice.

Geography has played an important role in the character of Northeast Indian cuisine. Since the states are isolated in a corner of the map, their culinary influences have come from neighboring countries instead of within. A number of dishes from Sikkim are largely influenced by Bhutan, with a combination of chiles and cheese, and Nepal, with dishes such as sadeko (a traditional peanut salad), piraloo (a spicy potato-based snack), and chhurpi achar (a pickle made from home-grown cheese found in Nepal). The indigenous Lepcha community of Sikkim have a simpler cuisine than those found in other parts of the region. They enjoy dairy and fresh fruits and vegetables, and rice is the most popular staple.

In this state, the tribals have their unique way of cooking. Take for instance two Bhutia tribes called Bari and Kinema that use unique cooking techniques such as fermenting beans in jute bags, wrapping food in banana leaves, sun-drying ingredients, and adding a small percentage of firewood ash to give the dish a unique flavor.

Meghalaya is known for its pork-laced recipes like jadoh, a pork rice, and dohkhlieh, a pig-meat salad, unique to this region alone. As a meat, pork is popular among the seven states, and especially in Meghalaya, which houses the Khasi, Garo, and Jaintia tribes. These tribes cook meats in a rustic style, with little oil, few spices, and lots of fragrant herbs.

Similar fare can be found in the adjoining state of Tripura, which is known for chakhwi, a light pork porridge, and muya bai wahan, pork-and-bamboo-shoot curry eaten with unprocessed rice.

Tribal gastronomy is evident in these regions and spreads across Arunachal Pradesh too. The beautiful, hilly state houses the Nyshi, Apatani, and Monpa tribes, whose recipes are almost oil- and spice-free. The Nepalese tribe Adi in Mebo, prepare a popular dish called gundruk, a fermented leafy vegetable, that is also one of the national dishes of Nepal. In more urban homes, rice plays an important role in every meal.

The same can be said for Mizo cuisine, which is one of the most well-known cuisines from this region. A must-try here is the typical Mizo dal, which is thick and made with a combination of toor, masoor, and moong lentils. A salad made from a boiled fruit (called chow chow, chayote, or iskut) stands out and is a special feature of the Mizo meal. The same fruit is also savored miles away in northern Vietnam, where it is known as su su xao and served along with sticky rice and a meat curry—just how the Mizos like it.

Further eastward, Nagaland has heavy tribal influences as a result of over a dozen different tribes living in this region. A Naga meal includes rice, some kind of meat (either dry or gravy based), boiled vegetables, and chile sauces for dipping.

Manipuri cuisine is more experimental. It does not shy away from spices and oil. Chakhao amubi, or black rice kheer, is a staple at local weddings and is unique for its stark color. There is also iromba, a popular dish made out of fermented fish, and several vegetarian dishes such as sana thongba (a curry made out of peas and cottage cheese—one of the rare instances where paneer is used) and alu kangmet, fried red chile and potato stir fry.

Food from the Northeast may be underrated, but its uniqueness allows us to savor a whole new variety of Indian cuisine.

# APPETIZERS

# GYATHUK

Hearty noodle soup laced with spices.

Cooking time: 30 minutes | Serves: 2        Origin: Sikkim

## INGREDIENTS

**For the paste**
1 medium-size onion
1 medium-size tomato
5 garlic cloves (*lasan*), peeled
1 (1-in. / 2.5-cm) piece peeled fresh ginger (*adrak*)
1 dried red chile (*sookhi lal mirch*)
Salt, to taste
Freshly ground black pepper (*kali mirch*), to taste
**For the gyathuk**
2 Tbsp (30 ml) vegetable oil
5 cups (1.25 L) vegetable broth
½ cup (80 g) shredded carrot (*gajar*)
½ cup (80 g) shredded cabbage (*bandh gobhi*)
Juice of 1 lemon (*nimbu*)
Salt, to taste
1 cup (175 g) rice noodles, cooked according to the package directions

## METHOD

1. **To make the paste:** In a blender, combine all the paste ingredients. Blitz well to form a paste.
2. **To make the gyathuk:** In a skillet over low-medium heat, heat the vegetable oil.
3. Add the paste. Stir well to combine.
4. Pour in the vegetable broth and let the mixture come just to a boil.
5. Add the carrot, cabbage, and lemon juice. Season to taste with salt.
6. To serve, divide the noodles between two soup bowls. Ladle the hot soup on top. Serve hot.

# OYING

Simple stew made from local vegetables.

Cooking time: 15 minutes | Serves: 2        Origin: Sikkim

## INGREDIENTS

1 tsp vegetable oil
1 Tbsp (15 g) ginger paste (*adrak*)
1 green chile, finely chopped
½ cup (35 g) sliced cabbage (*bandh gobhi*)
½ cup (65 g) sliced carrot (*gajar*)
½ cup (80 g) roughly chopped French green beans (haricots verts)
½ cup (80 g) green peas (*hara mattar*)
½ cup (112.5 g) cubed boiled potato
½ cup (15 g) finely chopped fresh spinach
Salt, to taste
Water, as needed

## METHOD

1. In skillet over medium heat, heat the vegetable oil.
2. Add the ginger paste and green chile. Cook for 1 minute until fragrant.
3. Add the cabbage, carrot, green beans, peas, potato, and spinach. Season to taste with salt and stir well to combine.
4. Cook until the vegetables begin to sweat. Increase the heat to high and continue to stir.
5. Add enough water to the stew to reach your desired consistency. Cook for 3–4 minutes more.
6. Serve hot.

## BEET AND RADISH SALAD 📷

Local salad with a mustard seed oil dressing.

Cooking time: 10 minutes | Serves: 2          Origin: Assam

### INGREDIENTS

**For the dressing**
1 Tbsp (10 g) minced garlic (*lasan*)
1 Tbsp (15 ml) freshly squeezed lemon juice
   (*nimbu*)
1½ tsp mustard seed oil (page 26)
1½ tsp minced peeled fresh ginger (*adrak*)
Salt, to taste
**For the salad**
½ cup (75 g) sliced beet (*chuqandar*)
½ cup (75 g) sliced radish
½ cup (75 g) sliced cucumber
1 medium-size tomato, sliced
½ cup (60 g) shredded fresh spinach
¼ cup (15 g) sliced spring onion (*hara pyaz*)

### METHOD

1. **To make the dressing:** In a small bowl, whisk the garlic, lemon juice, mustard seed oil, and ginger. Season to taste with salt.
2. **To make the salad:** In a large bowl, combine the beet, radish, cucumber, tomato, spinach, and spring onion.
3. Add the dressing and gently toss to coat. Serve immediately.

## KHAPSE

Tibetan-style biscuits.

Cooking time: 40 minutes | Makes: 10–15
Origin: Arunachal Pradesh

### INGREDIENTS

2 cups (250 g) all-purpose flour (*maida*)
¾ cup (180 ml) milk
3 Tbsp (45 ml) vegetable oil or ghee
½ cup (100 g) caster (superfine) sugar
Vegetable oil, for frying

### METHOD

1. In a medium-size bowl, combine the flour, milk, and vegetable oil. Stir to combine.
2. Add the sugar. Knead the mixture into a soft dough.
3. Cut the dough into 7–8 pieces and roll each piece into a large chapatti (flatbread). Cut these into strips and twist the strips.
4. Heat the vegetable oil to fry the prepared khapse.
5. Carefully add 2–3 at a time to the hot oil and fry until golden brown. Transfer to paper towels to drain. Continue with the remaining strips. Serve hot.

## ALUKANGMET
Potato and dried red chile stir-fry.

Cooking time: 15 minutes | Serves: 2     Origin: Manipur

INGREDIENTS

1 tsp mustard seed oil (page 26)
2 dried red chiles (*sookhi lal mirch*)
¼ cup (42.5 g) finely chopped onion
1 medium-size potato, boiled and mashed
Salt, to taste
¼ cup (4 g) fresh cilantro leaves (*hara dhaniya*),
   finely chopped

METHOD

1. In a skillet over low-medium heat, heat the mustard seed oil.
2. Add the red chiles and onion. Sauté until the onion turns golden brown.
3. Add the mashed potato and stir well to combine. Cook until heated through.
4. Season to taste with salt and garnish with cilantro. Serve with hot puris.

## BAMBOO SHOOT AND MUSHROOM STIR-FRY
Spice-coated mushroom and tender shoots stir-fry.

Cooking time: 20 minutes | Serves: 2     Origin: Assam

INGREDIENTS

¾ cup (180 ml) vegetable oil
1 cup (70 g) button mushrooms, chopped
1 spring onion (*hara pyaz*), sliced
1 dried red chile (*sookhi lal mirch*)
1 Tbsp (10 g) minced garlic (*lasan*)
1 tsp red chile powder
1 tsp ground cumin (*jeera*)
1 cup (150 g) tender bamboo shoots, sliced
½ cup (24 g) finely chopped garlic chives
1 Tbsp (15 ml) light soy sauce
1 tsp rice vinegar
Salt, to taste
Freshly ground black pepper (*kali mirch*), to taste

METHOD

1. In a deep skillet or saucepan over low-medium heat, heat the vegetable oil until hot.
2. Add the mushrooms. Deep-fry for 3–4 minutes until golden. Use a slotted spoon to transfer the mushrooms to a dish and set aside.
3. Remove the excess oil from the skillet and add the spring onion, dried red chile, garlic, red chile powder, and cumin. Stir well to combine. Cook for about 3 minutes until the onion softens.
4. Stir in the bamboo shoots and mushrooms. Cook until heated through.
5. Garnish with the garlic chives. Sprinkle with the soy sauce and vinegar.
6. Season to taste with salt and pepper and serve.

## LAU KHAR
Traditional bottle gourd side dish.

Cooking time: 30 minutes | Serves: 2        Origin: Assam

INGREDIENTS

2 cups (480 g) peeled, grated bottle gourd
  (calabash; *lauki*)
2 tsp baking powder
Salt, to taste
1 tsp mustard seed oil (page 26 )
1 tsp mustard seeds (*rai*)
1 tsp fenugreek seeds (*methi dana*)
1 bay leaf (*tej patta*)
1 Tbsp (15 g) ginger-garlic paste (*adrak-lasan*)

METHOD

1. In a small bowl, combine the bottle gourd and baking soda. Season to taste with salt and mix to combine. Transfer to a steamer basket and steam until soft.
2. In a skillet over medium-high heat, heat the mustard seed oil.
3. Add the mustard seeds and fenugreek seeds. Cook until the seeds begin to crackle.
4. Add the bay leaf, ginger-garlic paste, and steamed bottle gourd. Stir-fry until pleasantly brown. Taste and adjust the seasoning as needed.
5. Remove and discard the bay leaf and serve.

## VEGETABLE BAI
Light vegetable stew with bits of meat.

Cooking time: 30 minutes | Serves: 2        Origin: Mizoram

INGREDIENTS

1 tsp vegetable oil
1 bay leaf (*tej patta*)
1 tsp ginger-garlic paste (*adrak-lasan*)
1 green chile, chopped
1 cup (200 g) rice, rinsed
1 cup (240 g) cut mixed vegetables
5 cups (1.25 L) water
Salt, to taste
Freshly ground black pepper (*kali mirch*), to taste

METHOD

1. In a skillet over low-medium heat, heat the vegetable oil.
2. Add the bay leaf, ginger-garlic paste, and green chile. Cook for about 1 minute until fragrant.
3. Add the rice and stir well to combine.
4. Add the vegetables and the water.
5. Cook according to the package directions, or until the rice softens.
6. Remove and discard the bay leaf. Season to taste with salt and pepper and serve hot.

## PEANUT SADEKO
Quick and easy salad.

| Cooking time: 10 minutes | Serves: 2 | Origin: Sikkim |

### INGREDIENTS

1½ cups (300 g) roasted peanuts
½ cup (120 g) finely chopped tomato
¼ cup (4 g) fresh cilantro leaves (*hara dhaniya*), finely chopped
¼ cup (15 g) finely chopped spring onion (*hara pyaz*)
1 tsp red chile powder
1 tsp minced ginger (*adrak*)
1 tsp minced garlic (*lasan*)
1 tsp chaat masala
Juice of 1 lemon (*nimbu*)
Salt, to taste

### METHOD

1. In a small bowl, combine the peanuts, tomato, cilantro, spring onion, red chile powder, ginger, and garlic. Toss to combine.
2. Add the chaat masala and lemon juice, and season to taste with salt. Mix well and serve.

· · · · · · · · · · ·

## PIROALOO
Nepali-influenced Sikkimese potato appetizer.

| Cooking time: 15 minutes | Serves: 2 | Origin: Sikkim |

### INGREDIENTS

1 tsp mustard seed oil (page 26)
1 green chile, finely chopped
1 tsp minced garlic (*lasan*)
1 tsp red chile powder
1 tsp ground turmeric (*haldi*)
1 tsp ground cumin (*jeera*)
1 cup (225 g) parboiled cubed potato
Salt, to taste
¼ cup (4 g) fresh cilantro leaves (*hara dhaniya*), finely chopped

### METHOD

1. In a skillet over low-medium heat, heat the mustard seed oil.
2. Add the green chile, garlic, red chile powder, turmeric, and cumin. Stir to combine. Cook for about 1 minute until fragrant.
3. Add the potato. Cook, stirring, until crispy.
4. Season to taste with salt and garnish with cilantro. Serve hot.

· · · · · · · · · · ·

## SHILLONG ALU MURI
Flavorful teatime snack.

| Cooking time: 15 minutes | Serves: 2 | Origin: Meghalaya |

### INGREDIENTS

1 cup (14 g) puffed rice (*muri*; available at Indian markets)
¼ cup (40 g) sev (available at Indian markets)
¼ cup (50 g) Bengal gram (split chickpeas; *chana dal*)
¼ cup (50 g) roasted peanuts
¼ cup (50 g) mung beans (*moong*)
¼ cup (4 g) fresh cilantro leaves (*hara dhaniya*), finely chopped
¼ cup (56 g) chopped tomato
¼ cup (42.5 g) chopped onion
¼ cup (20 g) shredded tender fresh coconut (*nariyal*)
1 tsp chaat masala
Salt, to taste
Juice of 1 lemon (*nimbu*)
1 Tbsp (15 g) tamarind pulp (*imli*; page 30)
1 tsp mustard seed oil (page 26)

### METHOD

1. In a large bowl, combine the puffed rice, sev, chickpeas, peanuts, mung beans, cilantro, tomato, onion, coconut, and chaat masala. Season to taste with salt.
2. Add the lemon juice, tamarind pulp, and mustard seed oil. Toss well to combine and serve immediately.

# DOHKHLIEH
Popular pork salad.

Cooking time: 20 minutes | Serves: 2      Origin: Meghalaya

INGREDIENTS

1 tsp vegetable oil
2 green chiles
8 oz (225 g) pork, cubed
1 tsp minced peeled fresh ginger (*adrak*)
1 tsp minced garlic (*lasan*)
Salt, to taste
½ cup (85 g) sliced onion

METHOD

1. In a skillet over low-medium heat, heat the vegetable oil.
2. Add the green chiles. Cooking, turning, until they char slightly. Remove from the skillet and cool slightly. Finely chop the chiles and set aside.
3. Return the skillet to the heat and add the pork. Stir-fry for 3–4 minutes until cooked through. Transfer the pork to a serving bowl.
4. Add the chopped green chiles, ginger, and garlic. Season to taste with salt. Stir to combine.
5. Add the onion and serve.

# GAHORILAIHAAK
Pungent and rich pork stew.

Cooking time: 1 hour | Serves: 3      Origin: Assam

INGREDIENTS

12 oz (340 g) cubed pork
2 green chiles, roughly chopped
1 (1-in. / 2.5-cm) piece peeled fresh ginger (*adrak*)
2 cups (480 ml) water
Salt, to taste
1 tsp mustard seed oil (page 26)
4 garlic cloves (*lasan*), minced
½ cup (30 g) sliced spring onion (*hara pyaz*)
2 tsp red chile powder
1 tsp ground turmeric (*haldi*)
¼ cup (15 g) finely chopped fresh spinach
¼ cup (15 g) finely chopped sorrel leaves
¼ cup (15 g) mustard microgreens
¼ cup (4 g) fresh cilantro leaves (*hara dhaniya*), finely chopped

METHOD

1. In your pressure cooker cooking pot, combine the pork, green chiles, and ginger. Add the water and season to taste with salt. Lock the lid in place and close the pressure release valve. Select Manual/Pressure Cook and cook for 10 minutes.
2. Release the pressure and remove the lid. Strain the solids and set aside. Discard the broth.
3. In a skillet over low-medium heat, heat the mustard seed oil.
4. Add the garlic and spring onion. Stir well to combine. Cook for about 1 minute until fragrant.
5. Stir in the red chile powder and turmeric. Sauté further for 1 minute.
6. Add the spinach, sorrel, and microgreens. Cook, stirring, until the leaves begin to wilt.
7. Add the strained pork and continue to cook the gravy for 10 minutes more.
8. Taste and adjust the seasoning as needed. Garnish with cilantro and serve.

POULTRY AND EGGS

# CHICKEN AND BANANA FLOWER STIR-FRY

Flavorful curry served with soft chapattis.

Cooking time: 40 minutes | Serves: 3      Origin: Assam

## INGREDIENTS

9 oz (255 g) boneless, skinless chicken, cubed
1 Tbsp (15 g) ginger-garlic paste (*adrak-lasan*)
Juice of 1 lemon (*nimbu*)
1 Tbsp (15 ml) mustard seed oil (page 26)
1 Tbsp (15 g) whole spice mix (page 22)
1 bay leaf (*tej patta*)
¼ cup (60 g) onion paste
2 green chiles, finely chopped
1 tsp ground turmeric (*haldi*)
1 tsp ground coriander (*dhaniya*)
1 tsp red chile powder
½ cup (85 g) boiled, finely chopped banana flower (*mochar*; available at Indian markets), tough outer layers peeled, florets and stigma pulled out and the transparent petal-like portion discarded, and the florets then boiled for 10 minutes
Salt, to taste

## METHOD

1. In a medium-size bowl, combine the chicken, ginger-garlic paste, and lemon juice. Mix to combine. Refrigerate to marinate for 4 hours.
2. In a skillet over low-medium heat, heat the mustard seed oil.
3. Add the whole spice mix and bay leaf. Cook for 1–2 minutes until fragrant.
4. Add the onion paste and green chiles. Sauté until the paste turns brown.
5. Stir in the turmeric, coriander, and red chile powder.
6. Add the chicken. Sauté for 20–25 minutes, or until the chicken is cooked through.
7. Stir in the boiled banana flower. Cook until heated through. Remove and discard the bay leaf and serve.

# WOH

Fluffy lentil and chicken pancakes.

Cooking time: 1 hour | Makes: 8      Origin: Sikkim

## INGREDIENTS

2 cups (400 g) spilt black lentils (*urad dal*), soaked in water overnight, drained
3½ oz (100 g) boneless, skinless chicken, minced
2 green chiles, chopped
½ cup (8 g) fresh cilantro leaves (*hara dhaniya*), finely chopped
1 Tbsp (15 g) ginger-garlic paste (*adrak-lasan*)
1 tsp ground cumin (*jeera*)
1 tsp red chile powder
Salt, to taste
1 tsp vegetable oil

## METHOD

1. In a blender, blitz the lentils into a smooth paste. Transfer to a large bowl and add the chicken, green chiles, cilantro, ginger-garlic paste, cumin, and red chile powder. Season to taste with salt. Mix to combine and set aside to rest for 20 minutes.
2. In a shallow skillet or griddle over medium heat, heat the vegetable oil.
3. Pour the batter in small portions into the hot skillet. Use a spoon to spread the batter in a circular motion, as if you are making a pancake or crepe. These need to be small circles.
4. Cook until brown on both the sides and serve hot.

# BHUT JOLOKIA CHICKEN 📷

Chicken with the fiery, world famous ghost chile.

| Cooking time: 1 hour \| Serves: 2 | Origin: Nagaland |
|---|---|

## INGREDIENT

4 Tbsp (60 g) ghee, divided

½ Bhut Jolokia chile (ghost pepper), soaked in water for 4 hours, drained

½ cup (85 g) diced onion

4 garlic cloves (*lasan*), minced

1 Tbsp (6 g) minced peeled fresh ginger (*adrak*)

1 cup (240 ml) plus 3 Tbsp (45 ml) water, divided

1 Tbsp (6 g) ground coriander (*dhaniya*)

2 tsp ground cumin (*jeera*)

1 tsp ground turmeric (*haldi*)

¼ cup (62.5 g) tomato purée

8 oz (225 g) boneless, skinless chicken, cubed

Salt, to taste

Juice of 1 lemon (*nimbu*)

½ cup (8 g) fresh cilantro leaves (*hara dhaniya*), finely chopped

Plain cooked rice, for serving

## METHOD

1. In a skillet over low-medium heat, heat 1 Tbsp (15 g) of ghee.
2. Add the Bhut Jolokia chile (ghost pepper; adjust the spice level by reducing or increasing the amount), onion, garlic, and ginger. Stir-fry for 2–3 minutes and transfer to a blender. Add 3 Tbsp (45 ml) of water.
3. Blend it into a smooth paste.
4. In another skillet over medium-high heat, heat the remaining 3 Tbsp (45 g) of ghee.
5. Add the coriander, cumin, turmeric, and tomato purée. Stir well to combine. Stir in the remaining 1 cup (240 ml) of water.
6. Add the Bhut Jolokia (ghost pepper) paste and chicken to the skillet. Season to taste with salt. Reduce the heat.
7. Cover, and cook the curry for 25–30 minutes, or until the chicken pieces are cooked through. Taste and season with more salt if needed. Squeeze the lemon juice over and sprinkle with cilantro. Serve with plain rice.

MEAT AND PORK

## WAK BRENGA 🍲
Pork cooked in bamboo.

Cooking time: 1 hour 30 minutes | Serves: 2   Origin: Meghalaya

INGREDIENTS

1 (2-in. / 5-cm) piece peeled fresh ginger (*adrak*)
1 medium-size onion
10–15 green chiles, chopped
1 lb, 2 oz (500 g) pork, cubed (about 1-in. / 2.5-cm)
  pieces
Salt, to taste
½ tsp baking soda
Edible bamboo
Banana leaves

METHOD

1.  Using a mortar and pestle, roughly crush the ginger, onion, and green chiles.
2.  In a large bowl combine the crushed ginger, onion, and chiles with the meat. Season to taste with salt and add the baking soda. Toss well to combine the mixture.
3.  Stuff the mixture into one section of the bamboo (the open end of the bamboo should ideally be cut at the bottom joint and the bamboo should be of at least 4-in. / 10-cm in diameter). Making sure that the bamboo is not too full, use more than one bamboo if required.
4.  Stuff the bamboo opening with tightly rolled banana leaves so that it is almost airtight.
5.  Place the bamboo in a fire that has plenty of coals/ambers with less flames.
6.  Let the meat cook for a minimum of 45 minutes to 1 hour.
7.  Keep rotating the bamboo so that it does not burn (a little charring on the outside is fine, as long as it does not burn through).
8.  Scrape the burnt outer layer off the bamboo, as the burnt bamboo may fall into the dish while emptying it out.
9.  Empty out the contents of the bamboo into a dish and serve.

## WAK GALDA GISI 🍲
Pork cooked in dry powdered sorrel.

Cooking time: 40 minutes | Serves: 2        Origin: Meghalaya

INGREDIENTS

1 lb, 2 oz (500 g) pork, cubed (about 1-in. / 2.5-cm)
  pieces
Salt, to taste
1 Tbsp (6 g) *galda gisi* (powdered sorrel; available at Indian markets)
5–10 green chiles
Water
5 Tbsp (50 g) rice flour (*pura*)

METHOD

1.  In a skillet over medium-high heat, heat the pork. Season to taste with salt. Cook until the water that comes out of the meat evaporates. (The pork can alternately be cooked in a pressure cooker with salt until the meat is tender.)
2.  Add the *galda gisi* and chiles. Dry-fry the meat for 2–5 minutes.
3.  Add the water and let it simmer until it evaporates completely.
4.  Add more water until the meat is completely submerged. Bring the water to a boil.
5.  Drizzle the rice four, stirring continuously so that it does not form clumps.
6.  Let the rice flour cook and thicken.
7.  Once the flour does not feel grainy the dish is ready to be served.

## BAMBOO AND PORK STIR-FRY 📷

One-pot curry with a bit of sour tang.

Cooking time: 1 hour | Serves: 2     Origin: Assam

### INGREDIENTS

1 Tbsp (15 ml) vegetable oil

2 dried red chiles (*sookhi lal mirch*)

1 Tbsp (15 g) ginger-garlic paste (*adrak-lasan*)

1 lb (454 g) pork, cubed

1 cup (200 g) dried kidney beans (*rajma*), soaked in water overnight, drained

½ cup (85 g) finely chopped tender bamboo shoots

1 Tbsp (15 g) tamarind pulp (*imli*; page 30)

1 tsp ground turmeric (*haldi*)

1 tsp red chile paste

Salt, to taste

4 cups (960 ml) water

### METHOD

1.  On your pressure cooker, select Sauté and preheat the cooking pot.
2.  Add the vegetable oil to heat.
3.  Add the dried red chiles and ginger-garlic paste. Cook for about 1 minute, stirring, until fragrant.
4.  Add the remaining ingredients to the cooking pot. Lock the lid in place and close the pressure release valve. Select Manual/Pressure Cook and cook for 20 minutes.
5.  Release the pressure and remove the lid. Check the beans for doneness. Serve the curry hot.

## CHAKHWI

Pork dish with jackfruit seeds and bamboo shoots.

Cooking time: 45 minutes | Serves: 2     Origin: Tripura

### INGREDIENTS

½ cup (80 g) rice flour

2¼ cups (540 ml) water, divided

2 green chiles, finely chopped

2 tsp grated, peeled fresh ginger (*adrak*)

1 tsp ground turmeric (*haldi*)

½ cup (75 g) jackfruit seeds, peeled and halved

½ cup (85 g) tender bamboo shoots

4 oz (112 g) pork, cubed

½ cup (85 g) finely chopped papaya

Salt, to taste

### METHOD

1.  In a small bowl, stir together the rice flour and ¼ cup (60 ml) of water. Set aside.
2.  In a saucepan over high heat, combine the remaining 2 cups (480 ml) of water, the green chiles, ginger, and turmeric. Bring to a boil. Add the jackfruit seeds and bamboo shoots. Boil for 15–20 minutes, or until the seeds and shoots are tender. Add the pork and papaya to the pan. Reduce the heat to low and cook for 20 minutes more.
3.  Add the rice flour and stir vigorously.
4.  Add more water, as needed, to give it a smooth, slightly drippy consistency. Season to taste with salt and serve hot.

## NAGA-STYLE PORK CURRY 📷

Spicy pork curry best served with steamed rice.

| Cooking time: 1 hour \| Serves: 2 | Origin: Nagaland |
| --- | --- |

### INGREDIENTS

10 dried red chiles (*sookhi lal mirch*), soaked in water for 2 hours, drained
8 ounces (225 g) pork, cubed
¼ cup (42.5 g) finely chopped onion
2 Tbsp (30 g) ginger-garlic paste (*adrak-lasan*)
1 tsp freshly ground black pepper (*kali mirch*)
¼ cup (42.5 g) finely chopped tender bamboo shoots
1 cup (240 ml) water
Salt, to taste

### METHOD

1. In a blender, blend the soaked red chiles into a paste and set aside.
2. On your pressure cooker, select Sauté and preheat the cooking pot.
3. Add the pork and cook for 3 minutes, stirring constantly.
4. Add the onion, ginger-garlic paste, and pepper. Cook, stirring, for 3 minutes more.
5. Add the red chile paste and stir to combine. Add the bamboo shoots. Stir-fry for 3 minutes more.
6. Add the water to the cooking pot. Lock the lid in place and close the pressure release valve. Select Manual/Pressure Cook and cook the pork curry for 10 minutes.
7. Release the pressure and remove the lid. Season to taste with salt, and serve hot.

# FISH AND SEAFOOD

# MANIPURI IROMBA

Shrimp in spicy sauce with mushrooms and spring onions.

Cooking time: 20 minutes | Serves: 2          Origin: Manipur

## INGREDIENTS

1 tsp vegetable oil
1 green chile, finely chopped
1 lb (454 g) shrimp, peeled and deveined
½ cup (30 g) finely chopped spring onion
  (*hara pyaz*)
1 medium-size tomato, finely chopped
1 cup (70 g) chopped button mushrooms
1 medium-size potato, boiled
½ cup (120 ml) water
Salt, to taste

## METHOD

1. In a skillet over low-medium heat, heat the vegetable oil.
2. Add the green chile. Cook for about 2 minutes to soften.
3. Add the shrimp. Stir-fry for 2–4 minutes, depending on the size of your shrimp, or until cooked through. Remove from the pan and set aside.
4. Return the skillet to the heat and add the spring onion, tomato, mushrooms, and potato. Stir well to combine, almost mashing the potato.
5. Stir in the water to make it slightly mushy. Season to taste with salt. Top with the shrimp and serve.

# GRILLED SHRIMP

Indian-style tapa.

Cooking time: 30 minutes | Serves: 2          Origin: Mizoram

## INGREDIENTS

1 lb (454 g) shrimp, peeled and deveined
½ tsp ground turmeric (*haldi*)
Pinch salt
½ cup (120 ml) water
10 peppercorns (*sabut kali mirch*)
2 tsp coriander seeds (*dhaniya*)
1 tsp mustard seed oil (page 26)
Juice of 1 lemon (*nimbu*)

## METHOD

1. In a medium-size bowl, combine the shrimp, turmeric, and salt. Toss to coat. Let sit for 10 minutes.
2. In a medium saucepan over high heat, combine the water, peppercorns, and coriander seeds. Bring to a boil. Reduce to a simmer.
3. Add the shrimp. Simmer for about 3 minutes, or until cooked through. Remove from the water and set aside.
4. In a skillet over medium-high heat, heat the mustard seed oil.
5. Add the cooked shrimp and sauté until slightly charred.
6. Squeeze the lemon juice over and serve.

## NAGA FISH CURRY 📷
Crispy fish-topped curry.

Cooking time: 1 hour | Serves: 3    Origin: Nagaland

### INGREDIENTS

**For the fish marinade**
2 dried red chiles (*sookhi lal mirch*)
Juice of 1 lemon (*nimbu*)
1 Tbsp (15 g) ginger-garlic paste (*adrak-lasan*)
1 tsp ground turmeric (*haldi*)
Salt, to taste
**For the curry**
1 lb (454 g) rohu fish fillet, cubed, or carp or other
   white-fleshed fish (available at some Indian
   markets)
Vegetable oil, for frying
2 Tbsp (15 ml) mustard seed oil (page 26)
2 green chiles, finely chopped
1 medium-size onion, finely chopped
1 Tbsp (15 g) ginger-garlic paste (*adrak-lasan*)
1 medium-size tomato, finely chopped
1 tsp red chile powder
1 tsp ground turmeric (*haldi*)
Salt, to taste
½ cup (120 ml) water

### METHOD

1. **To make the fish marinade:** In a blender, blend
   all the marinade ingredients to combine.
2. **To make the curry:** In a resealable plastic bag,
   combine the marinade and fish. Seal the bag
   and refrigerate to marinate for 2 hours
3. In a skillet over low-medium heat, heat the
   vegetable oil until hot.
4. Remove the fish from the marinade and
   carefully add it to the skillet. Fry the fish for 2–3
   minutes until done. Remove from the oil and
   set aside.
5. In a medium-size saucepan over low-medium
   heat, heat the mustard seed oil.
6. Add the green chiles, onion, and ginger-garlic
   paste. Cook for about 2 minutes until the onion
   softens.
7. Stir in the tomato, red chile powder, and
   turmeric. Taste and season with salt.
8. Stir in the water. Reduce the heat to medium
   and let the curry bubble for 12–15 minutes.
9. Add the fried fish. Cook until heated through
   and serve hot.

## MASORTENGA
Rohu fish curry with spices.

Cooking time: 40 minutes | Serves: 2    Origin: Assam

### INGREDIENTS

5 pieces rohu fish, carp, or other white-fleshed fish
   (available at some Indian markets)
1 tsp ground turmeric (*haldi*)
Salt, to taste
5 Tbsp (75 ml) mustard seed oil, divided
   (page 26)
½ cup (85 g) finely chopped onion
1 green chile, finely chopped
1 Tbsp (15 g) ginger-garlic paste (*adrak-lasan*)
1 Tbsp (6 g) ground coriander (*dhaniya*)
2 tsp ground cumin (*jeera*)
1 tsp red chile powder
1½ cups (335 g) finely chopped tomato
Pinch brown sugar
1 medium-size potato, boiled and mashed
1 cup (240 ml) water
Juice of 1 lemon (*nimbu*)
2 Tbsp (2 g) fresh cilantro leaves (*hara dhaniya*),
   finely chopped

### METHOD

1. Season the fish with the turmeric and salt.
2. In a skillet over low-medium heat, heat 1 Tbsp
   (15 ml) of the mustard seed oil.
3. Add the onion, green chile, ginger-garlic paste,
   coriander, cumin, red chile powder, and tomato.
   Stir well to combine.
4. Cook for 3–5 minutes until the tomato and
   onion soften.
5. Add the brown sugar and mix well.
6. Stir in the mashed potato and water. Let simmer
   while you prepare the fish.
7. In another skillet over low-medium heat, heat
   the remaining 4 Tbsp (60 ml) of mustard seed
   oil. Working in batches, add the fish to the hot
   oil and fry until golden on each side. Transfer
   to the curry mixture and cook for 4–5 minutes
   more.
8. Season to taste with salt and the lemon juice.
   Garnish with cilantro.

VEGETARIAN

## MIZO DAL
Mixed lentil soup spiked with green chiles.

Cooking time: 30 minutes | Serves: 4          Origin: Mizoram

INGREDIENTS

1 tsp vegetable oil
2 tsp ginger-garlic paste (*adrak-lasan*)
1 medium-size onion, finely chopped
2 green chiles, finely chopped
½ cup (100 g) split green gram (*moong dal*)
½ cup (100 g) split pigeon peas (*toor dal*)
½ cup (100 g) split red lentils (*masoor dal*)
1 tsp ground turmeric (*haldi*)
4 cups (960 ml) water
Salt, to taste
Freshly ground black pepper (*kali mirch*), to taste
Cooked rice, for serving

METHOD

1. On your pressure cooker, select Sauté and preheat the cooking pot.
2. Add the vegetable oil, ginger-garlic paste, onion, and green chiles.
3. Stir well to combine. Cook for about 1 minute until fragrant.
4. Add the green gram, pigeon peas, red lentils, turmeric, and water. Lock the lid in place and close the pressure release valve. Select Manual/Pressure Cook and cook for 12 minutes. Release the pressure and remove the lid. Season to taste with salt and pepper. Serve hot with rice.

## ARUNACHAL ZAN
Rustic porridge topped with vegetables.

Cooking time: 15 minutes | Serves: 2  Origin: Arunachal Pradesh

INGREDIENTS

1 cup (240 ml) water
¼ cup (40 g) millet flour (*ragi*)
Salt, to taste
¼ cup (40 g) diced carrot (*gajar*), boiled
¼ cup (40 g) shredded cabbage (*bandh gobhi*), boiled

METHOD

1. In a small saucepan over high heat, bring the water to a boil.
2. Add the millet flour and season to taste with salt. Cook, stirring continuously, until it becomes semi-thick.
3. Top with the cooked carrot and cabbage and serve.

## CHHURPI STIR-FRY

Made using a local Northeastern cheese variety.

Cooking time: 35 minutes | Serves: 2     Origin: Sikkim

### INGREDIENTS

1 Tbsp (15 ml) vegetable oil
2 green chiles, finely chopped
1 Tbsp (15 g) ginger-garlic paste (*adrak-lasan*)
1 tsp Panch Phoran spice mix (available at Indian
    markets and online; page 32)
½ medium-size onion, finely chopped
1 cup (240 g) diced tomato
Salt, to taste
1 cup (240 g) cubed chhurpi (available online)
1 tsp freshly ground black pepper (*kali mirch*)
¼ cup (4 g) fresh cilantro leaves (*hara dhaniya*),
    finely chopped

### METHOD

1. In a skillet over low-medium heat, heat the
   vegetable oil.
2. Add the green chiles, ginger-garlic paste, and
   Panch Phoran. Stir in the onion and tomato.
   Season to taste with salt and cook until the
   vegetables are very soft.
3. Add the chhurpi. Cook, stirring, until the oil
   begins to pull away from the sides of the pan.
4. Stir in the pepper. Taste and season with more
   salt as needed. Garnish with cilantro and serve.

## TARO ROOT LEAF CURRY

Delicious curry rich in vitamins and dietary
fiber.

Cooking time: 30 minutes | Serves: 2     Origin: Assam

### INGREDIENTS

1 Tbsp (15 ml) vegetable oil
2 tsp minced garlic (*lasan*)
1 dried red chile (*sookhi lal mirch*)
¼ cup (42.5 g) finely chopped onion
1 tsp ground turmeric (*haldi*)
1 tsp ground coriander (*dhaniya*)
1 tsp red chile powder
½ cup (80 g) finely chopped tender taro root
    leaves (*arbi*)
2 cups (480 ml) water
1 cup (200 g) split red lentils (*masoor dal*), boiled
Salt, to taste
1 Tbsp (15 g) tamarind pulp (*imli*; page 30)

### METHOD

1. In a skillet over low-medium heat, heat the
   vegetable oil.
2. Add the garlic, dried red chile, and onion. Cook
   for 2–3 minutes until the onion softens.
3. Stir in the turmeric, coriander, and red chile
   powder. Add the taro root leaves and stir well
   to combine.
4. Add the water and lentils. Season to taste with
   salt. Reduce the heat to low and simmer the dal
   for 15 minutes.
5. Finish with the tamarind pulp and serve hot.

## LENTIL FRITTER CURRY

Wholesome curry with lentil fritters.

Cooking time: 1 hour | Serves: 2      Origin: Assam

### INGREDIENTS

**For the lentil fritters**
½ cup (100 g) split red lentils (*masoor dal*), cooked
1 red chile, finely chopped
Salt, to taste
Pinch ground asafoetida (*hing*)
¾ cup (180 ml) vegetable oil

**For the curry**
1 tsp mustard seed oil (page 26)
1 tsp Panch Phoran spice mix (available at Indian markets and online; page 32)
1 bay leaf (*tej patta*)
1 dried red chile (*sookhi lal mirch*)
½ cup (85 g) finely chopped onion
1 Tbsp (6 g) ground coriander (*dhaniya*)
1 tsp ground turmeric (*haldi*)
1 cup (240 g) finely chopped tomato
1 cup (240 g) cubed (peeled and seeded) bottle gourd (calabash; *lauki*)
1 cup (240 ml) water
Salt, to taste

### METHOD

1. **To make the fritters:** In a blender, combine the lentils and red chile. Blitz into a coarse paste. Season to taste with salt and add the asafoetida. Pulse to combine and set aside.
2. In a skillet over low-medium heat, heat the vegetable oil.
3. Add small (coin-size) portions of the lentil mixture and deep-fry, turning, until golden. Transfer to paper towels to drain.
4. **To make the curry:** In another skillet over medium-high heat, heat the mustard seed oil.
5. Add the Panch Phoran, bay leaf, and dried red chile. Heat until the spices begin to crackle.
6. Add the onion, coriander, and turmeric. Stir well to combine. Cook for about 3 minutes until the onion softens.
7. Stir in the tomato and bottle gourd. Cook until the bottle gourd is soft.
8. Stir in the water and add the fried lentil fritters. Taste and season with salt, if needed.
9. Remove and discard the bay leaf before serving.

## ELLICHAANA

Spicy yellow peas.

Cooking time: 30 minutes | Serves: 2      Origin: Manipur

### INGREDIENTS

1 tsp mustard seed oil (page 26)
½ cup (85 g) finely chopped onion
1 Tbsp (10 g) minced garlic (*lasan*)
½ tsp ground asafoetida (*hing*)
1 cup (200 g) cooked yellow peas
1 green chile, finely chopped
1 tsp ground turmeric (*haldi*)
1 tsp red chile powder
1 tsp ground coriander (*dhaniya*)
1 tsp ground cumin (*jeera*)
1 tsp chaat masala
¼ cup (4 g) fresh cilantro leaves (*hara dhaniya*), finely chopped
Salt, to taste

### METHOD

1. In a skillet over medium-high heat, heat the mustard seed oil.
2. Add the onion, garlic, and asafoetida. Stir well to combine. Cook for 2–3 minutes until the onion softens.
3. Add the yellow peas, green chile, turmeric, red chile powder, coriander, cumin, chaat masala, and cilantro. Season to taste with salt. Stir to combine and cook until heated through. Serve hot.

## PANEER AND PEA CURRY 📷

Paneer curry cooked in a creamy milk gravy.

Cooking time: 30 minutes | Serves: 2     Origin: Manipur

INGREDIENTS

2 tsp vegetable oil

1 tsp cumin seeds (*jeera*)

¼ medium-size onion, chopped

1 green chile, finely chopped

1 Tbsp (15 g) ginger-garlic paste (*adrak-lasan*)

1 tsp ground turmeric (*haldi*)

½ cup (80 g) green peas (*hara mattar*)

1 cup (225 g) paneer, cubed (available at Indian markets; page 28)

Salt, to taste

½ cup (120 ml) water

1 cup (240 ml) milk

¼ cup (4 g) fresh cilantro leaves (*hara dhaniya*), finely chopped

METHOD

1. In a skillet over medium heat, heat the vegetable oil.
2. Add the cumin seeds and onion. Sauté for 1 minute.
3. Stir in the green chile, ginger-garlic paste, turmeric, and peas.
4. Add the paneer. Season to taste with salt and cook until the paneer is slightly golden brown and the peas soften.
5. Add the water. Reduce the heat to low and simmer the gravy for 4–6 minutes.
6. Add the milk and continue simmering for about 3 minutes more. Once the gravy thickens slightly, taste and adjust the seasoning. Remove from the heat.
7. Garnish with cilantro and serve.

## SOYA THONGBA

Rich and creamy curry with chunks of soy.

Cooking time: 20 minutes | Serves: 2     Origin: Manipur

INGREDIENTS

1 Tbsp (15 ml) vegetable oil

1 tsp cumin seeds (*jeera*)

½ cup (85 g) finely chopped onion

1 green chile, finely chopped

2 tsp ginger-garlic paste (*adrak-lasan*)

1 cup (240 g) soya chunks, boiled and drained

½ cup (112.5 g) boiled cubed potato

¼ cup (40 g) green peas (*hara mattar*)

1 tsp ground turmeric (*haldi*)

1 cup (240 ml) milk

¼ cup (4 g) fresh cilantro leaves (*hara dhaniya*), finely chopped

Salt, to taste

METHOD

1. In a skillet over low-medium heat, heat the vegetable oil.
2. Add the cumin seeds. Cook until the seeds begin to crackle.
3. Add the onion, green chile, and ginger-garlic paste. Cook for about 3 minutes until the onion softens.
4. Stir in the soya chunks, potato, peas, and turmeric. Sauté for 4–5 minutes.
5. Add the milk, reduce the heat to low, and cover the skillet. Simmer for 3 minutes. Once the gravy thickens, season to taste with salt and garnish with cilantro. Serve hot.

## GREEN BEAN STIR-FRY

Vegan stir-fry made with local ingredients.

Cooking time: 30 minutes | Serves: 2      Origin: Tripura

### INGREDIENTS

1 Tbsp (15 ml) vegetable oil

2 green chiles, finely chopped

1 medium-size onion, finely chopped

4 garlic cloves (*lasan*), minced

½ cup (150 g) cubed firm tofu

1 cup (240 g) French green beans (haricots verts), parboiled

1 tsp ground turmeric (*haldi*)

Salt, to taste

Freshly ground black pepper (*kali mirch*), to taste

½ cup (8 g) fresh cilantro leaves (*hara dhaniya*), finely chopped

### METHOD

1. In a skillet over low-medium heat, heat the vegetable oil.
2. Add the green chiles, onion, and garlic. Cook for 2–3 minutes until the onion softens.
3. Add the tofu. Stir-fry until the tofu is slightly crispy.
4. Add the green beans and turmeric. Cook for 3–5 minutes more.
5. Season to taste with salt and pepper. Garnish with cilantro before serving.

## LASAN KERAO SANDHEKO

Spicy garlic-flavored green peas.

Cooking time: 30 minutes | Serves: 4-6      Origin: Sikkim

### INGREDIENTS

2 cups (320 g) green peas (*hara mattar*), boiled

Salt, to taste

2 bunches (20 pods) green garlic (*hara lasan*) with stems, dry-roasted, chopped

2 tsp ground cumin (*jeera*)

2 tsp dried red chiles (*sookhi lal mirch*), roasted, coarsely ground

2 tsp ginger (*adrak*), grated, dry-roasted

¼ tsp chukamilo (lemon concentrate) or 2 tsp lemon juice (*nimbu*)

3 green chiles, dry-roasted, slit into two

2 Tbsp (30 ml) mustard seed oil (page 26)

### METHOD

1. In a medium-size bowl combine the peas with salt to taste. Set aside for 30 minutes.
2. Add the garlic, cumin, dry red chiles, ginger, chukamilo or lemon juice, green chiles, and the mustard seed oil.
3. Toss well to combine and serve.

RICE AND BREAD

## TINGMO
Tibetan-style steamed bread.

Cooking time: 1 hour | Makes: 10      Origin: Sikkim

INGREDIENTS

1 Tbsp (12 g) dry yeast
2 tsp sugar
¼ cup (60 ml) warm water, plus more for kneading
1½ cups (190 g) all-purpose flour (*maida*)
1 tsp baking powder
1 tsp salt
1 Tbsp (15 ml) vegetable oil or ghee

METHOD

1. In a small bowl, combine the yeast and sugar with the warm water. Set aside in a dark place and let proof for 7 minutes.
2. In a medium-size bowl, mix together the flour, baking powder, and salt.
3. Add the yeast mixture to the flour mixture and knead into a soft dough. Add more warm water as needed to get the smooth texture.
4. Once the dough comes together, add the vegetable oil or ghee to give it sheen and softness. Turn to coat.
5. Cut the dough into 10 pieces and roll each piece into a 10-in. (25-cm) long (cinnamon-roll size) thick rope. Curl each rope like a cinnamon roll creating a snail-like circle and place in a steamer basket.
6. Steam the tingmos for 10–15 minutes and serve.

## KODOKO ROTI
Millet bread cooked in banana leaf.

Cooking time: 20 minutes | Makes: 10–15      Origin: Sikkim

INGREDIENTS

1 cup (120 g) millet flour (*ragi*)
2 green chiles, finely chopped
1 Tbsp (15 g) ghee
Salt, to taste
Water, for diluting
8 banana leaves, cut into circles

METHOD

1. In a small bowl, mix together the flour, green chiles, and ghee. Season to taste with salt.
2. Add some water, a bit at a time, and whisk well until a thick paste forms.
3. Divide the paste among 4 banana leaf circles and spread it out. Top each with another banana leaf circle and press together to seal. The paste will seal it loosely.
4. Preheat a griddle over medium heat.
5. Working in batches if needed, place the banana leaf parcels on the hot griddle. Cook for 4–5 minutes on both sides and serve hot.

## SANPIAU
Rice porridge infused with ginger and butter.

Cooking time: 15 minutes | Serves: 1        Origin: Mizoram

INGREDIENTS

1 cup (200 g) rice, rinsed
1 Tbsp (15 g) butter
1 tsp finely chopped garlic (*lasan*)
1 tsp finely chopped peeled fresh ginger (*adrak*)
Salt, to taste
Freshly ground black pepper (*kali mirch*), to taste
Fried onions (*birista*; page 30), for garnishing

METHOD

1. In your pressure cooker cooking pot, combine the rice, butter, garlic, and ginger. Season to taste with salt and pepper. Lock the lid in place and close the pressure release valve. Select Manual/Pressure Cook and cook for 15 minutes.
2. Release the pressure and remove the lid.
3. Garnish with fried onions and serve hot.

. . . . . . . . . . . .

## JANEIIONG
Strong rustic-flavored black sesame rice.

Cooking time: 20 minutes | Serves: 2        Origin: Meghalaya

INGREDIENTS

2 Tbsp (30 g) black sesame seeds, toasted
1 Tbsp (15 ml) vegetable oil
2 green chiles, finely chopped
2 tsp ginger paste (*adrak*)
1 cup (200 g) black rice, cooked
Salt, to taste

METHOD

1. In a blender, combine the black sesame seeds and 1 Tbsp (15 ml) of water. Blend into a smooth paste and set aside.
2. In a skillet over low-medium heat, heat the vegetable oil.
3. Add the green chiles and ginger paste. Stir well.
4. Add the black sesame seed paste and stir well to combine. Add the rice and season to taste with salt. Stir to combine and cook until heated through. Serve hot.

## FRIED RICE 📷
Turmeric-flavored fried rice.

Cooking time: 30 minutes | Serves: 2        Origin: Assam

INGREDIENTS

2 Tbsp (30 ml) sesame oil (*til*)
2 tsp ground turmeric (*haldi*)
1 tsp ginger paste (*adrak*)
1 tsp garlic paste (*lasan*)
¼ cup (42.5 g) finely chopped onion
1 tsp diced green chiles
1 Tbsp (15 g) ketchup or chile sauce
1 cup (200 g) long-grained rice, parboiled
1 cup (240 g) diced vegetables of choice (beans, carrot [*gajar*], corn, green peas [*hara mattar*])
1 egg
Salt, to taste
Freshly ground black pepper (*kali mirch*), to taste
½ cup (24 g) finely chopped garlic chives

METHOD

1. In a skillet over medium heat, heat the sesame oil.
2. Stir in the turmeric, ginger paste, and garlic paste. Add the onion and green chiles. Cook for 3 minutes, or until the onion is soft.
3. Add the ketchup, rice, and vegetables, stirring well to combine. Cook until the rice and vegetables are almost done (adding some water if needed).
4. Crack the egg into the center of the skillet and scramble it, stirring it into the rice.
5. Season to taste with salt and pepper. Garnish with garlic chives and serve.

# KHARZI

Dried red chile rice of the Monpa tribe.

Cooking time: 30 minutes | Serves: 2  Origin: Arunachal Pradesh

## INGREDIENTS

4 dried red chiles (*sookhi lal mirch*), soaked in
    water to rehydrate, drained
1 medium-size tomato, finely chopped
¼ cup (60 g) grated fermented cheese or (30 g)
    mozzarella cheese
1 Tbsp (15 g) ginger-garlic paste (*adrak-lasan*)
1 Tbsp (15 ml) vegetable oil
1 cup (200 g) rice, cooked
½ cup (30 g) sliced spring onion (*hara pyaz*)
Salt, to taste
Freshly ground black pepper (*kali mirch*), to taste

## METHOD

1. In a blender, combine the red chiles, tomato,
   cheese, and ginger-garlic paste. Process until a
   paste forms.
2. In a skillet over medium heat, heat the vegetable
   oil. Add the red chile mixture and sauté until
   the paste is thoroughly cooked and fragrant.
3. Stir in the rice and spring onion, stirring until
   the paste coats the rice grains well and the rice
   is heated through.
4. Season to taste with salt and pepper and serve.

# JADOH 📷

A staple pork rice from the Khasi tribe.

Cooking time: 40 minutes | Serves: 2        Origin: Meghalaya

## INGREDIENT

1 Tbsp (15 ml) vegetable oil
1 medium-size onion, finely chopped
1 green chile, finely chopped
1 bay leaf (*tej patta*)
1 Tbsp (15 g) ginger paste (*adrak*)
1 tsp ground turmeric (*haldi*)
8 ounces (226 g) pork, cubed
1 cup (200 g) Joha rice or flattened rice
    (*poha/chura*), rinsed
Salt, to taste
2 cups (480 ml) water
¼ cup (4 g) fresh cilantro leaves (*hara dhaniya*),
    finely chopped
Black and white sesame (*kala safed til*) seeds,
    for garnishing

## METHOD

1. In a skillet over low-medium heat, heat the
   vegetable oil.
2. Add the onion, green chile, bay leaf, ginger
   paste, and turmeric. Sauté for about 3 minutes
   until the onion is golden.
3. Add the pork. Fry for 3–4 minutes until golden
   brown.
4. Add the rice and season to taste with salt. Cook,
   stirring, for 3 minutes.
5. Add the water, lower the heat, and simmer the
   dish for 15 minutes, or until the meat and rice
   have thoroughly cooked. Remove and discard
   the bay leaf. Garnish with cilantro and black
   and white sesame seeds. Serve hot.

DESSERTS

## CHAKHAOAMUBI
Black rice kheer (pudding).

| Cooking time: 1 hour | Serves: 2 | Origin: Manipur |
|---|---|---|

### INGREDIENTS

1 cup (200 g) black rice, soaked in water for 3
    hours, drained
3 cups (720 ml) full-fat milk
½ cup (150 g) sweetened condensed milk
5 Tbsp (25 g) grated fresh coconut (*nariyal*)
Pinch ground cardamom
Slivered almonds (*badam*), for garnishing

### METHOD

1. In a medium-size saucepan, cook the black rice
   according to the package directions, about 35
   minutes, until completely softened.
2. In another medium-size pot over low-medium
   heat, bring the milk to a boil and stir in the
   sweetened condensed milk. Reduce the heat to
   low and cook to thicken slightly.
3. Stir in the black rice. The color will bleed into
   the milk. Continue to cook over low heat for 20
   minutes more until the rice absorbs the
   sweetness of the milk.
4. Stir in the coconut and cardamom. Remove
   from the heat.
5. Refrigerate the rice kheer to cool thoroughly,
   3–4 hours.
6. Garnish with almonds before serving.

## ANARASA
Rice flour delicacy.

| Cooking time: 1 hour | Serves: 2-4 | Origin: Sikkim |
|---|---|---|

### INGREDIENTS

2 cups (320 gm) rice flour, finely ground
1 cup (200 gm) sugar
4 tsp (20 ml) lemon juice (*nimbu*)
½ cup sesame seeds (*til*)
1¼ cups (250 g) ghee

### METHOD

1. In a medium-size bowl combine the rice flour,
   sugar, and lemon juice.
2. Cover the mixture with a deep dish turned
   upside down. Set aside for 4–5 hours.
3. Using just a little water knead the mixture into
   a dough.
4. Sprinkle the sesame seeds on a flat dish.
5. Divide the dough into small lemon-size balls
   and roll over the sesame seeds. Press the balls
   to form flat rounds, about 5-in. (12.5-cm) in
   diameter.
6. On a griddle over medium-high heat, heat the
   ghee.
7. In batches, fry the rice rounds until they turn
   golden.
8. Keep spooning the ghee (from the pan) over
   the rounds, but do flip them.
9. Transfer with a slotted spoon to paper towels to
   drain.

# NARIKOLORNARU
Coconut dessert.

Cooking time: 30 minutes | Makes: 15      Origin: Assam

INGREDIENTS

4 cups (320 g) grated fresh coconut (*nariyal*)
2 cups (400 g) sugar

METHOD

1. In a saucepan over medium heat, combine the coconut and sugar. Allow the sugar to melt.
2. Stir continuously until the mixture begins to pull away from the sides of the pan.
3. Cool the mixture slightly and roll it into balls.

# BAMBAISON
Cardamom-flavored milk sweet.

Cooking time: 1 hour | Serves: 4      Origin: Sikkim

INGREDIENTS

8 Tbsp (120 g) ghee, plus more to grease the plate
2 lb, 3 oz (1 kg) whole-milk fudge (*khoya*), grated, available at Indian markets (page 25)
1¼ cups (225 g) sugar
½ cup (120 ml) milk
1 tsp ground green cardamom (*choti elaichi*)

METHOD

1. In a heavy-bottomed skillet over medium heat, heat the ghee.
2. Add the whole-milk fudge and cook, stirring continuously, until light golden.
3. Add the sugar and milk; continue stirring until the sugar dissolves. Cook until the whole-milk fudge becomes a lumpy mass and begins to pull away from the sides of the pan.
4. Remove from heat and mix in the green cardamom. Grease a flat plate with ghee and transfer the mixture to the plate. Spread it out with a greased spatula or the back of a serving spoon. Cut into pieces while the mixture is still hot. Remove from the plate only when it cools, and serve.

ACCOMPANIMENTS

## CHHURPI ACHAR
Local cheese spiced and served as a side dish.

Cooking time: 10 minutes | Makes: 600 grams    Origin: Sikkim

INGREDIENTS

1 cup (240 g) soft chhurpi (available online) or
   ricotta cheese
½ cup (75 g) sliced radish (*mooli*)
½ cup (75 g) sliced cucumber (*kheera*)
½ cup (85 g) finely chopped onion
3 green chiles, finely chopped
1 tsp mustard seed oil (page 26)
Salt, to taste
Freshly ground black pepper (*kali mirch*), to taste

METHOD

1.  In a medium-size bowl, mix together the
    chhurpi, radish, cucumber, onion, and green
    chiles.
2.  Drizzle with mustard seed oil and season to
    taste with salt and pepper.
3.  Serve cold with chapatti, if desired.

· · · · · · · · · · · ·

## SEPEN
Tibetan-style hot sauce served with momos.

Cooking time: 10 minutes | Makes: 50 grams     Origin: Sikkim

INGREDIENTS

1 cup (240 g) dried red chiles (*sookhi lal mirch*),
   soaked in water overnight, drained
4 garlic cloves (*lasan*)
2 tsp peppercorns (*sabut kali mirch*)
1 (1-in. / 2.5-cm) piece peeled fresh ginger (*adrak*)
½ cup (8 g) fresh cilantro leaves (*hara dhaniya*),
   finely chopped
Salt, to taste
Water, as needed

METHOD

1.  Using a mortar and pestle or a blender, combine
    all the ingredients and blend together.
2.  Add water to adjust thick sauce-like consistency.

## MOOLA KO ACHAR
Radish pickle.

Cooking time: 20 minutes | Makes: 600 grams   Origin: Sikkim

INGREDIENTS

1 lb, 2 oz (500 g) radish (*mooli*), peeled, washed
3½ oz (100 g) red mustard seeds (*lal rai*)
4 tsp cumin seeds (*jeera*)
½ tsp timmur (optional)
4 tsp red chile powder
2 tsp ground turmeric (*haldi*)
Salt, to taste
2 cups (480 ml) mustard seed oil (page 26),
   divided
2 tsp lemon juice (*nimbu*)

METHOD

1.  Pat dry the radish and cut into 3-in. / 7.5-cm
    long pieces. Cut each piece diagonally into
    four. Replace if the radishes have a white tinge.
2.  Spread the radish out on a plate and sun-dry for
    5–6 hours.
3.  Using a grinder or mortar and pestle, coarsely
    grind the red mustard seeds, cumin seeds, and
    timmur (if using) together.
4.  Combine the prepared ground ingredients, red
    chile powder, and turmeric on another plate.
    Season to taste with salt.
5.  Add 2–3 Tbsp (30–45 ml) mustard seed oil and
    lemon juice. Stir well to combine.
6.  Add the radish pieces and toss well to coat the
    spice mix.
7.  In a dry glass jar, put in the radish slices in
    batches. Press down after each addition to pack
    them well. Cover and put out in the sun for 2
    days.
8.  On the third day, shake the jar well. There
    should be water in it. Add the remaining
    mustard seed oil and store. The pickle is ready
    to serve in 6–7 days.

## GOLBHENDA KO PAKAEKO
Tomato relish.

Cooking time: 30 minutes | Makes: 500 grams   Origin: Assam

INGREDIENTS

4 Tbsp (60 ml) mustard seed oil (page 26)
½ tsp fenugreek seeds (*methi dana*)
2 dried red chiles (*sookhi lal mirch*), halved, seeded
2 tsp garlic (*lasan*), chopped
2 tsp ginger (*adrak*), shredded
1 lb, 2 oz (500 g) chopped tomato
½ tsp ground turmeric (*haldi*)
Salt, to taste
1 tsp cumin seeds (*jeera*)
¼ tsp red chile powder

METHOD

1. In a skillet over medium-high heat, heat the mustard seed oil.
2. Add the fenugreek seeds and dried red chiles. Cook until the seeds begin to crackle.
3. Add the garlic and ginger. Cook for 2 minutes, or until the garlic turns brown.
4. Stir in the tomatoes, turmeric, and season to taste with salt. Stirring continuously, cook until the liquid gets absorbed.
5. Add the cumin seeds and red chile powder. Cook, stirring continuously till the liquid dries and the oil begins to pull away from the sides of the dish.
6. Transfer to a dish and let it cool. This can be refrigerated for up to one week.

## KORDOI CHUTNEY
Star fruit chutney—best enjoyed in summer.

Cooking time: 30 minutes | Makes: 100 grams   Origin: Assam

INGREDIENTS

5 star fruits, seeded and chopped
2 Tbsp (30 g) sliced jaggery (*gur*; unrefined cane sugar)
Water, as needed
2 Tbsp (30 ml) vegetable oil
¾ cup (109 g) palm sugar
2 dried red chiles (*sookhi lal mirch*)
3 Tbsp (45 g) raisins (*kishmish*)
1 Tbsp (7 g) ground cumin (*jeera*)
2 Tbsp (30 ml) rice vinegar
Indian black salt (*kala namak*), to taste

METHOD

1. In your pressure cooker cooking pot, combine the star fruit and jaggery. Add enough water to come up slightly above the level of the fruit. Lock the lid in place and close the pressure release valve. Select Manual/Pressure Cook and cook for 3 minutes.
2. Release the pressure and remove the lid. Use a potato masher to mash the fruit.
3. In a skillet over medium heat, heat the vegetable oil.
4. Add the palm sugar, dried red chiles, raisins, and cumin. Toss gently to combine.
5. Add the star fruit mash and stir well.
6. Finish with the vinegar and black salt before serving.

## BILAHITOK

Tomato sour chutney for every festive occasion.

Cooking time: 10 minutes | Makes: 250 grams    Origin: Assam

INGREDIENTS

1 Tbsp (15 ml) mustard seed oil (page 26), plus more as needed
1 bay leaf (*tej patta*)
1 tsp Panch Phoran spice mix (available at Indian markets and online; page 32)
1 dried red chile (*sookhi lal mirch*)
1 cup (240 g) finely chopped tomato
1 tsp ground turmeric (*haldi*)
1 tsp red chile powder
Pinch brown sugar
Salt, to taste

METHOD

1. In a skillet over low-medium heat, heat the mustard seed oil. Add the bay leaf, Panch Phoran, and dried red chile. Heat until the spices begin to crackle.
2. Stir in the tomato, turmeric, red chile powder, and brown sugar.
3. Cook for 3–5 minutes. Smash the tomato slightly and add more mustard seed oil if it gets too dry.
4. Season to taste with salt and remove from the heat.
5. Remove and discard the bay leaf before serving.

## RONGPU TAKENG

Egg chutney.

Cooking time: 10 minutes | Makes: 50 grams
Origin: Arunachal Pradesh

INGREDIENTS

2 hardboiled eggs, peeled and chopped
1 tsp grated ginger
Salt, to taste
Freshly ground black pepper (*kali mirch*), to taste

METHOD

1. In a small bowl, combine the eggs and ginger. Season to taste with salt and pepper. With a fork mash the ingredient into a coarse paste.

## MOSDENG SERMA
Fermented fish chutney.

Cooking time: 10 minutes | Makes: 500 grams   Origin: Tripura

INGREDIENTS

1 tsp mustard seed oil (page 26)
½ cup (85 g) finely chopped onion
2 Tbsp (30 g) garlic-chile paste (*lasan-mirch*)
1 cup (240 g) finely chopped tomato
2 dried red chiles (*sookhi lal mirch*), soaked in
   water to rehydrate, drained
2 Tbsp (30 g) *berma* or fermented dry fish
   (available online)
Salt, to taste

METHOD

1. In a small saucepan over low-medium heat,
   heat the mustard seed oil.
2. Add onion and garlic-chile paste. Stir well to
   combine. Cook for 2–3 minutes until the onion
   softens.
3. Stir in the tomato, rehydrated red chiles, and
   *berma*. Cook, stirring, until the tomato softens.
   Transfer the mixture to a blender.
4. Blitz to combine, season to taste with salt, and
   serve.

## AKHUNI CHUTNEY
Spiced and fermented soybean chutney.

Cooking time: 15 minutes | Makes: 50 grams Origin: Nagaland

INGREDIENTS

1 tsp vegetable oil
6 green chiles
1 medium-size tomato, roasted
1 (1-in. /2.5-cm) piece peeled fresh ginger
1 Tbsp (15 g) *akhuni* paste (available online)
Salt, to taste

METHOD

1. In a skillet over high heat, heat the vegetable oil
2. Add the green chiles. Cook, turning until the
   chiles are charred. Transfer to a blender.
3. Add the remaining ingredients and blend into a
   coarse paste.
4. Serve with a traditional Indian-style meal, thali.

## OAMBAL
Pumpkin chutney with sour tamarind pulp.

Cooking time: 20 minutes | Makes: 800 grams
Origin: Nagaland

### INGREDIENTS

1 lb (454 g) pumpkin chunks, boiled
5 Tbsp (75 g) tamarind pulp (*imli*; page 30)
1 Tbsp (15 ml) mustard seed oil (page 26)
1 Tbsp (15 g) mustard seeds (*rai*)
2 bay leaves (*tej patta*)
2 tsp red chile powder
5 Tbsp (75 g) grated jaggery (*gur*; unrefined
  cane sugar)
Juice of 1 lemon (*nimbu*)
1 Tbsp (15 g) raisins (*kishmish*)
Salt, to taste

### METHOD

1. In a medium-size bowl, mash together the
   pumpkin and tamarind pulp. Set aside.
2. In a skillet over low-medium heat, heat the
   mustard seed oil.
3. Add the mustard seeds and bay leaves. Cook
   until the seeds begin to crackle.
4. Stir in the red chile powder.
5. Add the pumpkin-tamarind mixture, stir, reduce
   the heat, and bring to a gentle simmer.
6. Stir in the jaggery until it dissolves completely.
   Remove the skillet from the heat. Add the
   lemon juice and raisins. Season to taste with
   salt before serving.

## TEMI ICED TEA
Chilled local tea with lemon.

Cooking time: 20 minutes | Serves: 2        Origin: Sikkim

### INGREDIENTS

6 cups (1.5 L) water
4 Temi tea bags (available at Indian markets and
  online)
1 cup (240 ml) sugar syrup (page 30)
½ cup (120 ml) freshly squeezed lemon juice
  (*nimbu*)

### METHOD

1. In a saucepan over low-medium heat, combine
   all the ingredients. Bring to a gentle boil and
   remove the tea bags.
2. Chill and serve.

# INDEX

●●●●●●

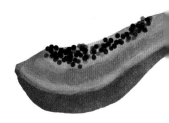

# INDIVIDUAL RECIPE CONTRIBUTORS

ADIL I. AHMAD (*Tehzeeb: Culinary Traditions of Awadh*): Pages 41 (left), 42, 54, 57, 60 (right), 69 (right), 82, 91 (right), 103, 105, 110 (right), 115 (right), 119 (left); ASHA VED: Pages 187 (right), 189 (right), 227, 228 (left), 230 (left), 239, 257 (left), 260 (right), 268 (top left); CHEF ANUJ WADHAWAN (ROSEATE HOTELS & RESORTS): Pages 81 (left), 156, 284 (right), 287 (left), 299 (left), 300 (right), 306 (right), 318 (right), 322 (right); CHEF FLOYD CARDOZ: Pages 204 (left), 216 (right), 219 (left), 235 (left), 252 (left); CHEF MANU CHANDRA: Pages 71, 91 (left), 92 (right); CHEF THOMAS ZACHARIAS: Pages 284 (left), 308 (right), 313 (left), (right) 317; GOMATHI MOHAN: Page 279 (right); ITI MISRA: Pages 389 (right), 408 (right), 409 (right), 432 (right); JAMES NOKSENG G MOMIN: Page 457 (both); KIRAN KAPOOR: Page 87 (right); LEENA MEHTA: Pages 188 (right), 189 (left), 190 (left); NUZHAT FAKIH: Pages 283 (right), 292 (left), 306 (left), 308 (left), 316 (right), 346 (right); ROCKY MOHAN (*The Art of Indian Cuisine*): Pages 46, 59, 60 (left), 62 (left), 69 (left), 76, 104, 106, 121 (left); SABA BASHIR: Page 72 (left); SABITA RADHAKRISHNA (*Annapurni: Heritage Cuisine from Tamil Nadu*): Pages 281, 283 (left), 290 (left), 291 (both), 293, 297, 300 (left), 302, 305, 315, 341 (left), 344 (below left), 345, 385 (left); SARLA RAZDAN (*Kashmiri Cuisine: Through the Ages*): Page 77 (right); VANDANA TOMAR: Pages 64 (right), 65 (left), 89 (left), 111 (left); VIDHU MITTAL (*Pure & Simple: Homemade Indian Vegetarian Cuisine*): Page 97 (both).

# RECIPES COURTESY

1000 GREAT INDIAN RECIPES: THE ULTIMATE BOOK OF INDIAN CUISINE: Pages 50 (right), 219 (right), 220 (right), 222 (right), 224 (left), 255 (right), 268 (right), 280, 282 (right), 292 (right), 303 (right), 312 (right), 317 (left), 324, 330 (left), 336 (both), 337 (both), 358 (left), 374 (right), 377 (left), 383 (both), 390 (left), 398 (left), 481 (right), 483 (right), 485 (right), 486 (left); ANNAPURNI: HERITAGE CUISINE FROM TAMIL NADU: Pages 309, 312 (left), 329, 338; DINING WITH THE NAWABS: Pages 73, 77 (left), 107, 148 (left), 151 (right); GOAN KITCHEN: Pages 203, 217, 220 (left), 222 (left), 245 (left), 252 (right), 255 (left), 271 (right); GUJARATI KITCHEN: Page 269 (left); INDIAN TIKKAS AND KEBABS: Page 56 (left); IYER KITCHEN: Pages 279 (left), 325, 326 (both), 353 (right); KASHMIRI KITCHEN: Pages 50 (left), 55 (right), 66 (right), 75 (right), 108 (right); KERALA KITCHEN: Pages 289 (right), 313 (right), 318 (left), 320 (both), 321 (left), 322 (left), 344 (top left), 349 (right), 359 (left); PARSI KITCHEN: Pages 204 (right), 212 (left), 214 (left), 224 (right), 251 (left), 256 (left), 269 (right); RAJASTHANI KITCHEN: Pages 199 (both), 210 (left), 258 (left), 270 (right).

# PHOTOGRAPHS

AASHISH MANDHWANI: Page 39 (above); ALAMY STOCK PHOTO: Pages 134 (above), 184 (above and below left), 277 (above right), 364 (all above and below left), 365 (above); DINODIA: Pages 134 (below left), 184 (below right), 185 (below); GETTY IMAGES: Pages 276 (above), 277 (above left and below), 364 (below right); HASHIM BADANI: Page 185 (above); KARAM K PURI: Pages 38, 39 (below left), 134 (below right); SRINIVASA PRASATH: Pages 39 (below right), 135, 276 (below); NILANJAN RAY: Page 365 (below); SANJIV VALSAN: Pages 442-443.

# CREDITS

Recipe photographs: ANSHIKA VARMA · Recipe preparation: CHEF ANUJ WADHAWAN (Roseate Hotels and Resorts) · Design: SNEHA PAMNEJA · Project Coordinator: ANISHA SAIGAL · Editors: NEELAM NARULA, PRIYA KAPOOR · Recipe editor: MARY CASSELLS · Layout: NARESH MONDAL · Design support: VAASAVI KAUSHIK · Prepress: JYOTI DEY · Production: YUVRAJ SINGH